Luke-apod Lukapod

Abbey!

Angelo

yeah
BoYYY!

V

DiT

Our United States

Silver Burdett Ginn

Parsippany, NJ

Atlanta, GA • Deerfield, IL • Irving, TX • Needham, MA • Upland, CA

PROGRAM AUTHORS

Juan R. García
Associate Professor of History and Associate Dean
 of the College of Social and Behavioral Sciences
University of Arizona
Tucson, AZ

Daniel J. Gelo
Associate Professor of Anthropology, Division of
 Behavioral and Cultural Sciences
University of Texas at San Antonio
San Antonio, TX

Linda L. Greenow
Associate Professor and Acting Chair,
 Department of Geography
S.U.N.Y. at New Paltz
New Paltz, NY

James B. Kracht
Professor of Geography and Educational
 Curriculum and Instruction
Texas A&M University
College Station, TX

Deborah Gray White
Professor of History
Rutgers University
New Brunswick, NJ

Silver Burdett Ginn
299 Jefferson Road, P.O. Box 480
Parsippany, NJ 07054-0480

UNIT 2

EXPLORATION AND COLONIZATION 44

UNIT 3 WAR AND INDEPENDENCE — 156

UNIT 4 EXPANSION AND CONFLICT — 208

UNIT 5 GROWTH AT HOME AND ABROAD

MAPS

Atlas Maps

Map Adventures

TIME LINES

GRAPHS, TABLES, CHARTS, AND DIAGRAMS

SKILLS

LITERATURE

The following books are recommended for optional reading and research.

Map Handbook

CONTENTS

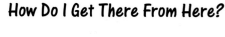

A MAP: When Is It Better Than a Photo?

If a picture is worth a thousand words, how many words would a map be worth? How many words would it take to describe going by land from one state to another or from one country to another? Luckily, you can use maps instead of words!

A map shows what Earth, or a part of it, would look like if seen from overhead. It gives you a picture that is very useful if you are trying to get from one place to another.

The photograph on this page was taken from about 1,500 feet above Earth's surface. In the map on page M3, a cartographer (kahr TAHG ruh-fur), or mapmaker, shows the same scene.

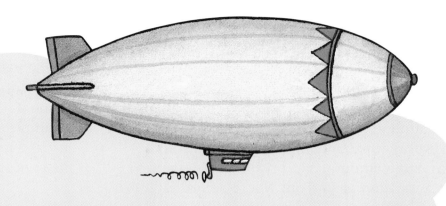

KEY

- Highways
- Other roads
- Buildings
- Parking lots
- Tennis courts
- Pond
- Trees
- Other land

Unlock the meaning.

The key on a map helps you to read the map. Another name for the key is the legend.

- What does this color symbol stand for?
- What color stands for trees?

Go from one kind of picture to another.

- Find a parking lot in the photograph. What color stands for it?
- Now find the parking lot on the map. Find a highway and the tennis courts, too.

Now Try This!

- Draw a map that shows what the top or the inside of your desk would look like if seen from above. Make up symbols to stand for books, rulers, pencils, and so on.

MAPS: Get the Most out of Them!

Maps are the most important tools we have for finding out where places are located. People use maps to help them understand the world around them. Maps are so much a part of our lives that we seldom stop to think about them. But, without maps, it would be difficult to plan a vacation or find out where Kenya is!

You will see many maps in this book. Each one has symbols that show different information. A symbol may look like the thing it stands for. For example, symbols for roads and mountains usually look like those things. Often, colors are used as symbols on maps.

The Compass Rose

The compass rose tells which way on the map is north. From this, you can figure out which ways are south, east, and west.

◆ Was the Louisiana Purchase east or west of the Mexican Cession?

Boundaries

The gray lines show boundaries between places.

◆ What two countries border the United States?

The Inset

An inset is a small map inside a larger one. It shows areas that are too large, too small, or too far away to show on a main map.

◆ Which states do the inset maps show?

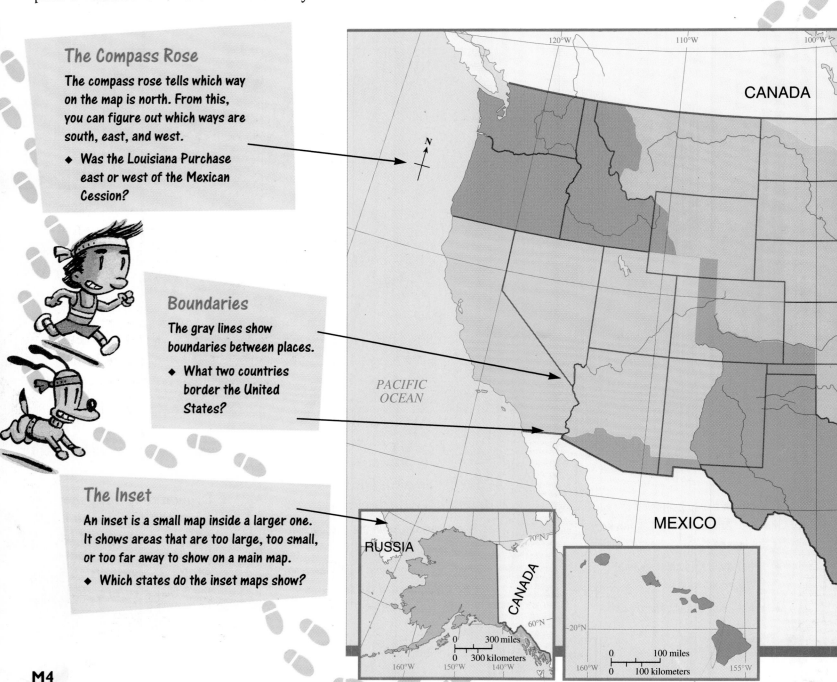

The Scale

The scale allows you to tell the distances between places.

◆ How many miles does this scale show?

Latitude and Longitude

Maps have lines to help locate places.

Latitude lines run east and west.

Longitude lines run north and south.

The latitude and longitude of a place tells exactly where it is located.

◆ Name two latitude lines that cross the Texas Annexation.

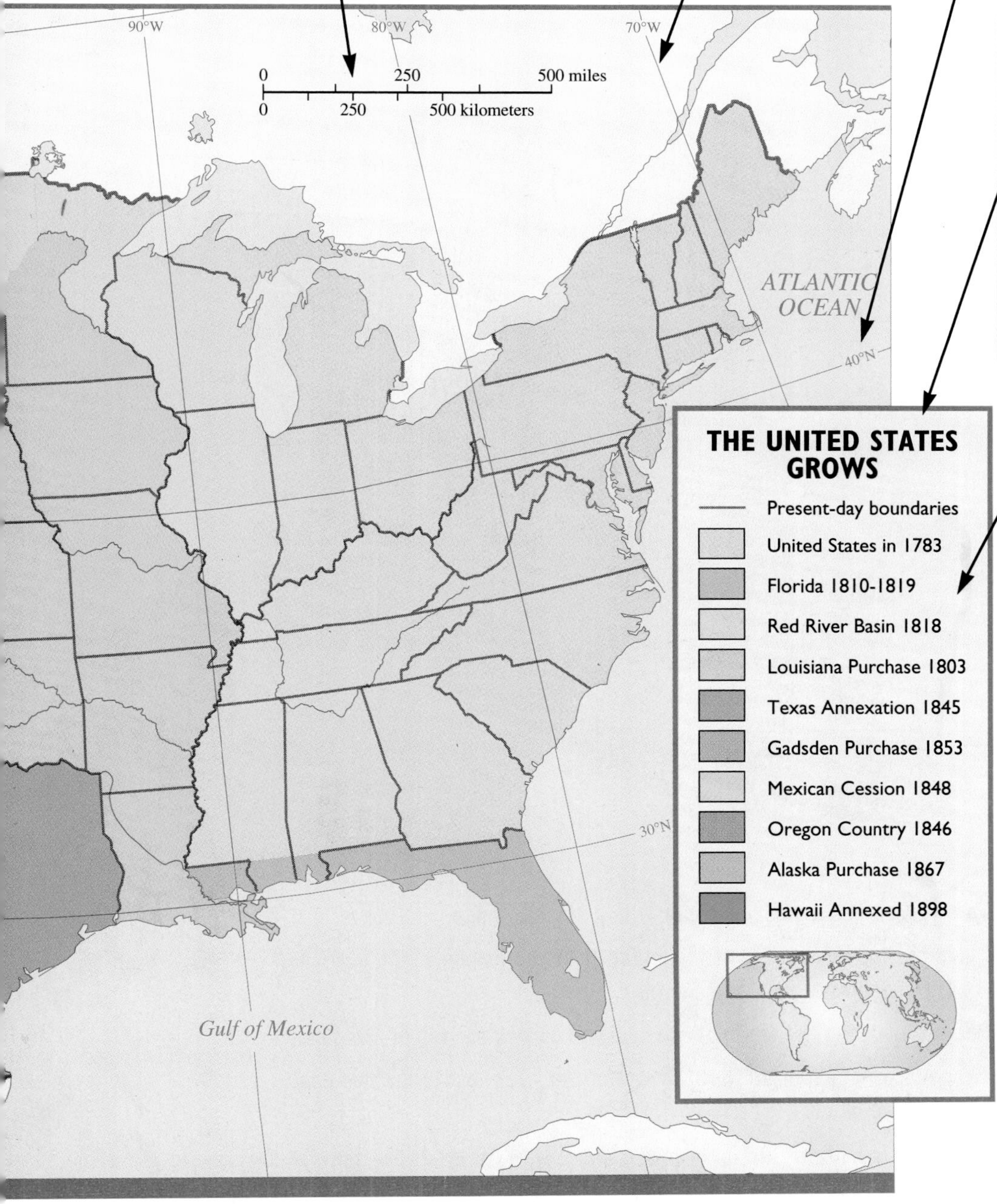

Map Titles

In this book, map titles are located at the top of the map key. The title tells you what kind of information you can find on the map.

◆ What is the title of this map?

The Key

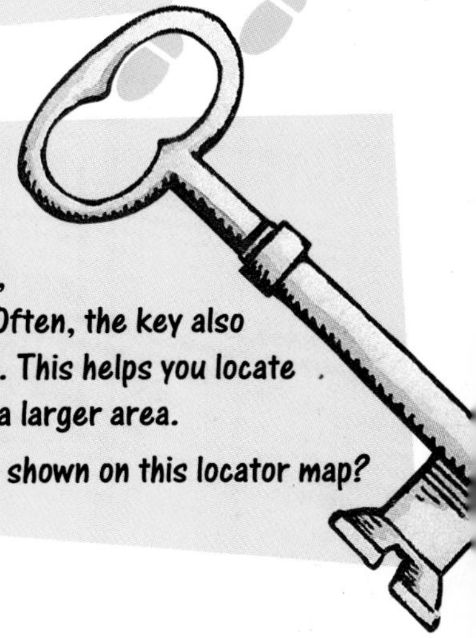

On most maps, a box called a key, or legend, explains the symbols. Often, the key also contains a locator map. This helps you locate the area in relation to a larger area.

◆ What larger area is shown on this locator map?

90°W   80°W   70°W

0   250   500 miles
0   250   500 kilometers

ATLANTIC OCEAN

40°N

30°N

Gulf of Mexico

THE UNITED STATES GROWS

— Present-day boundaries

United States in 1783

Florida 1810-1819

Red River Basin 1818

Louisiana Purchase 1803

Texas Annexation 1845

Gadsden Purchase 1853

Mexican Cession 1848

Oregon Country 1846

Alaska Purchase 1867

Hawaii Annexed 1898

Now Try This!

Draw a map of your neighborhood or town. First, sketch out the major streets. Then add places of interest. Later, as you master map skills, you will revise this map, using your new skills.

SCALE: How Far is It?

How long is a soccer field? How far is it from Phoenix to Chicago? To find out, you need a sheet of paper and a map that has a **distance scale**.

Distances on maps are smaller than the real distances on Earth. The distance scale shows how much smaller. A certain number of inches on a map stands for a certain number of feet, yards, or miles on Earth. If the map uses the metric system, centimeters stand for meters or kilometers.

Study the distance scale below. How many miles does one inch stand for? How many inches would show 400 miles? How many kilometers does one centimeter stand for?

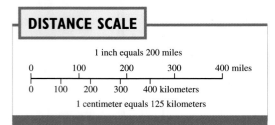

DISTANCE SCALE

1 inch equals 200 miles

| 0 | 100 | 200 | 300 | 400 miles |

| 0 | 100 | 200 | 300 | 400 kilometers |

1 centimeter equals 125 kilometers

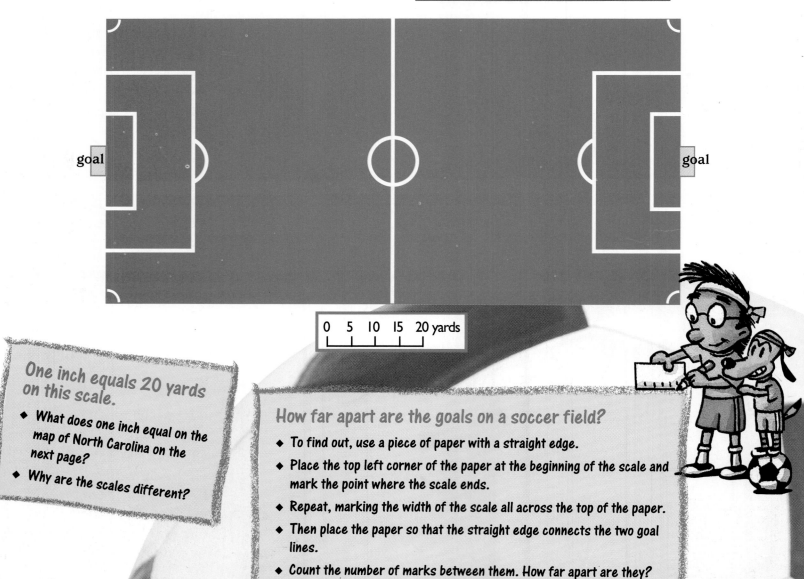

goal   goal

0   5   10   15   20 yards

One inch equals 20 yards on this scale.

- What does one inch equal on the map of North Carolina on the next page?
- Why are the scales different?

How far apart are the goals on a soccer field?

- To find out, use a piece of paper with a straight edge.
- Place the top left corner of the paper at the beginning of the scale and mark the point where the scale ends.
- Repeat, marking the width of the scale all across the top of the paper.
- Then place the paper so that the straight edge connects the two goal lines.
- Count the number of marks between them. How far apart are they?

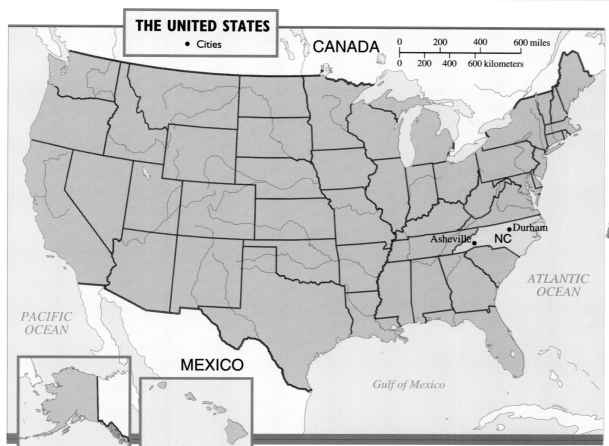

THE UNITED STATES

• Cities

CANADA

0   200   400   600 miles

0   200   400   600 kilometers

Durham

Asheville • NC

ATLANTIC OCEAN

PACIFIC OCEAN

MEXICO

Gulf of Mexico

Use your ruler.

◆ About how many miles are represented by one inch on the U.S. map?

◆ About how many miles are represented by two inches on the map of North Carolina?

NORTH CAROLINA

★   State capital

•   Other cities

40°N

N

Winston-Salem

Greensboro

Durham

Asheville   NC   ★ Raleigh

• Charlotte

35°N

ATLANTIC OCEAN

0   100   200 miles

0   100   200 kilometers

85°W   80°W   75°W

Large scale, small scale

◆ Use the scale on the map of North Carolina to find out how far it is from Asheville to Durham.

◆ Do this again, using the map of the United States. Did you get the same distance?

Now Try This!

With a group of classmates, map your classroom. Use a yardstick or tape measure to measure the room's length and width. Decide what scale of feet you will use to fit the map on a sheet of paper. Draw the map. Show windows, desks, and other features.

An INSET Map: Why Use It?

If all countries were about the same size, with even boundaries, it would be easy to create maps. Unfortunately, countries do not always cooperate with a mapmaker. Some countries have parts that do not touch each other. Other countries have some large parts and some small parts.

One nation that makes it hard for a mapmaker is the United States. At the beginning of 1959, the United States consisted of 48 states. Each state touched at least one other state. By the end of 1959, Alaska and Hawaii entered the Union, causing problems for mapmakers. Alaska and Hawaii are located far away from the other states. And Alaska is more than 400 times as large as Rhode Island, our smallest state!

This map shows the United States today, with Hawaii and Alaska in their correct locations.

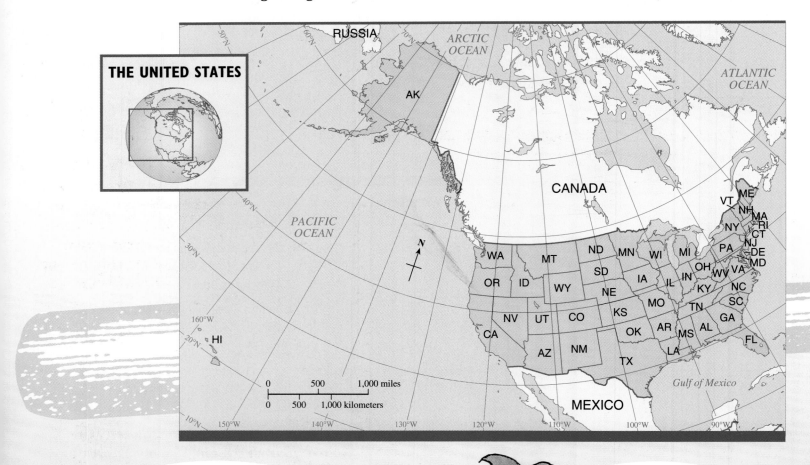

Find Alaska on the map.
- What other country has been included in order to show all of Alaska?

Find Hawaii on the map.
- Use the scale of miles to find the distance between Hawaii and its nearest neighbor in the United States.

The map on this page shows Alaska and Hawaii in a different way than the map on page M8 does. On the map below, Alaska and Hawaii are shown on **inset maps.**

To make the map fit, a different scale of miles is used for the main map and each inset. Alaska is shown much smaller than it actually is. It looks about the same size as Arizona, but it is actually much larger.

Hawaii appears in a small inset, close to the other states. This makes it hard to tell where Hawaii is in relation to the other states. To figure this out, you must use lines of latitude and longitude. You'll learn more about latitude and longitude on pages M14 through M16.

Use the scale of miles.

Using the scale on the inset map of Alaska, measure the distance from its northern to its southern boundaries. Now measure the distance from the northern to the southern boundaries of California.

◆ If you didn't understand scale, which distance would seem greater? Which is actually greater?

Now Try This!

On what floor of your school is your classroom? Draw a map of that floor, labeling the rooms. Then draw an inset map that shows your classroom. Work with a group of classmates to figure out two different distance scales for your main map and your inset.

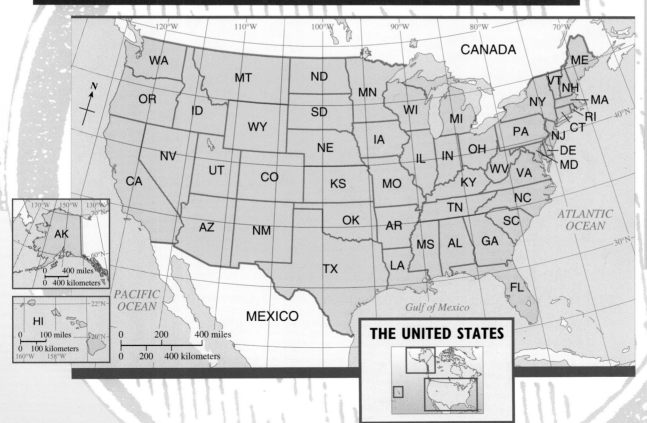

THE UNITED STATES

The COMPASS ROSE:
How Do I Get There From Here?

The tips of the compass rose on the map below point to the four **cardinal**, or main, directions: north, south, east, and west, marked N, S, E, and W. Between these directions are four **intermediate**, or in-between, directions. For example, in between north and east is northeast.

NE stands for northeast. What do NW, SE, and SW stand for?

The map below shows Harlem, a section of New York City. There, in the 1920s, many African American artists, writers, and musicians lived and created great works.

Visit Harlem in the 1920s.

Go from the Apollo Theater to Garvey's Liberty Hall.

◆ In which direction are you walking?

Which way is in-between?

From Garvey's Hall, go to Langston Hughes's home.

◆ In what intermediate direction are you walking?

Now Try This!

Use cardinal and intermediate directions to tell a partner how to get from one place to another on this map. Give a starting point, and give the directions. Did your partner end up in the right place?

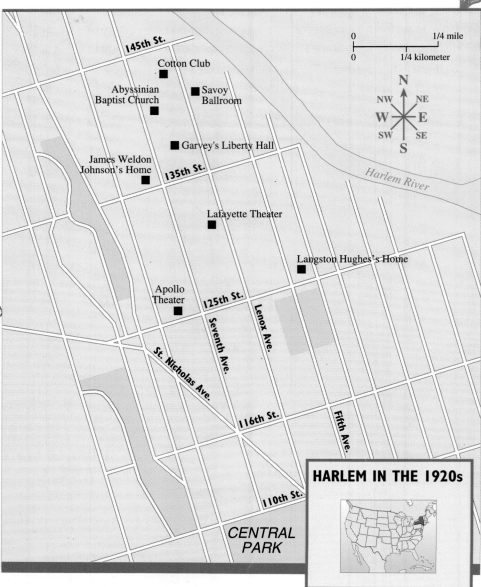

0   1/4 mile
0   1/4 kilometer

145th St.
Cotton Club
Abyssinian Baptist Church
Savoy Ballroom
Garvey's Liberty Hall
James Weldon Johnson's Home
135th St.
Harlem River
Lafayette Theater
Langston Hughes's Home
Apollo Theater
125th St.
Lenox Ave.
Seventh Ave.
St. Nicholas Ave.
116th St.
Fifth Ave.
110th St.
CENTRAL PARK

N
NW · NE
W · E
SW · SE
S

HARLEM IN THE 1920s

An ELEVATION Map:
What Do All Those Colors Mean?

A map has its own language. The "words" of this language are the symbols on the map. The mapmaker puts all the symbols together in one place. This part of a map is called the **key**, because it unlocks the meaning of the symbols.

Another term for the key is the **legend**.

On the **physical map** below, the symbols are colors that show differences in the **elevation**, or height, of land. Elevation is the height of land above or below sea level.

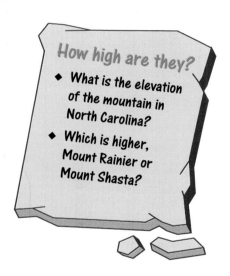

How high are they?

- What is the elevation of the mountain in North Carolina?
- Which is higher, Mount Rainier or Mount Shasta?

Now Try This!

- Find the place where you live. Use its color to find its elevation.
- Name two places that have a higher elevation than your home.
- Which color on the map stands for the lowest elevation?

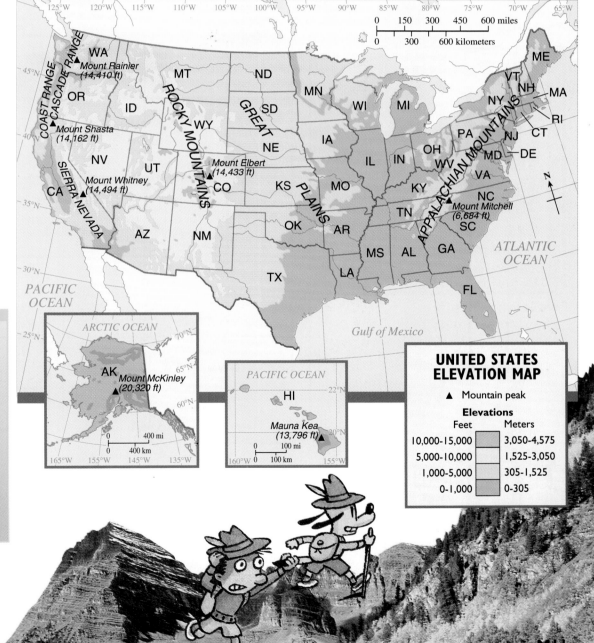

Mount Rainier (14,410 ft)

Mount Shasta (14,162 ft)

Mount Whitney (14,494 ft)

Mount Elbert (14,433 ft)

Mount Mitchell (6,684 ft)

Mount McKinley (20,320 ft)

Mauna Kea (13,796 ft)

UNITED STATES ELEVATION MAP

▲ Mountain peak

Elevations

Feet		Meters
10,000–15,000		3,050–4,575
5,000–10,000		1,525–3,050
1,000–5,000		305–1,525
0–1,000		0–305

Why Does This Road Map Have a GRID?

Places of interest are shown on the map of Anytown below. This map has a **grid**, or a set of crossed lines that form boxes on the map. The grid system helps you find places on street maps. Numbers run along the top, and letters run down the sides, giving each box an "address."

One museum in Anytown is called the Museum for the Study of Knockwurst. To find it, put a finger on the letter C, then put a finger of your other hand on the number 5. Move your fingers, one across and the other down, until they meet. Here you will find the box whose address is C5. Somewhere in that box is the museum.

Use the map key and the grid.

- What symbol stands for schools? How many schools are on the map?
- Is the library in box C2, or is it in box E5?
- The Chili Conservatory school is in box D3. What is the grid address of the other school?

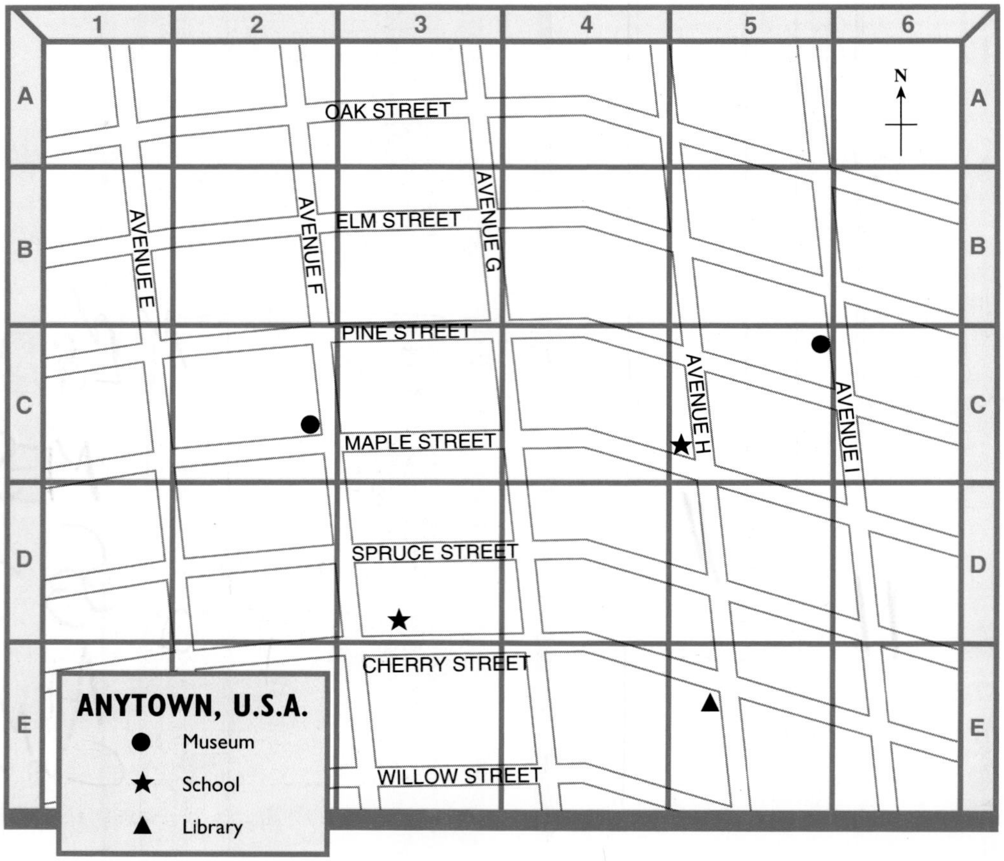

ANYTOWN, U.S.A.
- ● Museum
- ★ School
- ▲ Library

OAK STREET
ELM STREET
PINE STREET
MAPLE STREET
SPRUCE STREET
CHERRY STREET
WILLOW STREET

AVENUE E
AVENUE F
AVENUE G
AVENUE H
AVENUE I

CONSERVATORY
CHILI
KNOCKWURST MUSEUM

Road Maps

- On a road map the map key explains each symbol.
- The area is divided into squares that are identified at the top and left side of the map. The letter and number next to the name of each city listed in the **city index** identify the square in which that city is located.

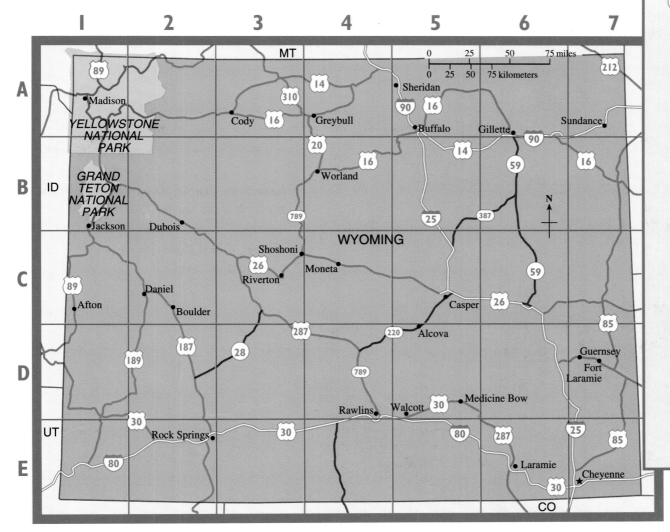

WYOMING ROAD MAP

★	State capital
•	Cities
90	Interstate highways
16	U.S. highways
59	State highways

Cities and Towns

Afton. C1
Alcova. D5
Boulder. C2
Buffalo. A5
Casper. C5
Cheyenne. E7
Cody. A3
Daniel. C2
Dubois. B2
Fort Laramie. . .D7
Gillette. A6
Greybull. A4
Guernsey. D7
Jackson. B1
Laramie. E6
Madison. A1
Medicine Bow. .D5
Moneta. C4
Rawlins. D4
Riverton. C3
Rock Springs. . .E2
Sheridan. A5
Shoshoni. C3
Sundance. A7
Walcott. D5
Worland. B4

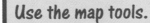

Use the map tools.

- Find Routes 16, 59, and 90. Which one is an interstate highway?
- Find Cody in the city index. Then find it on the map.

Now Try This!

- **Get out the map you drew of your neighborhood.**
- **Add a grid system to it.**
- **List places of interest in an index, giving each place an address.**

M13

LATITUDE and LONGITUDE:
Use Them to Find Places!

Mapmakers have created a special kind of grid system that gives us a way of finding the exact location of any place on Earth. This system uses two sets of lines that cross, called lines of **latitude** and **longitude**.

Latitude is the position of a place north or south of the equator. Lines of latitude run east and west around Earth. The **latitude** line that circles Earth at its center is called the **equator**.

North Pole

75°N
60°N
45°N
Minneapolis
San Diego
San Antonio
New Orleans
30°N
Jacksonville
15°N
0° Equator
15°S
30°S
45°S
60°S

Use lines of latitude.

Jacksonville, Florida, is near the 30° latitude line north of the equator (30°N). Find it on the map.

◆ What other U.S. cities are located near 30°N?

Consider the length.

◆ Do lines of latitude become shorter or longer near the North Pole?

◆ What is the longest line of latitude?

Northern Hemisphere

Equator ♪

Southern Hemisphere

The equator divides the Earth into a Northern Hemisphere and a Southern Hemisphere.

Another set of lines runs north and south on the globe. These are called **meridians**, or **lines of longitude**. They meet at the North Pole and the South Pole.

The line numbered 0° longitude runs through Greenwich, England. It is called the **prime meridian**. Lines east of the prime meridian, marked 20°E, 40°E, and so on, are called lines of east longitude. Lines west of the prime meridian, marked 20°W, 40°W, and so on, are called west longitude.

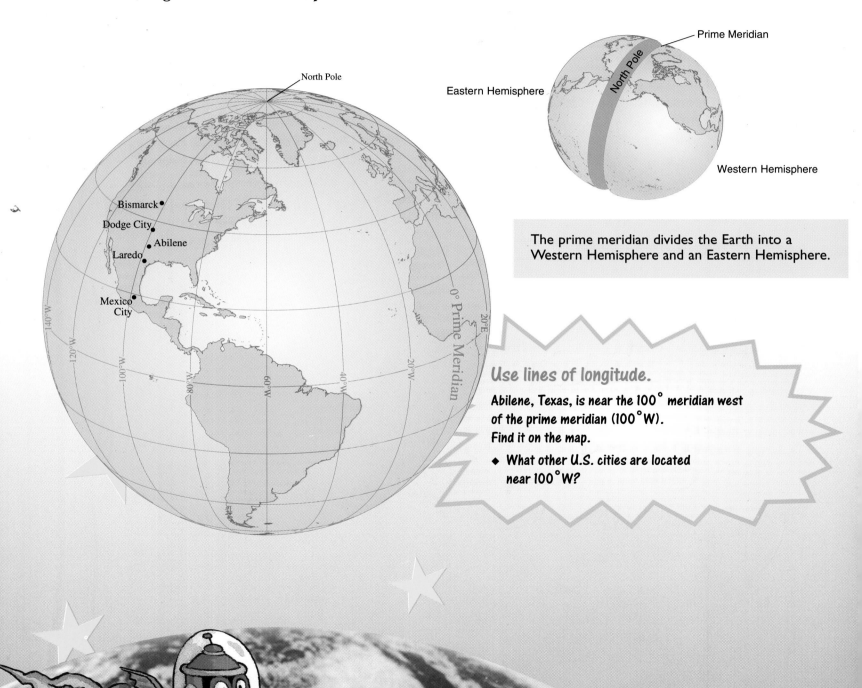

The prime meridian divides the Earth into a Western Hemisphere and an Eastern Hemisphere.

Use lines of longitude.

Abilene, Texas, is near the 100° meridian west of the prime meridian (100°W). Find it on the map.

◆ What other U.S. cities are located near 100°W?

Using Latitude and Longitude

Using latitude and longitude lets you give any place on Earth an exact "address." Jacksonville, Florida, is at 30°N. But so is New Orleans, Louisiana. Since the two cities are in different places, they can't have the same address. Combining latitude and longitude gives each city its own address. Use the map to see that Jacksonville's address is 30°N latitude, 82°W longitude. This address is written as 30°N/82°W. How would the location of New Orleans, Louisiana, be written?

Listen to an urgent message!

"This is the captain of the S.S. Peril. We are sinking fast. We are at 45°N/40°W. Help!"

◆ In which ocean should the rescue ship look?

◆ Should it look in the Northern Hemisphere or the Southern Hemisphere?

◆ What continent is west of the ship?

Now Try This!

Use an atlas to locate the route of a hot-air balloon trip. Start at 60°N/70°W, and end at 30°N/100°W. Then write a travel brochure that tells

◆ what continent you will fly over

◆ what countries you will be in

◆ what cities you might see.

A Precipitation Map

There are many kinds of maps. The most familiar is a **political map**. A political map uses color to show different countries or states.

The map below has a special purpose. It is a **precipitation map**. **Precipitation** is the amount of moisture that falls as rain, snow, sleet, or hail. However, since much of it falls as rain, this is also called a **rainfall map**. Color is used to show average precipitation over a one-year period.

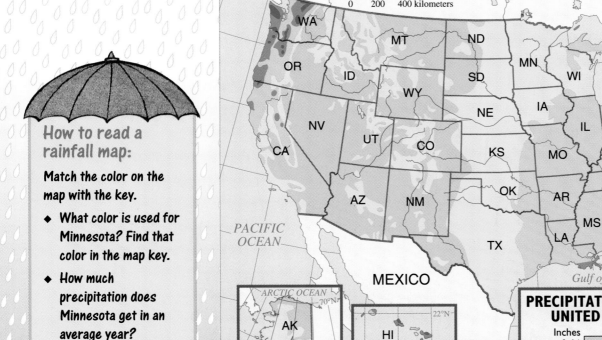

How to read a rainfall map:

Match the color on the map with the key.

- What color is used for Minnesota? Find that color in the map key.
- How much precipitation does Minnesota get in an average year?

PRECIPITATION IN THE UNITED STATES

Inches	Centimeters
0-16	0-41
16-32	41-81
32-64	81-163
64-96	163-244
Above 96	Above 244

Who gets more rain?

Annual precipitation is different from one place to another.

- Which state receives more precipitation, Pennsylvania or New Mexico?
- In general, which section of the United States is drier, the west or the east?
- Which areas tend to get more precipitation, coastal areas or inland areas?

Routes on a Map

Every map tells a story. This map tells how the explorers Lewis and Clark found their way across North America to the Pacific Ocean. How much of the story can you tell just by looking at the map?

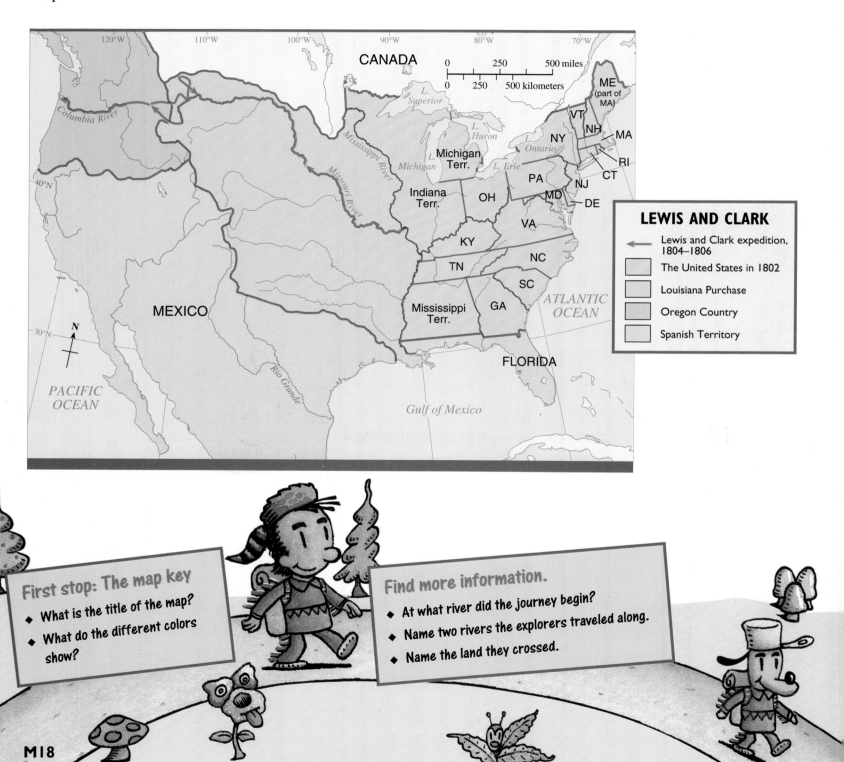

First stop: The map key

- What is the title of the map?
- What do the different colors show?

Find more information.

- At what river did the journey begin?
- Name two rivers the explorers traveled along.
- Name the land they crossed.

An Election Map

The **election map** below shows the results of the 1964 election for President. Presidential election maps show which states each candidate won.

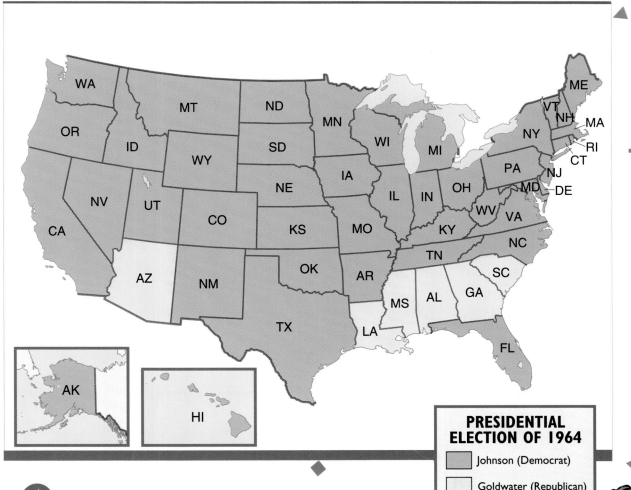

PRESIDENTIAL ELECTION OF 1964

■	Johnson (Democrat)
□	Goldwater (Republican)

Check the key and use the map.

Which Democrat ran for President in 1964? What color stands for that person?

◆ Can you tell at a glance which candidate won the election? How can you tell?

◆ How many states did Barry Goldwater win? Which states were they?

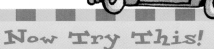

Now Try This!

To find two more election maps, turn to page 434.

◆ Which person won the Presidency in 1928?

◆ Which political party won in 1932?

◆ Why are Alaska and Hawaii not shown?

PROJECTIONS: Why Do Different Maps Show the Earth in Different Ways?

Maps are useful tools, but they all have one big problem. Maps are flat and Earth is curved. This means that maps are not entirely accurate. Globes are accurate, but what a problem you would have if you wanted to get from Elm Street to Spruce Avenue with only a globe to guide you!

Over the years, mapmakers have developed many map **projections**, ways of showing the curved Earth on a flat surface. Each projection is useful. However, each distorts, or changes, the shape of Earth in some way. Some maps are better for showing *shapes* accurately. Others show *distances* accurately.

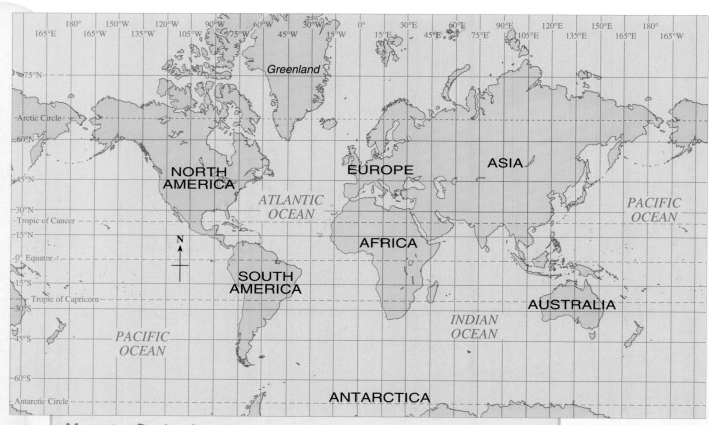

Mercator Projection

In the 1500s, sailors from Europe were exploring the oceans. They needed better maps. A mapmaker named Mercator created a map that shows direction accurately. The Mercator projection also gives an accurate view of land areas near the equator. However, it distorts the size and shape of lands near the Poles.

◆ How is longitude shown on this map? How is it different from longitude on a globe?

◆ Which is bigger on the map, Greenland or South America?

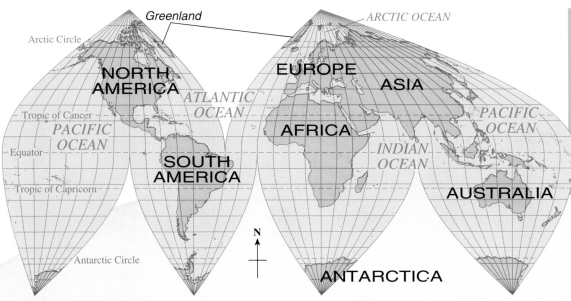

Greenland

Arctic Circle
NORTH AMERICA
ATLANTIC OCEAN
Tropic of Cancer
PACIFIC OCEAN
Equator
SOUTH AMERICA
Tropic of Capricorn
Antarctic Circle

ARCTIC OCEAN
EUROPE
ASIA
AFRICA
PACIFIC OCEAN
INDIAN OCEAN
AUSTRALIA
N
ANTARCTICA

Interrupted Projection

An interrupted projection shows the correct sizes and shapes of land. To do this, parts of oceans are separated.

◆ Can you measure the distance between the U.S. and Europe on this map?

Robinson Projection

This projection shows the correct sizes and shapes of most landmasses. It gives a fairly accurate view of the sizes of oceans and of distances across land.

◆ How does the Robinson projection show Greenland? How does the Mercator projection show it? How does the interrupted projection show it?

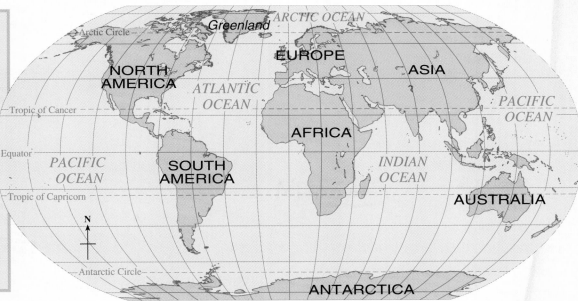

ARCTIC OCEAN
Greenland
Arctic Circle
EUROPE
ASIA
NORTH AMERICA
ATLANTIC OCEAN
PACIFIC OCEAN
Tropic of Cancer
AFRICA
Equator
PACIFIC OCEAN
SOUTH AMERICA
INDIAN OCEAN
Tropic of Capricorn
AUSTRALIA
N
Antarctic Circle
ANTARCTICA

Now Try This!

Trying to make a flat map out of a globe is like wrapping a round object in a piece of paper without making any creases. Try it with a small ball. Use scissors to cut out any bulges, creases, or bumps. Then unfold the paper. Does it look something like the interrupted projection on this page?

Photos taken of Earth from outer space seem to show a surface that is very much alike from one place to another. However, the closer one gets to the surface, the more differences one sees. On the surface itself, Earth is a complex, interesting place.

The diagram on these pages shows common forms of land and water. To find out about a certain form, check the number next to its description and find it on the diagram.

1. **bay**   A bay is a part of an ocean or lake that is partly enclosed by land.

2. **coast**   Coast is land that borders on the sea or ocean.

3. **delta**   A delta is an area formed by soil washed downstream by a river.

4. **glacier**   A glacier is a huge body of ice that moves slowly over land.

5. **island**   An island is an area of land surrounded by water.

6 **mountain range** A mountain range is a group of connected mountains or steep, high land areas.

7 **mouth of a river** A river mouth is the place where a river flows into a larger body of water.

8 **ocean** The oceans are the entire body of salt water that covers almost three fourths of Earth's surface.

9 **peninsula** A peninsula is a piece of land that is surrounded by water on three sides.

10 **plain** A plain is a broad stretch of level or nearly level land.

11 **plateau** A plateau is a large, level area of high land.

12 **source of a river** A river source is the place where a river begins.

13 **strait** A strait is a narrow waterway that connects two larger bodies of water.

14 **tributary** A tributary is a stream or river that flows into a larger river.

15 **volcano** A volcano is a mountain that builds up around an opening in Earth's surface. Under the opening is hot, melted rock.

Land AND People

How Do People in Different Places Live?

Explore the land that is America. Then learn how some Native Americans, Africans, and Europeans lived before they were thrust together in the Americas.

CHAPTER I

A LAND OF

The physical features of the United States affected the way our nation has developed and grown since it was first explored and settled.

▼ Find out what parts of America you can explore on page 12.

CONTENTS

SKILL POWER

Reading a Temperature Map   **4**
Explore what a temperature map can tell you about different sections of the United States.

GREAT VARIETY

These books tell about some people and places that are part of the story of our nation's geography and natural resources. Read one that interests you and fill out a book-review form.

READ AND RESEARCH

Adventures in Your National Parks **edited by Donald J. Crump** (National Geographic Society, 1988)
America's national parks help to preserve the country's natural beauty for all of us to see. Breathtaking photos show people taking part in park activities, such as wading in the Everglades and exploring Crater Lake. **(nonfiction)**

Going Places: The Young Traveler's Guide and Activity Book **by Harriet Webster, illustrated by Gail Owens** (Macmillan Publishing Co., 1991)
Reading this book will be fun as you learn tips on how to become a successful traveler in the United States. You will also learn much about what makes our country fascinating to explore. **(nonfiction)**

John Muir **by Eden Force** (Silver Burdett Press, 1990)
When you are thrilled by the sight of California's towering redwoods and struck by the majesty of Yosemite's granite cliffs, you can thank John Muir. Read how he heroically fought to save our wilderness areas for future generations. **(biography)**

The Nystrom Atlas of Our Country **edited by Charles Novosad** (Nystrom, 1996)
Use the variety of maps contained in this atlas to learn about the history and geography of the United States. With the help of photographs, time frames, art, and graphs, your knowledge of our country will grow. **(nonfiction)**

Skill Power

Reading a Temperature Map

You can use a temperature map to help you learn about different sections of the United States.

UNDERSTAND IT

Has your family ever taken a trip to another part of the United States? If so, how did you decide on what kind of clothes to pack? Did you take T-shirts and shorts? Or did you take a warm jacket and a sweater? Your decision probably depended on what your family knew about the average temperature of the place you were going to for the time of year in which you were traveling.

MESA VERDE NATIONAL PARK COLORADO

EXPLORE IT

Temperature measures the amount of heat in the air. A *temperature map* gives the average temperatures in an area over a period of time, such as a month. The map of the United States on the next page gives the average temperatures in July. The map key uses colors to show degrees Fahrenheit. Use the map and the map key to answer these questions.

1. What is the average July temperature in Indiana?

2. What are the average July temperatures in Texas?

3. What two states have areas that have average July temperatures above 90°F?

4. Which state has the lowest average July temperatures?

MOUNT RUSHMORE
BLACK HILLS SOUTH DAKOTA

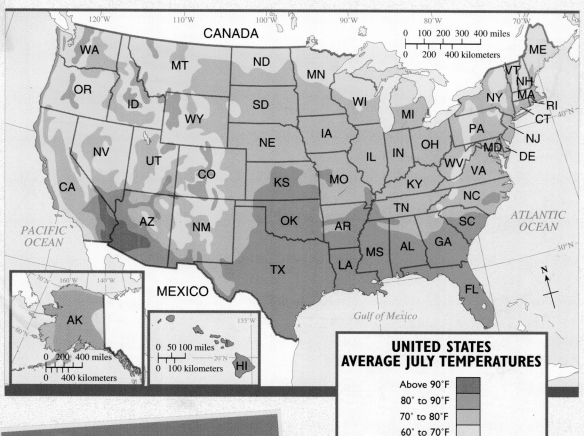

CANADA

**UNITED STATES
AVERAGE JULY TEMPERATURES**

Above 90°F
80° to 90°F
70° to 80°F
60° to 70°F
50° to 60°F
40° to 50°F

The ALAMO

TRY IT

Look at the map above and the map on page 10 that shows average January temperatures. Choose a part of the country that has average January or July temperatures that are different from the area in which you live. Plan a trip to that part of the country. Describe the kinds of clothes you would take. Include clothing you would take in case the actual temperature is 20° cooler or warmer than the average.

Colonial Williamsburg
Visitor's Companion

SKILL POWER SEARCH
Use the temperature map on page 10 to write five questions. Trade questions with a classmate and answer them.

Setting the Scene

⭐ **KEY TERMS**

history
geography
metropolitan area
natural resource
region
climate

OUR COUNTRY

FOCUS The United States has spectacular mountains, lakes, rivers, valleys, deserts, and plains. People from many different cultures live and work together here.

> This land is your land, — This land is my land
> From California — to the New York island;
> From the redwood forest — to the Gulf Stream waters;
> This land was made for you and me.
>
> Woody Guthrie

Our Wonderful Land

Look around you—at your city or town, your county, your state, your country. Just by looking, you can tell that the United States is a land of great variety. Your community is not exactly like any other community in your state. And your state does not look just like the state next to it.

That is because the United States contains seacoasts, mountains, lakes, rivers, marshes, valleys, deserts, canyons, and grasslands. Each of these landforms features different kinds of plant and animal life. The area in which you live has grown and developed differently than other areas of our nation. Our country's landforms have affected our country's **history** in many ways. But before we begin to study our country's history, we must first understand its **geography**.

history The study of past events and people
geography The study of the earth and how people use it

A Snapshot of America

A snapshot is a photo. Could you take *one* photo to show what our country looks like? As you have read, the country is different in different areas. You might be able to take a picture of your neighborhood or a natural wonder. But it would be hard to capture the country's variety in just *one* photo.

One reason is that our country is very large. Find the United States on the world map on pages 586–587 in the Atlas. With its 3.6 million square miles, the United States takes up about 6 percent of the world's land area. That makes it the fourth largest country, after Russia, Canada, and China.

More than 250 million people live in the United States. That's about 5 percent of the world's 5.4 billion people. Only China and India have larger populations. Compared with its neighbors, the United States has a huge population. It has about three times as many people as Mexico and nearly ten times as many people as Canada.

Who We Are

The United States is a diverse country made up of people from many different backgrounds. Many thousands of years ago the first Americans came here from Asia. Beginning in the late 1400s, people began arriving here from Europe. Over the years, people came here from many countries throughout the world. Immigrants, or people who were born in other countries, continue to come to the United States. Almost 20 million people living here today were born in other countries. That's 8 percent of the population. The largest group of immigrants in the 1980s and 1990s has come from Mexico. The second largest group immigrated from the Philippines. Between the 1970s and the 1990s large numbers of immigrants also came from Cuba, Vietnam, China, Korea, and Russia.

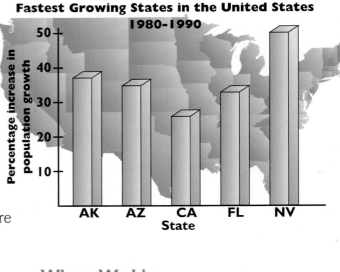

Fastest Growing States in the United States 1980–1990

Percentage increase in population growth — AK, AZ, CA, FL, NV — **State**

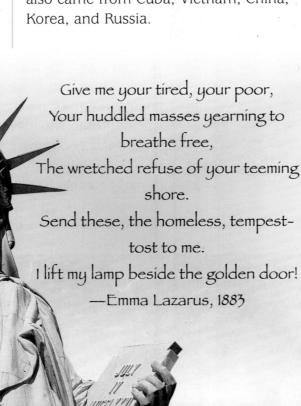

Emma Lazarus's poem "The New Colossus" is inscribed on the Statue of Liberty.

Give me your tired, your poor,
Your huddled masses yearning to breathe free,
The wretched refuse of your teeming shore.
Send these, the homeless, tempest-tost to me.
I lift my lamp beside the golden door!
—Emma Lazarus, 1883

Where We Live

Americans have always been on the move. Up until the 1800s, many Americans made their living farming, hunting, and fishing. Then some Americans moved to cities as industries grew there. Although farming is still a major occupation in the United States, today about 80 percent of all Americans live in or near cities. About half of them live in **metropolitan areas**.

In recent years, Americans have been moving to southern and western states. These areas have experienced more population growth than the North or the East. This movement has resulted in rapid population growth in states such as Alaska, Arizona, California, Florida, and Nevada. Today about 56 percent of the population lives in either the West or the South.

⭐ **metropolitan area** An area made up of a large city or several large cities and the surrounding towns, cities, and other communities

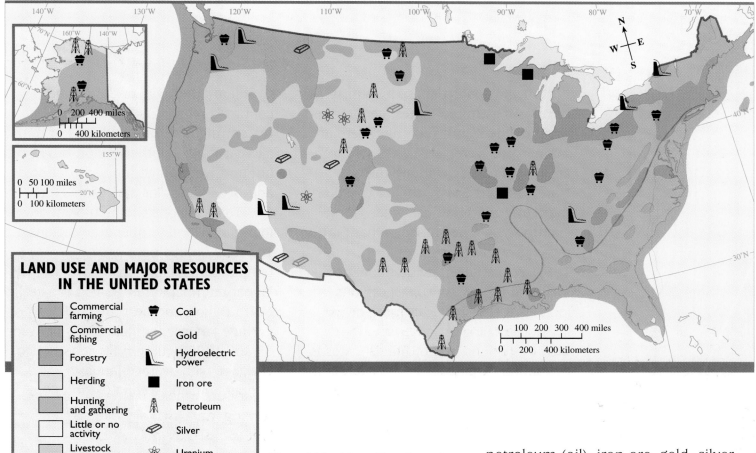

LAND USE AND MAJOR RESOURCES IN THE UNITED STATES

- Commercial farming
- Commercial fishing
- Forestry
- Herding
- Hunting and gathering
- Little or no activity
- Livestock raising
- Manufacturing and trade

- Coal
- Gold
- Hydroelectric power
- Iron ore
- Petroleum
- Silver
- Uranium

How We Use the Land

The United States has a great wealth of **natural resources**. Two of them are farmable land and an abundant supply of water. When early European settlers arrived on the Atlantic coast, they cut down trees and turned land into farms. Some people fished the abundant ocean waters. Still others used the fine coastal harbors to make their living in shipping and trade.

As time passed, and America became more settled, other great resources were tapped. As you can see on the map, the United States has such natural resources as coal, petroleum (oil), iron ore, gold, silver, and uranium. These resources affect what people do for a living. For example, vast oil reserves are located in parts of the United States. As a result, the production of petroleum has been key to Louisiana and Texas. Likewise, mining is an important industry in Rocky Mountain states such as Colorado and Wyoming.

Resources can also be used for recreation. Americans can enjoy swimming, boating, water skiing, and fishing on their country's oceans, lakes, and rivers. In addition, spectacular forests, valleys, mountains, and deserts are popular with skiers, campers, and backpackers.

★ **natural resource**   Things such as coal, water, or farmable land that are provided by nature and are useful to people

9

What Is a Region?

To help us learn about a country as large as the United States, geographers often divide it into **regions**. There are many types of regions. The ones we are most familiar with are the Northeast, the South, the Midwest, and the West, which we use when, for example, we tell someone what part of the country we live in.

But we can also divide the nation into land-use, or *economic*, regions by looking at forestry or farming or livestock-raising. Another way to identify regions in the United States is by natural resources, as you saw on the map on page 9.

Climate Regions

Still another way to define the country's regions is by **climate**. One region might be hot, with lots of rain all year long. Another region might be hot and wet part of the year but cold and dry in another part of the year.

Climate regions can be broken down into rainfall and temperature regions. The map on this page shows temperature regions, using average January temperatures. As you can see, North Dakota can be quite cold. Its average January temperature is between 0° and 10°F. Southern Florida, though, is warm, with average January temperatures between 60° and 80°F.

 region An area with one or more common characteristics that make it different from surrounding areas

climate The pattern of weather that a place has over a period of years

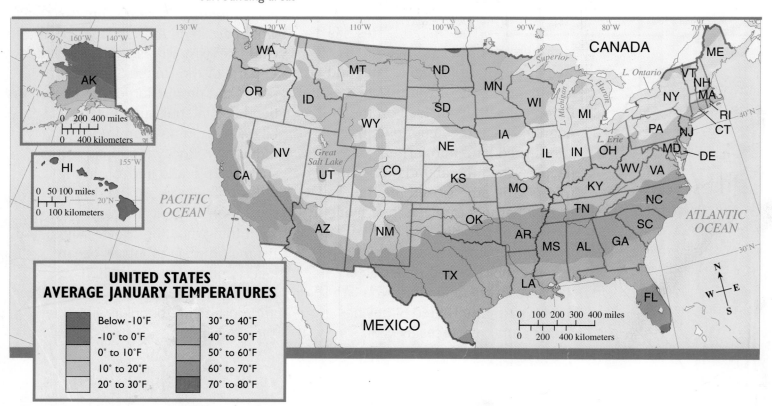

UNITED STATES AVERAGE JANUARY TEMPERATURES

Below -10°F	30° to 40°F
-10° to 0°F	40° to 50°F
0° to 10°F	50° to 60°F
10° to 20°F	60° to 70°F
20° to 30°F	70° to 80°F

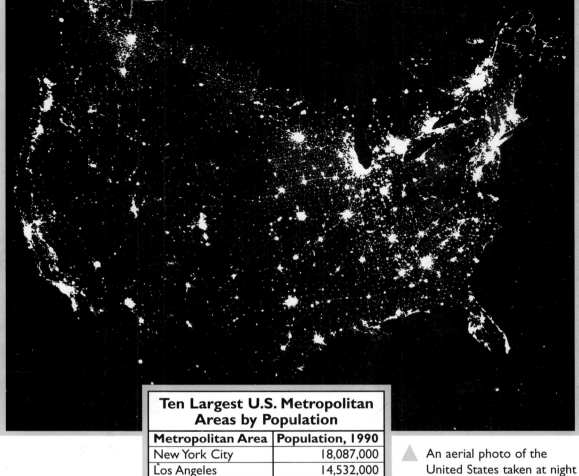

Ten Largest U.S. Metropolitan Areas by Population	
Metropolitan Area	Population, 1990
New York City	18,087,000
Los Angeles	14,532,000
Chicago	8,066,000
San Francisco	6,253,000
Philadelphia	5,899,000
Detroit	4,665,000
Boston	4,172,000
Washington	3,924,000
Dallas	3,885,000
Houston	3,711,000

An aerial photo of the United States taken at night

SHOW WHAT YOU KNOW!

REFOCUS
COMPREHENSION

1. Where do most Americans live?

2. Name three kinds of regions.

THINK ABOUT IT
CRITICAL THINKING

Why is it important for our country to have resources?

WRITE ABOUT IT
ACTIVITY

Describe the climate of your state and tell how it affects the way you live. Use the maps on pages 5 and 10 for reference.

Population Regions

Look at the photo of the United States on the top of this page. It was taken at night from a satellite in space. The lighted spots in the photo show the areas in which the greatest number of people live. Even though the photo isn't labeled, you can easily see where the largest cities are. The brightest glow on the Atlantic Coast includes Boston, New York City, Philadelphia, and Washington, D.C.

There are good reasons that people choose to live in certain places. Many American cities are located on the seacoast, along major rivers, or on the Great Lakes. These waters provide transportation, which is essential for trade. Take a look at the list of the top ten metropolitan areas. Four of the top five cities are located on either the East Coast or the West Coast. The other city, Chicago, is located on Lake Michigan. Some cities also grew because they were located close to natural resources needed to fuel industry.

Spotlight

REGIONS OF THE UNITED STATES

FOCUS *The United States has nine physical regions. Each has unique features that distinguish it from other regions of the nation.*

Nine Special Regions

You have already learned about some ways to study regions of the United States. Another common way to study the country is to look at its distinct landforms, or physical regions. Geographers have identified seven physical regions within the 48 contiguous (kun TIHG yoo us), or adjoining, United States, shown on the large map on page 13. These regions are the Coastal Plain, the Appalachian (ap uh LAY chun) Highlands, the Interior Lowlands, the Great Plains, the Rocky Mountains, the Intermontane West, and the Pacific West. In addition, the United States includes two other distinct regions—Alaska and Hawaii. They are shown in the two inset maps on page 13.

Most of the early Europeans and Africans who came to North America arrived on the Atlantic Coast. They moved westward over the years, eventually reaching all of the landform regions of the United States. Native Americans, who reached America long before Europeans and Africans, arrived in present-day Alaska and moved east and south from there.

THE PHYSICAL
REGIONS OF THE
UNITED STATES

The Coastal Plain

As you can see from the regional map on page 13, most of the land along the Atlantic Ocean and the Gulf of Mexico is a plain, or area of flat land. The Coastal Plain reaches from southern New England to Texas. Along the Atlantic Ocean the plain is often very narrow—sometimes only 20 or 30 miles wide. Along the Gulf of Mexico, it is much wider, reaching several hundred miles inland. The soil in this region is sandy and makes good farmland.

Many rivers, such as the Potomac (puh TOH muk) and the Savannah (suh-VAN uh), cut through this region. Several of our nation's largest cities began as ports where the rivers meet the ocean. The Coastal Plain has fine beaches along the Atlantic and the Gulf of Mexico. The region's low elevation gives it many swamps, marshes, and ~goons. One of the world's best-known ~tlands is the Everglades in Florida.

in A wide area of flat or gently rolling land
vation The height of land above sea level

Alligators call the southern part of the Coastal Plain home.

The Appalachian Mountains are popular with hikers.

The Coastal Plain also includes the most southerly part of the Mississippi River. This part of the plain, known as the Mississippi Delta, is a vast area of sand, silt, and mud. Because the land is so low, it is in constant danger of flooding.

Appalachian Highlands

Find the Appalachian Highlands on the map on page 13. The mountains in this region have different names in different states. They are the Green Mountains in Vermont, the Catskill Mountains in New York, and the Blue Ridge Mountains in Virginia and North Carolina. A few peaks are over 5,000 feet high. The Appalachians were a major barrier to transportation and moving west for early settlers.

The population of the Appalachian Highlands is fairly low. That's because

Wheat grows in the Interior Lowlands.

cattle, and dairy cows.

The region is also rich in natural resources such as coal and petroleum. Such resources are essential for the development of heavy industry. Two great cities in the Interior Lowlands grew up around railroads or industry. Chicago's growth revolved around railroads. And Detroit's growth came from manufacturing automobiles.

the land is rugged and the soil is poor for farming. But it does have grazing land for cattle and sheep. Also, parts of the region are rich in resources such as coal, oil, and timber.

Interior Lowlands

The Interior Lowlands covers the center, or *interior*, of the United States and is lower than the regions around it. The great feature of this region is the Mississippi River. Several other large rivers cut through the region and empty into the Mississippi. These include the Ohio and Missouri rivers.

Sediment from these rivers has helped to enrich the soil. This, plus a humid climate and flat land, makes the region one of great agricultural productivity. Farmers here specialize in raising crops such as corn, wheat, and soybeans. In addition, they raise hogs,

Great Plains

The Great Plains is a large, flat, fairly dry area between the Rocky Mountains and the Interior Lowlands. The land's elevation rises gently as you travel westward. Near the Rockies, the Great Plains reaches more than 5,000 feet in elevation. The region gets less than 20 inches of rain a year, and there are few trees except along the edges of rivers. The region's grassland, however, is ideal for grazing cattle.

Rodeos are common in the flat Great Plains.

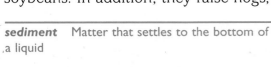

sediment   Matter that settles to the bottom of a liquid

15

"Old Faithful" is one of the natural wonders in Yellowstone National Park.

Large rivers, such as the Platte and the Kansas, flow west to east from the Rockies. Some of these rivers were followed by early settlers heading westward in covered wagons. The dryness of the Great Plains kept most people from settling there. That's why today the region has few large cities. Denver began as a small mining town but became a major city. It is on the Great Plains and also on the edge of the Rocky Mountains.

Rocky Mountains

Many peaks in the Rocky Mountains, such as Pike's Peak and Snowmass in Colorado, are over 14,000 feet in elevation. The Rocky Mountains, like the Appalachians, were a barrier to transportation. Severe, unpredictable weather made the Rockies a hazard to pioneers trying to move west. Early adventurers came to the Rockies to mine the region's rich deposits of gold, silver, and copper.

The rugged land and cold weather have kept this region sparsely settled. Some small cities have grown up as important ski resorts. These include Vail and Aspen in Colorado and Sun Valley in Idaho. Tourists flock to the Rockies to enjoy skiing, hiking, and backpacking. Two famous **national parks** are found here—Yellowstone, mostly in Wyoming, and Glacier in Montana.

Intermontane West

The Intermontane West is located between the Rocky Mountains and the mountains of the Pacific West. *Intermontane* means "between the mountains." This region is a vast area of deserts and dry lands. In this region, mountains alternate with flat areas called **basins**.

These areas are flat because over the ages they filled with sediment. When it

national park   An area of scenic beauty maintained by the federal government for the public to visit

basin   A wide, deep area bounded by higher elevations

A cactus blossoming in the desert ▶

Redwood trees are found only in the Coast Ranges ▶

rained, many streams overflowed into the deserts and then dried up, leaving the sediment behind. The Great Salt Lake in Utah formed in this way.

Only a few rivers cut through this region. But the results can be spectacular. The Colorado River, for example, has carved out the Grand Canyon. Some of the nation's largest dams, including the Hoover Dam on the Colorado River, are here. They provide a steady source of water, making it possible for cities such as Las Vegas and Phoenix to grow.

Pacific West

The Pacific West is a region of mountains and valleys. The Coast Ranges are located near the Pacific Ocean and extend through Washington, Oregon, and California. Farther inland there are more mountains—the Cascades in the north and the Sierra Nevada in the south.

In between the mountain ranges are some of the most fertile valleys in the world. These include the Willamette Valley in Oregon and the Central Valley in California. The Pacific West region is also rich in resources such as petroleum, fish, minerals, and forests.

Alaska and Hawaii

Alaska and Hawaii are two regions that are not located in the contiguous United States. Alaska is a vast,

mountainous region that lies far to the north. The climate is very cold, with long, bitter winters. In the summer, temperatures rise well above freezing. Most people who live in Alaska live in the southern part of the state where temperatures are warm enough in summer to allow for some farming.

Hawaii is made up of a series of islands in the Pacific Ocean. These islands are the tops of volcanic mountains that rise from the floor of the ocean. Much of Hawaii's income comes from tourists who enjoy its warm climate, pretty scenery, and beautiful beaches. Sugar, pineapple, and coffee are also important sources of income.

SHOW WHAT YOU KNOW!

REFOCUS
COMPREHENSION

1. List nine regions of the United States.

2. Compare and contrast the Coastal Plain and the Appalachian Highlands.

THINK ABOUT IT
CRITICAL THINKING

National parks are public property—they belong to all Americans. Why is it important to take care of and preserve these areas?

WRITE ABOUT IT
ACTIVITY

Which region do you live in? Describe its landforms and natural resources.

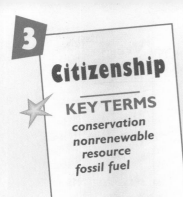

3

Citizenship

KEY TERMS

conservation
nonrenewable
resource
fossil fuel

CONSERVING OUR RESOURCES

FOCUS *More and more Americans have begun to realize the importance of conserving our country's resources.*

▲ Students in Los Angeles found ways to recycle plastic and build a playground.

Testing riverbeds for pollutants ▶

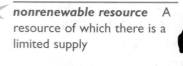

Taking Action

You have learned about the great natural beauty and variety of the United States. All over the country, people are now taking action to preserve that beauty and variety. In Everett, Washington, they have stopped companies from dumping waste into a nearby creek. In West Milford, New Jersey, they have convinced schools not to use disposable plastic food trays in cafeterias. In Austin, Texas, they have organized the Children's Alliance for Protection of the Environment to clean up local beaches.

★ *conservation* The care, protection, or management of natural resources

Why Conservation Is Important

These people—adults as well as children—are part of a growing movement to preserve the environment. As they have shown, this movement is not limited to powerful lawmakers or wealthy foundations. It has been started and helped along by people of all ages.

Conservation is important in assuring that our nation's natural resources are not being wasted or destroyed. Many natural resources are **nonrenewable resources**. *Nonrenewable* means we can't make any more of

★ *nonrenewable resource* A resource of which there is a limited supply

Conserving Resources

Here are a few simple things that you can do to help save the environment and our natural resources.

- Recycling aluminum cans, glass bottles, plastic bottles, and paper products reduces what we throw away.
- Conserving water helps save our limited usable water supply.
- Disposing of trash properly keeps the environment clean and safe for animals.
- Joining an organization or writing a letter to your representative or senator will let people know your concerns about the environment.
- Planting a tree provides homes for birds and animals and air for people and animals to breathe.

them. Once they are used up, they are gone from our lives forever. All **fossil fuels**—coal, petroleum, and natural gas—are nonrenewable resources.

Some resources are *renewable*. Renewable energy sources include water power, wind, and the sun. Although some resources are renewable, they must still be used wisely. For example, forests are renewable, but if we cut down too many trees at once, we may later face wood and paper shortages. Trees provide oxygen, which is necessary to maintain life on the earth.

fossil fuel   A nonrenewable energy source found underground

Saving Our Natural Resources

The chart above offers some simple ideas for conserving the earth's resources. Consider how you might use these ideas in your own life. After all, the earth belongs to all of us. We share the responsibility of caring for it.

As you read the remaining chapters in this book, think about how well the land and its resources have served us over the many years of our nation's history. Remember that if we use resources wisely, they will provide for us long into the future.

LINKING OUR LAND

FOCUS In the 1950s, President Eisenhower began the Interstate Highway System to link the nation's regions. The resulting **interstate highways** made cross-country travel easier and safer, so Americans could explore their country.

NATIONAL PARKS AND INTERSTATE HIGHWAYS

- National parks
- 90 Interstate highways
- ⊛ National capital
- ★ State capitals

Adventure in Our National Parks

The Interstate Highway System stretches from the Pacific Coast to the Atlantic Coast and from our border with Canada to our border with Mexico. Each highway has a number and passes through many different states. By learning the way the highways are numbered, you can travel around the nation. Use the interstate highways on the map to reach many national parks.

Map Legend

1 Everglades National Park Created in 1934, this park is responsible for protecting the endangered ecosystem of southern Florida. Visitors take nature walks and boat rides to see exotic plants and animals.

2 Great Smoky Mountains National Park This is the nation's busiest national park, with over 8 million visitors a year. It covers 800 square miles and has over 270 miles of roads and 900 miles of trails. Hiking the trails, you can see the homes of people who lived here before the area became a park.

3 Badlands National Park This park is famous for its 100-mile strip of cliffs known as "the Wall." Carved over many years by water, these cliffs attract hikers and campers year-round. The park also has 35-million-year-old fossils embedded in its cliffs.

4 Yellowstone National Park Almost as big as the state of Rhode Island, Yellowstone National Park is the site of Old Faithful, the world-famous geyser. Near Old Faithful is the Upper Geyser Basin, a one-mile-long trail of geysers and boiling hot springs.

5 Grand Canyon National Park Every year over 4 million people visit the Grand Canyon. This park offers a 277-mile long canyon, hiking, mule trails, museums, and Native American ruins.

6 Redwood National Park This park has 110,000 acres of redwood trees, some of which are over 200 feet high. The federal government created it in 1968 to preserve the redwood trees, estimated to be over 400 years old.

---

interstate highway One of the network of highways connecting the regions of the United States
ecosystem A group of plants and animals and their environment
geyser A hot spring that shoots steam

MAP IT

Your family in Boston is planning to visit some national parks.

1. What interstate highways will you take to get to the Great Smoky Mountains National Park? In what direction will you travel on each road?

2. You are now on Interstate 40, headed from the Great Smoky Mountains to Badlands National Park. What are some north-south routes you could take to get from Interstate 40 to Interstate 90? What pattern do you see in the numbers of the north-south routes as you travel toward Badlands?

3. After you leave Badlands National Park, your next stop is Yellowstone National Park. What points of interest will you see there?

4. You are on your way to Redwood National Park from Yellowstone. You want to visit relatives in Olympia, Washington, on the way. What interstates will you take to Redwood National Park?

EXPLORE IT

Plan a route from Redwood National Park to the Everglades. Choose the national parks you want to visit on the way and the interstate highways that can take you there.

SUMMING UP

1 DO YOU REMEMBER . . .
COMPREHENSION

1. How does the United States compare in size and population with other countries?

2. Give some examples to show that the United States has many kinds of landforms.

3. You can divide a climate region into two other kinds of regions. What are they?

4. Name the physical regions of the United States.

5. Name three features of the Coastal Plain.

6. What is the most important river in the Interior Lowlands?

7. Why does the Great Plains region have few large cities?

8. What two regions are not located in the contiguous United States?

9. What might happen if Americans do not practice conservation?

10. Which national park is home to alligators? Where could you see 400-year-old trees?

2 SKILL POWER
READING A TEMPERATURE MAP

In this chapter you have learned to read temperature maps. Work with a small group to make your own temperature map. Use your local newspaper or television station to track the daily temperatures in several communities in your state for one month. Then make a map that shows the average temperatures in those communities for that month. Repeat your project in six months.

3 WHAT DO YOU THINK?
CRITICAL THINKING

1. Why have Americans been moving to the southern and western states recently?

2. Which natural resources found in the United States do you think early settlers considered most valuable? Would a person today have a different answer? Why?

3. Why are both the Appalachian Mountains and the Rocky Mountains no longer barriers to settlement?

4. If you could live in any of the nine physical regions of the United States, which would you choose? Why?

5. The President of the United States has appointed you head of a commission to decide what qualifies a place to become a national park. What will your rules be?

4 SAY IT, WRITE IT, USE IT
VOCABULARY

You are the teacher. Make up a quiz to test your students' understanding of the words below. Give your quiz to classmates and see how they do.

basin	interstate highway
climate	metropolitan area
conservation	national park
ecosystem	natural resource
elevation	nonrenewable resource
fossil fuel	plain
geography	region
geyser	sediment
history	

5 GEOGRAPHY AND YOU
MAP STUDY

Use the maps on pages 13 and 20 to plan a two-week automobile trip for your family.

1. You have decided to visit three places in three different physical regions. What are they? Where are they located?

2. What highways will you take to your first stop?

3. What highways will link the three places you want to visit?

4. List the states you will go through on your trip.

6 TAKE ACTION
CITIZENSHIP

It is very important to protect the environment and help with conservation. With a small group of classmates, find out about organizations in your community that work to save natural resources and preserve the environment. Choose an organization that you would like to work with. Call and ask what you can do to help. With permission, volunteer to work with the organization of your choice.

7 GET CREATIVE
SCIENCE CONNECTION

Find out more about conservation and find a subject that interests you. (An environmental organization in your community will help you find a subject of interest.) With a partner or by yourself, create a poster that promotes conservation in your school or community. You can use original art, take photographs, or create a collage to emphasize your message. Present your poster with other posters made by your classmates.

LOOKING AHEAD
In Chapter 2, learn about life in Europe, Africa, and the Americas before 1500.

THREE

The first people to live in North America began to migrate from Asia many thousands of years ago. People from Europe and Africa also came here, but only after 1500. What was life like for some of these people before 1500?

CONTENTS

What is this girl holding? Turn to page 30 to find out.

HOMELANDS

These books tell about some people, places, and important events before 1500. Read one that interests you and fill out a book-review form.

READ AND RESEARCH

Morning Girl by **Michael Dorris** (Hyperion Books for Children, 1992)
Listen to 12-year-old Morning Girl and her brother, Star Boy, describe their peaceful lives on an island in the Bahamas just before the arrival of Columbus in 1492. What will happen when the explorers arrive? *(fiction)*

The Iroquois: A First Americans Book by **Virginia Driving Hawk Sneve, illustrated by Ronald Himler** (Holiday House, 1995)
Among the first people to live in what is now New York State were the Iroquois. From the peacemaker Hiawatha to women in the nation, you will learn about many different people in the Iroquois society. *(nonfiction)*

The Discovery of the Americas
by **Betsy and Giulio Maestro** (William Morrow & Co., 1991)
At least 20,000 years ago, the discovery of the Americas began. Read about the groups of people and explorers who found their way to the Americas by land and by sea. *(nonfiction)*

Fine Print: A Story About Johann Gutenberg
by **Joann Johansen Burch, illustrated by Kent Alan Aldrich** (Carolrhoda Books, 1991)
For over 30 years Johann Gutenberg struggled to invent a machine that would print books faster. Find out how important Gutenberg's contribution was to the world. *(biography)*

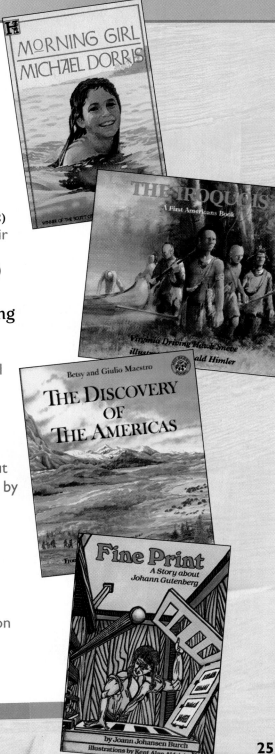

Writing a Research Report

Learning some simple steps to write a report will make your work easier and faster.

UNDERSTAND IT

You have to write a two-page social studies report. You've decided to do it on *Native American Ways of Life*. Right away, though, you have a problem. The encyclopedia article on *Native Americans* is 70 pages long, and you don't see anything about *ways of life*. What should you do?

Step 1 in writing a report is finding a suitable topic. *Native American Ways of Life* is too big and general for two pages. You have to narrow the topic.

To narrow a topic, get more specific. What group of Native Americans most interests you—the Hopis, Cheyennes, Iroquois, Seminoles? What is it about this group's way of living that gets your attention—their hunting or farming methods, their houses or religions or weapons? You can't cover them all in a short report, so choose one—Iroquois houses—and check the encyclopedia again.

EXPLORE IT

Once you've narrowed the topic, you're ready for *Step 2*—gathering information.

• Remember, your information should come from a variety of sources. Encyclopedias—in book version or on CD-ROM—are good places to start. Then check the library for other books and magazines. Your librarian can help you use databases, too.

• As you read, take notes on index cards. Write down any information that you might need. Don't copy anything word for word. Use your own words. On each index card, be sure to give the source of the information.

• Keep a list of the sources you use. Write the name of the source, the author, the publisher, the date of publication, and the page reference.

Step 3 is organizing your information. Organize ideas and information into categories. Then write a heading for each category: *Materials for Long Houses, How They Were Built,* and so on.

Step 4 is writing a first draft. Get your ideas down on paper in an order that makes sense.

Step 5 is the final draft. Make sure every sentence says exactly what you want it to say. Also be sure to check your spelling and punctuation.

TRY IT

Now write your own two-page report. To choose and narrow your topic, write the name of the Native American group or nation that interests you most. Then focus on one thing about this group's culture.

After you select your topic, make a plan of action. Set dates for finishing each of the five steps, allowing enough time for each one. Plan an illustration or two for your report. Then share the report with your classmates.

Hopi Pottery

by Sally Davis
Mrs. Walters
Grade 5

SKILL

POWER SEARCH As you read this chapter, think about the research. What sources might the writers have used? How did they organize their information?

1 Setting the Scene

KEY TERMS

migrate
nomad
environment
culture
mesa
long house

NATIVE AMERICANS

FOCUS By the 1400s the Pueblos of the Southwest and the Iroquois of the Northeast were among the more than 500 nations of Native Americans living in North and South America.

The First Americans

In Chapter 1 you looked at the geography of the United States. Now you will find out about the people. But there was a time, many thousands of years ago, when no people lived in the Americas. Over a very long period of time, people came here from Asia and then from Europe and Africa. In this chapter you will read about how some of these people lived in their homelands before 1500. In later chapters you will explore how, why, and when some of these diverse people left their homelands and came to the Americas.

The first people who came to North America **migrated** from Asia between 20,000 and 36,000 years ago. As shown on the map, Asia and North America are separated by a body of water called the Bering Strait. But 36,000 years ago, land connected Asia and North America.

This land bridge was over 1,000 miles wide. People crossed into North America on foot, looking for plants to

migrate To move from one place to another

ROUTES OF THE FIRST AMERICANS

→ First Americans

Present-day land area

Bering Strait Land Bridge

Other land area during Ice Age

Ice sheet

eat and animals to hunt. Over thousands of years these people spread out through North and South America. You can see their migration routes on the map. Because they were the first people to populate the Americas, we refer to them as Native Americans or American Indians.

Hunters killed animals with sharp stone points attached to wooden handles.

Nomads and Farmers

Early Native Americans were **nomads**, people who wander in search of food. They knew how to make spear points from hard stones. Their tools helped them hunt large animals, such as the woolly mammoth.

About 10,000 years ago the climate gradually became warmer. Much grassland turned to desert or forest, and many large animals didn't survive. Native Americans had to hunt smaller animals, fish, and gather fruits, nuts, and other vegetation. In time, some learned to farm, and this allowed them to become settled.

Native people lived in many areas of North America. Four of the major groups are shown on the map on page 30. Different **environments** greatly affected the way each group lived. As the members of each group found ways to cope in their new environment, they formed a unique **culture**.

Eventually there were more than 500 groups or nations of Native Americans. By the 1400s these nations totaled about 10 million people. Two groups who lived in very different environments were the Pueblos of the Southwest and the Iroquois of the Northeast.

▲ Pueblo ruins at Mesa Verde, Colorado

The Pueblo People

Native Americans who were later called Pueblos lived in permanent villages. In fact, the word *pueblo* comes from the Spanish word meaning "village." The Pueblos built their homes, groups of which were also called *pueblos*, from materials found in their environment. Walls were made of local stone, and roofs were made of timber covered with tree branches and

★ **nomad** A person who moves from place to place
environment The physical setting of a place, including everything that affects the way people live there: the land, air, water, plants, animals

★ **culture** The ideas, values, tools, skills, arts, and way of life of a certain people

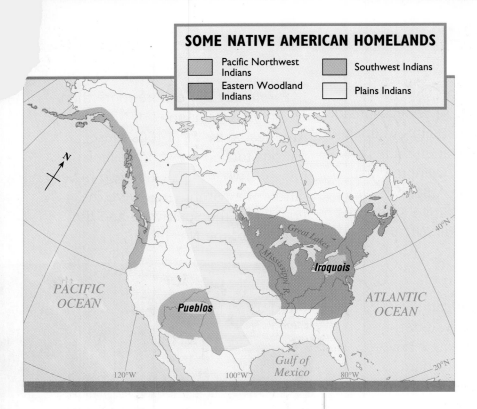

Pacific Northwest Indians

Eastern Woodland Indians

Southwest Indians

Plains Indians

PACIFIC OCEAN

Iroquois

Pueblos

ATLANTIC OCEAN

Gulf of Mexico

Pueblo Farming

The dry land and rocky cliffs made the Southwest a difficult place in which to live. But the Pueblos found ways to farm the land successfully. They watered their crops to make up for the lack of rain. People who didn't live near rivers made reservoirs to collect and store rainwater and mountain runoff. They even rolled huge snowballs off the mountains to melt in the reservoirs.

This water was used for growing crops such as corn, beans, peppers, and squash. Corn was the most important crop. Most days, and especially at times of celebration, Pueblos ate a corn bread called *piki* (PEE kee). They also grew cotton, which they wove into cloth for blankets and clothing.

earth. In some areas the Pueblos built their homes on top of flat plateaus or hills, called **mesas**. Houses were box-shaped, and as more houses were needed, they were built next to or even on top of others.

In areas where stone was scarce, houses were built out of a clay mixture called adobe (uh DOH bee). These homes, too, were built side by side and stacked on top of each other. Homes built closely together helped make villages safe from enemy attacks. Cliff-top locations, small doorways, and removable ladders made pueblos easier to defend.

mesa A flat-topped hill or small plateau with steep sides

Pots like this one were used to store food and water. Squash and beans were Pueblo crops.

Women and Men Share Work

Women made grinding stones, pottery, and baskets. Women also prepared and stored the food. Food storage was important because lack of rain could ruin crops. Men worked in the fields, collected building stones, and in many pueblos did the weaving, knitting, and embroidery. They also made arrows and other necessary tools.

A reconstructed Iroquois long house

The Iroquois

The Iroquois also began building permanent homes and growing crops. The map on page 30 shows the extent of their territory. The Iroquois lived in long rectangular buildings called **long houses**. These were made of poles covered with bark shingles and were about 60 feet long, 18 feet wide, and 18 feet high. As many as 10 to 12 related families, each with its own living space and fire, occupied a long house. Usually a woman and her husband, their unmarried children, and their married daughters and families made up the household. When a son married, he moved into his wife's long house.

Sharing Responsibility

Iroquois divided work between men and women. Women grew corn and other crops, gathered wild vegetation, cooked, and prepared animal skins to make clothes and moccasins. Men fished and hunted for deer and elk.

Women and men shared political power. Women headed each household, but they chose male leaders to represent their households in village meetings. Men were the warriors, but women could prevent military excursions by withholding food and moccasins.

An Iroquois mask, or false face, worn for prayers and offerings

⭐ **long house** A large house built by Native Americans in which a number of families lived

SHOW WHAT YOU KNOW!

REFOCUS
COMPREHENSION

1. How did people first arrive in North and South America?

2. How did the environment of the Southwest affect the Pueblos' way of life?

THINK ABOUT IT
CRITICAL THINKING

What were some benefits for Native Americans of learning to farm?

WRITE ABOUT IT
ACTIVITY

Do some research to find out more about the Iroquois. Write about their family life.

LIVING IN A HOPI PUEBLO

FOCUS *The Hopis were a Pueblo group living in an arid section of the Southwest. Finding water for crops in this region was difficult. However, the Hopis succeeded in building villages and growing a variety of crops.*

WHERE PUEBLO INDIANS LIVED

Pueblo peoples

Hopi pueblos

Adventure in a Hopi Pueblo

Hot days, cold nights, and about ten inches of rain each year made life difficult in a Hopi (HOH-pee) pueblo. The sun sucked up each drop of water, leaving the earth dry and lifeless. Summer rainfalls brought water, but their floods often spelled doom for young unprotected corn plants. The Hopis walked miles to their fields and toiled for hours, hoping that some of these plants would survive.

Map Key

1 Pueblo To protect themselves from attack, the Hopis built their pueblos on top of high mesas. Hopi pueblos were as large as five stories high. As many as 1,000 people might call a pueblo home.

2 Corral Here the Hopis kept animals, including wild turkeys. They also kept eagles. Corrals were made of either stones and mud or wooden posts.

3 Rainwater pools The Hopis dug pools in the top of the mesas to collect rainwater. In the winter, snowballs were put into the pools to melt.

4 Gardens Each family had a garden, where beans, peppers, and onions were planted. Small walls were built around each plant to keep in the water. Gardens were often located at the base of the mesas to catch the rain running down from the top.

5 Underground spring Underground springs were often found where the rain running down from the top of the mesa landed. Finding the underground water was difficult. Digging up too much of the hard topsoil might cause the underground water to dry up.

6 Corn The Hopis traveled miles to find the best places to plant corn and other crops. These were often at the base of mesas or near small streams. Corn was the most important crop. It was grown in the summer to take advantage of rainstorms. Seeds were planted deep into the ground so that roots could reach the underground springs.

7 Field Shelters Shelters were built on the edges of fields to provide shade from the sun. Many were built out of tree branches or stones. If fields were far from home, farmers built small pueblos to live in until the harvest.

★ **topsoil** The upper layer of soil

8 Storage Storing food was important for the Hopis, who faced cold winter months and frequent droughts (drouts), or dry spells. Each family had a room in the pueblo where a two-year supply of food was dried and stored.

MAP IT

Think about being a Hopi child living in a pueblo. Your mother is grinding corn into meal, using her metate (muh TAHT ay), or stone. She asks you to get more corn from your father, who is out in a field. Describe what you see as you go to find him.

1. As you near the fields, you hear men talking about planting a new field. Where might be a good spot? Why?

2. You cannot find your father. The villagers tell you he is resting from the hot sun. Where will you find him?

3. Your father tells you that the family's garden needs water. Where are you likely to find water for the plants? Trace the route you will take to get the water.

EXPLORE IT

The pueblo is getting crowded. Some people decide to build a new pueblo and plant their own cornfields. Look at the drawing and locate a good place for a new pueblo. Explain why you chose that spot.

PEOPLE OF WEST AFRICA

FOCUS *By the 1400s, kingdoms such as Ghana, Mali, and Songhai were among several large kingdoms that had flourished in West Africa.*

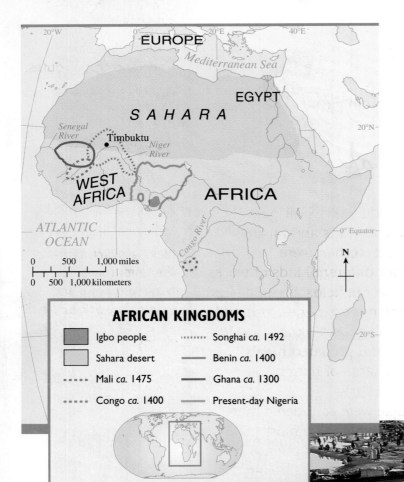

AFRICAN KINGDOMS

■	Igbo people	⋯⋯⋯	Songhai *ca.* 1492
■	Sahara desert	▬▬	Benin *ca.* 1400
⋯⋯⋯	Mali *ca.* 1475	▬▬	Ghana *ca.* 1300
⋯⋯⋯	Congo *ca.* 1400	▬▬	Present-day Nigeria

An Ancient Society

The first people who lived in Africa, about 2 million years ago, were nomads. Around 7,000 years ago they learned how to farm and raise animals. Although some groups remained nomadic, many settled to farm in small villages.

By the 1400s several great kingdoms had arisen in West Africa. You can find some of them on the map. The supply of gold and ivory in West Africa helped form these wealthy and powerful kingdoms. There were extensive trading networks and large cities where the arts and education flourished. Scholars studied science, law, and religion. Artists created sculptures, ceramics, and metalwork.

The Kingdom of Ghana

The first of these great kingdoms was Ghana. It controlled an important trade route through the Sahara Desert between West Africa, northern Africa,

Present-day salt market on the Niger River ▶

This head, made of zinc and brass, represents a king from West Africa.

and southern Europe. Ghana traded items within Africa, such as gold and salt. In fact, salt was so important that it was literally worth its weight in gold. In hot climates, people needed salt in their bodies to keep from losing too much water. Salt was also needed to season some foods and preserve others, especially meats.

In addition, the traders of Ghana exchanged gold, ivory, salt, and other objects for European clothes, horses, glassware, swords, and books. Ghana traders also bartered enslaved people, who were **slaves**.

Mali and Songhai

In the mid-1000s, Ghana was conquered. Soon, Mali replaced Ghana as the largest kingdom in West Africa. Like Ghana before it, Mali controlled important Saharan trade routes. In Mali, the city of Timbuktu (TIM buck TOO), was a center of culture and learning.

Mali eventually lost control of its outermost regions and by the early 1400s was replaced by Songhai (SAWNG-gye), the largest and most powerful of the three kingdoms. Other kingdoms of this time period were Congo and Benin. Congo reached its height between the 1300s and 1600s. Benin, known for its brass work, survived well into the 1800s.

Life in West Africa

Farmers lived in small villages, growing rice and yams and raising cattle. Men and women were responsible for different kinds of work. Both worked in the fields, breaking up the soil. Women tended the crops and traded food and goods in the marketplaces and prepared meals. Men were in charge of hunting, fishing, and warfare.

Some people were considered more important than others. The most respected were nobles and priests, usually elderly men. Next came farmers, the largest category. Least respected were the slaves. People became enslaved in different ways. Some were captured in war, others were criminals, and still others sold themselves into slavery to repay debts. By the early 1600s, enslaved Africans were being forced on ships headed to the Americas.

⭐ *slave* A person who is enslaved and owned by another person

SHOW WHAT YOU KNOW!

REFOCUS
COMPREHENSION

1. Name the three largest West African kingdoms.

2. Describe Ghana trade and trade routes.

THINK ABOUT IT
CRITICAL THINKING

Why were many people in these kingdoms farmers?

WRITE ABOUT IT
ACTIVITY

Make a chart showing the differences between men's and women's work in West African villages in the 1400s.

GROWING UP IN AN IGBO VILLAGE

FOCUS *Like children everywhere, African children had to learn many things on the road to adulthood.*

A Child's Life

What would it be like to grow up in West Africa in the 1400s? The answer would depend, in part, on which African society you lived in. Just as there were many groups of Native Americans, each with their own way of life, so too were there many African communities. One group, called the Igbo (IHG boh), lived in what is now Nigeria.

Suppose you were born into an Igbo family. Your first three years of life would be spent surrounded by family and friends and being showered with affection. Adults let you do just about anything you want.

▼ West African girl carrying sticks

Soon, though, your carefree life comes to an end. By the age of three or four, you have chores to do. If you are a boy, you carry messages for your father. If you are a girl, you collect firewood for cooking. By age five or six, boy or girl, you also work in the fields. You spend long hot hours helping your parents grow yams and rice for the village.

As a young child, much of your free time is spent in the center of the village, mixing with other children. You do not go to a formal school. You often play games in the sand or wrestle with your friends.

▲ This mask is for a play in Igbo villages.

 society People living together as a group with the same way of life

West African mother and child gathering rice

Girls Learn From Their Mothers

As Igbo children grow older, boys and girls begin to be separated from each other. Igbo girls spend much time with their mothers. They learn to sweep floors, prepare food, and polish the clay walls of their homes by using wet banana leaves. Since women do the trading, girls accompany their mothers to market, where they learn to bargain for oils, peppers, fish, and other goods.

Beginning at age four, girls also have to learn to carry water. No village can survive without fresh water, and often the nearest supply is a long way off. To bring water back, girls have to balance water pots on their heads. Imagine trying to carry a full pot of water on your head. Now imagine doing it while walking two miles through the hot morning sun in bare feet as insects swarm all around you!

Secret Societies for Girls

Mothers are not the only ones who teach Igbo girls. Some training comes from so-called secret societies. These groups, led by older unmarried girls, teach girls to make up songs, create new dances, sew special costumes, and prepare elaborate feasts. Igbo girls also take part in wrestling matches to see who is the strongest and most powerful among them.

These secret societies have rules governing girls' behavior. If you are an Igbo girl and you break the rules, you are fined. Did you leave trash lying around? Were you too lazy to help polish the walls of

Woman and child from Mali carrying water on their heads

37

Calabash, or gourd, carver of West Africa

a neighbor's new home? Did you skip some of your cleaning duties? If so, it will cost you. After paying a few fines, you will probably change your ways. This is how you will learn appropriate behavior.

Boys' Societies

Boys, meanwhile, have secret societies of their own. The boys' groups are even more organized and more secret than the girls' societies are. The boys' groups are set up in a separate part of the village and are off-limits to all girls and women—no sisters,

girlfriends, or mothers are allowed to visit here.

Boys learn many things in their secret societies, including archery and wrestling. They also learn the rules of fighting and become experts at using a long sharp knife called a machete (muh SHET ee).

From age five, boys spend most of their time in these secret societies. Their mothers still feed them. Their fathers still expect them to help with farm work and to carry clay from nearby pits so that new houses can be built. But beyond that, parents have little control over their sons. Whatever a boy needs to know, he learns from the other boys in his society.

Boys quickly figure out that life in a secret society is tougher than life with parents. If you are an Igbo boy and you misbehave around your parents, they may smile or shake their heads. But discipline is strong in your secret society. You need to learn how to behave before you can take your place as an adult in the village.

SHOW WHAT YOU KNOW!

REFOCUS
COMPREHENSION

1. What chores did Igbo boys do?
2. What chores did Igbo girls do?

THINK ABOUT IT
CRITICAL THINKING

Why were the secret societies so important to the Igbo people?

WRITE ABOUT IT
ACTIVITY

Write a paragraph telling what chores you are expected to do and how these differ from those of an Igbo child.

LIFE IN EUROPE

FOCUS *Europeans in the 1400s had clear ideas about how the world was ordered. By the end of the century, they were also developing national identities.*

Kings and Peasants

Europeans in the 1400s had different lives according to their rank, or position, in society. A person's position was based on wealth, political power, and the status of his or her parents.

Most powerful and important were kings. With the help of soldiers, kings tried to acquire territory.

People in a king's territory were expected to pay taxes, increasing his wealth. A king's power depended on the support of rich men who ran the local governments.

Most people were peasants, who had the lowest rank in society. Peasants were farmers who either owned or rented land in villages. But because farming was such hard work, villagers shared the work of

plowing, planting, and harvesting crops such as wheat, rye, barley, and oats. Many villages also had some land for grazing cattle and other livestock that everyone shared.

Work for Men and Women

Men were responsible for much of the work in the fields. At planting and harvest time, however, women helped,

▼ Working in the fields is the subject of this painting from the 1400s.

EUROPE IN 1450

• Major cities

— National boundaries

ENGLAND
London •
Antwerp •
Paris •
FRANCE
HOLY ROMAN EMPIRE
Milan •
SPAIN
Venice
• Lisbon
Seville •
Rome •
Naples •
Constantinople •
Black Sea
PORTUGAL
AFRICA
Mediterranean Sea
ASIA

60°N
50°N
40°N
30°N

0°   10°E   20°E   30°E   40°E

too. Some men also herded livestock, such as sheep for wool, and goats, pigs, and cattle for food.

Peasant women worked hard, milking cows and raising poultry. They cared for children, preserved food, cooked, spun thread for making clothing, and did other jobs necessary for maintaining the household.

Some poor peasants moved from the country to the cities in search of a better living. But even if they found jobs, they often remained poor.

Whether peasant or royalty, women in Europe had less status than men. Most Europeans believed that men were better suited than women to be political and religious leaders. Even though peasant women had huge responsibilities, men were considered heads of households.

Culture Flourishes

Important changes in education, art, architecture, and literature took place in Europe before 1500. Johann Gutenberg invented a printing press with moveable type in the 1440s. Within 50 years many presses were built. Now books and other printed materials were available in European cities.

Art and architecture flourished, often around religious themes. Huge cathedrals were built to glorify Christianity. These buildings had stained-glass windows that often depicted biblical scenes. Since most people couldn't read or write, they could "read" the Bible by looking at the windows. Elaborate paintings and **tapestries** served a similar purpose.

▲ Cathedral of Notre Dame de Paris and a stained-glass window from the cathedral

 tapestry An elaborate, heavy cloth with designs and scenes woven into it

Many fine works of literature were also produced. Some, called illuminated manuscripts, were hand-written, with decorative initial letters, designs in gold and silver, and miniature pictures.

Europe in a State of Change

Europe was emerging from a difficult period in the 1400s. During the 1300s there was not only widespread starvation but also a terrible plague, a deadly disease that travels from person to person. This Black Death killed one third of Europe's population.

Warfare, too, took its toll. Between 1337 and 1453, France and England, in a struggle for territory, fought a series of wars known as the Hundred Years' War. But this warfare helped

bring about great changes in Europe. People began thinking in terms of national, rather than local, interests. A feeling of **nationalism**, or pride in one's country, developed. With this new way of looking at themselves, and with the years of famine and plague behind them, Europeans soon looked beyond their own borders and set out to explore other parts of the world.

Three Cultures Meet

As a result of exploration, Native Americans and Europeans came into contact for the first time in the Americas. Eventually, enslaved Africans were also forced to come. By the 1600s, Native Americans, Europeans, and Africans were living side by side in the Americas.

---

nationalism A feeling of pride, loyalty, and devotion to one's country

This page from a French book of the 1400s shows the activities of the farm year.

SHOW WHAT YOU KNOW!

REFOCUS
COMPREHENSION

1. What kind of work was done by peasant men and women?

2. Describe some ways in which culture flourished in Europe before 1500.

THINK ABOUT IT
CRITICAL THINKING

Why was the availability of books, made possible by Gutenberg's printing press, an important development?

WRITE ABOUT IT
ACTIVITY

Write a paragraph telling why a person might be proud of his or her nation.

SUMMING UP

1 DO YOU REMEMBER . . .
COMPREHENSION

1. When did the first Native Americans settle in North America?

2. About how many Native Americans lived in North America in the 1400s?

3. How were Pueblo houses different from Iroquois houses?

4. Why were Hopi homes built on mesas?

5. What led Ghana to become a great kingdom in Africa?

6. What types of work did women do in West Africa? What work did men do?

7. If you were an Igbo girl, what might you learn in your secret society?

8. What did Igbo boys learn in their secret societies?

9. Why was Johann Gutenberg's invention so important?

10. What serious disease killed one third of Europe's population in the 1300s?

2 SKILL POWER
WRITING A RESEARCH REPORT

In this chapter you read about many possible topics for a research report. Choose three topics you've read about and narrow them to about the right size for a report. Then list three likely sources you might use to find out more information about each topic.

3 WHAT DO YOU THINK?
CRITICAL THINKING

1. The land bridge crossed by the first Native Americans is no longer there. (See map on page 28.) Tell what you think happened to it.

2. Would you rather live in a Hopi village or in an Iroquois village? Give reasons for your choice.

3. Why did trade instead of farming lead to the rise of large kingdoms in Africa?

4. What institutions in your community might play some of the same roles that secret societies did for the Igbo?

5. Why do you think Europeans wanted to explore other parts of the world?

4 SAY IT, WRITE IT, USE IT
VOCABULARY

You've just traveled by time machine to North America in the 1400s to visit Iroquois and Hopi settlements. In a letter to a friend, describe what you see. Try to include most of the vocabulary words in your letter.

culture	nomad
environment	slave
long house	society
mesa	tapestry
migrate	topsoil
nationalism	

5 GEOGRAPHY AND YOU
MAP STUDY

Use the map below and the ones on pages 28, 30, and 34 to answer the following questions.

1. Name the major cities in Europe in 1450.

2. What body of water now separates Asia and North America?

3. Which Native American group lived near the Pacific Ocean?

4. In what direction would you travel to go from West Africa across the Sahara Desert to Europe?

6 TAKE ACTION
CITIZENSHIP

Taking pride in one's country is very important. With a group of classmates, make a list of things about the United States that make you very proud. Tell what it is about each item that gives you this sense of pride. What other things make you proud?

7 GET CREATIVE
LANGUAGE ARTS CONNECTION

Look at the traditional designs on the Pueblo pot and the African calabash in this chapter. Or find other traditional Native American and African designs in library books. Choose one design and describe something about that design.

LOOKING AHEAD
In the next chapter you will learn more about why Europeans set out to explore other parts of the world.

Exploration AND Colonization

UNIT 2

CHAPTER 3
EXPLORATION

CHAPTER 4
EARLY EUROPEAN SETTLEMENTS

CHAPTER 5
THE NEW ENGLAND COLONIES

CHAPTER 6
THE SOUTHERN COLONIES

CHAPTER 7
THE MIDDLE COLONIES

Why Do People Explore and Colonize?

Go back in time and find out what made people explore and colonize. Learn what happened when people from different cultures encountered one another and how people adapted to a new environment.

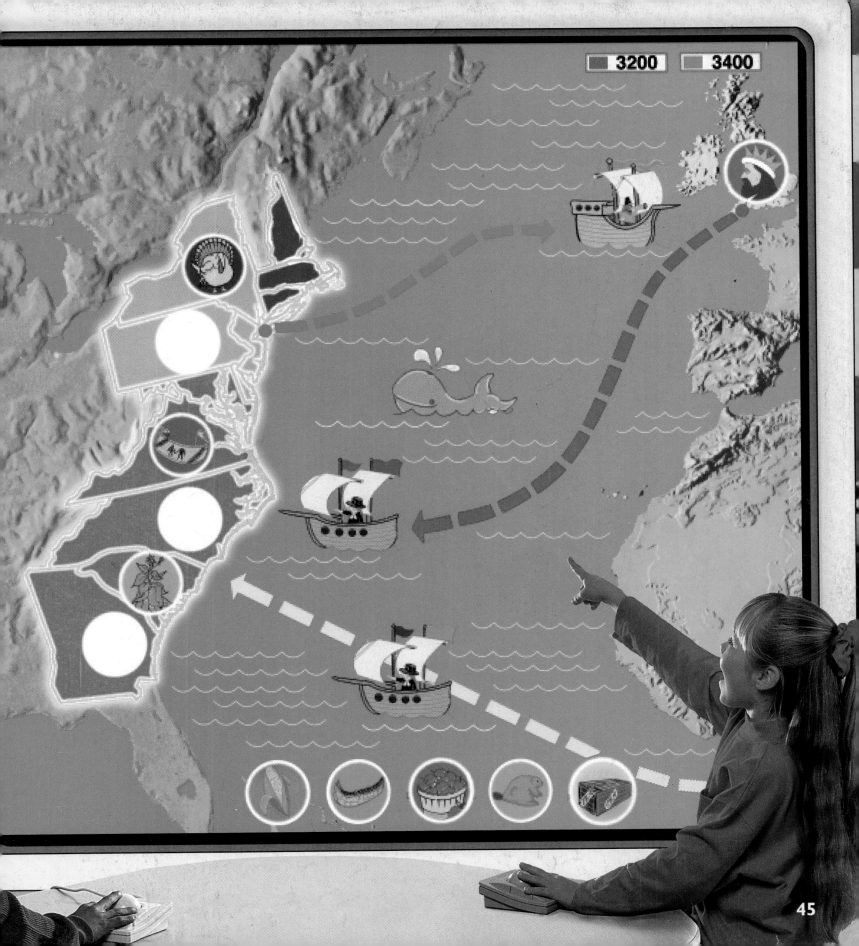

EXPLORATION

By the 1400s, Europeans' desire for riches had inspired them to travel to unknown places. At first the goal was to find a water route to Asia. In 1492, Christopher Columbus reached the Americas, and Europeans' knowledge of the world changed forever.

▼ This girl is holding a sextant. Find out what it was used for on page 52.

Skill Power CONTENTS

These books tell about explorers and explorations of the 1200s, 1400s, and 1500s. Read one that interests you and fill out a book-review form.

READ AND RESEARCH

Pedro's Journal by **Pam Conrad** (Scholastic, 1992)
Pedro de Salcedo is a ship's boy aboard Christopher Columbus's *Santa María*. Read Pedro's journal about the excitement of finally reaching land. *(historical fiction)*
- *You can read a selection from this book on page 58.*

Around the World in a Hundred Years: From Henry the Navigator to Magellan by **Jean Fritz** (G. P. Putnam's Sons, 1994)
In 1400 all maps had a space at the edge representing the "Unknown," a dangerous area that no one could explore and hope to return from. Travel with many different explorers on their journeys to find out more about the "Unknown." *(nonfiction)*

Marco Polo by **Zachary Kent** (Childrens Press, 1992)
Read about the life and journeys of the remarkable Marco Polo. Use the map at the end of the book to follow him as he travels through China and other Asian lands. *(biography)*

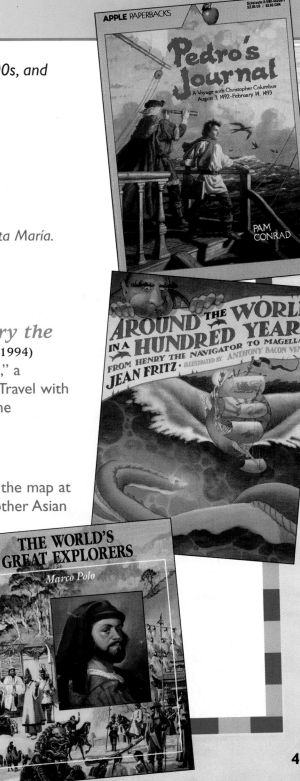

Tracing Routes on a Map

Knowing how to trace routes on a map can help you understand important information about the past.

UNDERSTAND IT

Have you ever had to explain to a friend how to get to your home or tell a new student where the cafeteria is? Then you know what a difference a map can make. Even if it's just a rough sketch on a scrap of paper, a good map clears up the confusion over where you're going in no time.

At one time there were very few maps. There was even a time when there weren't any maps of the continent of North America. That was the case when Spaniards began to explore what is now America. As explorers, part of their job was to create the first maps.

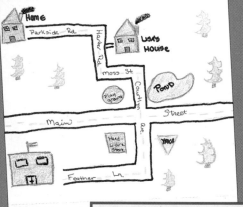

This is a modern-day map showing the routes that Cabeza de Vaca took. ▶

EXPLORE IT

Álvar Núñez Cabeza de Vaca (AHL vahr NOO nyethh kah BE thhah thhe VAH kah) could have used a good map. In 1528, after sailing across the Gulf of Mexico from Florida, he was shipwrecked near what is now Texas. Hoping to find a Spanish settlement, Cabeza de Vaca wandered for eight years across unmapped territory. Eventually, he reached a Spanish settlement in Mexico.

Cabeza de Vaca's route is shown on the map below. How many present-day states did he pass through during his long journey? According to the map key, when did his exploration take place?

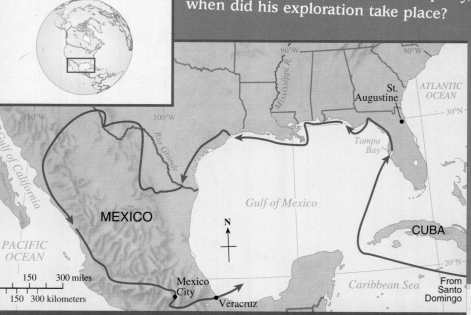

CABEZA DE VACA'S EXPLORATION

◀— Cabeza de Vaca, 1528–1536

—— Present–day boundaries

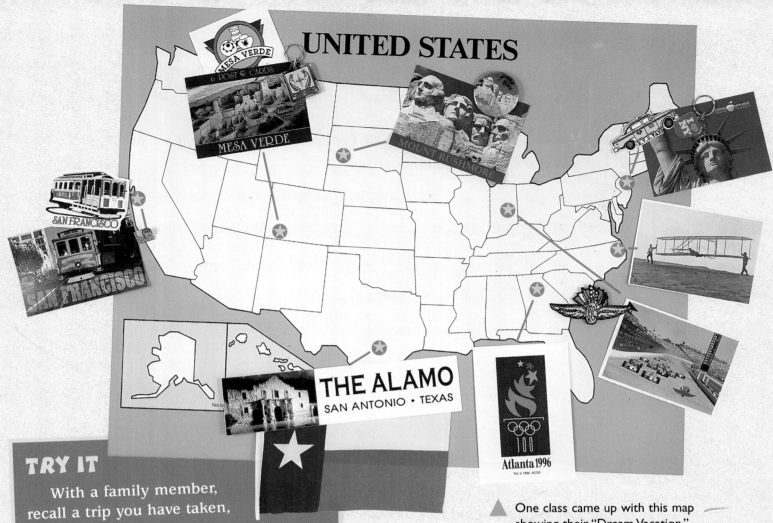

UNITED STATES

One class came up with this map showing their "Dream Vacation."

TRY IT

With a family member, recall a trip you have taken, whether to another state or simply in your neighborhood. You might have made the trip by car, bus, train, or plane. On a local map, state map, or map of the United States, mark the two locations between which you traveled. Then draw in the route you followed between the two places.

With a group of classmates, create a "Dream Vacation" map. Each member of your group should first name one place in the United States that he or she would like to visit. Mark these locations on a map of the United States. Then trace the best route to follow to visit all these places and return home. You can decorate your map with pictures of the things you would see at each place.

SKILL POWER SEARCH

Can you find other maps in this book that show the routes of different explorers?

49

1
Setting the Scene

⭐ **KEY TERMS**

Crusade
empire
cartographer
northwest passage
conquistador
economy

EXPLORING THE WORLD

FOCUS *In the 1400s and 1500s, Europeans discovered that the world was a much larger place than they had previously imagined.*

Looking Outward

In the early 1400s, most Europeans had no idea that the continents of North and South America existed. It was by accident that their view of the world was changed forever.

Even though they didn't know about the Americas, Europeans were curious about the world outside their borders. European fascination with foreign lands began with the **Crusades**, a series of wars fought between Christians and Muslims. Muslims are followers of the religion of Islam. Christians believe in the religion of Christianity. The two groups were fighting over the Holy Land—a wide area around Damascus, Bethlehem, and Jerusalem, along the eastern coast of the Mediterranean (med ih tuh RAY-nee un) Sea. For many years Muslim rulers from Arabia had allowed Christians to travel to Jerusalem, a city sacred to Christianity. But in the late 1000s, Turkish Muslims conquered the area and cut off Christians' access to the city. For the next 200 years, thousands of Christian soldiers joined the Crusades to take the Holy Land from the Muslims.

Muslim Trading Centers

The tales that these crusaders brought back to Europe taught Europeans about the Muslims, who knew much about science, geography, and medicine. Europeans were also dazzled by news of Muslim trading centers full of exciting goods.

In the late 1200s the stories of an Italian merchant named Marco Polo again captured the

▼ This map, made for Columbus, shows how some Europeans thought the Earth was shaped.

⭐ **Crusade** A Christian expedition to take the Holy Land from Muslims

1298 Marco Polo first tells about his journeys	1394 Prince Henry is born	1488 Bartholomeu Dias rounds the tip of Africa	1492 Columbus reaches North America	1507 America is named

1300	1375	1400	1450	1475	1500

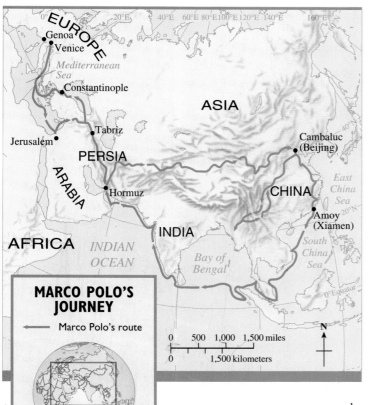

MARCO POLO'S JOURNEY

← Marco Polo's route

0 500 1,000 1,500 miles

0   1,500 kilometers

widely throughout Europe and influenced explorers for 200 years.

The Silk Road

For many years there had been a long overland trade route between Asia and some Arab and European cities on the Mediterranean Sea. Camels were used to carry goods 4,000 miles across mountains and deserts. This route is known as the Silk Road, for Asian silk was one of the main goods traded. The stories of crusaders and Marco Polo heightened the demand for Asian goods. But the few merchants who controlled the trade routes charged high prices for their

imagination of Europeans. Polo had traveled from Europe to China, India, and other places in Asia between 1271 and 1295. The map above shows the routes he took. Polo told of rich Asian empires, brilliant scholars, golden palaces, spices, silks, and jewels. A book describing his journey was read

empire The lands and peoples ruled by a powerful ruler or group

▼ One artist of the 1300s depicted Marco Polo greeting China's ruler, Kublai Khan.

goods in the rest of Europe.

In the 1400s, parts of the Silk Road were blocked by Muslims, making the movement of goods along the route even more difficult. Europeans all over the Continent wanted easier access to Asia and its wealth. Would it be possible to *sail* there? Prince Henry of Portugal wondered.

Henry the Navigator

Born in 1394, Prince Henry was fascinated with ships, maps, and riches. And he had a dream—he wanted the Portuguese to find a water route east around Africa to Asia.

Prince Henry started a school to teach navigation, the science of figuring the course of a ship. Students at his school learned how to use a compass, which shows direction, and an astrolabe, an instrument used for determining location. They learned how to use a sextant, which measured distance to determine latitude and longitude. They learned how to read a map, and they learned about ocean currents. Students also learned how to use these skills to sail farther and farther away from the sight of the coast without getting hopelessly lost. By the late 1400s

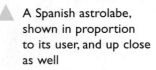

▲ A Spanish astrolabe, shown in proportion to its user, and up close as well

new and better ship designs made ships faster and easier to sail. Sea captains then began to make voyages that reached farther and farther down the west coast of Africa. In 1488, Bartholomeu Dias (bahr too loo ME oo DEE us), who studied at the school, was the explorer who first rounded the southern tip of Africa.

Sailing West

Another of Prince Henry's students was Italian navigator Christopher Columbus. Columbus had read Marco Polo's stories of Asia. He hoped to find a water route to Asia, but he wondered: why not sail *west* to get there?

In 1492, Christopher Columbus sailed westward across the Atlantic Ocean.

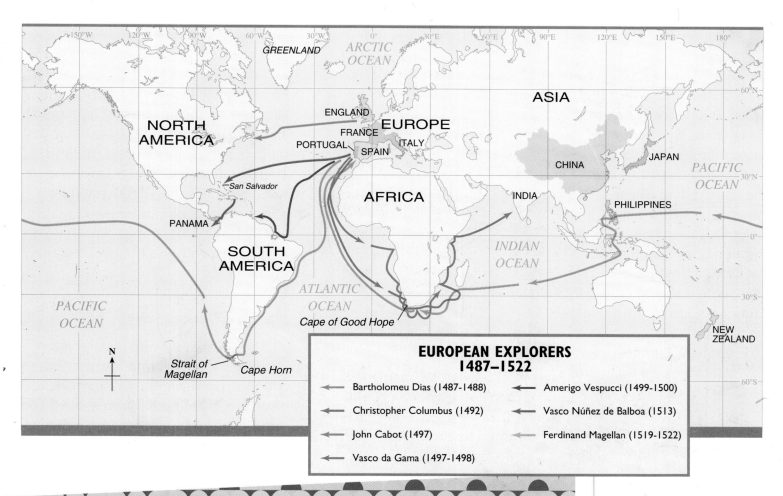

EUROPEAN EXPLORERS 1487–1522

← Bartholomeu Dias (1487-1488)	← Amerigo Vespucci (1499-1500)
← Christopher Columbus (1492)	← Vasco Núñez de Balboa (1513)
← John Cabot (1497)	← Ferdinand Magellan (1519-1522)
← Vasco da Gama (1497-1498)	

EXPLORER	SPONSORING COUNTRY	PLACE REACHED
Bartholomeu Dias	Portugal	Rounds the southern tip of Africa
Christopher Columbus	Spain	Bahamas
John Cabot	England	North America
Vasco da Gama	Portugal	India
Amerigo Vespucci	Spain	South America
Vasco Núñez de Balboa	Spain	Reaches the Pacific Ocean by crossing Central America
Ferdinand Magellan	Spain	Philippines; His expedition is the first to sail around the globe

We were three months and twenty days without fresh food. We ate biscuit, which was no longer biscuit, but powder of biscuit swarming with worms. —Pigafetta, shipmate of Magellan

53

He reached land, which he claimed for Spain. But where were the glittering trade centers? Where were the spices, the perfumes, the silks?

Although Columbus didn't know it at the time, he had reached North America, not Asia. Still, Columbus's achievement inspired other countries to sponsor voyages west. You can read more about other European explorers beginning on page 60.

Eventually, European navigators realized Columbus's error. In 1500, Italian sailor Amerigo Vespucci (ah me REE-goh ves POOT chee) reached the coast of South America. His journey helped convince Europeans that a huge landmass lay between Europe and Asia. In 1507 a **cartographer**, or mapmaker, honored Vespucci by putting his first name, Amerigo, on this land. From then on, this landmass would be known as North America and South America.

A Northwest Passage?

Europe was still interested in finding a water route to Asia. Some explorers hoped they could sail around North America to get there. France sponsored several voyages in search of a **northwest passage** to Asia. In 1534,

A SHORTE AND briefe narration of the two Nauigations and Difcoueries to the Northweaft partes called NEWE FRAVNCE:

Firft tranflated out of French into Italian, by that famous learned man *Gio : Bapt: Ramutius*, and now turned into Englifh by *Iohn Florio* : Worthy the rea-ding of all Venturers, Trauellers, and Difcouerers.

IMPRINTED AT LON-don, by H.Bynneman, dvvelling in Thames ftreate, neere vnto Baynardes Caftell.

Anno Domini. 1 5 8 0.

This pamphlet is an English translation of the story of Jacques Cartier's journeys in America.

French sailor Jacques Cartier (zhahk kahr tee AY) sailed across the Atlantic and reached the shores of present-day Canada, which he claimed for France. There he followed the St. Lawrence River for miles, hoping it would lead him to Asia. It didn't. Instead, it brought him into contact with Native Americans from the Iroquois (IHR uh-kwoi) nation.

Spanish Conquerors

The Spaniards were disappointed that they hadn't found a water route to Asia. However, they soon decided that they didn't need to reach Asia to find riches. The American continents had treasures of their own. Beginning in the early 1500s, Spanish explorers came to South America searching for gold and silver. Some of the routes they took are shown on the map on page 55.

As you learned in Chapter 2, America was already home to a great many peoples. To get to the gold and silver, the Spanish explorers attacked many Native American societies and claimed their lands for Spain. These explorers were called **conquistadors**, which is Spanish for "conquerors."

The Columbian Exchange

Columbus's voyage brought together two worlds—Europe and the Americas. By

---

★ **cartographer** A person who makes maps
northwest passage A water route from the Atlantic Ocean to the Pacific Ocean through the arctic islands of Canada

★ **conquistador** Spanish conqueror of America in the 1500s

This Portuguese ship, painted by an artist of the day, was one that participated in the Columbian exchange.

the 1600s the relationship between Europeans and Native Americans had changed the way both groups lived. The exchange of goods and ideas between these two worlds became known as the Columbian exchange.

From Native Americans, Europeans learned to grow potatoes, corn, squash, pumpkins, and beans. These new sources of nutrition led to rapid population growth in Europe. Also, Europe's **economy** became stronger with the new supply of American gold and silver.

Native Americans, meanwhile, saw a new side to farming when Europeans arrived with cattle, pigs, and horses. The native people also learned to grow wheat,

rice, sugar, coffee, and bananas. But more than goods and ideas were exchanged. Disease, too, traveled across the sea. Native Americans had no resistance to European diseases, such as smallpox, chicken pox, whooping cough, and measles. These and other diseases killed hundreds of thousands of Native Americans.

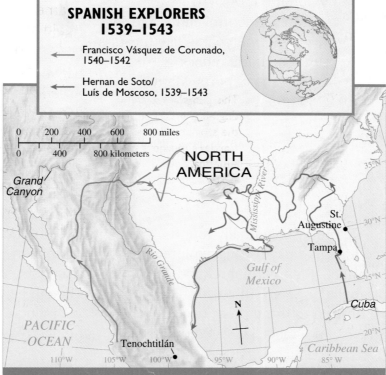

SPANISH EXPLORERS 1539–1543

← Francisco Vásquez de Coronado, 1540–1542

← Hernan de Soto/ Luís de Moscoso, 1539–1543

0   200   400   600   800 miles
0   400   800 kilometers

NORTH AMERICA

Grand Canyon

Mississippi River

St. Augustine

Tampa

Gulf of Mexico

Cuba

Rio Grande

PACIFIC OCEAN

Tenochtitlán

Caribbean Sea

N

35°N
30°N
25°N
20°N
110°W   105°W   100°W   95°W   90°W   85°W

★ **economy** The way in which natural resources and workers are used to produce goods and services

SHOW WHAT YOU KNOW!

REFOCUS
COMPREHENSION

1. What were some ways in which Europeans learned about Asia?

2. Why were Europeans looking for a water route to Asia?

THINK ABOUT IT
CRITICAL THINKING

Which of the explorers you read about do you think had the greatest impact on history? Give reasons for your answer.

WRITE ABOUT IT
ACTIVITY

Use pictures and words to describe the Columbian exchange.

CHRISTOPHER COLUMBUS

FOCUS *The voyages of Christopher Columbus opened new doors to European exploration of the world.*

▲ Portrait of Columbus and one of several versions of his signature

A Teenage Boy, A Bold Idea

Christopher Columbus was born in Genoa in 1451. At that time Genoa was one of the great Italian port cities that traded goods arriving from the Silk Road. At the age of 14, Columbus took a job on a ship, and from then on the sea was his life.

By the late 1400s all the countries of Europe were competing to find an easy route to Asia—one that wasn't controlled by a few greedy merchants like those in Genoa and other Mediterranean ports. Many hoped to find a water route to Asia. Columbus took a fresh look at this idea. While everyone else was looking *east* to reach Asia, he looked *west*.

The First Voyage

Columbus eventually found sponsors to pay for his exploratory voyage—King Ferdinand and Queen Isabella of Spain. In return he promised to bring them back great riches. In August 1492, Columbus set sail with three small ships—the *Niña*, the *Pinta*, and the *Santa María*—and a crew of about 90 sailors.

Early on the morning of October 12, one of his men spotted the small island that Columbus called San Salvador. After reaching the island, Columbus and his men were greeted by the local people, the Arawaks. Because Columbus believed he had reached the **East Indies**, he called these people "Indians." Columbus had actually come upon an island in what we now call the Bahamas, close to present-day Florida. Unknown to him, or to any other Europeans, two large continents lay between Europe and Asia—North America and South America.

Columbus presented the Arawaks with gifts of blue glass beads, red cloth caps, and small copper bells. The Arawaks gave gifts to Columbus, but none of these were the spices and gold he expected.

Columbus sailed on through the Caribbean Sea, searching for the great Asian cities described by Marco Polo. Though he found no gold and had not yet found China or Japan, he was sure he had reached Asia.

 ★ **East Indies** The islands of Indonesia; in older times the East Indies also included India, Indochina, and the Malay Peninsula

A Colony in the Caribbean

In 1493, Columbus returned to the Caribbean and set up a Spanish colony on the island of Hispaniola (hihs pun-YOH luh). The Arawaks who lived there were described by Columbus as "very gentle." But Columbus believed that the Arawaks were inferior to Europeans, partly because he thought they had no religion.

The Arawaks did "not know what it is to be wicked, or to kill others, or to steal," wrote Columbus—but the sailors did. They stole from the Arawaks. Many Arawaks were enslaved and sold in Spain. An enslaved person is someone who is forced to work for another, often under brutal conditions.

From the sailors, the Arawaks also caught European diseases, which their bodies could not fight. Fifty years after Columbus's arrival, nearly all the Arawaks of Hispaniola were dead.

The Final Voyages

Columbus made two more voyages between 1497 and 1502, still looking for the fabulous cities of Asia. He sailed to Central America and South America, but he never reached his goal.

Although Columbus never found Asia, explorers from many European countries followed his route west, exploring what was to them a "new

world." This world, however, had been home to many peoples for a great many years. The presence of Europeans in the Americas changed the lives of the native people forever as Europeans began to claim these lands as their own. The Americas would never be the same again.

he land is "full of trees of endless varieties, so high that they seem to touch the sky, and I have been told that they never lose their foliage. I saw them as green and lovely as trees are in Spain in the month of May."—Christopher Columbus, 1493, on the land he sighted that he named San Salvador

Pedro's Journal

by Pam Conrad

Pedro de Salcedo worked aboard Christopher Columbus's Santa María *in 1492. He captured major events of the voyage in his journal.*

October 10: I am certain of this. . . . There is nothing out here. Surely we are lost. . . . This morning the men responded slowly to orders, scowling and slamming down their tools and lines. They whispered in pairs and small groups on deck and below. The air was thick with mutiny and betrayal, until finally everything came to a dead stop. . . . "Enough," one of the men said. . . . "This is enough. Now we turn back."

Columbus paced the deck, telling them how close he figured we must be, that land could be right over the next horizon. He told them again of the fame and fortune that would be theirs if they could only last a little longer. And they laughed at him, the cruel laughter of impatient and defeated men.

"Let me offer you this," Columbus finally said. "Do me this favor. Stay with me this day and night, and if I don't bring you to land before day, cut off my head, and you shall return."

The men glanced at each other. Some nodded. "One day," they said. "One day, and then we turn around."

October 11 Through the day, the day that was to have been our last day traveling westward, many things were seen floating in the water, things that stirred everyone's hopes and had the men once again scanning the horizon. We saw birds in flocks . . . and even a stick was recovered that had iron workings on it, obviously man-made.

No one asked about turning back. . . . The men dispersed to their watches and their bunks, and the Captain paced the deck. I don't know why, but this night I stayed with him. I stayed still by the gunwale, watching over the side. Once in a while he would stand beside me, silent, looking westward, always westward.

Then, an hour before moonrise, the Captain froze beside me. "Gutierrez!" he called to one of the king's men on board, who came running. He pointed out across the water. "What do you see?"

Gutierrez peered into the west. "I don't see anything," he said. "What? What? What do you see?"

"Can't you see it?" the Captain whispered. "The light? Like a little wax candle rising and falling?"

The man at his side was quiet. I was there beside him, too, straining my own eyes to the dark horizon.

Suddenly another seaman called out across the darkness, "Land! Land!"

"He's already seen it!" I shouted. "My master's already seen it!" And the Captain laughed and tousled my hair.

Want to find out more about Pedro and Christopher Columbus? Check the book out of your school or public library.

SHOW WHAT YOU KNOW!

REFOCUS
COMPREHENSION

1. How was Columbus's plan for finding a water route to Asia different from other people's plans?

2. Why did Columbus call the Arawaks "Indians"?

THINK ABOUT IT
CRITICAL THINKING

Why did Europeans claim lands in the Americas even though people already lived there?

WRITE ABOUT IT
ACTIVITY

Write how you would have felt about "turning back" on October 11, 1492, as a mate on Columbus's voyage.

WORLD EXPLORERS

FOCUS *During this period, Europeans set out to explore the world beyond their borders. Although they didn't always reach their goals, their journeys vastly expanded European knowledge of the world.*

FAILURE FOR ENGLAND

Like Spain, England sought a western route to Asia. In 1497, England paid for Italian John Cabot's trans-Atlantic voyage. Cabot and his crew spotted what they thought was Asia, but it was actually an island off Canada.

In 1498, Cabot headed west again, this time with a fleet of four ships in which to take home the riches he expected to find. But something went terribly wrong with Cabot's voyage. No one knows exactly what happened, but John Cabot and his small crew were never seen again. Disappointed, England sponsored no more westward journeys until the late 1500s.

TO AFRICA, AGAIN

In 1497, Portuguese sailor Vasco da Gama picked up where Bartholomeu Dias had left off. With a fleet of four ships, Da Gama rounded the southern tip of Africa, as Dias had done, and sailed on to reach India in 1498. At last, a water route to Asia had been found.

BRAZIL, NOT AFRICA

In 1500, Portuguese navigator Pedro Cabral was instructed by his king to duplicate Da Gama's voyage. Cabral set out from Portugal to sail down the west coast of Africa. But tradewinds directed his ship away from Africa's coast, and he landed on the east coast of South America in the present-day country of Brazil. Cabral claimed this land for Portugal.

| 1498 | 1498 | 1500 | | 1513 | | 1519–1522 | 1524 |
| Da Gama reaches India | Cabot lost at sea | Cabral claims Brazil for Portugal | | Balboa sees the Pacific Ocean | | Magellan's crew sails around the world | Verrazano looks for northwest passage |

1495   1500   1505   1510   1515   1520   1525

PANAMA TO PACIFIC

In 1501, conquistador Vasco Núñez de Balboa (VAHS-koh NOOnyethh thhe bahl-BOH ah) sailed from Spain to the Americas in search of gold. He settled on the island of Hispaniola.

In 1513, Balboa sailed from Hispaniola to explore present-day Panama. Slashing through jungles and climbing over mountains, he crossed over Panama and was amazed to see a great ocean—the Pacific!

AROUND THE WORLD

In 1519, Ferdinand Magellan set out from Spain to reach Asia by sailing around South America. Over a year later he found the waterway he was looking for. His ships sailed on for three months without seeing land and with no fresh supplies. The sailors were so hungry they became ill and weak. Many died.

They eventually reached the Asian islands called the Philippines. Magellan planned to sail west all the way back home, but he was killed in a battle with the local people.

Magellan's crew continued on to Indonesia, where they traded for spices. From there they followed the route that Da Gama had discovered 25 years earlier. They arrived back in Spain in 1522, three years after they had left. Of the five ships and nearly 240 sailors that had started the voyage, one lone ship with 18 crew members made it home. But those 18 were the first people to have sailed around the world.

NO WATERWAY TO ASIA

Of course, no one who wanted to go from Europe to Asia would choose Magellan's route. It was far too long and dangerous. Some European rulers, however, hoped to find a northwest passage around *North* America that would lead to Asia.

One of these rulers was the king of France, who in 1524 hired Italian sailor Giovanni da Verrazano (joh VAHN nee duh vayr raht SAHN OH) to find such a route. Verrazano explored the coast of North America from what is now North Carolina northward to Canada. But to his great disappointment, he found no sign of a waterway to Asia.

61

| 1528-1539 | 1539–1542 | 1540–1542 | 1610 | 1673 |
| Estevan explores America | De Soto explores America | Coronado explores America | Hudson explores Hudson Bay | Marquette and Joliet explore America |

| 1530 | 1540 | 1550 | 1610 | 1670 | 1680 |

SEARCH FOR CITIES OF GOLD

Estevan, an enslaved person of African descent, was a guide to Spanish explorer Álvar Núñez Cabeza de Vaca. Their group was part of a failed 1528 trip to explore Florida. Most were killed, but Estevan, Cabeza de Vaca, and two others were captured by Native Americans in what we now call Texas.

The four men later escaped and headed south to Mexico. They heard stories of golden cities that sounded like an old Spanish legend about bishops who had left Spain to found the Seven Cities of Gold, Cíbola (SEE buh luh), across the ocean. The search for Cíbola began.

LAND CLAIMS

Conquistador Hernando de Soto had heard that what we call Florida was a land of gold. Perhaps, he thought, that's where Cíbola could be found.

In 1539, De Soto began exploring much of what is now the southeastern United States. He and his men killed many Native Americans in their search for gold.

De Soto died in 1542, having found no gold. He did, however, claim the lands he explored for Spain.

MORE LAND FOR SPAIN

In 1540, Spain's Francisco Vásquez de Coronado began exploring the American Southwest. Like De Soto, who at the same time was exploring the American Southeast, he was looking for the legendary Cíbola.

Coronado and his men found many things, including the Grand Canyon and Pueblo Indian villages, but no golden cities. Coronado took a Native American, called Turk, prisoner. Turk told Coronado what he wanted to hear—that cities of gold did exist. So in 1541, Coronado continued his search, exploring what would later become New Mexico, Texas, Oklahoma, and Kansas. Though he found no gold, Coronado did claim these lands for Spain.

ENGLAND TRIES AGAIN

In 1610, Henry Hudson of England still believed in a northwest passage to Asia. He thought he had found it in what is now Canada. He sailed through what was later named Hudson Strait. This waterway led to Hudson Bay.

But the bay was just that—a bay. It did not lead to Asia. Hudson's men, weary of the harsh winter voyage, took control of his ship. They set Hudson, his son, and seven others adrift in a small boat with no food. Then the crew sailed back to England. No one ever heard from Hudson again.

DOWN THE MISSISSIPPI

In 1673 a French explorer, Father Jacques Marquette (zhahk mahr-KET), and a French Canadian fur trader, Louis Joliet (lwee JOH lee et), set off to search for a western river to Asia. Traveling by canoe, they reached the Mississippi River, which they thought was that route. They found catfish so large that when one struck their canoe, Marquette thought they had hit a big tree. Joliet and Marquette traveled as far south as the Arkansas River. They discovered that the Mississippi flowed to the Gulf of Mexico, not to the Pacific Ocean.

SHOW WHAT YOU KNOW!

REFOCUS
COMPREHENSION

1. What did Magellan's crew accomplish?

2. How were Native Americans treated by some of these explorers?

THINK ABOUT IT
CRITICAL THINKING

If you could travel with one of these explorers, which one would you choose? Explain your choice.

WRITE ABOUT IT
ACTIVITY

Describe the effects the European explorers might have had on the native people.

THE MAYA, INCAS, AND AZTECS

FOCUS *The Americas were home to several highly developed, complex cultures before Europeans arrived in the 1500s.*

Maya Civilization

Hundreds of years before the arrival of the Spaniards, three great civilizations flourished in Central and South America. Find them on the map on page 65. The earliest of these was the Maya (MAH yuh) Empire. The Maya moved south into the green valleys of Mexico and Guatemala (gwah tuh- MAH luh) more than 1,500 years ago.

They found that corn grew well there—so well that they raised more than they could eat. They stored away their extra corn so that they would be sure of a food supply.

Since they no longer had to worry about finding food, the Maya settled down and built permanent homes. They began creating works of art from wood and stone. They learned to make beautiful pottery, jewelry, and statues.

Maya Achievements

The Maya civilization reached its height between A.D. 300 and 900. During that time the Maya built more

▲ A Maya stone sculpture, A.D. 500–800

▲ What does this look like to you? It is a stucco mask on a Maya stone temple now covered by jungle plants.

than 40 cities. These cities were home to great pyramid-temples, with which the Maya honored their gods. The temples were made of huge blocks of stone atop large mounds of earth. Some rose more than 150 feet high. No one today knows exactly how the Maya were able to create such gigantic structures.

The Maya had a remarkable understanding of mathematics and astronomy. By carefully observing the movement of the sun, planets, and stars, they were able to create a very accurate calendar—far better than any calendar used in Europe at the time.

The Maya also developed a system of writing. Using pictures and symbols, they began recording information about their history, calendar, mathematics, and religious ceremonies. They carved these symbols on stone or painted them on strips of plant fiber.

By the early 1100s, the Maya world had fallen apart. No one knows why, but the Maya left their cities. Their wooden art works began to rot. Their fields were overgrown with vines and trees. When Europeans arrived in the 1500s, even the great Maya temples were crumbling.

The Inca Empire

The Incas settled along the western coast of South America during the 1100s, as you can see on the map on the right. They built dozens of cities along 2,500 miles of Pacific Ocean coastline. They conquered other societies to build an empire of perhaps 7 million people.

The region they settled was both dry and mountainous. In the desert lowlands there was not enough water to grow crops. Although plenty of rain fell in the mountains, it washed the soil away, down the steep hillsides. Despite this, the Incas used their remarkable skills to prosper in this difficult land.

Developing the Land

To water the deserts, they built **aqueducts** that carried water from mountain streams. Some of these aqueducts were 500 miles long. To keep soil from washing down the steep mountains, they cut terraces, or rows of wide steps, into the mountainsides. The edge of each step was walled with stone for support. Rain now fell gently from terrace to terrace, watering the soil but not washing it away. The Incas used their now fertile land to grow potatoes, beans, corn, and squash.

The rugged land also made travel difficult. Again the Incas put their skills to work. The Incas built paved roads that stretched up to 2,000 miles. They created sophisticated rope bridges to cross the deep canyons and built **causeways** over swamps and streams. This great road system was used for travel, trade, and even as a postal highway.

aqueduct A structure that carries water to an area from a distant site
causeway A roadway built above water

MAYA, AZTEC, AND INCA EMPIRES

- Aztec Empire
- Maya Empire
- Inca Empire
- Pizarro's route
- Cortés's route

The Incas honored their gods by creating tapestries, such as this one, and other images of them.

The Incas were also great architects. They carved up huge blocks of stone for use in building homes and temples and to surround their capital city, Cuzco. Using rope, rollers, and human muscle power, they moved blocks as heavy as 200 tons. These blocks were cut so precisely that they fit together perfectly.

End of the Inca Empire

The Incas worshiped a sun god. They mined large amounts of gold, a symbol for the sun, to use in religious ceremonies and for decoration. They also worshiped a moon god, represented by silver.

In 1532 a conquistador, Francisco Pizarro (frahn THHEES koh pee THHAHR-roh) and his small army attacked the unsuspecting Incas with guns and cannons. They killed thousands and kidnapped the Inca ruler, Atahualpa (ah-tuh WAHL puh). The Incas gave Pizarro huge amounts of gold and silver, for which Pizarro had agreed to release

The Incas made this counting device, or *quipu*, out of strings made to look like gold and silver.

Atahualpa. But instead, Pizarro murdered him. Soon Pizarro's army overran the Inca capital. The beautiful gold and silver statues and ornaments meant to save Atahualpa were melted down into bars. The Inca Empire had been crushed.

Aztec Culture

In the 1200s the Aztecs, or Mexica (me CHEE cah), settled in what is now central Mexico. By the 1500s they had conquered enough neighboring societies to claim a dazzling empire of 10 million people.

The Aztec capital was called Tenochtitlán (te nawch tee TLAHN). It was built on an island in Lake Texcoco (tay SKOH koh). People and goods moved along the city's many roads and canals. Aqueducts brought water from distant freshwater lakes. Long causeways connected the island city to the shore.

Although it was one of the world's biggest cities, Tenochtitlán was clean and orderly. Every day the streets were swept and washed, and garbage was hauled away.

Tenochtitlán buzzed with activity. Thousands gathered daily to trade at its great marketplaces. Towering above all this bustle were glorious pyramids. These temples were as central to the city as religion was to Aztec life.

The Aztecs believed in many gods, but the most important was

An Aztec urn being restored by an archaeologist, who studies the remains of early civilizations

Huitzilopochtli (wee-tsee loh POHCH tlee), the god of sun and war. Because Aztecs believed that the first gods sacrificed themselves to create the world, sacrifice was important to their religion. Warriors could gain honor by capturing prisoners to offer as sacrifices. These sacrifices were thought to be honorable and welcomed by the gods.

The Aztecs were great astronomers and created accurate calendars. They also knew how to set broken bones, fill dental cavities, and even do brain surgery. They used hundreds of herbal medicines, some of which are still used today. Anything they couldn't make from local resources they got by demanding payments from the cities they conquered.

The Aztecs believed they could appease their gods by making masks such as this.

An Empire Disappears

In 1519 the Spaniards, led by Hernán Cortés, marched toward Tenochtitlán in search of gold. Helping him were warriors from neighboring cities that were tired of making payments to Tenochtitlán.

Aztec warriors were no match for Spanish guns and cannons, which they had never seen before. And Aztecs had never battled soldiers mounted on horses, huge beasts the Spaniards had brought with them. In just two years Aztec gold was in the hands of Europeans, and the mighty Aztec Empire was gone forever.

Mexican painter Diego Rivera's vision of Tenochtitlán

SHOW WHAT YOU KNOW!

REFOCUS
COMPREHENSION

1. What were some results that followed after the Maya had built a food supply?

2. How were the Incas able to farm, even though they lived in a mountainous area?

THINK ABOUT IT
CRITICAL THINKING

Compare the accomplishments of the Maya, the Incas, and the Aztecs.

WRITE ABOUT IT
ACTIVITY

What would you do if you were an Aztec living in Tenochtitlán in 1519? Write a journal entry about the advance of the Spaniards.

SUMMING UP

1 DO YOU REMEMBER . . .
COMPREHENSION

1. What effect did Marco Polo and the Crusades have on Europeans in the 1200s?

2. What was the Silk Road?

3. Why did Europeans want to find easy access to Asia?

4. What was Prince Henry the Navigator's dream?

5. What were French and English explorers looking for on their first voyages to the New World?

6. What important discovery did Jacques Marquette and Louis Joliet make?

7. What did early Spanish explorers—Balboa, De Soto, Coronado—most want to find?

8. Describe the Columbian exchange.

9. What were some achievements of the Maya, Inca, and Aztec cultures?

10. What were some similarities in the way the Incas and the Aztecs were conquered?

2 SKILL POWER
TRACING ROUTES ON A MAP

In this chapter you used maps to trace the routes of explorers. Work with other students to draw a larger version of the map on page 53. The map should be large enough to display in your classroom. Be sure to include the routes of the explorers. Then have each member of your team choose one or more of these explorers to write a report about. Display your reports with your map.

3 WHAT DO YOU THINK?
CRITICAL THINKING

1. Why might Native Americans have wished that the Europeans had never come to their land?

2. Who do you think made the greater contribution—Columbus or Magellan? Explain.

3. Why do you think people want to become explorers? What are people exploring today?

4. No one knows why the Maya abandoned their cities about 900 years ago. List three possible reasons why they did so.

4 SAY IT, WRITE IT, USE IT
VOCABULARY

Write a paragraph about the world's explorers as discussed in this chapter. Try to use as many vocabulary words as possible. If you include four or more, you are a very talented word worker!

aqueduct	East Indies
cartographer	economy
causeway	empire
conquistador	northwest passage
Crusade	

5 GEOGRAPHY AND YOU
MAP STUDY

Use the map and chart on page 53 to answer the following questions.

1. Which explorers sailed for Spain?

2. Whose voyage was longer—Vespucci's or Da Gama's?

3. Which explorer traveled along the coast of South America?

4. In what year did Balboa cross Panama?

6 TAKE ACTION
CITIZENSHIP

Explorers expanded their knowledge of the world by going beyond borders. With videotapes you can go beyond the borders of your school and community. Make a poster, audio tape, or videotape about your class, showing your special projects and interests. Then send it to a class in another community or state. Include a note that asks the class to reply with information about themselves. By being a "pen pal," you will expand your knowledge of the world.

7 GET CREATIVE
ART CONNECTION

With a group of classmates, create a mural that shows scenes of the Maya, Inca, and Aztec cultures. Begin by drawing a giant map of Central and South America. Place the scenes of each culture in the correct region. Use the illustrations on pages 64–67, encyclopedias, library books, and other resources for art ideas.

LOOKING AHEAD
In the next chapter you'll find out what happened as Europeans began to settle the lands they explored.

Early European

Spain, France, England, and the Netherlands had all established settlements in North America by the 1600s. Each nation had different goals for its settlements and treated the Native Americans they encountered in different ways.

CONTENTS

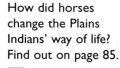

How did horses change the Plains Indians' way of life? Find out on page 85.

Settlements

These books tell about some people, places, and events of interest during the time of the early European settlements. Read one that interests you and fill out a book-review form.

READ AND RESEARCH

St. Augustine: America's Oldest City by Linda R. Wade
(Rourke Enterprises, 1991)
Travel back 400 years and find out about the history of America's oldest city. Notice how the past affects life in the city today. *(nonfiction)*

North American Indian Sign Language by Karen Liptak
(Franklin Watts, 1992)
Without sign language, Plains Indian nations would not have been able to communicate so easily. Explore the world of symbols that many of these people used to express their feelings and ideas. *(nonfiction)*

The Jews of New Amsterdam by Eva Deutsch Costabel
(Simon and Schuster Children's Publishing, 1988)
What historical events led to the arrival of 23 Jews in the Dutch colony of New Amsterdam? Find out about their contributions to the colony. *(nonfiction)*

Reading a Time Line

Knowing how to read a time line will help you understand when different events happened.

UNDERSTAND IT

When you're really busy, it's easy to lose track of the time. That's why people use calendars like this to show when things are planned to happen.

Saturday, May 13

9:00 A.M. Soccer game

11:30 A.M. Orthodontist

2:00 P.M. Help Dad at store

4:30 P.M. Guitar lesson

6:00 P.M. Pizza party at Eric's

When keeping track of past events, people use a time line, which is similar to a calendar. A time line organizes historical information by putting events in sequence.

EXPLORE IT

The city of St. Augustine, Florida, has been governed by many nations, including Spain and the United States. Who first settled the city? When did it become part of the United States?

1565 The Spaniards settle St. Augustine

1586 The English sack and burn St. Augustine

1672 The Spaniards begin building San Marcos, a fort, to protect the city

1763 Britain gains control of Florida

Look at the time line on page 73. Since the earliest date is on the left, the first event took place in 1565—the Spaniards settled St. Augustine.

The second date, 1586, is placed to the right of the first event. When making a time line, it is important to have a scale for the number of years. For instance, every one-inch space might represent 20 years.

Look at the time line again. When did Britain gain control of St. Augustine? How long had the Spaniards been in St. Augustine before they built San Marcos? Time lines can answer many questions about the order of events in history.

History of St. Augustine

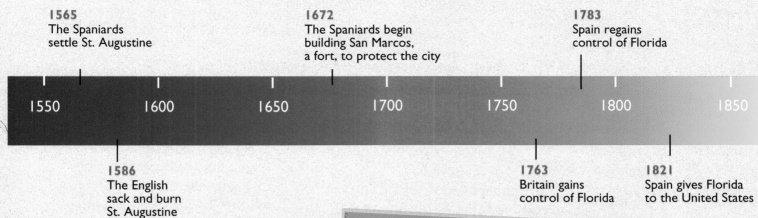

1565
The Spaniards
settle St. Augustine

1672
The Spaniards begin
building San Marcos,
a fort, to protect the city

1783
Spain regains
control of Florida

1550   1600   1650   1700   1750   1800   1850

1586
The English
sack and burn
St. Augustine

1763
Britain gains
control of Florida

1821
Spain gives Florida
to the United States

TRY IT

With a group of your classmates, create a time line. Here are some topic ideas.

- The history of your town or city

- The history of your school

- Figure skating from 1945 to the present

- The life of a famous person

- The history of desktop computers

When all the groups have finished, all the time lines can be combined in a booklet.

▲ Fort at St. Augustine ▶

SKILL POWER SEARCH

Look for other time lines in this chapter. How many years are shown on each one?

73

1 Setting the
Scene

KEY TERMS
missionary
mission
presidio
trading post

Europeans Settle in America

FOCUS *Various groups of Europeans settled in North America for different reasons. They often pursued their goals at the expense of the Native Americans.*

Spaniards in America

The Spaniards who settled the islands of the Caribbean, shown on the map below, were looking for gold. But they were unwilling to do the dangerous work of mining for gold themselves. Instead, they enslaved the local Native Americans, the Arawaks. The terrible working conditions and European diseases caused the Arawaks to die at a horrifying rate. Soon the Spaniards were using enslaved Africans to replace the Arawak slaves who died. By the end of the 1500s, most of the enslaved workers were African.

As Spanish explorers pushed northward during the 1500s, they

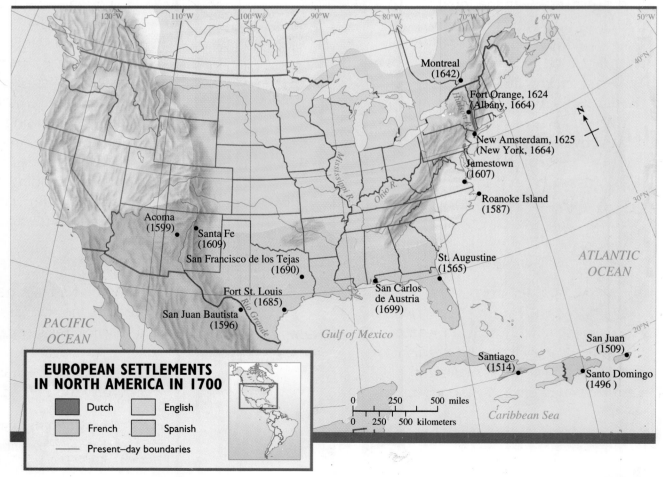

**EUROPEAN SETTLEMENTS
IN NORTH AMERICA IN 1700**

- Dutch
- French
- English
- Spanish
- Present–day boundaries

1565	1585	1613	1682
Spaniards settle St. Augustine	England sends first settlers to Roanoke	Dutch establish New Netherland	La Salle claims Mississippi Valley for France

1560   1580   1600   1620   1640   1660   1680

claimed more and more land for Spain. Spain soon began to establish colonies in present-day Mexico, New Mexico, Texas, and California.

Many Spaniards came to North America with an *encomienda,* or royal grant. The grant gave the holder control over a certain number of Native Americans in a particular area. The grant holder could demand payment from the Native Americans in the form of gold, goods, or labor. In return, the grant holder was supposed to protect the Native Americans and teach them Catholicism, the religion of Spain.

This *encomienda* system was created by Spain, not by the Native Americans. It let Spaniards take over Native American lands and became, in practice, a form of slavery.

Catholicism Spreads

Gold was not the only reason Spain settled North America. The Catholic church of Spain wanted to spread Catholicism. The Spanish government saw the spreading of Catholicism as a way to expand its

▲ Native Americans and Spaniards building a settlement

empire. Spain sought to convert Native Americans into tax-paying Christians under Spanish rule.

Spanish priests worked as **missionaries** to convert Native Americans to Catholicism. They built **missions** in which to carry out their work.

These missionaries wanted not only to spread Catholicism but also Spanish culture—they expected Native Americans to give up their own religion and culture. Missionaries also taught European methods of farming and cattle raising. But they forced Native Americans to do the work needed to keep the missions running. Sometimes mission life for Native Americans was little better than slavery.

Presidios Protect Spain's Claims

Many Native American groups, such as the Apaches, Comanches, and Navajos, resisted Spanish rule and sometimes fought missionaries and settlers. Other Europeans, such as the French and the English, also disliked

---

⭐ **missionary** A person sent to teach religion to people of a different faith
mission A settlement of religious teachers

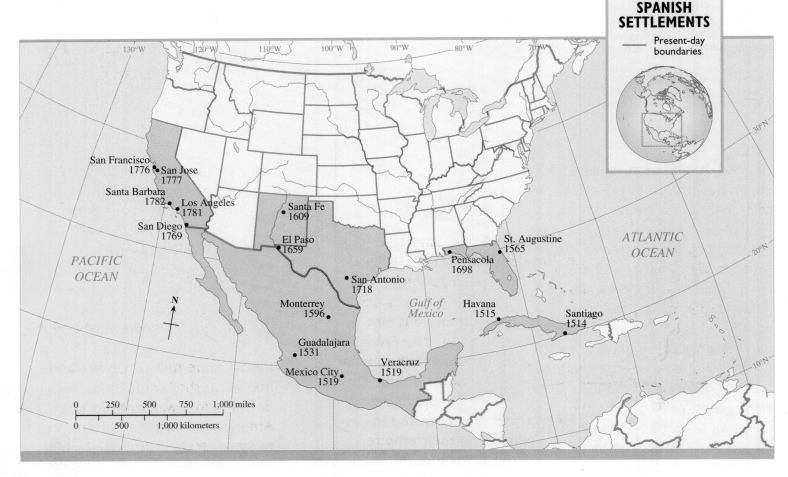

Spain's presence in North America and envied the gold and silver that Spain was accumulating. To help protect their claims in North America, Spaniards built fortified settlements called **presidios**.

Spain claimed a large part of North America, and its many presidios helped it protect those claims. In the western part of North America, Spain had settlements, missions, and presidios as far south as Mexico and as far north as California. In the east, Spain claimed part of the

▲ This Native American bowl illustrates the Spanish influence on Pueblo art.

Caribbean and took over French settlements in Florida.

In 1565, the Spaniards built St. Augustine in a spot where they had destroyed a French settlement. St. Augustine is today the oldest European settlement still standing in North America.

As you can see on the map above, Spaniards were building settlements in North America for over 250 years. What were some of Spain's earliest settlements? What were some of the latest settlements?

presidio   A Spanish military base on the edge of a settlement

It is likely that the floral design on these Iroquois moccasins was learned from French nuns in Quebec. ▼

French Settlements

Although Spain claimed a huge portion of the Americas, other European countries laid claim to North America. Having lost their southern settlement to Spain, the French took their interests north to what is now Canada. Unlike the Spaniards, the French weren't interested in expanding their empire. Instead, they wanted to trade with the Native Americans. They set up **trading posts**, where they could get beaver and other furs that they could sell in Europe for a huge profit. Furs were used for hats, coats, and other clothing and were in great demand in Europe. The French traded beads, tools, firearms, brass and iron kettles, and rum in exchange for furs.

Relations With Native Americans

The French took care to establish good relations with Native Americans because the French depended on them to obtain the valuable furs. The fur traders were few in number and knew that they could easily be defeated in a war with Native Americans. It was to their advantage to stay friendly with the Native Americans. Because the French didn't want Native American land, the Native Americans didn't see them as a threat.

France soon discovered, though, that without colonies it couldn't protect its trading posts. In 1608 the French founded the settlement of Quebec. Later they established Montreal. In 1682, French explorer Robert Cavelier, Sieur (syoor) de La Salle, claimed the Mississippi River valley for France. He named it Louisiana after the French king, Louis XIV.

Like the Spaniards, the French also sought religious converts. But instead of trying to wipe out Native

A French fur trader

⭐ *trading post* A place where people trade goods with the people who live in the area

James Fort

Built in the period of
May 14 to June 15, 1607.

▲ A painting of early Jamestown

American beliefs, the French missionaries studied those beliefs and tried to blend them with Catholicism. As a result, French missionaries had better relationships with Native Americans than Spanish missionaries did.

Early English Settlements

England also began establishing North American settlements during this time. The English first tried to set up a colony in 1585. Sir Walter Raleigh sent 108 men and boys to Roanoke Island, off the coast of present-day North Carolina. Unprepared for the hard work needed to maintain a settlement, the colonists gave up and returned to England after 10 months.

Raleigh tried again in 1587. He sent 91 men, 17 women, and 9 children to Roanoke. But when supply ships returned to the island three years later, the colony had vanished.

Twenty years after the Roanoke disaster, the English tried yet again. This time they started a settlement, called Jamestown, on an island in the James River in present-day Virginia. The first 104 settlers arrived in May 1607. They had high hopes of finding large supplies of gold, as Spaniards had found in Mexico and South America. And they expected to make the Native Americans who lived there do all the hard work, as the Spaniards often did. But there was no gold to be found, no empires to conquer.

▲ A helmet from Jamestown

Lacking eager missionaries and government and military support, the English were unable to enslave the Native American population.

Jamestown Survives

Being aristocrats who were not used to doing hard work, the English were unwilling to do the labor needed for successful farming. As winter arrived, food supplies decreased. Many settlers died from disease and malnutrition. By January 1608 only 38 were still alive. Things didn't look good for the settlement. Yet a few years later, Jamestown found a way not only to survive but to prosper.

Although local Native Americans taught English settlers how to grow new crops, relations between the two groups rapidly grew worse. The English, like most Europeans, believed Native Americans were inferior and not worthy of respect. Europeans felt that if land was not heavily farmed, it belonged to no one. So they settled on lands the Native Americans used for hunting and growing crops. Conflicts over land occurred again and again as more and more English settlers arrived in America.

The Dutch Arrive

In the early 1600s the Dutch came to America. They were interested in the area explored by Henry Hudson, who was working for a Dutch company when he explored the Hudson River.

Like the French, the Dutch wanted to trade with local Native Americans for furs. But they, too, found that trading posts needed the support of colonies. In 1613 they therefore started the colony of New Netherland.

New Netherland had trouble attracting settlers, for the Dutch enjoyed prosperity at home. So the Dutch invited others to come to their settlements, including Germans, Swedes, and Norwegians seeking religious freedom. Still, Dutch settlements remained small.

Dutch relations with Native Americans were peaceful until the Dutch began settling Native American land. Native American groups also started fighting with each other for control of the fur trade. By 1664 few Native Americans remained in New Netherland.

Dutch traders took furs back to the Netherlands for use in clothing, such as this coat.

SHOW WHAT YOU KNOW!

REFOCUS
COMPREHENSION

1. What were the purposes of the Spanish missions and presidios?

2. How was the French treatment of Native Americans different from the treatment of other Europeans?

THINK ABOUT IT
CRITICAL THINKING

If you were a leader of the Jamestown colony, what would you do to make it more successful?

WRITE ABOUT IT
ACTIVITY

Look at the map on page 74. Make a time line showing when the different European settlements shown on the map were established.

Spanish Culture in America

FOCUS *As Spaniards settled in America, they set up several different kinds of communities. They brought Spanish life to the Americas, but in some ways they adapted their culture to the new area.*

Transplanting Spanish Culture

For Spanish settlers, life in America often proved extremely difficult. In Florida, settlers struggled with isolation, harsh conditions, pirate raids, and hostile relationships with other European settlers. For instance, French and English ships sometimes cut St. Augustine off from Cuban supply ships. The Spaniards would then face hunger and hardship. Settlers in Texas, New Mexico, and California faced similar problems. Throughout the Southwest they dealt with dry, dusty climates. And

almost everywhere they dealt with poor soil, angry Native Americans, and a lack of supplies.

Spaniards who came to America didn't plan to change their lifestyle. They wanted to live as they had in their homeland. Spanish settlers tried to transplant as much of their culture as they could, including their language, religion, traditions, architecture, and social class structure.

They even dressed as they had in Spain. They wore ruffled shirts, leather

▼ Father Ignacio Tirsch returned to Spain in 1768 with this drawing of a California mission.

This drawing explains the different parts of the soldier's outfit.

boots, and Spanish suits. They used linen handkerchiefs and fancy hats.

Settlers also hauled Spanish furniture to America. They brought Spanish kitchen items, paintings, and jewelry. They also planned settlements to look like towns back in Spain.

Adjusting to a New Land

Despite their best efforts, however, settlers could not duplicate Spain on this side of the Atlantic Ocean. Things simply were not the same. When leather boots wore out, there were no shoemakers around to make new ones. So Spanish settlers wore Native American moccasins. They needed to eat, so they learned to like corn, beans, and squash. They didn't always have enough silverware, so they began scooping up food with tortillas.

Similarly, the Spaniards soon gave up on European-style towns. Settlers needed to live out in the countryside. They needed to be near their animals, fields, and water supply.

In addition, the houses varied from settlement to settlement, based on the climate or environment. In Florida, houses had big windows to catch the cooling breezes. In the Southwest they had small windows to keep out the sun. In Florida, roofs were made with palm leaves. In New Mexico, roofs were made of wood and dirt.

In all the settlements the homes were small and simple. Often there was not much furniture. Many settlers slept on mats on the floor. The settlers quickly learned to do without many things, especially since they had to make whatever they lacked.

Life in the Presidios

Even more difficult than a civilian's life in a settlement was a soldier's life in a presidio. Soldiers lived with bare walls, dirt floors, and little furniture. While all faced death from disease or enemy arrows, soldiers were at greater risk from enemy attacks.

In addition, soldiers dressed very uncomfortably. They wore long leather coats and carried lances and leather shields. The coats were heavy—about 18 pounds each. The coats protected soldiers from arrows, but in the heat of the desert, they were brutally hot.

Spanish soldiers also faced loneliness. Most of them were unmarried men who came to the **frontier** alone. Some eventually married Native American women and set up their own huts near the presidio. Others, however, lived and died without any family nearby.

 frontier A newly settled area that separates older settlements from the wilderness

Establishing Missions

Since the Spanish people believed that Native American souls were at risk, they sent priests to become missionaries and to build missions. In the missions the priests would teach Spain's religion, Catholicism, and culture to the Native Americans.

Once the priests had converted enough people, they could begin building a mission. This would include a church, workshops, housing for the priests, and separate housing for the "mission Indians." Some Native Americans liked mission life. They learned to speak Spanish. They learned Spanish methods of sewing, farming, and pottery making. However, mission Indians had to give up their old customs and beliefs.

Not all Native Americans wanted to give up their beliefs. Some didn't want to wear European clothes. Either way, many Native Americans didn't like being ordered around all day long.

In missions Native Americans learned skills such as blacksmithing.

Some mission Indians tried to run away. The ones who were caught were locked up or whipped. Other Native Americans tried to drive priests out by attacking the missions.

In the end, missions did not do well in Arizona, New Mexico, and Texas. But they did succeed in California. And some California missions, such as San Diego and San Francisco, eventually grew into major cities.

A mission bell

SHOW WHAT YOU KNOW!

REFOCUS
COMPREHENSION

1. How did the Spaniards try to recreate their old lifestyle?

2. What were some ways in which they learned to adapt?

THINK ABOUT IT
CRITICAL THINKING

Why do you think the Spaniards insisted on wearing clothes from their homeland when they moved to a very different climate?

WRITE ABOUT IT
ACTIVITY

Draw a picture or diagram showing what a Spanish settlement house might have looked like on the inside.

3

Living on America's Plains

FOCUS *Plains Indians lived on the land that stretches from present-day Canada to Texas and from the Rocky Mountains to the Midwest. At their height the Plains Indians numbered around 250,000.*

The Plains Indians

In the 1600s and 1700s, some Plains Indians lived in settled farming villages and hunted during different seasons. They lived in grass houses or earthen lodges.

Other Plains Indians were truly nomadic hunters. They did not live a settled life at any time of the year. Nomadic Plains Indians lived in **tipis** (TEE peez). Read about life growing up as a nomadic Plains Indian.

Searching for Food

You certainly put a lot of miles on your moccasins. Every few months, as the seasons change, your family packs up and moves—and you walk every step of the way. You do have some dogs that are harnessed to pull your belongings, but there are no animals to carry you.

The reason for all your traveling is simple: food. In the summer your family may gather wild fruits and roots. But you mostly eat buffalo meat.

So each year, as the buffalo herds migrate, or move, the people in your camp migrate, too.

Hunting buffaloes on foot requires great skill. Hunters must either **stampede** the buffalo off a cliff or drive the animal into a trap. To get the buffalo over the cliff or into the trap, hunters will sometimes disguise themselves with animal skins. This way the hunters will look and smell like animals the buffalo is used to.

You will want to set up camp near where you will hunt, because buffaloes weigh more than 1,000 pounds each.

▲ Plains Indians often disguised themselves with animal skins when hunting buffalo.

---

 tipi   A Native American tent made of animal skins

stampede   To cause a herd of animals to panic and run

How will you carry all that weight? You will cut up the buffalo to make it easier to carry. And you will not waste any parts of the buffalo.

On a good day you eat buffalo meat. But on a bad day you may not eat at all. With food supplies so scarce, you can't be a picky eater. You are expected to eat whatever is given to you, whether you like it or not.

There are other rules to follow as well. You are not allowed to sit down inside your tipi until an adult gives you permission. And you cannot interrupt older people when they talk.

Time to Play

You will probably take a toy or two with you wherever you move. The first present girls get is a doll made of wood or animal skin. Boys receive a bow and arrow. Later on, both boys and girls are given puppies. Sometimes these animals are raised as pets, but often they are used to do work.

You may also play games with other children in your nation. You might play war or you might pretend to hunt buffaloes, with some of the children acting as the animals. In the winter you probably sled on the ice, using animal bones for runners.

This picture, from a later time period, shows Native American children with their dogs.

A Social People

In your community there are social rules to follow. When you are a guest in someone else's tipi, you take your own bowl and spoon. When your host cleans his pipe, it is time for you to leave.

You do not spend all your time with people of your own nation. You may get together with other Plains Indians. Sometimes your meetings are friendly. Other times there are disagreements.

The pictures on this buffalo skin tell a part of Plains Indian history.

Most of the people you meet speak different languages. So how do you communicate with each other? You use sign language. The Plains Indians have a highly developed system of signs that enable you to share stories, ideas, and warnings with each other.

Help From Horses

When the Europeans arrive with horses, your way of life as a Plains Indian completely changes. On horseback your hunters can travel faster and farther than ever before. This gives Plains Indians a new freedom. It is now easier to reach fresh water supplies. And your next meal of buffalo meat is just a horseback ride away.

Horses also enable you to carry much more weight when you move around. In fact, one horse can carry up to 250 pounds. It doesn't take many horses to enable your hunters to bring a buffalo back to the camp. Moving your tipi is much easier, too. So your home gets bigger and more comfortable.

Not every Native American nation gets horses right away, of course. The northernmost nations do not get horses until 1800. Since the horse makes living on the plains easier, other Native American groups from the east and west move onto the plains. The map above shows some Plains Indian nations after the arrival of the horse. By the mid-1700s, horses are a central feature in the lives of most Plains Indians.

PLAINS INDIAN NATIONS

Present-day boundaries

SHOW WHAT YOU KNOW!

REFOCUS
COMPREHENSION

1. How did the buffalo affect the way the Plains Indians lived?

2. How did the people of different Plains Indian nations communicate with each other?

THINK ABOUT IT
CRITICAL THINKING

How did the horse change the Plains Indians' hunting and living patterns?

WRITE ABOUT IT
ACTIVITY

Your nation has just been introduced to the horse. In your journal describe your reaction to this new animal.

From Roanoke to California

FOCUS *European settlements were scattered across the continent of North America, from east coast to west coast. Not all settlements were successful, but some developed quickly and grew stronger over time.*

ROANOKE SETTLERS LOST

In August 1590, John White brought fresh supplies for English settlers who had come to Roanoke Island three years earlier.

As he walked along the shore, White saw footprints in the sand. But he found no other sign of life. The houses were torn down, and some rusty armor was lying among the weeds.

White saw the word *CROATOAN* carved on a tree. Did this mean that the settlers had fled to the nearby island where the Croatoan Indians lived? Bad weather kept White from going to the island to find out. So the lost colonists of Roanoke are still a mystery.

THE DUTCH BUY AN ISLAND

Peter Minuit was looking for land. As director of a Dutch trading company, he wanted to expand New Netherland. In 1626 he asked the Canarsie Indians if they would sell him the island of Manhattan.

It wasn't the Canarsies' land to sell. It really belonged to the Manhattan Indians. Nonetheless, the Carnarsies and Minuit made a deal. Minuit gave the Canarsies $24 worth of beads and trinkets. Today that $24 would really be thousands of dollars.

Minuit then founded New Amsterdam on the island. Later the Dutch did pay the true owners of Manhattan.

TROUBLE IN NEW MEXICO

Pueblo Indians were furious with Spaniards who were charging them taxes. In addition, the Spaniards were whipping—even hanging—Pueblos who practiced their native religion.

Finally, one Pueblo man, named Popé, had had enough. He gathered his people and planned a revolt. On August 9, 1680, the Pueblos attacked Santa Fe. Of the 2,800 settlers, 400 were killed, and 2,000 fled to El Paso, Texas. No one knows what happened to the other 400. The Pueblos controlled Santa Fe until Spain regained control after Popé's death in 1692.

| 1590 | 1626 | 1680 | 1701 | 1769 |
| John White brings supplies to Roanoke | Peter Minuit pays the Carnarsies for Manhattan | The Pueblos attack Santa Fe | Cadillac founds Detroit | Junipero Serra leaves for California |

1590   1610   1630   1650   1670   1690   1710   1730   1750   1770

CADILLAC BUILDS DETROIT

Detroit's founder had quite a name—Antoine de La Mothe Cadillac (ahn twahn duh lah mawt kah dee YAHK). Actually, when he was born, he was named Antoine Laumet. But as a young man, he changed his name so that people would think he was more important.

Cadillac loved money, sword fights, and his country—France. In 1701 he was sent to start a French fur settlement on the Detroit River. Cadillac headed off with 102 men. After 49 days of canoeing, on July 24, they reached what is now Detroit. Cadillac made friends with local Native Americans, and soon the settlement of Detroit was thriving.

NEW MISSIONS IN CALIFORNIA

Father Junípero Serra (hoo NEE pay-roh SER rah) desperately wanted to bring Catholicism to Native Americans. He spent 20 years as a missionary in Texas and Mexico. Then he had an opportunity to spread his faith even farther. The king of Spain asked him to establish missions in California.

In 1769, Serra, who had been sickly throughout his whole life, had an infection in his left leg that wouldn't heal. But he set out for California anyway. On some days he couldn't walk at all and was carried on a stretcher. Still, by 1782, Serra had founded nine missions throughout California, in places such as San Diego and San Francisco.

SUMMING UP

1 DO YOU REMEMBER . . .
COMPREHENSION

1. Why was the death rate of Native Americans so high in Spanish settlements?

2. In what part of North America did France set up its first colony?

3. What colony did the English try unsuccessfully to start in 1585 and again in 1587?

4. Why did the Dutch set up the colony of New Netherland?

5. What type of lifestyle did the early Spanish settlers try to create in the New World?

6. Why did the Spaniards want Native Americans to live in missions?

7. Why did Plains Indians move so often?

8. How did horses change the way of life of the Plains Indians?

9. Why did the Pueblo Indians revolt in 1680?

10. Who was Antoine de La Mothe Cadillac?

2 SKILL POWER
READING A TIME LINE

In this chapter you learned how to make and use time lines. Make a time line of the last ten years. At the top, place important events from your own life. At the bottom, place major events that have happened in our nation and in the world.

3 WHAT DO YOU THINK?
CRITICAL THINKING

1. Which Europeans seemed to have the best relationships with Native Americans? Explain.

2. What do you think might have happened to the early settlers at Roanoke?

3. Why do you think some Native Americans resisted mission life?

4. Not all Plains Indians had contact with European settlers. How do you think they got horses?

5. What do Peter Minuit's experiences in buying Manhattan Island tell you about early land deals between Europeans and Native Americans?

4 SAY IT, WRITE IT, USE IT
VOCABULARY

Write a conversation that might have taken place between an early Spanish settler and a Native American. Have the characters describe their ways of life. Use as many of the vocabulary terms as you can.

frontier   stampede
mission   tipi
missionary   trading post
presidio

5 GEOGRAPHY AND YOU
MAP STUDY

Use the map below and the map on page 74 to answer these questions.

1. What European nations had settlements along the east coast of the United States?

2. What river connected the Dutch settlements of Fort Orange and New Amsterdam?

3. Name five present-day states that have land once claimed by Spain.

4. Which European nation settled in the area around the Great Lakes?

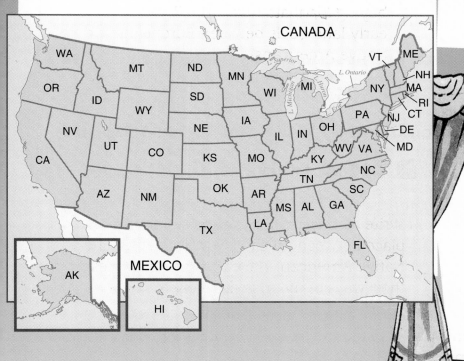

6 TAKE ACTION
CITIZENSHIP

In 1680 the Pueblo Indians were angered by Spanish taxes, and they revolted against Spanish rule. Almost one hundred years later, antitax feelings on the part of British colonists led to the American Revolution. Taxes are still a necessary part of citizenship. Talk to adults at home and school to find out more about taxes. Is there a state income tax where you live? Are the schools in your community funded with real estate taxes? Make charts to show the different taxes that people pay and what people get in return for these taxes.

7 GET CREATIVE
LANGUAGE ARTS CONNECTION

Create a short skit based on one of the events in this chapter. Your skit could show a Spanish family trying to adjust to life in the Southwest, a group of Plains Indians learning to use horses, or Peter Minuit trying to buy Manhattan Island.

LOOKING AHEAD
In the next chapter, read about English settlements that were started by Pilgrims and Puritans.

THE NEW

Pilgrims and Puritans left "old" England and settled in New England, with strong religious beliefs. They produced a close-knit, structured society, but their society was soon threatened by problems of disease, hunger, conflict, and rebellion.

How can a gravestone tell you about early New England? Find out on page 103.

CONTENTS

SKILL POWER

Here lyes y Body of Stephen Cooke Dec'd Dec y 24th 1749 in y 19 year of his Age

ENGLAND COLONIES

These books tell about people, places, and events of interest in New England in the 1600s. Read one that interests you and fill out a book-review form.

READ AND RESEARCH

Stranded at Plimoth Plantation, 1626 **by Gary Bowen**
(HarperCollins, 1994)
Christopher Sears is 13 and an orphan at the struggling Plymouth Colony in 1626. No wonder he feels stranded! In his journal he recounts the details of his life in one year at Plimoth Plantation. *(historical fiction)*

The Children of the Morning Light: Wampanoag Tales
as told by Manitonquat (Simon & Schuster Books for Young Readers, 1994)
An Assonet Wampanoag storyteller retells tales and legends of his people, including stories of the creation of the world and of how the Wampanoags ended up near Plymouth in 1620. *(folk tales)*

Indians of the Northeast Woodlands **by Beatrice Siegel**
(Walker, 1992)
Northeast Woodland Indians—the Wampanoags, Narragansetts, and Pequots—lived and still live in New England. Find out all about their history, culture, language, and art. *(nonfiction)*

SKILL POWER

Reading a Table

Tables organize information so that it is easier to understand.

UNDERSTAND IT

Do you have a paper route? If so, how do you organize information about your customers? Do you organize it by the order in which you deliver papers or by the customers' last names? Whichever way you use, a table would help you organize the information. A table has a title, columns, and rows to make information easier to find and use.

CUSTOMER LIST

Name	Address	Instructions
Chan, Lu	12 Park St.	none
Johnson, Sam	16 Park St.	Leave at door
Doty, Ellen	24 Park St.	Inside gate
East, Olivia	110 East St.	none
Dughan, Sam	124 East St.	Inside door
Goldman, Sol	130 East St.	Leave at door

▲ This table is organized by order of delivery.

EXPLORE IT

When you have to organize names, dates, sizes, or locations, a table may be a good way to do so. When you read a table, first look at its title to see what information is included in it. To find information, you can look for the **row** you want and move your finger across it until you find the **column** you want. Another way is to look for the column you want and run your finger down it until you find the row you want. Use the table below to answer these questions.

● Was Rhode Island the first, second, third, or fourth place shown to become a colony?

● On what date did Connecticut become a state?

● Which other colonies in the table also became states in 1788?

● What is the nickname for New Hampshire?

TITLE

SUMMARY OF NEW ENGLAND COLONIES

	SETTLED BY EUROPEANS	BECAME A COLONY	BECAME A STATE	RANK OF STATEHOOD	NICKNAME TODAY
Connecticut	1636	1639	Jan. 9, 1788	5th	Constitution State
Massachusetts	1620	1630	Feb. 6, 1788	6th	Bay State
New Hampshire	1623	1679	June 21, 1788	9th	Granite State
Rhode Island	1636	1663	May 29, 1790	13th	Ocean State

ROWS

COLUMNS

◀ This table gives a lot of information about early New England colonies.

TRY IT

Try your hand at making a table. First, think of information that could be put in the form of a table. Perhaps your family needs to keep track of phone numbers. Maybe your baseball card collection needs to be sorted so that you know if you have duplicates. Or maybe your class wants a list of who plays what position on your softball team, and their birthdays.

How will you organize your table? You could list the names in alphabetical order, like the table on the above right, so that it would be easy to look up the names of your teammates. But maybe you're really interested in when the team members' birthdays are. The table to the right shows you one way to do that.

When your table is finished, make up questions based on the information it includes. Then trade your table and questions with a classmate.

STUDENT	POSITION	BIRTHDAY
Anderson, Jan	Pitcher	June 4
Czerny, Tom	left field	May 11
Franklin, Tom	first base	September 8
Garces, Jose	Short stop	January 8
Green, Debby	right field	February 6
Lin, Janet	second base	November 13
Martelli, Ellen	Catcher	June 14
Morris, Monique	Center field	January 3

BIRTHDAY	STUDENT	POSITION
January 3	Monique Morris	center field
January 8	Jose Garces	short stop
February 6	Debby Green	right field
May 11	Tom Czerny	left field
June 4	Jan Anderson	pitcher
June 14	Ellen Martelli	catcher
September 8	Tom Franklin	first base
November 13	Janet Lin	second base

SKILL POWER SEARCH   *As you read this chapter, think about how information about the New England colonies could be organized in a table.*

1 Setting the Scene

KEY TERMS
- Puritan
- separatist
- Pilgrim
- Mayflower Compact
- charter
- delegate

SETTLING NEW ENGLAND

FOCUS *The people who settled New England hoped to create a model society. In some ways they succeeded beyond their wildest dreams. In other ways they fell short of their goals.*

Trouble in England

By 1600, life in England had become particularly difficult for many groups of people, including those known as **Puritans**.

What was so bad about life in England for people at that time? Cities were growing rapidly. Prices were rising. Unemployment was high, and wages were low. But for Puritans, life was also difficult because they didn't like many things about the Church of England. They felt that the church encouraged people to ignore the rules of the Bible as the Puritans interpreted them. People danced and played cards. Worship services were elaborate. The Church of England was the official church—the *only* legal church in the country. So Puritans saw it as responsible for what was wrong with England.

In truth, the country was ripe for change. But James I, king of England, and his successor, Charles I, were resistant to Puritan demands for change. James didn't like the way the Puritans spoke out against the Church of England. He did whatever he could to make their lives miserable. He even had some Puritans thrown in jail.

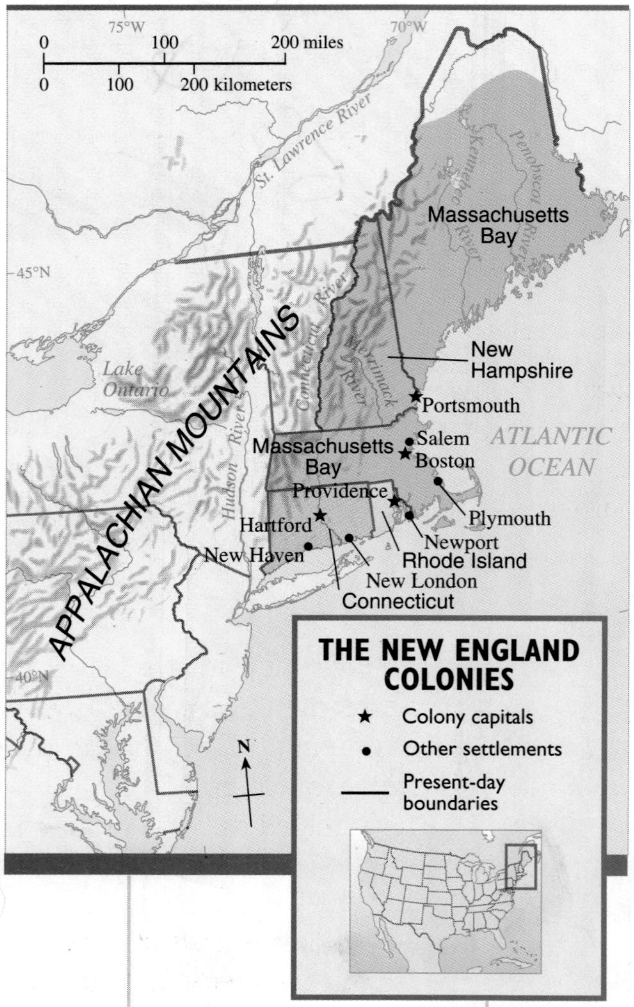

THE NEW ENGLAND COLONIES
Colony capitals
Other settlements
Present-day boundaries
0
100
200 miles
0
100
200 kilometers
75°W
70°W
45°N
40°N
St. Lawrence River
Kennebec River
Penobscot River
Massachusetts Bay
Merrimack River
Connecticut River
Hudson River
Lake Ontario
APPALACHIAN MOUNTAINS
New Hampshire
Portsmouth
Salem
Boston
ATLANTIC OCEAN
Massachusetts Bay
Providence
Hartford
Plymouth
New Haven
Newport
Rhode Island
New London
Connecticut
N

Most Puritans believed they could change the church and still remain a part of it. But a small group of them wanted to form their own church, *separate* from the Church of England. People in this group were known as **separatists**. For them, it was time to leave England and move to a new land, where they could worship as they believed. If they could create a truly religious society, perhaps other English people would recognize their accomplishments and follow their examples.

Puritan A person in the 1600s in England who thought the English church should be made "pure"

separatist A person who wished to separate from the Church of England

| 1620 | 1630 | 1636 | 1636 | 1652 | 1679 |
| Pilgrims land at Plymouth | Massachusetts Bay Colony settled | Connecticut is settled | Rhode Island is settled | Maine joined to Massachusetts Bay Colony | New Hampshire Colony is formed |

1620   1630   1640   1650   1660   1670

Leaving Home

In 1608 the separatists left England for the Netherlands, where they could worship as they pleased, without interference from a church. By 1620, though, this group had returned to England because they were not comfortable with Dutch ways and customs. They set their eyes on America. Their ship, the *Mayflower*, set sail from Plymouth, England, in September 1620.

Not all 101 passengers on board were separatists, however. About half were *strangers*—the English term for those who were unfamiliar. Generally these men and women were farmers who simply hoped to get a fresh start, away from England. Together the people on the *Mayflower* became known as the **Pilgrims**. For two months the Pilgrims sailed west, expecting to go to Virginia, where the English had already settled. When at last they spotted land, it was the coast of New England, not Virginia! But they could not turn back—this was to be their new home.

The Mayflower Compact

The Pilgrims had to deal with two problems right away. They needed a government, and they had to make it through the winter.

They tackled the first problem before they got off the ship. Separatist Puritans and strangers naturally might have had different ways of seeing things, but they were able to agree to make rules for their new colony in the **Mayflower Compact**. Those who signed the compact agreed to live by the rules and to work together to

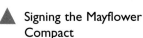

Signing the Mayflower Compact

Pilgrim A person who travels for religious reasons

Mayflower Compact An agreement to obey the rules of Plymouth Colony, signed aboard the *Mayflower*

A high chair like this was brought to America for the first Pilgrim child born at Plymouth, Peregrine White.

support them. Their settlement was called Plymouth because that is what Captain John Smith, who had mapped the coast of New England, named it.

The next problem for the Pilgrims was how to survive a cold winter that was much harsher than England's. They barely had time to throw together shelters before the first snow came. More than half of the Pilgrims died during the winter of 1620–1621. They *all* might have died if it hadn't been for Native Americans. The Wampanoags (wahm puh NOH agz) lived near Plymouth Colony. They taught the colonists where to plant corn and where to fish.

By the fall of 1621, the Pilgrims were still facing tough times. But they had made it through one whole year in Plymouth. To show their gratitude, they held a three-day harvest festival, known to us today as the feast of Thanksgiving.

The Massachusetts Bay Colony

By the late 1620s another, larger group of English settlers began to talk of heading for America. The Puritans, like the Pilgrims, were fed up with things in England. Unlike the Pilgrims, these Puritans did not believe that they had to *separate* from the Church of England. They hoped to create a Puritan society in the new Massachusetts Bay Colony.

More than 1,000 Puritans founded the Massachusetts Bay Colony in 1630. John Winthrop was the colony's governor for most of its first 20 years. Winthrop believed that Boston, the heart of the colony, should be a "City of God." It would show the world how society should be run. This colony and other New England colonies are shown on the map on page 94.

Plymouth Colony has been recreated as Plimoth Plantation.

Many Puritans who settled in the Massachusetts Bay Colony shared Winthrop's vision. They expected to work hard and live a pure life. If they did, they hoped that God would bless their colony with economic success. They thought that their success might be proof that God's grace had been given to them. Puritans believed that only with God's grace would they enter heaven.

How the Colony Worked

The Puritans who set up the Massachusetts Bay Colony had to deal with many of the same hardships the Pilgrims had endured. They suffered through long winters and struggled farming rocky soil. Still, this second group of settlers didn't have to worry about creating a new government. They already had one in place.

Back in England the king had granted these Puritans a **charter** allowing them to settle in Massachusetts. The charter, which they brought with them, gave them the right to elect their own leaders.

Puritans expected their government to support their church. They expected, for instance, that government leaders would pass a law requiring everyone to go to church. But Puritans did not want the government to *control* the church, as it did in England.

Laws for the Massachusetts Bay Colony were made in Boston. At first a small group of men made the laws. But as the colony grew, people in new towns wanted input. So each town was allowed to send a **delegate** to Boston to help make laws. Towns voted on who would be sent.

However, only free white men were allowed to vote. And they had to be members of the Puritan church. To join the church, a person had to pass a test by standing up in front of fellow churchgoers and describing how he or she had experienced God's grace.

Complaints

Almost from the beginning many settlers had problems with some of the colony's rules. For example, a Puritan minister named Roger Williams didn't like the idea that only church members could vote. He thought that this rule too closely linked the government and the church. In 1635, Williams was forced out of the Massachusetts Bay Colony. The next year he established a settlement that later became the colony of Rhode Island.

Thomas Hooker had similar complaints and left Massachusetts. In 1636 he founded what became the colony of Connecticut. Anne Hutchinson also spoke up. She saw no reason why church members always had to agree with their ministers. In 1637 she was put on trial for her ideas and was banished from Massachusetts. She fled to Rhode Island.

"Whatsoever we did or ought to have done when we lived in England, the same must we do, and more also, where we go. . . . We must bear one another's burdens. . . ." —John Winthrop, 1630

▲ John Winthrop

★ **charter** An official paper in which rights are given by a government to a person or company

★ **delegate** A representative

Changing Times

As time passed, more people arrived in Massachusetts. Many were single people, not people with families. They came not for religious reasons but to make money.

These settlers helped build the farming colony into a center for fishing, shipbuilding, and trading. The map on this page shows some of the trade routes that developed and the goods traded between the colonies and other places. Frontiers were extended as older settlements along the coast became overcrowded. People moved from Boston to lands farther north, west, and south, across hills and rivers into western Massachusetts and into what became Maine and New Hampshire. They also moved into Rhode Island and Connecticut.

But it wasn't just strangers and newcomers who caused change. The children of the original settlers found some Puritan rules too rigid. For example, they weren't interested in taking a test to join the church. In 1662 the Puritans changed

Cod, important to New England's economy, was traded for goods from other countries.

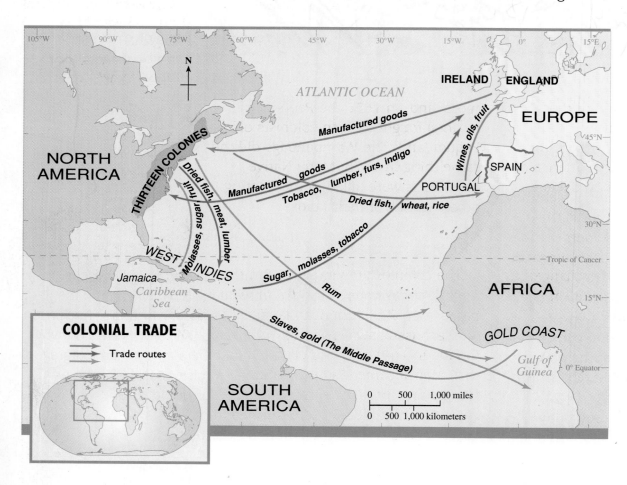

COLONIAL TRADE

→ Trade routes

98

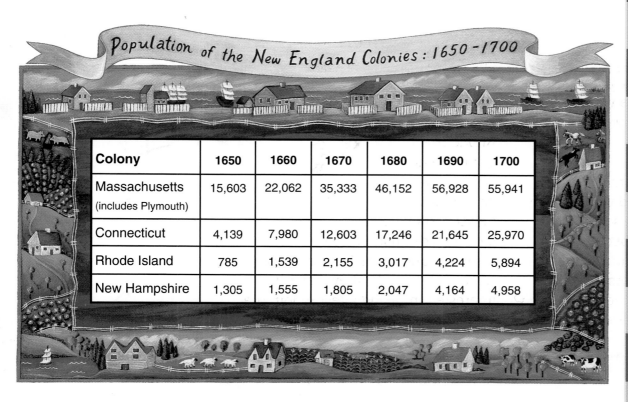

Population of the New England Colonies: 1650-1700

Colony	1650	1660	1670	1680	1690	1700
Massachusetts (includes Plymouth)	15,603	22,062	35,333	46,152	56,928	55,941
Connecticut	4,139	7,980	12,603	17,246	21,645	25,970
Rhode Island	785	1,539	2,155	3,017	4,224	5,894
New Hampshire	1,305	1,555	1,805	2,047	4,164	4,958

this rule, allowing children of the original Puritan settlers to become church members, even if they hadn't experienced grace. The importance of the Puritan church began to decline.

Relations With Native Americans

Over the years the settlers' dealings with Native Americans also changed. At first, relations with Native Americans had been quite friendly. The Wampanoags, after all, had assisted the settlers that first year.

But things soon turned ugly. Native Americans were hurt by diseases brought from Europe. They were angry that colonists were settling more and

more land. In 1636 the Pequots (PEE-kwahts) fought to keep colonists off Pequot land. The Wampanoags did the same thing in 1675. Many Native Americans were killed in the fighting; others lost all of their lands.

Growing by Leaps and Bounds

The colonies grew rapidly after the English colonists took control of what had been Native American lands. Massachusetts swallowed up Plymouth Colony in 1691 and also claimed land that later became Maine and New Hampshire. By 1700, Massachusetts had more than 50,000 settlers. New England as a whole had about 90,000.

SHOW WHAT YOU KNOW!

REFOCUS
COMPREHENSION

1. Most people who settled New England in the 1600s came from what country in Europe?

2. What New England colony was settled first?

THINK ABOUT IT
CRITICAL THINKING

Compare New England in 1635 with New England in 1700. What major changes took place? Why?

WRITE ABOUT IT
ACTIVITY

If you were a settler who did not agree with the Puritan rules in Boston in 1650, what would you do? Where would you go?

You Are There

KEY TERMS

meeting house
common
apprentice
primer

LIFE IN A NEW ENGLAND VILLAGE

FOCUS *People in Puritan New England had a strong sense of family and community. These values were evident in many aspects of everyday life.*

Nosy Neighbors?

If you suddenly found yourself transported from your home today to a Puritan village of the 1600s, you would think that your neighbors were pretty nosy. They would be watching every move you made. But if you felt as if your privacy were being invaded, you'd be missing the point. In Puritan society your neighbors were *supposed* to watch you.

As you have learned, Puritans believed that you needed God's grace to get into heaven. You and your Puritan neighbors cannot be sure how to obtain it, but you feel it can't hurt to try to live a perfect life. That means following every rule. It means you have to read the Bible and listen to your minister. It means doing plenty of good deeds. By keeping an eye on you, your neighbors are really trying to help you make sure that you live as good a life as possible.

▶ Meeting houses were simple, but communion cups, such as this one that belonged to John Winthrop, were fancy.

▲ A meeting house built in the 1700s in Sudbury, Massachusetts

Much in Common

To watch over each other, Puritans have built their houses close together. The fields you farm might lie on the outskirts of your village, but chances are your home is right in the center of town. You see your neighbors every day. You also see your neighbors at your village's **meeting house**. Every village has one or more of them. Meeting houses are simple wooden buildings, sometimes called Lord's barns. Across from or near the meeting house is the **common**, where

meeting house A building used for both public and religious meetings
common Land available for use by all people of a village or town

villagers meet to discuss events of the day, as well as to graze their animals.

At the meeting house, townspeople gather at least twice a week—every Sunday, plus one day in the middle of the week. You listen for hours as the minister tells you what God expects of you. And then you are expected to go back home and do it!

Most Puritans, of course, like being part of a strong community. On the map on this page, you can see that Boston is an example of a Puritan community. Its meeting house and common are right in the middle of town! You enjoy being with neighbors who care about and think like you. If you get sick, neighbors will bring you meals. If your barn burns down, neighbors will help you rebuild it. Often the people who settled a town were relatives. But even those who were not related were, in a way, like brothers and sisters.

Family All Around

If you lived in Puritan New England, you would not only be part of the community but you would also be part of a family. Family life isn't just nice; it is necessary.

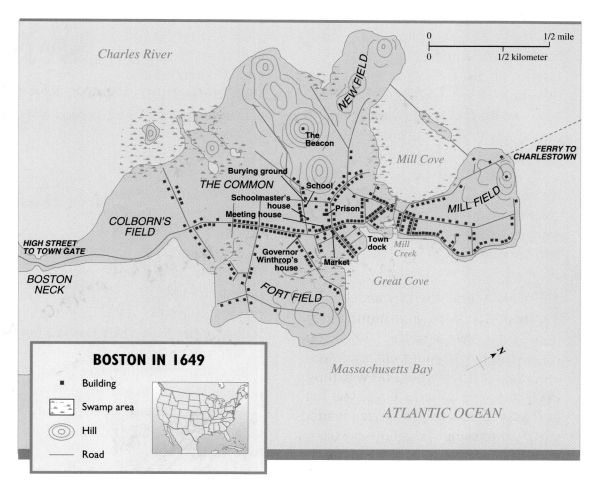

BOSTON IN 1649

- ■ Building
- Swamp area
- ◎ Hill
- — Road

Only families are granted land. In fact, single people aren't welcomed into early Massachusetts at all. They aren't allowed to move to the colony unless they can find a family to live with. This is because New Englanders think single people are more likely to cause trouble than married people or family members. They might break laws and live lives different from those lived by families. They might gamble or dance, for example.

Both mothers and fathers play important roles in family life. Puritan mothers handle household chores. They take loving care of their children.

Mothers are especially gentle with infants, as disease is a constant worry. Still, fathers are in charge of Puritan families. Puritan men, who make the laws and cast the votes, believe that men are wiser than women.

Your father decides how much of the family's land or money you will get when you grow up. And he has to say yes before you can marry the person you want to marry.

Growing Up Quickly

Childhood for Puritans didn't last as long as it does for people today. Today most people consider you to be an adult when you reach age 21. But in the 1600s you were expected to act like an adult at the age of 6 or 7. You have to dress like an adult. You work alongside your parents. Girls begin cooking, spinning, and making soap. Boys work outdoors, tending to farming chores, such as caring for animals, planting crops, and making and mending fences.

When you are just a little older, you might become an **apprentice**. This means leaving your home and spending several months or even years learning a skill from an experienced laborer. Skills such as barrel making, cabinet making, and silversmithing are commonly taught.

Chances are your father will teach you to read and write. There are very few schools in early New England. Yet reading is an important skill in New England. You have to be able to read the Bible. A **primer** (PRIHM ur), an early version of a school book, is used by Puritan fathers to teach reading and other skills to their children. Mothers are less likely to be able to read and write.

Ministers have to be especially well educated. After all, they have to explain God's word to the community. No one is more important to a town than its minister. In 1636, Puritans start Harvard College to train these ministers.

Staying Healthy . . .

With their emphasis on reading, New Englanders are very well educated settlers. They are also very

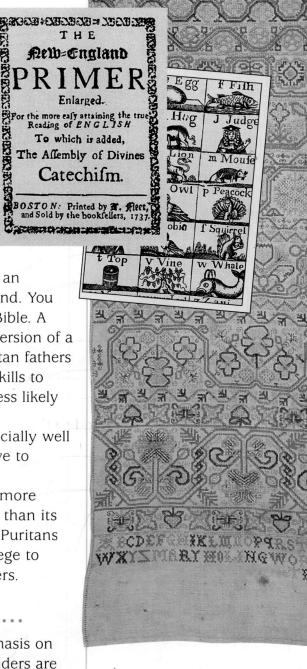

▲ Work and fun — a primer, and a sampler embroidered for fun

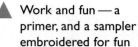

★ **apprentice** A person who works in return for instruction, room and board, or payment

★ **primer** A simple book for teaching reading to beginners

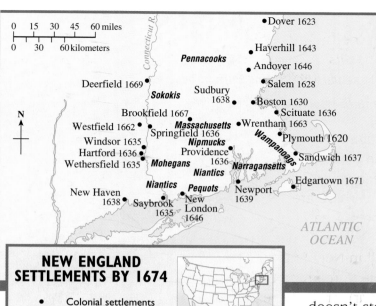

NEW ENGLAND SETTLEMENTS BY 1674

- Colonial settlements
- *Pequots* Native Americans

Map labels: Dover 1623, Haverhill 1643, Andover 1646, Pennacooks, Deerfield 1669, Sokokis, Sudbury 1638, Salem 1628, Boston 1630, Scituate 1636, Brookfield 1667, Massachusetts, Springfield 1636, Wrentham 1663, Westfield 1662, Nipmucks, Plymouth 1620, Windsor 1635, Providence, Wampanoags, Hartford 1636, 1636, Sandwich 1637, Wethersfield 1635, Mohegans, Narragansetts, Niantics, New Haven 1638, Niantics, Pequots, Newport 1639, Saybrook 1635, New London 1646, Edgartown 1671, ATLANTIC OCEAN

Connecticut R.

0 15 30 45 60 miles
0 30 60 kilometers

N

healthy. As a New England settler—if you have survived childhood—you are likely to live a long, healthy life. One reason for this is New England's cold climate. For nearly half the year, bad weather keeps you from traveling far. If you don't move around, you don't carry disease with you. Also, your town is not as crowded as European cities are. This means that diseases tend not to sweep through whole towns. (Many of the early towns are shown on the map on this page.) Finally, everyone around you has enough land to grow plenty of food. With a healthy diet, your body can fight off diseases.

...But Accepting Death

Puritans are generally pretty healthy, but that doesn't stop them from thinking about death. Most Puritan families experience the death of at least one or two children. And they know that New England, as good as it is, is not perfect. They feel that heaven is the only perfect place. Therefore Puritans work hard at gaining God's favor so that they might enter heaven after they die. You and your family and friends also spend much of your life wondering what heaven is like.

Gravestones show this interest in life and death. Their inscriptions tell stories of people who lived, worked, and died for faith.

◀ In New England you can find gravestones from the 1600s.

SHOW WHAT YOU KNOW!

REFOCUS
COMPREHENSION

1. How was life in a Puritan village different for boys and girls?

2. Why was education so important to Puritans?

THINK ABOUT IT
CRITICAL THINKING

What aspects of life in a New England village might have made an outsider feel unwelcome? What about it made others feel right at home?

WRITE ABOUT IT
ACTIVITY

If you lived in a New England village of the 1640s instead of in your town or city today, how would life be different for you?

NEW ENGLAND CHANGES

FOCUS *Some of New England's first settlers had strong Puritan beliefs. The beliefs began to change over time as people challenged them.*

SQUANTO'S HELP

In early 1621 the Pilgrims were cold, sick, and hungry. They wouldn't have survived had it not been for Squanto. This Native American had been captured by European explorers some years earlier. He had been taken to England, but he was back now, living with the Wampanoags and their leader, Massasoit (MAS uh-soit). As a result of his captivity, he spoke English. Squanto was willing to live with the Pilgrims, teaching them how to survive in a land that was strange to them. He introduced them to new methods of farming and fishing. When he died in 1622, many in Plymouth Colony felt the loss.

ROGER WILLIAMS'S TROUBLES

When Roger Williams settled Rhode Island in 1636, he did so fuming over the Massachusetts rule that only church members could vote. It was a law, he said, that "stinks in God's nostrils." Williams wouldn't have that kind of rule in his colony. In Rhode Island, the government would not make *any* laws about religion.

As a result, people in Rhode Island were free to worship any way they wanted to. The colony encouraged people of different faiths to live together.

ANNE HUTCHINSON'S QUESTIONS

Anne Hutchinson was in big trouble. She had questioned the wisdom of ministers in the Massachusetts Colony. She held meetings in her home to discuss the ministers' sermons. Soon she started to express opinions about religion that differed from those of the colony's ministers. The ministers weren't used to anyone—especially a woman—challenging what they taught. At Hutchinson's trial, in 1637, ministers and lawmakers tried to show that she was wrong. Hutchinson knew the Bible so well that she tripped them up. But they didn't care. They decided she was "a woman not fit for our society." When they forced her out of the colony, she fled to Rhode Island with her husband and children.

1621	1636	1637	1662	1675–1676
Squanto begins helping the Pilgrims	Roger Williams settles Rhode Island	Anne Hutchinson is put on trial	Puritans adopt Halfway Covenant	King Philip's War fought

1620　1630　1640　1650　1660　1670　1680

THE HALFWAY COVENANT'S COMPROMISE

Children and grandchildren of the original Puritan settlers weren't eager to join the church. Many of the rules for joining—and maintaining church membership—were very strict. And these second and third generations of Puritans didn't like what had happened to people who had questioned church authority—people such as Roger Williams and Anne Hutchinson.

As a result, church membership was down. This worried the original Puritan settlers. To get their children to join the church, they adopted the Halfway Covenant in 1662. This allowed children of church members to join the church, even if they hadn't experienced grace. So original church members could pass on membership to their children, who in turn could pass it on to their children. But what kind of church would those children want? Something much different from that of 1630, for sure.

KING PHILIP'S SAD END

It was a sad time for Metacomet (met uh KAHM iht), known as King Philip, leader of the Wampanoags. For 60 years his people had been friends with New Englanders. His father was the legendary Massasoit. But times had changed since his people were so generous to the Pilgrims and the Pilgrims were so thankful in return. Throughout the 1600s, Puritan settlers had taken Wampanoag land and brought much disease. Anger and distrust now filled the air.

In June 1675, King Philip led a war against the colonists, in which both sides committed terrible acts. By the end of 1676, hundreds of settlers had been killed.

Most significantly, though, *40 percent* of the Native American population in New England—including King Philip himself—had been killed.

REFOCUS
COMPREHENSION

1. Why did Anne Hutchinson leave Massachusetts Bay Colony?

2. Why was King Philip's War fought?

THINK ABOUT IT
CRITICAL THINKING

How would you compare Roger Williams's Rhode Island Colony with the Massachusetts Bay Colony?

WRITE ABOUT IT
ACTIVITY

Make a map that shows where the major events in New England took place between 1621 and 1676. Then write a key that works with your map.

4

WHY WE HAVE TOWN MEETINGS

FOCUS *Starting with the Mayflower Compact, New Englanders developed a tradition of self-government. That tradition can still be seen in town meetings across New England and America.*

The Roots of Self-government

The Pilgrims hadn't planned on governing themselves. If their ship hadn't strayed off course, they wouldn't have had to. Remember, they thought they were going to Virginia. There an English settlement was already in place, with a charter and rules of order clearly spelled out.

But the Pilgrims had landed in a very different place from Virginia! Luckily they didn't panic. Before leaving their ship, they wrote the Mayflower Compact. It wasn't very long—only about 200 words. Yet it was a great accomplishment. It contained the seeds of self-government that would, years later, help America become independent. It proved that separatists and strangers on board the *Mayflower* could agree on basic ideas about how their new homeland would be run.

▲ People have been speaking out at town meetings for centuries.

Rules of the Compact

The Mayflower Compact set the stage for town meetings at which everyone who could vote would play a part in making laws. At these meetings, decisions would be made by **majority rule**. In other words, if most people voted in favor of an idea, that idea would become law.

The Mayflower Compact worked! It kept everyone, separatists and strangers alike, united in the new colony. The compact remained in place until 1691, when Plymouth became part of the larger, more powerful Massachusetts Bay Colony. The Pilgrims then came under that colony's rules. But the idea of town meetings didn't die. In fact, many laws and rules in the Massachusetts Bay Colony were similar to those of Plymouth. All across New England settlers picked up on this form of

---

majority rule   Rule by more than half the population

government. It became the way New Englanders made their local laws. Many New Englanders took this form of government with them when they went on to settle in other areas.

Town Meetings Live On

Even today, town meetings are alive and well in many communities across the country. Once a year, or more often if necessary, people gather at a public place, such as a school or town hall. They talk, debate, and sometimes even shout at each other. Should the town pass a leash law for dogs? Should it spend money constructing new basketball courts? Each townsperson might have his or her own point of view on issues such as these. And each townsperson has the right to express that point of view, just as the people are doing in the picture on these pages. After all the talk a vote is taken. The decision is made by majority rule, just as it was in Plymouth Colony.

Town meetings remain popular because they allow for **direct democracy**. This means that the people vote on laws. Town meetings are about the only places left where Americans get to do this. Americans don't vote directly on state or national laws. Instead, we vote to elect lawmakers, and the lawmakers actually make the laws.

Will town meetings always be around? It's hard to say. As towns become larger, it gets harder to make town meetings work. Many towns have gotten so big that it's impossible to fit all the voters into one meeting hall. Still, town meetings are such an important part of New England's—and America's—history that it's unlikely they will disappear anytime soon.

★ **direct democracy** A principle of American government that allows citizens to participate in making laws

SHOW WHAT YOU KNOW!

REFOCUS
COMPREHENSION

1. Where did the tradition of town meetings begin?

2. What is the major reason town meetings remain popular?

THINK ABOUT IT
CRITICAL THINKING

What are some possible problems with town meetings?

WRITE ABOUT IT
ACTIVITY

Write a letter to your newspaper saying whether you believe your town should have town meetings. If so, why? If not, why not?

SUMMING UP

1 DO YOU REMEMBER . . .
COMPREHENSION

1. Why did the Puritans come to America?

2. What was the Mayflower Compact?

3. How did the English colonists depend on Native Americans at first?

4. What did economic success prove to the Puritans?

5. What rights did their royal charter give the Puritans?

6. How were Roger Williams's and Anne Hutchinson's ideas different from those of most Puritans?

7. Why did Puritan townspeople gather at meeting houses?

8. Who could vote in Puritan villages?

9. How did the Puritans make decisions at town meetings?

10. What was the Halfway Covenant?

2 SKILL POWER
READING A TABLE

Make a table that shows the accomplishments of John Winthrop, Roger Williams, and Thomas Hooker. List the colonies they started. Also give their reasons for starting these new colonies.

3 WHAT DO YOU THINK?
CRITICAL THINKING

1. The Puritans wanted to show the world how society should be run. Tell whether you think they succeeded.

2. Would you have wanted to live in Massachusetts when the Puritans ruled the colony? Explain your answer.

3. Would you say the Massachusetts colony was run in a democratic or undemocratic fashion? Explain.

4. How do you think Puritan beliefs influenced daily life in early New England?

5. Why, do you think, did the Massachusetts colony grow so rapidly?

4 SAY IT, WRITE IT, USE IT
VOCABULARY

If you were a tour guide in a typical Puritan village in 1650, how would you tell a group of visitors from another country about what they see as they ride through town? Use as many of the vocabulary words below as you can.

apprentice	Mayflower Compact
charter	meeting house
common	Pilgrim
delegate	primer
direct democracy	Puritan
majority rule	separatist

5 GEOGRAPHY AND YOU
MAP STUDY

Use the map below and the map on page 94 to help you answer the following questions.

1. What New England river ran through two colonies, splitting each in half?

2. Name the capitals of the New England colonies.

3. What settlements, established by very small groups, were founded between 1620 and 1630?

4. List the ten earliest New England settlements on this map.

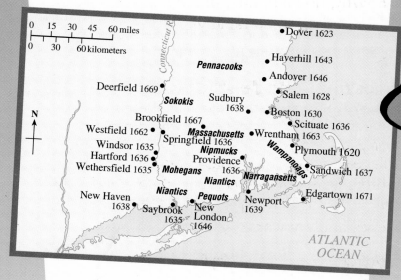

6 TAKE ACTION
CITIZENSHIP

You probably agree that it was unfair that only white male church members could vote in Massachusetts Bay Colony. Over the centuries the vote has been given to all American citizens over 18. Yet in many elections, less than half of all eligible voters bother to go to the polls!

Make a poster that tells why you think voting is important. Include information about how people can register to vote. Hang your poster in a place where adults will see it.

7 GET CREATIVE
HEALTH CONNECTION

With room enough to fish, hunt, and grow plenty of food, New Englanders had a healthy diet. Do some research to find out about the typical foods that New Englanders ate in the 1600s and 1700s. Then make a chart that compares their typical meals with those of your family. Finally, decide who ate the healthier foods.

LOOKING AHEAD
Find out in the next chapter why the Southern Colonies were different from those in New England.

The Southern

The English began settling the Southern Colonies in the early 1600s. The settlers grew tobacco and rice, which required many workers and lots of land. The need for both land and workers greatly impacted the lives of Native Americans and Africans.

Where might you see a weather vane like this? Look on page 124 for one example. ▶

CONTENTS

Colonies

These books tell about some interesting people, places, and events during the settlement of the Southern Colonies. Read one that interests you and fill out a book-review form.

READ AND RESEARCH

An Introduction to Williamsburg by Valerie Tripp
(Pleasantry Press, 1985)
Picture yourself living 200 years ago in Colonial Williamsburg. Find out about the daily lives and activities of various people at that time. *(nonfiction)*
• *You can read a selection from this book on page 126.*

Pocahontas and the Strangers by Clyde Robert Bulla
(Scholastic, 1987)
Trouble starts for Pocahontas and her nation when the Europeans arrive. After her people capture Captain John Smith, Pocahontas saves his life. Will her life change forever? *(biography)*

Who Owns the Sun? by Stacy Chbosky (Landmark Editions, 1988)
A father and son have a conversation about beautiful things in the world that belong to no one. Read slowly as the boy sadly discovers the truth about his own situation. This book was written by a 14-year-old. *(historical fiction)*

SKILL POWER   Making an Outline

Writing an outline can help you organize information for a report.

UNDERSTAND IT

Notebook

Are you an organized person? If you are, your loose-leaf notebook is probably organized according to subjects—social studies, science, and so forth.

How can you organize your thoughts and ideas before writing a report? A good way is to use an outline, organizing your information into a title, main ideas, and supporting ideas.

To make an outline:

• Center the title at the top.

• Label each main idea, or topic, with a Roman numeral and a period. List the topics in a logical order.

• Indent the supporting ideas, or subtopics. Label each subtopic with a capital letter and a period.

• Use a capital letter for the first word of each main topic and subtopic.

EXPLORE IT

American colonists in the 1600s, especially in what is today South Carolina, grew rice. The outline below describes this kind of farming.

Rice Farming

I. Conditions for growing

  A. Type of soil

  B. Temperature

II. Planting and cultivating

  A. Sowing the seeds

  B. Water supply

  C. Weed control

Where would you add the subtopic *Rainfall?*

Which would be a good topic for the next entry—III—Making rice pudding or Harvesting the crop?

Work in groups of four. As a group, decide on a topic you all know about, such as "An Ordinary Day" or "Planning a Surprise Party." Have each person, without consulting the others, make an outline to organize information about the topic. When everyone in the group has finished, compare your outlines. Are they different in some ways? Do they all work? Do they all organize information in a clear and logical way?

Guest List
Music
Food
Balloons
Games

Planning a Surprise Party

I. Guest list

    A. Relatives

    B. Friends

    C. Neighbors

II. Decorations

    A. Crepe-paper streamers

    B. "Congratulations" banner

    C. Balloons

    D. Paper plates, cups, and napkins

III. Food

    A. Appetizers

    B. Main dishes

    C. Desserts

IV. Entertainment

    A. Music

    B. Games

SKILL POWER SEARCH *As you read the next lesson, Setting the Scene, make an outline of the main topics.*

1 **Setting the Scene**

⭐ **KEY TERMS**

work ethic
export
cash crop
indentured servant
buffer zone
plantation

People in the South

FOCUS *The development of the Southern Colonies was often slow and painful. It was hard for the settlers, but it was worse for Africans and Native Americans.*

Trouble in Jamestown

As you read in Chapter 4, the early years of the Jamestown settlement in Virginia were not easy. Many of the settlers died, and others wasted their time looking for gold. These early settlers also made enemies of the Algonquian Indians in the area. The settlement seemed unlikely to survive.

However, things changed in 1608, when Captain John Smith took control of Jamestown. Smith brought a new **work ethic** and announced a new rule—only people who worked would get food. It was a tough policy, but it worked. People stopped digging for gold and started planting crops. Smith also improved relations with the Algonquians. He met with their powerful chief, Powhatan, and traded with him for corn.

Despite Smith's new plan, there were still problems. Many settlers were weakened by a mosquito-borne disease called malaria. And during the winter of 1609–1610, the settlers ran out of food. They had to eat dogs, rats, and snakes. So many people died that the population of Jamestown dropped from 500 to 60 within a few months.

Again help came. In the summer of 1610, a ship

⭐ **work ethic** A belief in working hard

▼ This picture shows early settlers arriving in Jamestown.

114

1610	1619	1634	1680
300 more English settlers arrive in Jamestown	The first African slaves are brought to Virginia	The first settlers arrive in Maryland	Algonquian population drops below 1,000 in Virginia

1600	1610	1620	1630	1640	1650	1660	1670	1680

arrived from England bringing food, supplies, and 300 more settlers. Virginia would soon become the first English colony in America to succeed. Find Virginia and the other Southern Colonies on the map on this page.

An Important Crop

In 1612, John Rolfe made a discovery that would dramatically affect the settlement of Jamestown and the colony of Virginia. He learned that tobacco would grow in Virginia. Settlers then began to grow tobacco and **export** it to Europe.

Tobacco became popular in Europe after explorers took it home from North America in the 1500s. However, not everyone liked tobacco. Even King James I of England said, "Smoking is a custom loathsome to the eye, hateful to the nose, harmful to the brain, [and] dangerous to the lung." Many people disagreed with the king. And by 1638, Virginians exported 3 million pounds of this **cash crop** annually.

A Need for Workers

Tobacco helped Virginian colonists but not Native Americans. To grow tobacco, settlers needed lots of land and workers. The colonists took land from Native Americans. They also tried to force Algonquians to work in tobacco fields. The Algonquians fought successfully to keep their freedom, but they were still devastated by war

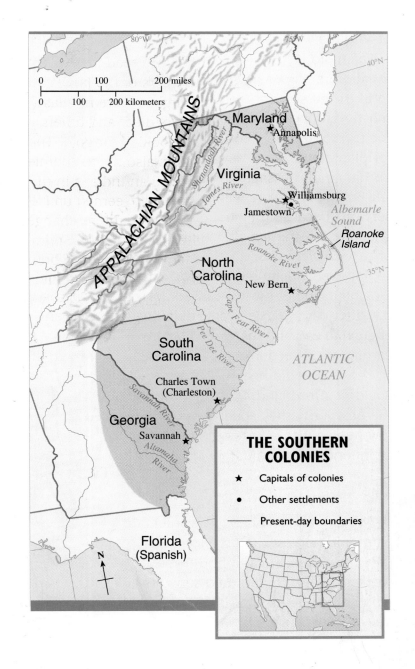

THE SOUTHERN COLONIES

★ Capitals of colonies

● Other settlements

— Present-day boundaries

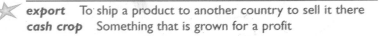

---

export To ship a product to another country to sell it there
cash crop Something that is grown for a profit

115

and European diseases. The Algonquians had never been exposed to European diseases, such as smallpox. As a result, many of them died from these diseases. By 1680 there were fewer than 1,000 Algonquians left in the colony of Virginia.

Failing to get the Native Americans as laborers, the colonists tried using indentured servants. These were mostly Europeans who couldn't afford the trip to America. So they worked for planters for up to seven years in exchange for passage to Virginia. They left Europe and were willing to become servants because they hoped for a good life in America after their years of service were over.

However, indentured servants worked long hours in hot mosquito-filled fields day after day. Some servants didn't get enough to eat, and many died before earning their freedom.

Those who did become free couldn't afford land. Most did not find the prosperity they sought. By 1660 few people wanted to come to Virginia as indentured servants.

The Slave Trade

The planters still needed workers to plant and harvest their tobacco. So they turned to Africa to find those workers. Unlike indentured servants who had come to America voluntarily, these Africans were brought here

against their will. And unlike indentured servants who rode as passengers on boats, these Africans traveled like cargo beneath the decks of ships. Also, unlike indentured servants who could eventually gain freedom, most of these Africans would never become free.

The process of enslaving Africans began in Africa. Often European slave traders, armed with guns, crept into African villages and forests. They captured unarmed men, women, and even children. Sometimes Africans were captured and enslaved by rival African groups.

After being captured, enslaved Africans were chained together, forced to march to the west coast of Africa, and sold to the highest bidder. The map on page 117 shows how many Africans were forced into slavery.

Once they reached the coast of Africa, these captives were forced into

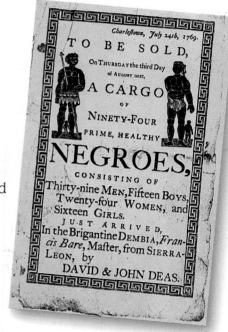

▲ An announcement of a slave auction

---

indentured servant A person who sold his or her services for a certain period of time in exchange for free passage to America

116

ships that would take them across the ocean. Called the *Middle Passage*, this voyage took from four to six weeks.

For the Africans, every moment was torture. There were so many people forced into the bottom of the ship that they had no room to move. The high waves of the open sea made many of them seasick. The conditions were so bad that many Africans did not survive the trip. Those who did survive were forced to lie in filth at the bottom of the ship. They did not know why they had been ripped from their families or where they were going.

The Life of a Slave

When Africans arrived in America, they were treated like animals and sold at auctions. Their masters now completely controlled their lives and their children's lives. Any baby born to an enslaved woman automatically became a slave.

In the 1600s most enslaved people had masters, or owners, who did not give them enough food, decent clothing, or shelter. Many slaves were also whipped. Some slaves fared better, depending on their masters.

Africans had been torn from their homelands and confronted with a new language, a new culture, and a grim new life. However, they adapted to this life and used their skills to help build the colonies.

Over time the Southern Colonies purchased even more Africans. In

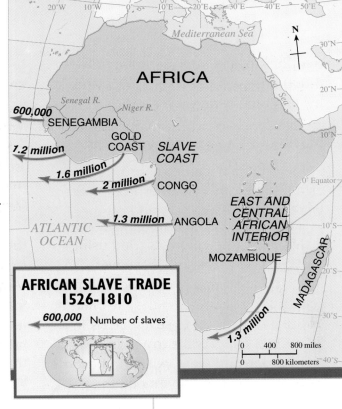

AFRICA

AFRICAN SLAVE TRADE
1526-1810

600,000 Number of slaves

600,000 SENEGAMBIA
1.2 million GOLD COAST / SLAVE COAST
1.6 million
2 million CONGO
1.3 million ANGOLA
EAST AND CENTRAL AFRICAN INTERIOR
MOZAMBIQUE
1.3 million MADAGASCAR

ATLANTIC OCEAN

Mediterranean Sea
Senegal R. Niger R.
Red Sea

0 400 800 miles
0 800 kilometers

▼ Slaves on a forced march to the African coast

the Chesapeake area alone there were 4,000 enslaved people in 1675, and by 1760 there were over 185,000.

Maryland and the Carolinas

As Virginia became more established, other Southern Colonies were settled. Find Maryland on the map on this page. In Maryland, settlers learned from Virginia's mistakes. They planted food crops and developed good relationships with the Native Americans.

Another colony took a very different approach. In Carolina, settlers didn't want friendship from Native Americans. Instead they wanted land and workers because they grew tobacco and rice, which required a great deal of land and labor.

The Carolinians used force to take the lands they wanted from Native Americans. Fierce fighting broke out between the two groups.

Carolinians, like Virginians, turned to Africans for labor. By 1720, enslaved people outnumbered free colonists two to one in the southern part of Carolina.

Since most of Carolina's settlers lived near Albemarle Sound in the north or near Charleston in the south, they considered splitting into two colonies. In 1729 the colony was split into North Carolina and South Carolina.

The Georgia Colony

Georgia was the last English colony to be established in America. It grew much more slowly than the other colonies. One reason was that Georgia was too hot for many Europeans.

The few colonists in Georgia created a great problem for Native Americans. Before the colonists arrived, the area that was later called Georgia was used as a **buffer zone** for Native Americans. When settlers were fighting the Yamasees (YAH muh seez) in Carolina, some Yamasees fled south, retreating into the area of Georgia. It wasn't

Population of the Southern Colonies 1630 – 1750

	1630	1670	1710	1750
Virginia	2,500	35,309	78,281	231,033
Maryland		13,226	42,741	141,073
North Carolina		3,850	15,120	72,984
South Carolina		200	10,883	64,000
Georgia				5,200

CHESAPEAKE SETTLEMENTS 1607–1700

Maryland
Annapolis 1649
St. Marys 1634
Virginia
Henrico 1611
James River
Williamsburg 1699
Yorktown 1631
Fort Henry (Petersburg) 1645
Jamestown 1607
Hampton 1610
Norfolk 1682
PIEDMONT
TIDEWATER
ATLANTIC OCEAN
Potomac River
Chesapeake Bay
Delaware Bay
FALL LINE

buffer zone An area of safety between people in conflict

the best land, but it was safe. When English settlers moved into Georgia, these Native Americans had to face Spanish settlers in Florida if they moved farther south.

Plantations and Farms

Throughout the Southern Colonies most farms were small. The farmers worked the land themselves, growing a few crops, raising a few animals, and basically surviving year to year.

Over time, farming in the Southern Colonies changed. There were always many small farms in the South. But later, planters set up some very large farms, called **plantations**. Often on a plantation, only one main crop, such as tobacco, would be grown.

---

plantation A large farm where one main crop is grown

Many people in the Southern Colonies lived more isolated lives than people in the New England Colonies. In New England, many people lived in towns and farmed fields on the edge of town. New Englanders might have friendly conversations with neighbors on the way out to the fields each morning. Many southerners lived on farms or plantations that were widely scattered. So they often had few neighbors. Also, since the Southern Colonies didn't have many towns, many Southerners didn't have the opportunity to go to weekly church services or attend town schools as New Englanders did. Life on plantations was not as lonely as on small farms, since plantations had more people.

Cultivating tobacco on a Virginia plantation

SHOW WHAT YOU KNOW!

REFOCUS
COMPREHENSION

1. How did John Smith improve the work ethic in Jamestown?

2. What were the major differences between indentured servants and enslaved people?

THINK ABOUT IT
CRITICAL THINKING

In what ways did the African slave trade affect the development of the Southern Colonies?

WRITE ABOUT IT
ACTIVITY

It is 1695 and you live in Carolina. Write a letter to a friend in England explaining how the colonists' relationship with the Native Americans has deteriorated in the Carolinas.

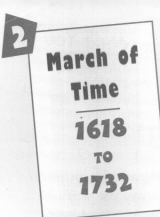
Colonizing the South

FOCUS *The story of the Southern Colonies was full of false starts and dashed hopes. Still, some important lessons were learned, and the colonies survived.*

50 ACRES FREE

It was difficult to get people to move to Virginia. In 1618 the Virginia Company of London, which owned the colony, introduced the *headright system*.

This meant that the company would give 50 acres to every person who paid for his or her own passage to America and then settled in Virginia. The company also would give these settlers an extra 50 acres of land for every person they brought with them.

Since thousands of people lived in overcrowded cities in England, many people were attracted to Virginia through this plan, and the colony grew.

THAT WAS QUITE A GIFT

In 1632, King Charles I gave George Calvert a gift—the large territory around the Chesapeake Bay. It was named Maryland, in honor of the king's wife, Henrietta Maria. Being Catholic, Calvert wanted Catholics to be able to worship in public and to hold public office in his colony.

Calvert died before anyone moved to Maryland. But his son, Lord Baltimore, carried out his father's plans by offering land to wealthy English people who would settle the land. In 1634 the first 200 settlers arrived in Maryland.

Fewer Catholics came than Baltimore had hoped for, so he invited Protestants. Before long, more Protestants than Catholics lived in Maryland. In 1649 they passed the Toleration Act, which allowed all Christians—Catholic or Protestant—to worship as they pleased.

1618	1649	1663		1732
The Virginia Company introduces the headright system	Toleration Act is passed in Maryland	The King approves plan for colony of Carolina		Parliament charters colony of Georgia

1600	1620	1640	1660	1680	1700	1720	1740

RAISING SILKWORMS IN CAROLINA

Eight rich Englishmen planned to earn a fortune by starting a colony in America. They hoped to send other people to live in the colony and raise silkworms for silk, olives for oil, and grapes for wine. Then the Englishmen thought they could sell the products in Europe.

The king of England approved the plan for the colony of Carolina in 1663. But things didn't go the way the Englishmen had hoped. Few Carolina settlers wanted to raise silkworms, olives, or grapes. Instead they grew rice, indigo, and tobacco.

In 1670 the settlers built Charles Town, which attracted people from England, Scotland, and English colonies in the West Indies. Huguenots (HYOO-guh nahts), or French Protestants, also came to Carolina. They had been persecuted in France, and Carolina offered them religious freedom.

GEORGIA

James Oglethorpe wanted to help give released prisoners a second chance. In 1732, Parliament chartered the colony of Georgia as a refuge for people who had been jailed for not paying their debts. In Georgia, Oglethorpe hoped these people would live reformed lives. He also planned for them to raise silkworms and make him rich.

And Oglethorpe didn't want slavery in his colony. So Georgia became the only colony where slavery was illegal.

Oglethorpe had good intentions, but his plans mostly failed. The silkworms didn't survive in Georgia, the settlers didn't change their ways, and in 1750, slavery was legalized.

121

3

Africans in Carolina

FOCUS *Africans who came to America as slaves brought skills they had learned in their homelands. By using these skills, Africans helped the colony of Carolina survive and develop.*

A Struggling Colony

During colonial times the southern coastal area of the colony of Carolina was miserable, especially in the summer. There was no relief from the heat and humidity. Mosquitoes buzzed over the swampy land, carrying a variety of diseases, including yellow fever and malaria.

By the 1680s, new settlers avoided the southern region of the colony. Some settlers who were already there left. Many who stayed were sickly. However, the southern region of the colony did survive and even flourished due to the hard work and abilities of the settlers and the African slaves.

To begin with, Africans didn't get as sick as European settlers. Having come from lands where malaria and yellow fever were common, they were often **immune** to these diseases. Thus, Africans were able to work more days than the European settlers.

Cultural Influences

In addition, enslaved Africans brought from Africa many skills that were useful in Carolina. For instance, in the southern region of Carolina there were many rivers and few roads. So travel was easiest by boat. The Africans knew how to handle boats, and they knew how to hollow a canoe out of a single cypress tree log. Africans taught settlers how to make these **dugout canoes**.

A region full of rivers also meant that fishing was a good source of food. Africans made fishing nets that worked better than the ones the English made. Africans also knew more efficient ways of catching fish.

immune To be protected from an illness because of previous exposure to it
dugout canoe A boat that is made by hollowing out a log

▼ Fishing with a net in Albemarle Sound

One way was to dam up a river. Then the Africans added a mixture to the water that calmed the fish and made them easier to catch.

Another skill the Africans brought with them was cattle-herding. In Europe, cattle grazed in closed areas. In Africa they grazed in open fields. Since the colonists were from Europe, they tried to have their cattle graze in closed areas, as they had done in Europe. However, when this practice didn't work, the Africans showed the colonists how to graze cattle in open fields. The cattle thrived.

Having grown rice along the West African coast, Africans were able to teach the colonists more efficient ways of planting, hoeing, and processing rice. In addition, Africans designed baskets for "fanning" the grain in the sun. Carolinian colonists,

▲ The Banjo Lesson was painted by Henry O. Tanner in 1893.

with the Africans' help, were able to turn rice into a profitable **staple crop**.

Africans also wove baskets and mats out of reeds and grass. And they carved out gourds that could be used to hold drinks and food.

Cultures Are Blended

Africans also made other important contributions to American culture. Some Africans crafted musical instruments, such as the banjo, based on similar instruments they had played in their homeland.

They also had a long tradition of storytelling. By passing along old stories and folk tales, Africans were able to keep their history alive. Folk tales have long been appreciated as a special form of American literature.

As African traditions were adapted to an American setting, something new began to develop—an African American culture.

staple crop   The most important crop grown in an area

SHOW WHAT YOU KNOW!

REFOCUS
COMPREHENSION

1. How did Africans use their skills to help the colony survive?

2. What are some ways that Africans preserved their past and their culture?

THINK ABOUT IT
CRITICAL THINKING

How might life have been different in Carolina without the Africans and their contributions?

WRITE ABOUT IT
ACTIVITY

Write a short story about something that has happened in the history of your family or write your own folk tale.

4

Citizenship

KEY TERMS

legislature
veto
represent

LITERATURE

An Introduction to
Williamsburg

The House of Burgesses

FOCUS In 1619, Virginia settlers elected people to the House of Burgesses. It began a tradition of representative government in America that continues today.

Governing a Colony

How do you run a colony? The Virginia Company of London was a small group of merchants who had provided the money to start the colony of Virginia. The company planned to keep all the lawmaking power for the colony in England. A few colonists would set things up without making any laws. Then these colonists would carry out instructions sent from England.

When the Virginians needed a law changed, they had to send a request to England and wait for someone to bring back the news of the change (if it was granted). It became obvious that the colonists really needed local leaders who had power. In 1610 the Virginia Company sent a governor with more power to Jamestown.

Nine years later the Virginia Company decided to give the settlers a voice in the colony's government. Then Virginians set up their own **legislature**. This legislature would share power with the governor. The

legislature A group of people who make laws

legislature could create laws, and the governor had the right to **veto** any laws passed by the legislature.

The First Legislature

Virginia's new legislative body was named after Parliament, the lawmaking body in England. Since members of the English Parliament were called burgesses, the new legislature in Virginia was named the House of Burgesses.

Members of the House of Burgesses were elected by the "free men" of the colony. These did not include enslaved people or women. The first assembly had 22 elected burgesses to **represent** the colonists. They met for the first time on July 30, 1619, in a little church near the James River.

It could be brutally hot in the Tidewater, or lowland, of Virginia. The burgesses made it worse by wearing the same kinds of robes and felt hats as members of the English Parliament did. The heat was so bad that several burgesses fell ill, and one died. After six hot, sweaty days, the burgesses ended the very first legislative meeting in the English colonies.

The burgesses passed a series of laws about distributing land. They also passed laws against drunkenness, gambling, and idleness. And they set penalties for "excess in apparel," meaning that settlers had to dress properly.

▲ A reenactment of a meeting at the House of Burgesses

They also made it a law that everyone had to attend church twice on Sunday. Also, anyone who owned a gun or sword had to take it to church. This was a time of peace with the Native Americans, but this law showed that the settlers weren't quite sure it would last.

Creating a Tradition

As the years passed, the House of Burgesses continued to meet. The idea that people could govern themselves had taken hold, and colonists didn't want to give it up.

This independent spirit would, in time, lead Americans to fight for their own nation. And when the United States of America was established, it would be based on the same kind of representative government that began with the House of Burgesses.

veto To reject a proposed law
represent To act and speak for another in a lawmaking body

◀ This is the capitol in Williamsburg, Virginia. Note the flag of England and the weather vane.

An Introduction to Williamsburg

by Valerie Tripp

Colonial Williamsburg in Virginia is a living museum, where people experience colonial America. Williamsburg was a very important colonial city, especially during the American Revolution. Most of Colonial Williamsburg represents the late 1700s. Read about Colonial Williamsburg and enjoy the sights, smells, and sounds of this exciting town as if you were actually taking a tour there.

Walk down Williamsburg's deep-shaded streets and walk back into history. Back to the eighteenth century, when ladies in elegant gowns and gentlemen in powdered wigs rode in horse-drawn carriages down the dusty streets. Back to colonial times, when the king of England ruled America and the British flag flew above the housetops you pass.

Williamsburg was born as the eighteenth century dawned. The original capital of Virginia had been located in the crowded village of Jamestown. When the statehouse there burned in 1699, the legislators voted to rebuild it in a new place. They named the new town Williamsburg in honor of their king, William III. Here was a chance for a fresh start, the opportunity to create a noble capital city where before there had been little more than fields and forests. To guard against haphazard growth, a town plan was drawn up that was both practical and artistic. Williamsburg's main street was to be long and broad, skirted by wide greens and open spaces. Houses were to be set back six feet from the streets on lots of one-half acre. The main street, named for the Duke of Gloucester, would stretch nearly a mile from the College of William and Mary, past the church and the market square, to the new statehouse called the Capitol. Soon there would be an elegant Palace for the governor of the colony, who was the king's appointed representative there.

By 1750 Williamsburg had become the most important city in Virginia. People came here from remote parts of the colony to learn of the latest fashions from England and Europe in clothing, furnishings, music, amusements, and ideas. It was a major business center where tobacco planters, farmers, craftsmen, shippers, and merchants came to buy, sell, and trade. And because Williamsburg was the capital of Virginia, it was the political center of the colony where affairs of government were conducted. Laws made in the Capitol and enforced in the courts here affected everyone in Virginia and even influenced other colonies far beyond its borders.

Want to read more? You can continue exploring Colonial Williamsburg by checking the book out of your school or public library.

SHOW WHAT YOU KNOW!

REFOCUS
COMPREHENSION

1. How was power divided between the governor and the House of Burgesses?

2. Who could and who couldn't vote for members of the House of Burgesses?

THINK ABOUT IT
CRITICAL THINKING

Why is it important to have people who represent us in our government?

WRITE ABOUT IT
ACTIVITY

Make a brochure that would encourage people to visit Colonial Williamsburg.

SUMMING UP

1 DO YOU REMEMBER . . .
COMPREHENSION

1. What rule did John Smith announce to make sure Jamestown would survive?

2. What important product did Jamestown settlers export to Europe?

3. What was the Middle Passage?

4. What caused the fighting between early Carolinian settlers and Native Americans?

5. Why was life on a southern farm lonelier than life in a New England village?

6. What was the *headright system*?

7. What did James Oglethorpe hope to achieve in Georgia?

8. What important skills of Africans helped the Carolina colony survive?

9. Describe the first government of the Virginia colony.

10. Who could vote in Virginia's first elections?

2 SKILL POWER
MAKING AN OUTLINE

Make an outline showing what you learned in this chapter. For each main topic, list at least three subtopics. These subtopics should be the important supporting ideas in the chapter. You can use each of the Southern Colonies as a main topic for your outline.

3 WHAT DO YOU THINK?
CRITICAL THINKING

1. Do you think the work ethic that John Smith imposed on the first Virginians was fair? Why or why not?

2. In what ways was farming in the Southern Colonies different from farming in the New England Colonies?

3. What skills might be needed to settle a colony on the moon?

4. How might the Southern Colonies have developed differently if slavery had been outlawed from the beginning?

5. What makes the founding of the House of Burgesses so important?

4 SAY IT, WRITE IT, USE IT
VOCABULARY

Write sentences that show what you've learned in this chapter. Include at least two of the vocabulary words in each sentence. Try to use as many of the words as you can.

buffer zone	legislature
cash crop	plantation
dugout canoe	represent
export	staple crop
immune	veto
indentured servant	work ethic

CHAPTER 6

5 GEOGRAPHY AND YOU
MAP STUDY

Use the map below and others throughout this chapter to answer these questions.

1. What present-day states made up the Southern Colonies?

2. What borders the western edge of the Southern Colonies?

3. From what part of Africa were the most African slaves taken?

4. How far was Charles Town from New Bern?

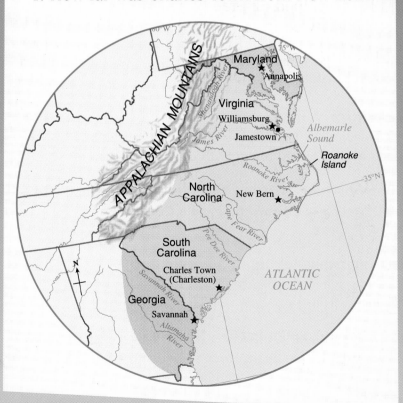

6 TAKE ACTION
CITIZENSHIP

The House of Burgesses provided Virginians with local leaders who had power. With a group of classmates, find out who the local elected leaders are in your community. Is there a mayor, a town supervisor, or a town council? Draw a chart that identifies some local officials and the powers they have.

7 GET CREATIVE
HEALTH CONNECTION

In the United States, people rarely get diseases such as polio and smallpox because of vaccines. In tropical areas of the world, some people still get yellow fever, even though a vaccine is available. Research how a vaccine works. What are some reasons that people don't get vaccines for diseases that are prevalent in their part of the world?

LOOKING AHEAD
In the next chapter read about the rest of the English colonies in North America—the Middle Colonies.

EXPLORE

CHAPTER 7

The Middle

New Jersey, New York, Pennsylvania, Delaware—do you know anyone who lives in one of these states? If you do, you already know something about the Middle Colonies. Clearing forests, planting crops, trading, learning from other groups—that's what this chapter is all about.

Can you guess what he's holding? You can find out on page 144.

CONTENTS

Colonies

These books tell about some people, places, and events of interest during the settlement of the Middle Colonies. Read one that interests you and fill out a book-review form.

READ AND RESEARCH

Night Journeys **by Avi** (William Morrow & Co., 1994)
In this story Peter York has a chance to help two young indentured servants. Will he lose his own freedom if he chooses to help them? *(historical fiction)*
• *You can read a selection from this story on page 150.*

The Lenape Indians **by Josh Wilker** (Chelsea House, 1993)
The Lenapes are a peaceful people who struggle for survival when Europeans settle on their land. Their feelings after they are scattered across many states and Canada are part of their story. *(nonfiction)*

Charlie's House **by Clyde Robert Bulla** (Alfred A. Knopf, 1993)
This is the story of a boy who is tricked into becoming an indentured servant but remains determined to fulfill his dream. *(historical fiction)*

They Led the Way: 14 American Women
by Johanna Johnston (Scholastic, 1987)
Included in this book about great women in America is the story of Lady Deborah Moody. You might be surprised to learn what Moody does with the land she buys from the governor of New Amsterdam. *(biography)*

SKILL POWER

Using Primary and Secondary Sources

Knowing how to identify and use a primary source can give you important information about the past.

UNDERSTAND IT

Historians rely on two kinds of sources to get information about the past. The kind they prefer is called a primary source. This can be a firsthand account of an event by an eyewitness. It can be a letter, a book, or a newspaper article. Photographs that have not been tampered with and artifacts such as tools can also be primary sources.

Secondary sources use facts from other books to describe or interpret an event. These sources are written by people who did not witness the event.

If you have old photographs, you have primary sources that tell about your own history.

EXPLORE IT

William Penn wrote this letter from Pennsylvania in 1683. As the governor of the new English colony of Pennsylvania, Penn wanted to attract settlers. He tried in this letter to convince people that Pennsylvania was a better place to live than Europe. Penn's colorful words and detailed descriptions give us a good idea about the climate of Pennsylvania more than 300 years ago!

° Is Penn's letter an example of a primary or a secondary source?

A brief Account of the
Province of Pennsylvania,
Lately Granted by the
KING,
Under the GREAT
Seal of England,
TO
WILLIAM PENN
AND HIS
Heirs and Assigns.

"The air is sweet and clear, rarely overcast. The waters are generally good, for the rivers and brooks have mostly gravel and stony bottoms. . . . From December to the beginning of March, we had sharp frosty weather; not foul, thick black weather, as in England. The air [is] dry, cold, and piercing, yet I [did not wear] more clothes than in England. From [March] to June, we enjoyed a sweet spring, no gusts, but gentle showers and a fine sky. . . . And whatever mists or fogs foul the heavens, in two hours time [they] are blown away."

Letters written by William Penn ▲ spread the word about the benefits of Pennsylvania.

This family photograph was taken in 1921. ▶

TRY IT

Ask family members to help you find primary sources that tell about your family. You might bring in printed material, such as a newspaper clipping, postcard, or photograph, or an artifact, such as baby shoes or a medal. Share your primary source with your classmates and tell what you learned from it.

As a class you could create a display that shows what everyone has brought in (a bulletin board is good for this). You could call the display "Exploring Our Past" or whatever title the class chooses. Small cards that tell about each primary source would help visitors understand the display.

This Civil War medal was awarded to a soldier in 1865.

EXPLORING OUR PAST

My great-grandparents' wedding day (1914)

Jamie Mahoney

A hand-carved wooden toy (1921)

Carmine Ferraro

A Civil War medal (1865)

Megan Honeyman

St. Mary's Hospital

Aunt Judy's birth certificate (1938)

Jennie Bracken

Family picture (1921)

Alethia Carter

A shoe-buttoner (1890s)

Elissa Knoerr

My grandma came to America as a war bride. (1946)

Ryan Tettemer

Baby shoes worn by a relative (about 1904)

Lee Chin

My aunt's family (1955)

Elaine Soares

SKILL POWER SEARCH *There are more primary sources in this chapter. How many can you find?*

133

WHEN CULTURES MEET

FOCUS *Many different groups of people helped create the Middle Colonies. To survive in their new surroundings, they borrowed and learned from each other.*

Coming to a New Land

William Penn's letters advertising his colony were a great success. By the late 1600s, thousands and thousands of European settlers were packing their belongings and sailing to the Middle Colonies. These colonies were called Pennsylvania, New York, and New Jersey. At that time the present-day state of Delaware was part of the Pennsylvania colony. Locate the colonies on the map on this page.

The Middle Colonies offered several advantages over New England and the Southern Colonies. For one thing, the climate was more inviting. Much of the Middle Colonies did not have the scorching heat of the South or the bone-chilling cold of New England. In addition, the land was rich and fertile, perfectly suited for farming. It was better than the hard, rocky soil of Massachusetts and better than the swampy fields of the Carolina colony.

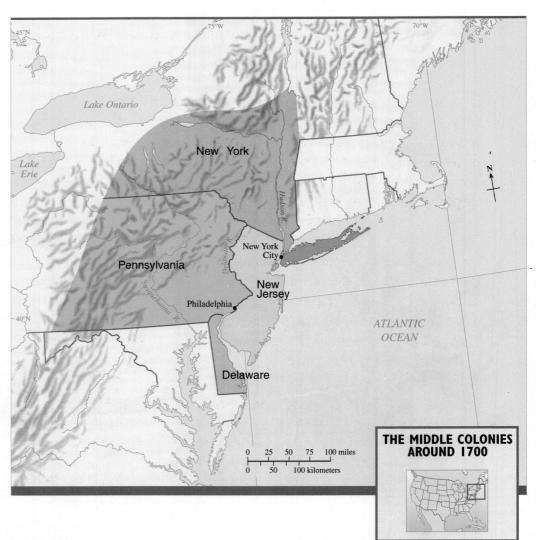

THE MIDDLE COLONIES AROUND 1700

| 1664 | 1664 | | 1681 | | 1704 | |
| New Netherland becomes New York | New Jersey is founded | | Pennsylvania is founded | | Delaware gets its own legislature | |

| 1660 | 1670 | 1680 | 1690 | 1700 | 1710 |

Freedom of Religion

The Middle Colonies also offered religious freedom, which means that people were free to practice the religion of their choice. Pennsylvania especially welcomed settlers of different religions. As early as 1682, Pennsylvania's **Frame of Government**, or plan of government, guaranteed people the right to worship God as they saw fit.

The settlers did not think of their new homeland as the Middle Colonies. That label was used later to distinguish the area from the New England Colonies and the Southern Colonies.

So how did the settlers view themselves? Most thought of themselves as members of a religious group. They were Quakers, Jews, Mennonites, or Anglicans. They were Presbyterians, Dunkards, Moravians, or Baptists. Almost every settler felt a burning commitment to his or her religion. It was a central feature in people's lives.

Africans who came to America as enslaved persons had not lived in areas of Africa where Christianity was practiced. Many, however, became Christians in the colonies.

Furs, Farms, and Cities

As people arrived from Europe, they spread out into the Middle Colonies. Some settled in Philadelphia or New York City. Others traded for furs with Native Americans at trading posts along the Hudson River in the New York colony. Other people looked for farmland in the rolling hills of Pennsylvania, New York, and northern

Colonists traded with Native Americans in New York.

⭐ **Frame of Government** William Penn's plan for the government of the Pennsylvania colony

New Jersey. These settlers had to clear the forests before they could plant crops in the rich soil. The sandy soil of Delaware and southern New Jersey also proved good for farming.

The Native Peoples

As the settlers of the Middle Colonies spread out across the land, they cut deeper and deeper into Native American territory. Several Native American nations lived in this region. The Lenapes (LEN uh peez) made their home in what is now New Jersey and in nearby parts of New York, Pennsylvania, and Delaware. Farther south, in southern Delaware, lived the Nanticokes (NAN tih-kohks). The Susquehan-nocks (sus kwuh HAN uks) lived in southern Pennsylvania. And the Iroquois had settled in northern Pennsylvania and New York.

There were important differences among these Native American nations. But they all shared a respect for the land. Their families had lived here for centuries. They knew where the best hunting grounds were and how to travel the complex network of trails through the forests. They knew how to live on the land without changing it very much. Yet change was on its way. As the number of European settlers in the Middle Colonies grew, some Native Americans must have sensed that things would never again be the same.

The Iroquois League

While the Middle Colonies were just beginning, the **Iroquois League** had been running smoothly for well over a hundred years. This league consisted of five Indian nations: the Oneidas, Onondagas, Mohawks, Cayugas, and Senecas. According to legend, two heroic Indians—a Huron named Dekanawidah and a Mohawk named Hiawatha—took a stand for peace. They convinced five warring Indian nations to join together to form the Iroquois League, also called the League of the Great Peace. The result was an effective and democratic system.

The people in the league were governed by a council of chiefs. The chiefs had the power to settle disagreements, make treaties, and declare war. They were chosen by important women of the clans that made up each nation. These women could also remove the chiefs from

A painting created in 1946 by Tom Two-Arrows Dorsey, an Onondaga artist, showed respect for the earth.

The Iroquois League

Oneidas (oh NYE duz)   **Cayugas** (kay YOO guz)
Onondagas (ahn un DAW guz)   **Senecas** (SEN ih kuz)
Mohawks (MOH hawks)   **Tuscaroras** (tus kuh RAWR uz)

⭐ *Iroquois League* A political union of five, and later six, Iroquois nations who were governed by a council of chiefs

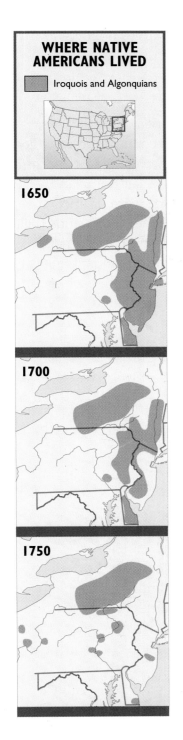

1650

1700

1750

power. Iroquois women owned the cornfields, and they had an equal say with men in making important decisions, such as when to harvest crops.

About 1722 a sixth nation, the Tuscaroras, joined the league. The Iroquois League worked so well that some Americans later studied it as a model when they were creating the United States government.

Impact on Native Americans

Over time, more and more Europeans moved into areas where Native Americans lived. The European colonists came to view Native Americans as obstacles to expansion and settlement. The maps on this page show where Native Americans lived in the years 1650, 1700, and 1750. As you can see on the maps, by 1750, Native Americans had been forced to move to the north and west of where they had been in 1650.

Forcing them off their land was not the only effect that the arrival of Europeans had on Native Americans. Smallpox and other diseases brought by the Europeans spread like wildfire through Native American communities. Native Americans had never been exposed to these diseases before, and their systems could not handle them. As a result, the death rate from disease was very high.

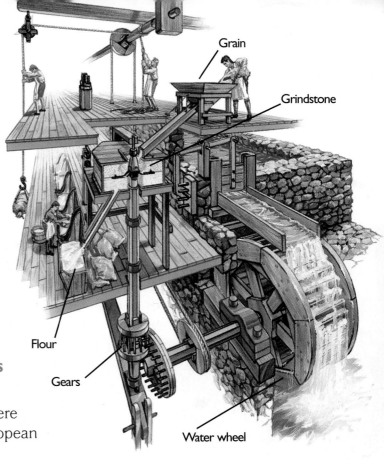

Grain

Grindstone

Flour

Gears

Water wheel

▲ **GRISTMILL**
The river current turned the water wheel, providing the power to turn the gears. The gears operated the grindstone, which then ground the grain into flour.

"The Bread Colonies"

It didn't take long before settlers in the Middle Colonies were able to grow all the food they needed and more. They had enough left over to sell. Farmers began taking wheat and rye to **gristmills** that sprang up along the rivers. At these mills the grains were ground into flour. Then the flour was sold to settlers throughout the English colonies. This is how the Middle Colonies earned the nickname "the bread colonies."

 gristmill A structure where grain is ground into flour

A Need for Workers

Throughout the Middle Colonies there was a shortage of workers to farm the land and to do the many other jobs that needed to be done. As you learned in Chapter 6, a need for labor was sometimes met by indentured servants. In exchange for having his or her passage to America paid, a person agreed to work as an indentured servant for a period of five to seven years. Indentured servants lived with the families they worked for. Most indentured servants in the Middle Colonies were English, Scots-Irish, and German.

Africans in the Middle Colonies

Some indentured servants came from Africa. Other Africans came to the Middle Colonies as enslaved persons. They were all brought to this area to supply much-needed labor.

Africans did many kinds of jobs. Some worked as skilled artisans or craftspersons. Some worked as farmhands. Others did household chores. Those who lived in cities often labored alongside the people they worked for and learned a trade. They might have worked as carpenters, coopers, or tailors. Other Africans

Africans learned trades, like soap making, by laboring alongside skilled workers.

worked on the wharves, loading and unloading ships.

Ties to the Past

At first the European colonists identified with the countries from which they had come. They clung to customs and manners from their homeland. Settlers from France wore distinctive wigs. Settlers from the Netherlands built Dutch-style homes and barns. English settlers tried to plant traditional English flower gardens. In addition, each group brought its own style of food, clothing, and entertainment.

Learning to Change

These distinctions began to fade as time passed. Life in the colonies demanded a new outlook. People had to adapt to their new surroundings. They needed to learn from each other's mistakes and to take advantage of each other's successes. In that sense the great variety of people in the Middle Colonies helped all settlers.

Some Swedish settlers showed Welsh newcomers how to build log homes. English settlers might learn to bake pies from German neighbors. A farmer from Scotland could learn new farming techniques from German neighbors on the next farm. After a

---

cooper A person who makes or repairs wooden barrels, tubs, or casks

while, Dutch families might begin to dress more like the English families they met.

Cultural Borrowing

Again and again different groups borrowed and learned from each other. Before long, even differences in religion and language began to blur. Some Quakers became Lutherans. Some Germans turned to the Dutch Reformed Church. Children from different backgrounds learned to speak English. These are all examples of **cultural borrowing**—that is, learning new ideas, customs, languages, and ways of doing things from different groups of people.

Settlers also learned from Native Americans who lived in the area of the Middle Colonies. These people already knew how to live on this land. They taught settlers to grow corn and beans, eat a kind of fish called sturgeon, and make dugout canoes, as shown below. Settlers also learned to like Native American dishes, such as succotash, a mixture of corn and beans. Popcorn covered with maple syrup was a popular dish, too.

▲ Native Americans carved bowls and spoons from wood.

A New Culture

By 1750 most of the settlers living in the Middle Colonies had been born there. The American colonies were the only homes they knew. Most who had a European background had never seen Europe. Although they still valued their European roots, they were becoming less European with each passing generation. Some Africans, however, still wanted to return to their homeland.

The mixing and blending of cultures was changing the way people in the Middle Colonies lived and worked. By 1750 a new, distinctive culture was beginning to emerge. Whether they knew it or not, the settlers were becoming less European and African and more what we would eventually call American.

⭐ **cultural borrowing** The exchange of ideas, languages, customs, and ways of doing things among different groups of people

▼ A dugout canoe was hollowed out of a large log.

SHOW WHAT YOU KNOW!

REFOCUS
COMPREHENSION

1. What different groups of people helped create the Middle Colonies?

2. What did the different groups learn from one another?

THINK ABOUT IT
CRITICAL THINKING

What, do you think, were the most important lessons the settlers had to learn to survive?

WRITE ABOUT IT
ACTIVITY

It is April 4, 1724. You came to the Middle Colonies three years ago from France. Write a letter to a friend you left behind, telling about your new life and the adjustments that you've had to make.

WILLIAM PENN

FOCUS *William Penn founded Pennsylvania on his belief in the value of peace and toleration. Part of his plan was a government that reflected democratic ideals.*

An English Quaker

In the late 1670s, William Penn was a wealthy Englishman living on his country estate. Yet he was not happy. He constantly had to defend his religious views. Penn had joined the Society of Friends. The Friends claimed that the spirit of God lay inside every person. This spirit was so strong, some said, that it made them quake. The Friends were called **Quakers**.

If God's spirit lay inside *everyone*, then no one was better than anyone else. So the Quakers saw no reason to give special treatment to the rich or powerful. For example, they did not tip their hats when they met a wealthy man. Quakers were also **pacifists**—they did not believe in fighting or going to war. Many people in England despised the Quakers and considered them to be troublemakers. They feared the spread of Quaker beliefs.

A Pennsylvania Governor

Penn wanted to form a perfect Quaker society in America. He asked the king of England to give him land there. To pay a debt owed to Penn's father, the king agreed. In 1681, Penn became owner and governor of a new colony named Pennsylvania—"Penn's Woods"—in honor of his father. He set up a government that allowed settlers to choose their own lawmakers and to practice their own religion.

William Penn advertised far and wide for settlers from different backgrounds and countries. He believed everyone could thrive in his colony if people treated each other fairly and with respect.

Penn also wanted to treat Native Americans fairly. He viewed them as people with rights and ideas of their own. His attitude toward

I am very sensible of the unkindness and injustice that has been too much exercised towards you by [Europeans]. . . . But I am not such a man. . . . I have great love and regard toward you, and I desire to win and gain your love and friendship by a kind, just, and peaceable life. . . . I am your friend.

William Penn

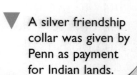

▼ A silver friendship collar was given by Penn as payment for Indian lands.

▼ A wampum belt honors a 1682 treaty of friendship between the Delaware Indians and William Penn.

Quaker A member of a religious society whose beliefs include equality and nonviolence

pacifist A person who does not believe in fighting or going to war

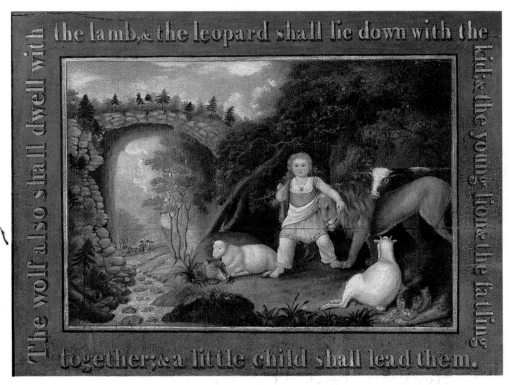

The Peaceable Kingdom of the Branch was painted in 1830 by Edward Hicks, a Quaker minister.

Native Americans is evident in a letter he wrote to the Lenape nation. You can see part of his letter on page 140.

Within a few years Pennsylvania was booming. But the results of this prosperity did not always please Penn. He feared that Quaker ideas were slipping away. He thought the settlers now had too much interest in money and not enough interest in God.

After Penn's Death

In fact, after Penn's death, his own sons cheated the Lenapes of almost 1 million acres of land. In the Walking Purchase of 1737, the Native Americans agreed to give up the amount of land that a man could cover *walking* in a day and a half from a certain tree. Penn's sons hired athletes to *run* the distance, much of it on roads.

Generally, Pennsylvania was a success. It became the fastest-growing of the 13 colonies. It produced some of the best craftspersons, farmers, and merchants. It also had a public library, a general hospital, and an organized postal service. And Quaker ideas had made a difference. They led to 40 years of peace with local Native Americans and to some of the first written protests against slavery in America.

SHOW WHAT YOU KNOW!

REFOCUS
COMPREHENSION

1. How did William Penn put his beliefs into action?

2. How did William Penn view Native Americans?

THINK ABOUT IT
CRITICAL THINKING

What was William Penn's dream for Pennsylvania? Why did he have difficulty putting his dream into practice?

WRITE ABOUT IT
ACTIVITY

How would William Penn have felt about the role his sons played in the Walking Purchase of 1737? You can use Penn's letter, a primary source, to help you write an answer.

SETTLING THE MIDDLE COLONIES

FOCUS *The years 1664 to 1750 saw the emergence of the Middle Colonies—New York, New Jersey, Pennsylvania, and Delaware. As the colonies grew in size, Native Americans were forced to give up their lands.*

ENGLAND GAINED NEW YORK

For 40 years the Netherlands had controlled New Netherland, the area between New England and Maryland. In Europe the Netherlands and England were often at war. In 1664, England's Duke of York sent warships to take over New Netherland. The ships sailed into the port city of New Amsterdam. New Netherland's cruel governor, Peter Stuyvesant, wanted to fight. But he had few weapons, and his colonists refused to fight. Stuyvesant surrendered. The colony was renamed for the Duke of York. The English now controlled the Atlantic coast from Maine to Carolina.

TROUBLE IN NEW JERSEY

The Duke of York, feeling generous, gave part of the New York colony to his friends John Berkeley and George Carteret. They called their new colony New Jersey, after the English island of Jersey.

By 1676, trouble was brewing in the colony. Some thought the land belonged to Berkeley and Carteret. Others said it belonged to settlers from New York. Finally, the king of England declared that Berkeley and Carteret were the rightful owners. The men divided the colony into East and West Jersey. Carteret kept East Jersey. Berkeley sold West Jersey to a group of Quakers.

PENNSYLVANIA NEEDED DELAWARE

William Penn, governor of the new colony of Pennsylvania, had a problem. The colony had no direct access to the ocean. In 1682 the Duke of York solved the problem by giving Penn the area called Delaware. Now Penn's colony had access to the Atlantic Ocean by way of Delaware Bay. Delaware got its own legislature in 1704.

In 1682 an Irishman named Thomas Holme worked with William Penn to design a new city on the Delaware River. This city would have a logical design for streets. Penn called it Philadelphia, "the city of brotherly love."

1664	1676	1682	1686	1702	1750
England controls New Netherland	New Jersey is divided	William Penn gains Delaware	Mennonites protest slavery	East and West Jersey are rejoined	Nearly 30 percent of Middle Colonists are Africans

| 1660 | 1670 | 1680 | 1690 | 1700 | 1710 | 1720 | 1730 | 1740 | 1750 |

A PROTEST AGAINST SLAVERY

The Mennonites, a religious group in Pennsylvania, believed that slavery was wrong. In 1686 the Mennonites wrote an important document addressed to the Quakers of Pennsylvania, some of whom owned slaves. It stated the following.

We should do to all men [as we would have them do to us]; making no difference of what generation, descent or colour they are. . . . To rob and sell [people] against their will, we stand against.

The statement was the first protest against slavery in the English colonies. The protest embarrassed many Quakers. In 1696 the Quakers themselves passed a resolution saying that slavery violated the teachings of the Bible.

NEW JERSEY AGAIN

People in East Jersey and West Jersey were still arguing over who owned what. In 1702, King William III of England rejoined the two colonies, once again calling the area New Jersey. This time it became a royal colony. However, New Jersey continued to have two capital cities—Perth Amboy in the east and Burlington in the west.

A GROWING POPULATION

Between 1680 and 1750 the population of the Middle Colonies grew considerably. A mix of people from all over Europe flocked to these colonies for a better life.

By 1750 almost 30 percent of the people in the Middle Colonies were Africans. The proportion of Native Americans to white settlers had changed dramatically. As more and more white settlers moved to the Middle Colonies, Native Americans were forced to give up their land.

SHOW WHAT YOU KNOW!

REFOCUS
COMPREHENSION

1. Why were the years between 1664 and 1750 important to the Middle Colonies?

2. Which group was the first to protest against slavery in the English colonies?

THINK ABOUT IT
CRITICAL THINKING

Why, do you think, did William Penn need Delaware's access to the Atlantic Ocean?

WRITE ABOUT IT
ACTIVITY

Use pictures and words to chart the major events that occurred between 1664 and 1750.

LIVING IN A NEW LAND

FOCUS *A new life in a strange land was filled with challenges and new experiences. From letters and journals that settlers wrote, we know what ordinary people faced when moving to the Middle Colonies.*

Leaving Home

If you think about leaving your home in Europe, traveling across an ocean, and carving out a new life in a strange land, it may sound exciting. In fact, it probably was for the settlers who came to the Middle Colonies in the late 1600s. But it was also scary and dangerous. The map below shows the areas in Europe and Africa from which people came to the Middle Colonies.

Crossing an Ocean

The ocean voyage itself is a challenge. It is probably your first journey out onto the open sea. Feel the spray of salt water on your face. Enjoy the power of the wind and the waves as they move you along. After a while, though, the rolling of the ship might make you sick. You might experience headaches, fever, or vomiting. Even if you don't get sick on the voyage, other people probably will. Some might even die. Their bodies will be buried at sea.

The ship is crowded and dirty. The meat you eat has been heavily salted to keep it from rotting. It burns your mouth and leaves you with sores on your tongue. By now, every inch of the ship smells. Bugs are everywhere. They even crawl over your face as you sleep. At last, after six or seven weeks at sea, you arrive in America.

A New Land

When you reach your new land, many things look strange but wonderful. You see animals you've never seen before. Imagine seeing a raccoon for the very first time! You might catch a glimpse of a wild turkey, a wood turtle,

▲ The oak footwarmer had hot coals inside. You would rest your cold feet on top.

The long-handled pan filled with embers would be used to warm your bed.

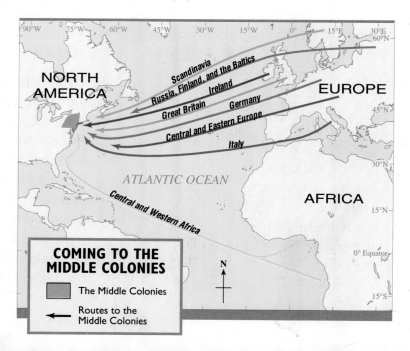

COMING TO THE MIDDLE COLONIES

- ▢ The Middle Colonies
- ← Routes to the Middle Colonies

NORTH AMERICA

Scandinavia
Russia, Finland, and the Baltics
Ireland
Great Britain
Germany
Central and Eastern Europe
Italy

EUROPE

Central and Western Africa

ATLANTIC OCEAN

AFRICA

or a white-tailed deer. Don't forget all the new kinds of flowers, bushes, and trees you can discover.

Building a Home

You and your family will probably build your new home. You might even live in a cave until a hut can be put up. When the hut is finished, it is small—perhaps only 18 feet by 20 feet. Your entire family—father, mother, and several brothers and sisters—live in one room. A fire in the fireplace is the only source of heat and the only way to cook your food. Clouds of smoke from the fire hang in the room, and you can't draw a breath without taking in dry, dusty air. But outside, the air is crystal clear—far better than the smoke and smog of European cities, like London, England.

▲ This reconstructed hut was made from materials at hand—branches, sticks, and leaves.

What's for Dinner?

You eat some of the same foods you had back in Europe. Day after day you eat bread, buttermilk, and roasted or boiled meat. Some food, though, is new to you. You get your first taste of corn, potatoes, pumpkins, and squash. You might also taste Native American dishes, such as the flavorful mixture called succotash.

What Will You Wear?

Boys and girls in the colonies are dressed alike, often in long gowns, until they are about five or six years old. Then they start wearing hand-me-down clothes from their parents or older brothers or sisters. At about this same age, children are given duties and chores.

Do Your Chores!

The colonists never run out of work to do. Everybody in the family has chores. Boys spend hours helping their fathers clear trees, plow the land, plant and harvest crops, build fences, chop wood, and care for livestock.

Most of what is used in the home is made there. Girls help plant gardens and care for the younger children. The girls help prepare food, preserve vegetables, smoke meats, milk cows,

▲ Children in the colonies played with dolls made from corn husks.

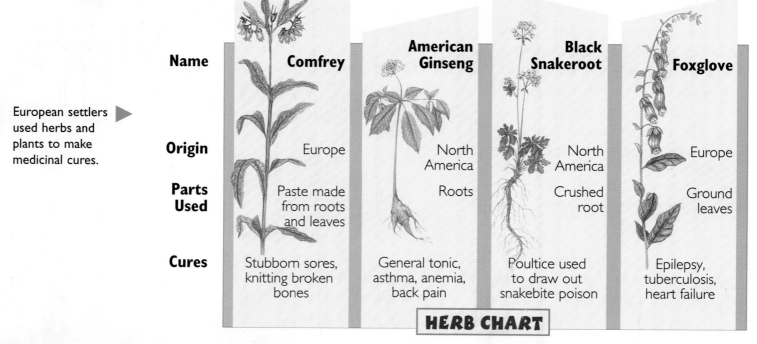

make butter and cheese, and make clothes. Before you can make clothes, you first have to spin the thread, weave the thread into cloth, and then dye the cloth. Once a month, girls help gather up all the dirty clothes in the house and wash them, using homemade soap. Three or four times a year, girls help pluck the feathers off the geese to get goose down for feather beds. The geese put up a terrible fight. You might have to pull a stocking down over each bird's head to keep it from biting you. Although the chores might seem difficult at times, children go to bed at night knowing that their family can take care of themselves.

▲ Women and girls spent hours at spinning wheels.

Do You Have a Cure?

There are very few trained doctors in the colonies. If you get sick, you will probably be cared for by your mother or some other female settler. Sometimes she uses cures brought over from Europe. Many of these are herbal cures. Your mother might learn more about herbal medicines from local Native Americans. They know which plants can ease the pain of a sprained ankle and which soothe an upset stomach.

The colonists don't know what causes certain illnesses. But they use a variety of remedies to treat various symptoms. Feeling feverish? Eat seven insects. Depressed? Go gather ants by the light of the moon. If that doesn't work, some people think that letting a person bleed will get the sickness out of the body.

European settlers used herbs and plants to make medicinal cures. ▶

Name	Comfrey	American Ginseng	Black Snakeroot	Foxglove
Origin	Europe	North America	North America	Europe
Parts Used	Paste made from roots and leaves	Roots	Crushed root	Ground leaves
Cures	Stubborn sores, knitting broken bones	General tonic, asthma, anemia, back pain	Poultice used to draw out snakebite poison	Epilepsy, tuberculosis, heart failure

HERB CHART

Still, your best hope is to stay healthy. For many diseases there is no effective treatment. Diseases such as smallpox, yellow fever, and malaria are passed easily from person to person. They pose a special threat in the cities, where living conditions are the most crowded. You might step on a rusty nail and die of blood poisoning. You could die from rabies after being bitten by a rabid animal. You could die from bee stings or snakebites. With no fire departments in existence until 1736, your entire family could die in a house fire.

A Little Learning

Chances are you won't have much schooling, especially if you live in the country. Maybe your parents will use a **hornbook**, such as the one shown here, to teach you to read the Bible. The rest of your education is learning to follow in your parents' footsteps. Boys usually learn their father's trade—farming, woodworking, or other crafts. Girls usually master the many skills needed to run a household.

hornbook A piece of wood with the letters of the alphabet, often protected by a thin layer of transparent horn

Life in a City

You and your family might make your way to a city in search of work. Although America in colonial times is mostly countryside dotted with farms and small villages, a few cities are thriving. You might choose to make your home in New York City or in Philadelphia (the biggest city of the time). As you arrive, you see a built-up area, a busy harbor with ships of all sizes coming and going, and streets lined with dwellings, shops, and churches. And on those streets you hear many languages spoken.

One of your chores might be to walk to a main street of the city to buy fruit for your family. As you approach the marketplace, you see hundreds of farmers, fishers, fur traders, and sellers of all kinds.

Before journeying home, you stop to visit your older brother, who is working as an apprentice for a printer. Your brother and his master have signed a contract. The master feeds, clothes, and trains your brother. In exchange, your brother works hard until he is experienced and old enough to open his own shop.

SHOW WHAT YOU KNOW!

REFOCUS
COMPREHENSION

1. What challenges and new experiences did the Middle Colonists face?

2. What were some of the cures the colonists used for injury or sickness?

THINK ABOUT IT
CRITICAL THINKING

If you were a Middle Colonist, would you rather live in a city or out in the country? Why?

WRITE ABOUT IT
ACTIVITY

What have you done today—plucked a goose or made soap? Write a journal entry as a Middle Colonist might have written it.

147

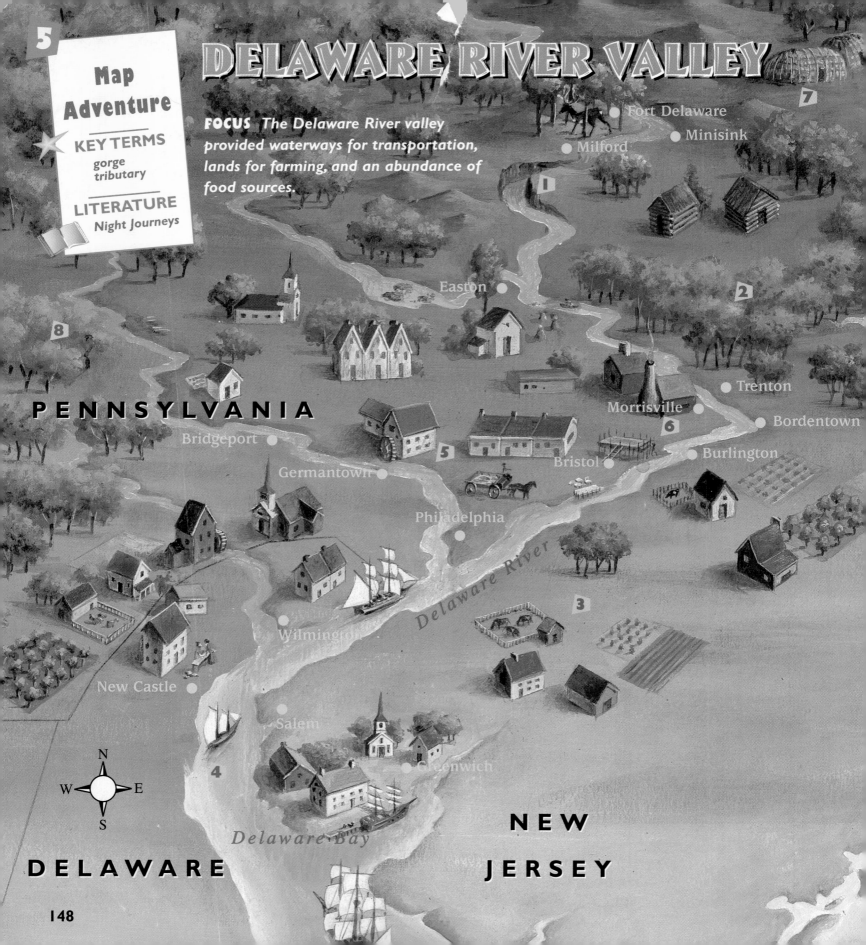

DELAWARE RIVER VALLEY

5

Map Adventure

★ **KEY TERMS**
gorge
tributary

LITERATURE
Night Journeys

FOCUS The Delaware River valley provided waterways for transportation, lands for farming, and an abundance of food sources.

PENNSYLVANIA

Fort Delaware

Minisink

Milford

Easton

Trenton

Morrisville

Bordentown

Bristol

Burlington

Bridgeport

Germantown

Philadelphia

Wilmington

Delaware River

New Castle

Salem

Greenwich

NEW

JERSEY

Delaware Bay

DELAWARE

N
W E
S

148

Adventure on the Delaware

The Delaware River begins its life in the high hills of southern New York. It then flows south, zigging and zagging its way through hills, valleys, and lowlands. After a 280-mile journey, the river reaches the Delaware Bay. The river forms part of the border between Pennsylvania and New York, the entire border between Pennsylvania and New Jersey, and—for a few miles—the border between New Jersey and Delaware.

Map Legend

1 Delaware Water Gap This beautiful gorge is two miles long, with steep stone wall cliffs on both sides.

2 Woodland Trees provided the settlers with logs for buildings and wood for fuel.

3 Crops and livestock Throughout the Delaware Valley, settlers grew wheat (the most important crop), rye, potatoes, and corn. They also raised pigs, cattle, and horses.

4 Fish and crustaceans The waters of the valley were an important source of food for the Native Americans and the European settlers. The Delaware Bay provided oysters, crabs, and clams. The Delaware River provided trout, bass, and shad.

5 Small industry Sawmills, gristmills, and ironworks built along the Delaware River and its tributaries supplied lumber, flour, and iron for the settlers.

6 Towns and cities Towns sprang up along the Delaware River, often near the site of a mill or ironworks. Trade spurred the growth of some towns into cities.

7 Lenape villages The Lenapes used saplings and trees to build their homes.

8 Animals in the forests Europeans saw strange new animals, such as the white-tailed deer, the red squirrel, and the passenger pigeon. Settlers trapped or shot wild animals for their meat and fur.

⭐ **gorge** A narrow pass or valley between steep heights
tributary A stream or river that flows into a larger one

MAP IT

What if you lived in the village of Minisink, which is north of the Delaware Water Gap? Locate the village on the map with your finger. You have trapped beaver and mink all winter, and now the skins can be taken by boat down the Delaware River.

1. Use your finger to trace your boat journey on the map. Traveling south, what is the name of the first town you reach? What do you see near that town?
2. Passing the town of Easton, you begin paddling southeast. What do you see as you make your way to Burlington?
3. You are headed to Wilmington to sell your furs. In what direction must you travel as you leave Burlington? What settlements do you pass along the way?

EXPLORE IT

You could design a travel plan for a partner, using the map as your guide. Invite your partner to follow your directions and explore your route, making observations along the way.

ATLANTIC
OCEAN

149

Night Journeys

by Avi

During the 1700s a child just about your age has an adventure on the Delaware River. Read about Peter, an orphan taken into the home of a Quaker, Mr. Everett Shinn. Mr. Shinn and his family live about 60 miles north of Philadelphia. Mr. Shinn and Peter are helping to search for two escaped indentured servants. Join Peter and Mr. Shinn as they keep watch at Morgan's Rock, an island that lies between Pennsylvania and New Jersey.

At that point the Delaware River is fairly wide, almost a quarter of a mile, wider than anywhere else for some miles north or south. There in the river lies Morgan's Rock, set at unequal distances from the river's banks: fifty yards from the Pennsylvania side and perhaps three hundred or so from Jersey.

A narrow island, Morgan's Rock is much in the shape of a teardrop, its pointed end to the south. At the northern end a mass of rock thrusts against the river's flow like the prow of a great ship, making the river split into two different paths.

On the eastern—Jersey—side of the island the water runs wide and fairly shallow, making it wild and fierce. On the western—Pennsylvania—side, it's the reverse. There the narrow channel runs to a greater depth but is quiet as church. But on that side a line of broken rock juts halfway into the river: the dangerous Finger Falls.

Night Journeys

Peter can help Robert and Elizabeth, or himself.
It's his choice.

by Avi

Thus, while one side of the island is rough and fast, there is no obstruction; the other side is soft but obstructed. Boats coming down the river must decide which route to take. To the unknowing, the silent side looks easier. To those who know, the rough side is the wiser choice. Too late a decision is the greatest danger of all, for at the dividing point, where the rock stands, the river is at its worst, tearing itself like mad dogs in battle. Many a boat has broken there; and men have drowned. The island's very name—Morgan—recalls a man who so drowned.

The land directly behind the rock itself is an island clear of water. The northern section, some sixty yards or more, is solid and fertile, being heavily overgrown with trees, bushes, and whatever else can grow there. Indeed, the foliage is so thick that it's hard to enter. Moreover, it holds masses of logs and branches, hurled up on the island by the rolling waters around the rock.

The island's southern end is but an ever narrowing strip of sand and silt, which lengthens and shortens depending on the river's height.

Curiously, the island is known as a good place to ford the river. Indeed, it *is* a good place, but only when the river is low, such as might occur in summer. Then one can drive a wagon across the shallow side, cross the island, and float across the narrow channel.

At one place near the middle the sand and trees commingle. Mostly

open and easy to cross, it was there we meant to take our watch.

We tied Jumper loosely to a tree, but kept her saddle on, not knowing when, or if, we would be called upon to use her.

The place to which we had come was a little landing area. There, a small flat-bottomed boat was kept, which belonged to a man who fished for shad. A low-sided craft (no more than eight inches in height), it was steady but so easily swamped as to make it useless for anything except the calm waters we intended to cross. At the bottom of the boat lay the two poles used to push it.

Having set the lantern at one end of the boat, I fixed the rifle on Mr. Shinn's back, then each of us took up a pole. Standing on either side we edged off into the channel and began to push.

As I have said, the western channel of the island is far calmer than the eastern. Even so, with the water rising, the river ran swiftly. We had to work in unison, Mr. Shinn and I, or else the boat would most certainly have spun.

Beginning at the prow, we pushed the poles into the river bottom, and firmly holding the poles, walked toward the stern. This moved the boat forward and kept it on an even course. We reached the other side in moments.

I leaped ashore and tied the boat's rope securely to a nearby tree.

"The water's still rising," I said to Mr. Shinn.

"That will make it easier for us," he answered.

"Why?" I asked.

"I'll show thee." Still holding his lantern carelessly, he led me over the narrow width of the island across the slight rise in its center. We stood then upon the eastern side.

It was yet night, but the high half-moon was bright and unobstructed so that I could look across. The Jersey side was a black mass of trees. The river before us, swollen and shapeless, had flecks of foam that caught the moonlight, revealing the water's speed.

What I saw made my heart sink. Anyone attempting to cross the river there and then would have to be a fool. He would be swept away, never to reach the island.

"We'll win no rewards here," I complained.

Mr. Shinn shrugged.

Swinging about, he moved a few feet up the island's rise to a place where we could look down on the river, keep our feet from getting wet, yet lean comfortably against the trees.

"Now," he whispered, settling his back and trimming the lantern to a lower light so that the night seemed to come that much closer. "Let us wait and hope that no one comes. Thee wished to come, Peter. Look to thy silence."

Want to read more? You can find out what becomes of Peter by checking the book out of your school or public library.

SHOW WHAT YOU KNOW!

REFOCUS
COMPREHENSION

1. Why did so many people choose to settle in the Delaware River valley?

2. What was the most important crop grown in the Delaware Valley?

THINK ABOUT IT
CRITICAL THINKING

What do you think might happen next to Peter and Mr. Shinn? Share your prediction with your classmates.

WRITE ABOUT IT
ACTIVITY

Suppose that you are a Lenape on a scouting mission to observe the newcomers and their activities along the Delaware River. Report your findings to a partner.

SUMMING UP

1 DO YOU REMEMBER...
COMPREHENSION

1. Describe the climate and land of the Middle Colonies.

2. What groups of people made up the population of the Middle Colonies?

3. What happened to Native Americans as more and more settlers came to the Middle Colonies?

4. What kinds of work did Africans in the Middle Colonies do?

5. What was William Penn's purpose in founding Pennsylvania?

6. How was each of the Middle Colonies started?

7. Tell about the chores boys and girls performed in the Middle Colonies.

8. How were children educated in the Middle Colonies?

9. Describe city life in the Middle Colonies.

10. What were the food sources for settlers in the Delaware River valley?

2 SKILL POWER
USING PRIMARY AND SECONDARY SOURCES

In this chapter, primary sources helped provide you with information. Can you find more examples of primary sources that tell about the Middle Colonies? How many can you find? Team up with a partner. Set a time limit. Then begin the search! Track down magazines, like *Cobblestone;* books with historical paintings; and other sources. Share what you find.

3 WHAT DO YOU THINK?
CRITICAL THINKING

1. How did the settlers learn to survive? What were the most important lessons they had to learn?

2. Based on what you have read, rate William Penn on a scale of 1 to 10 as a leader of Pennsylvania. Write a short defense of your rating.

3. Why, do you suppose, were the Native Americans willing to teach the settlers how to hunt, trap, fish, make canoes, and grow crops?

4. How do you think the Middle Colonies would be different if the region had been settled by people from only one European country?

5. Many settlers saw themselves as members of religious groups from countries with different customs. How do you see yourself? Write a brief description.

4 SAY IT, WRITE IT, USE IT
VOCABULARY

Write a short paragraph that summarizes what you learned about the Middle Colonies. Try to include as many vocabulary words as possible. If you include four or more, you are a very talented word worker!

cooper	hornbook
cultural borrowing	Iroquois League
Frame of Government	pacifist
gorge	Quaker
gristmill	tributary

5 GEOGRAPHY AND YOU
MAP STUDY

Use the map below and others throughout this chapter to answer these questions.

1. What four present-day states made up the Middle Colonies?

2. What are the three main rivers found in the Middle Colonies?

3. Which river forms the border between Pennsylvania and New Jersey?

4. In what colony were Trenton and Burlington located?

6 TAKE ACTION
CITIZENSHIP

Think about how hard it is to start a new life in a strange land. Welcome newcomers to your school or community by thinking of helpful things that you could do. You might offer to help with school work or point out the bus stop. You can think of lots more! As you get to know your new friends, you will learn new ideas and ways of doing things from them, too!

7 GET CREATIVE
COMPUTER CONNECTION

On the computer create an advertisement that encourages others to settle in your community. Use William Penn's letter as an example. You might want to decorate your advertisement by hand or with a graphics program, if you have one.

LOOKING AHEAD
Find out in the next unit what happened when the colonies take a stand and declare their independence from England.

War AND Independence

What Is a Revolution?

How far would you go to support a cause you believed in? Would you be willing to fight a war? Explore the revolution that changed the world and has an impact even today.

THE WAR

After the French and Indian War, the colonists were upset by changes in British policy. Peaceful colonial protests gave way to battles at Lexington and Concord. The War for Independence, or the Revolutionary War, had begun.

CONTENTS

To find out what this tool is used for, turn to page 172.

FOR INDEPENDENCE

These books tell about some people, places, and events of interest during America's struggle for independence. Read one that interests you and fill out a book-review form.

READ AND RESEARCH

Hand in Hand: An American History Through Poetry
collected by Lee Bennett Hopkins (Simon & Schuster, 1994)

As you read poetry, you will travel back to many different periods in history. Find out about Molly Pitcher and other people and places of the Revolutionary War. Read these poems aloud with your classmates. *(poetry)*

• *You can read a poem from this book on page 180.*

George Washington: The Man Who Would Not Be King
by Stephen Krensky (Scholastic, 1991)

Learn how George Washington became general of the colonial troops during the Revolutionary War. See how his courage and leadership inspired the new nation when he was made President. *(biography)*

Phillis Wheatley **by Victoria Sherrow** (Chelsea House, 1992)

In 1761, Phillis Wheatley, a young African girl, arrived in Boston and served as a domestic slave. Find out how she later became known as a poet. *(biography)*

The Fighting Ground **by Avi** (HarperTrophy, 1984)

When the tolling of a bell is heard throughout the New Jersey countryside, Jonathan hopes for a battle against the British and the Hessians. But when he becomes a soldier in that battle, he learns more about war than he ever could have known. *(historical fiction)*

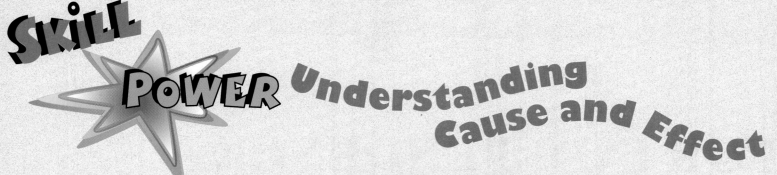

SKILL POWER — Understanding Cause and Effect

Identifying the relationships between causes and effects can help you understand history better.

UNDERSTAND IT

If you touch a hot stove, you'll burn your hand. You know this so well that you don't even think about it anymore. That is because you've learned a lesson in cause and effect. The cause of the burn is touching the hot stove. The effect is a burned hand. Here is another cause and its effect: If you work hard at something, you improve at it. The cause is that you work hard. The effect is that you improve.

In many ways, history is the study of cause and effect. For example, a historian looking at the Revolutionary War has to study many causes and their effects. Each action (or cause) by the British resulted in a reaction (or effect) by the colonists. The string of causes and effects led to war.

EXPLORE IT

On the night of April 18, 1775, Paul Revere was one of two riders who crept out of Boston to warn their neighbors of the British advance on Concord, Massachusetts. Because of their warning, the farmers and militia weren't caught by surprise. They prepared to fight.

In a famous poem the poet Henry Wadsworth Longfellow describes Paul Revere's historic ride. Part of the poem appears on this page. It describes a cause and effect. If the lantern is hung in the belfry (cause), Boston will know that it is in danger (effect).

He said to his friend, "If the British march
By land or sea from the town tonight,
Hang a lantern aloft in the belfry arch
Of the North Church tower
as a signal light—
One, if by land, and two, if by sea;
And I on the opposite shore will be,
Ready to ride and spread the alarm
Through every Middlesex village
and farm,
For the country folk to be up
and to arm."

Recall at least five things you have learned about the American colonies in Chapters 5, 6, and 7. Then, using large index cards, make a cause-and-effect quiz. On one side of each card, write an action (cause) you learned about. On the other side, write the action's effect.

With a group of your classmates, take turns displaying one side of a card, either a cause or its effect. Let group members give a cause for each effect and an effect for each cause.

CAUSE

The British were taxing tea.

EFFECT

The Boston Tea Party!

Stamp Act!

CAUSE & EFFECT FLASH CARDS

SKILL POWER SEARCH *You'll find many examples of cause and effect in this chapter. Think about how history would be changed if any of the causes and effects had been different.*

★ KEY TERMS
proclamation
Loyalist
Patriot
Minuteman
revolution
Declaration of
Independence

MAKING A NEW NATION

FOCUS *After 1763, Americans grew increasingly angry about British rule. Finally, they declared their independence and waged a successful war to guarantee it.*

French and Indian War

You have already learned that England had established colonies in America. By 1750, Great Britain, of which England was now a part, still had those 13 colonies. The population in these colonies was growing and so was the need for land. By 1754, colonists tried to expand into the Ohio River valley, but France already claimed this area for itself. French trappers and traders did not welcome the British settlers.

This dispute over land led to a war between France and Great Britain. For nine years, French and British troops

Young Washington meets with Iroquois chiefs during the French and Indian War.

fought this war in America. Because some Native Americans fought on the French side, colonists called the war the French and Indian War.

Britain won the war in 1763, and France lost most of its land in North America. The cost of the war had been high. Thousands of British

Soldiers carried gunpowder in powderhorns like this.

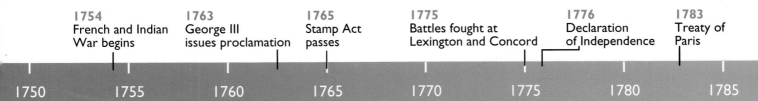

1754	1763	1765	1775	1776	1783
French and Indian War begins	George III issues proclamation	Stamp Act passes	Battles fought at Lexington and Concord	Declaration of Independence	Treaty of Paris

| 1750 | 1755 | 1760 | 1765 | 1770 | 1775 | 1780 | 1785 |

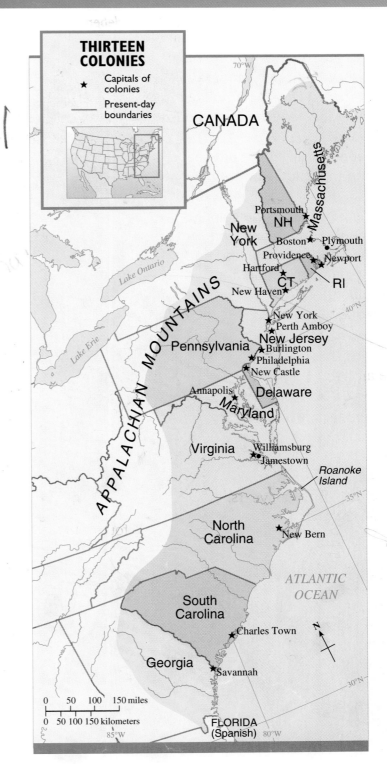

soldiers had been killed. There were also casualties among Americans who had fought in the war.

Proclamation of 1763

In 1763, Britain's King George III issued a **proclamation**. He called for a line to be drawn on a map along the top of the Appalachian Mountains, from New York to Georgia. The colonists were to stay on the east side of the line; Native Americans would stay on the west side.

The king and his ministers felt that keeping the colonists east of the line would make them easier to control. The colonists were angered. They had fought for the land west of the line. Now their king was telling them they couldn't use it. Their anger grew when British soldiers were sent to the colonies to enforce the proclamation.

New Taxes

A second event made colonists even angrier. Parliament announced it was imposing new taxes. This made sense to the British government. The war had cost a lot of money. Since the war had been fought to help the colonists, it was only fair that the colonists should

⭐ **proclamation**   An official announcement

help pay for the war. Americans saw things differently. They felt they *had* paid for the war—with their blood.

As the colonists grumbled, it became clear that many didn't think of themselves as British anymore. Also, for years they had pretty much governed themselves. What made Britain think it could step in and push them around?

Few people realized it, but Great Britain and the colonies were now on a collision course. Britain was determined to remind the colonies who was boss. Americans were determined not to buckle under to some distant king. Within a dozen years these two sides would be at war.

Boston citizens, angered by the Stamp Act, burned the stamps.

Colonists Revolt

Between 1764 and 1775 the colonists felt increasing pressure from the British. By means of the Stamp, Sugar, and Townshend acts, Parliament imposed new taxes on such items as paper, sugar, and tea. Some Americans vowed to fight back. In Boston, Sam Adams and John Hancock spoke out strongly against the new taxes. Patrick Henry did the same in Virginia.

Some of these colonists joined the Sons of Liberty, a group formed to fight British control. These men held rallies, gave speeches, and sang songs. They also harassed British tax collectors, dumped British tea into Boston Harbor, and set fire to the house of a British customs official.

Colonial women protested, too. They formed the Daughters of Liberty to show that Americans could survive without British goods. Daughters of Liberty set up spinning wheels in public places, spinning wool hour after hour to prove they could get along without British cloth. They stopped buying British tea and began drinking tea made from local herbs.

Not all colonists wanted to break away from Britain. Some, called **Loyalists** or Tories, wanted to stay under British control. But as time passed, more and more Americans were convinced that they could not be happy under British rule. They joined the side of the **Patriots**.

Loyalist A colonist who was a supporter of Great Britain and King George III
Patriot A person who supported the American cause for independence from Britain

Preparing for the Worst

By the spring of 1775, tempers were flaring. Britain had sent thousands of soldiers to America. Dressed in their fancy red coats and polished black boots, these "redcoats"—as the colonists called them—tried to calm the restless Americans. This only made the colonists angrier.

The colonists meanwhile were building up militias, groups of ordinary Americans who agreed to act as soldiers if the need arose. In Massachusetts, militiamen were especially active. Some of them were called **Minutemen**, as they were to be ready to fight at a minute's notice.

The Shot Heard Round the World

The fighting began on April 19, 1775, as British troops marched from Boston toward the town of Concord, 20 miles away. Find Concord on the map on the right. There they planned to seize weapons belonging to the Massachusetts militia. The militia rushed to block their way. The two sides met in the town of Lexington, east of Concord. As they stood face to face, a pistol shot rang through the early morning air. No one knows who fired the weapon, but it later became known as "the shot heard round the world." A **revolution**—the American

Revolution—had begun. By the end of the day, 50 Americans had been killed. Another 39 had been wounded. The British casualties were much worse, with 73 dead and 174 wounded.

THE WAR IN MASSACHUSETTS 1775

- ✴ Battle site, American victory
- ✴ Battle site, British victory
- --→ Dawes's route
- --→ Revere's route
- → British route

North Bridge · REVERE CAPTURED · Lexington · Concord · Lexington Green · REVERE AND DAWES · Medford · REVERE · Arlington (Menotomy) · Cambridge · Bunker Hill · Old North Church · DAWES · Boston · Brookline · Roxbury · Mystic River · Concord River · Charles River · Boston Harbor

0 — 5 miles
0 — 5 kilometers

Minuteman   A member of a militia of citizens who claimed to be ready to fight the British at "a minute's notice"

revolution   A sudden, complete change

▼ A Minuteman is plowing, ready to move out with his weapon on a moment's notice.

Declaring Independence

By 1776 many Americans had shaken off their lingering loyalty to the king. Thomas Paine, who had moved to America from England, helped with a pamphlet he wrote called *Common Sense*. In the pamphlet he argued that it was wrong for kings to be in charge just because they were born into a certain family. True power to govern, Paine suggested, came only when people gave that power to someone.

By the summer of 1776, Americans were ready to break from Britain. A group of colonial leaders called on Thomas Jefferson to write the Declaration of Independence. This was America's formal announcement that it was becoming a separate nation—the United States of America. The Declaration of Independence was signed on July 4, 1776.

Advantages and Disadvantages

Americans had declared themselves an independent nation. Now they had to fight a war with Great Britain to make that independence a reality. Several things, however, were working in America's favor. Great Britain had plenty of resources, but they were all thousands of miles away. Weapons, soldiers, ammunition—everything had to be shipped across the Atlantic Ocean.

In addition, while British soldiers were better trained than Americans, they were not as determined. British soldiers fought because it was their job. Americans fought because their homes, their families, and their beliefs were at stake.

Americans adopted a Native American style of fighting. This was guerrilla warfare, sneaking up on the enemy to stage hit-and-run attacks. George Washington, the leader of America's Continental army, taught this

You can read the Declaration of Independence on pages 612–615.

THE ILLUSTRIOUS PATRIOTS OF 1776 AND AUTHORS OF THE DECLARATION OF INDEPENDENCE. 1844

In UNITY there is STRENGTH

The signing of the Declaration of Independence, painted in 1844 by American artist Edward Hicks

Declaration of Independence The document that stated the reasons for the desire of the American colonies to be independent of British control

166

approach to his men. Francis Marion's use of this style of fighting in the swamps of South Carolina gained him the nickname Swamp Fox.

Perhaps the biggest boost to the Patriots came in 1778, when France agreed to help the United States fight the war. France had no particular reason to do this other than that it disliked having the British in North America. Great Britain and France had fought many wars over the years, including the French and Indian War just a few years earlier. To help the new nation defeat Britain, France provided the Americans with troops, money, and supplies.

Surrender!

By 1781 the British were growing weary. On October 19, British general Charles Cornwallis found himself outnumbered and trapped on a small peninsula on Chesapeake Bay in Yorktown, Virginia. Knowing that it was useless to keep fighting, Cornwallis surrendered his troops. Yorktown was the last great battle of the war. Peace talks began the next year, and in 1783 the Treaty of Paris was signed. Great Britain agreed that its colonies were now "free and independent states."

British troops surrender to General George Washington at Yorktown. The British general, Lord Cornwallis, did not attend this ceremony.

SHOW WHAT YOU KNOW!

REFOCUS
COMPREHENSION

1. What were some effects of the French and Indian War?

2. Name some advantages and disadvantages for both the British and the Americans during the Revolutionary War.

THINK ABOUT IT
CRITICAL THINKING

Why, do you think, did the British fight a war with the Americans after the Declaration of Independence was issued?

WRITE ABOUT IT
ACTIVITY

Write a letter to a relative in Great Britain about American reactions to the new taxes. Describe some of the ways in which the colonists protested the taxes.

STEPS TO INDEPENDENCE

FOCUS *From 1765 to 1776 there was a steady stream of stern British actions and bitter American reactions. American anger built until it exploded in revolution.*

STAMP ACT

The colonists were angry. It was bad enough when the British Parliament put taxes on goods coming into the colonies. But the Stamp Act of March 22, 1765, was something new. Now a tax was added to things made right here in America. Some 50 kinds of paper used in the colonies were to be taxed. To prove that the tax had been paid, a special stamp was placed on everything from calendars and newspapers to playing cards.

STAMP ACT CONGRESS

Furious about the Stamp Act, nine colonies decided to send representatives to New York to talk things over. At this Stamp Act Congress, held in October 1765, Americans declared the new tax illegal. They said that only colonial legislatures had the power to tax them.

On March 11, 1766, Parliament backed down. It got rid of the Stamp Act. But Parliament warned the colonists that it did indeed have the power to pass any laws it wanted to for the colonies— including tax laws.

BOSTON MASSACRE

On a cold winter night, five people died in the streets of Boston, Massachusetts. The incident began as a kind of one-sided snowball fight. Bostonians didn't like having British soldiers stationed in their city. On March 5, 1770, they expressed their disgust by throwing snowballs at the soldiers. Some colonists turned mean and started throwing rocks.

A few redcoats lost control and fired into the crowd. One of those killed was Crispus Attucks, a runaway slave who worked as a sailor. Attucks was the first African American to die for the cause of American liberty but not the last. The incident became known as the Boston Massacre.

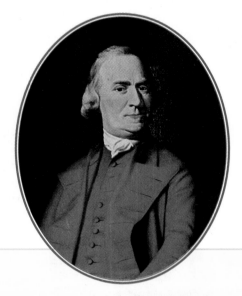

BOSTON TEA PARTY

Americans loved their tea. They drank it morning, noon, and night. But when Britain tried to collect a tax on tea, the Americans took a stand. They wanted nothing to do with taxed tea. When three ships brought a new supply of tea into Boston Harbor, the Sons of Liberty took action. On December 16, 1773, about 60 of them disguised themselves as Mohawk Indians. They crept onto the ships and dumped 342 chests of tea overboard.

COMMITTEES OF CORRESPONDENCE

Samuel Adams worked hard to build Patriot support in Boston. But local efforts were not enough, and Adams knew it. Other towns and colonies needed to be involved. In November 1772, Adams formed a Committee of Correspondence. Whenever something happened in Boston, this group sent messages out across the colonies.

Soon other areas set up similar committees to send and receive messages. A network was created from New England to the Carolinas. Now all Americans could be kept informed of British actions.

INTOLERABLE ACTS

King George was furious about the Boston Tea Party. He wanted to punish the entire city of Boston. Parliament agreed. In the spring of 1774, it passed a series of tough acts. It closed Boston Harbor until the tea that had been dumped was paid for. Another law took away most of the colony's rights of self-government.

Americans labeled the measures the "Intolerable Acts." The British hoped that the measures would teach the colonists a lesson. Instead, the acts simply stirred up more anti-British feelings. Until now, the trouble had been confined mostly to Massachusetts. But now, people in all 13 colonies were angry.

1774	1774	1775	1775	1775	1775	1776
Intolerable Acts	First Continental Congress	Paul Revere's ride	Battles of Lexington and Concord	Second Continental Congress	Battle of Bunker Hill	Declaration of Independence

1774   1775   1776

FIRST CONTINENTAL CONGRESS

The Committees of Correspondence called for action. They felt that the Intolerable Acts were simply—well—intolerable! On September 5, 1774, representatives from 12 colonies met in Philadelphia. Among the representatives were Samuel Adams, Patrick Henry, and George Washington.

These men wrote down their complaints and sent the list off to the king, asking him for help. They also agreed to meet again in May 1775.

THE MIDNIGHT RIDE OF PAUL REVERE

Paul Revere jumped onto his horse and galloped off through the night. Revere was a Boston silversmith and one of the Sons of Liberty. On the night of April 18, 1775, he learned that the British were headed to Concord. Revere rushed to warn local leaders and military commanders that their supplies were about to be seized. He and a man named William Dawes rode like the wind. Thanks to them, and other riders, the militia was ready and waiting when the British reached Lexington the next morning.

BATTLES OF LEXINGTON AND CONCORD

Things hadn't gone well for the Americans in Lexington on April 19, 1775. Eight Patriots were killed and nine were wounded. But things changed as the day went on. In Concord the British destroyed some of the Patriots' military supplies. But the militia continued to advance toward the British, and more fighting broke out. Soon the British turned and headed back to Boston. Americans hid behind trees, fences, and stone walls. They shot at the redcoats all along the way, picking them off one by one. By the time the British reached Boston, they had suffered defeat. The day was considered a big victory for the colonists.

SECOND CONTINENTAL CONGRESS

As planned, representatives met for the Second Continental Congress on May 10, 1775. But things had changed since their first meeting. Now war had broken out. John Adams told his fellow representatives that they must rise to the challenge. At his urging, they created an official American army, called the Continental army. To lead the new army, Adams said, Congress was fortunate to have the right man for the job in that very room—George Washington. With his military experience in the French and Indian War, his ability to remain calm, his strong will, and his determination, George Washington was indeed the perfect man for the job.

THE BATTLE OF BUNKER HILL

Before Washington could take command of his new army, more fighting broke out near Boston. On June 17, 1775, the British tried to drive Americans off Breed's Hill and Bunker Hill. Americans had no ammunition to waste, so Israel Putnam, a major general in the Continental army, cried out, "Don't fire until you see the whites of their eyes!" The Americans obeyed. When British soldiers got close, militiamen fired.

The British managed to capture the hill, but more than 1,000 redcoats were killed or wounded in the process. The battle of Bunker Hill convinced Americans that they *did* stand a chance against the mighty British army.

DECLARATION OF INDEPENDENCE

Americans wanted the world to know why they were breaking away from Great Britain. So in 1776, when Thomas Jefferson wrote the Declaration of Independence, he listed the "long train of abuses" the colonists had suffered. He said that governments didn't have the right to interfere with "Life, Liberty, and the pursuit of Happiness." Because Britain had done this, Americans had a duty to revolt.

GEORGE WASHINGTON

FOCUS *Americans were fortunate to have George Washington on their side. This bold, brave leader saw Americans through some of their bleakest moments.*

Nerves of Steel

George Washington was a brave, determined man. He faced many dangers in his life, yet he seldom panicked and never gave up. Instead, he worked his way through each problem as calmly and bravely as possible.

As a boy in Virginia, Washington learned to love music, drama, and books. But he also loved adventure. In 1749, at the age of 17, he became a **surveyor**. As part of his work, he traveled through tangled wilderness for weeks at a time. Washington fed himself by shooting wild turkeys, and at night he slept under the stars.

Then came the French and Indian War. Washington was a young man—just 22 years old. Still, he took charge of more than 150 men and headed off to face the French. He ended up fighting hundreds of enemy soldiers in the pouring rain. Two horses were shot out from under him. Four bullets whizzed through his coat. Washington lost the battle, but he had survived. By the time he left the army four years later, he had earned a reputation as a man who could deal with anything.

Peaceful Years

In 1759, Washington married a widow, Martha Dandridge Custis. He lived the life of a Virginia planter at his Mount Vernon plantation, attending the theater and going on fox hunts and fishing trips. He danced, played cards, and watched horse races.

But the Revolutionary War changed Washington's life. Americans needed an army, and they needed someone to lead it. On June 15, 1775, the Second Continental Congress appointed George Washington to lead the Continental army.

▼ Washington surveys a tract of land, using measurements known as chains and links.

★ **surveyor** A person who determines the location, form, and boundaries of a tract of land

General and Mrs. Washington attend a formal reception in 1789.

Doing His Duty

Washington agreed to take the job, but he refused a salary. He believed in the American cause. More than that, he believed in doing his duty.

For eight years Washington led the American forces. He led them on long marches through snow and rain. Like his troops, he sometimes went without food or rest. During the frightful winter of 1777–1778 at Valley Forge, Pennsylvania, he was the strength that held the army together. Men watched him to see if his spirits sank. When they saw he wasn't giving up, some decided they could hang on, too.

An American Hero

In the end George Washington became a hero. He was more than just a good general. He had the ability to take command and inspire his soldiers to do the impossible. Also, as commander of the revolutionary army, he was quick to understand the importance of geography in a way that the British never did. He learned the dangers of having his soldiers in any location where their retreat or escape might be cut off. When Americans were looking for their first President, it is no wonder they turned to George Washington.

SHOW WHAT YO KNOW!

REFOCUS
COMPREHENSION

1. What were some skills that Washington developed as a young man?

2. Why did Washington agree to lead the American forces during the Revolutionary War?

THINK ABOUT IT
CRITICAL THINKING

What, do you think, are some essential qualifications that a military leader needs?

WRITE ABOUT IT
ACTIVITY

You are a soldier in the Continental army. Write a letter home telling your family why you think George Washington is the right person to lead the army.

WINNING THE WAR

FOCUS *Showing remarkable grit and determination, the American troops defeated the more powerful British army. As a result, the colonies had truly gained their independence.*

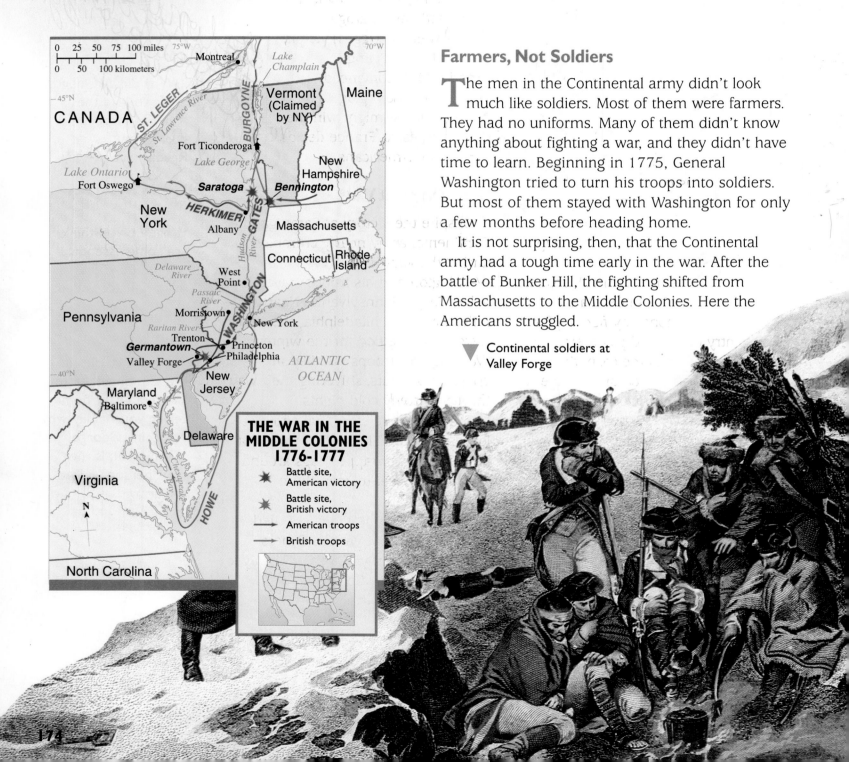

THE WAR IN THE MIDDLE COLONIES 1776-1777

✴ Battle site, American victory

✳ Battle site, British victory

→ American troops

→ British troops

Farmers, Not Soldiers

The men in the Continental army didn't look much like soldiers. Most of them were farmers. They had no uniforms. Many of them didn't know anything about fighting a war, and they didn't have time to learn. Beginning in 1775, General Washington tried to turn his troops into soldiers. But most of them stayed with Washington for only a few months before heading home.

It is not surprising, then, that the Continental army had a tough time early in the war. After the battle of Bunker Hill, the fighting shifted from Massachusetts to the Middle Colonies. Here the Americans struggled.

▼ Continental soldiers at Valley Forge

In August 1776 the two sides met near New York City. By December, Washington's troops had been pushed back across New Jersey all the way into Pennsylvania. Washington looked at his tired, confused men. "The spirits . . . [are] quite shrunk," he told a friend. "Without fresh troops . . . I think the game is pretty near up."

Glimmers of Hope

Washington knew he had to do something fast. On Christmas night, 1776, he led his men across the icy Delaware River. They staged a lightning-quick early-morning raid at Trenton, New Jersey. Find Trenton on the map on page 174.

The attack was not on British soldiers but on **Hessians.** These German soldiers earned money by fighting for any country that would pay them. Since the British had the cash, the **mercenaries** had signed on with them.

Washington's plan worked. The Americans overwhelmed the enemy troops. A few days later Washington's men scored again by taking control of Princeton, New Jersey.

These successes kept Americans going. But the war was far from over, and it still looked to many as though Britain would ultimately win.

Victory at Saratoga

In the spring of 1777, British troops moved into northern New York. They planned to take control of the Hudson River, cutting New England off from the other colonies. But the redcoats didn't coordinate their attack. On October 17, 1777, they lost a huge battle at Saratoga.

This was the biggest victory yet for the struggling Americans. It convinced France that the ragtag Americans just might win the war. As a result, France decided to help the Americans.

Hard Times at Valley Forge

Despite the victory at Saratoga, the Continental army nearly crumbled during the winter of 1777–1778. Washington and his troops stayed in Valley Forge, Pennsylvania. Nearly 20 miles away, in Philadelphia, the British were snugly settled for the winter. Washington's troops huddled in crudely built huts, shivering their way through bitterly cold nights.

The troops ate stew "full of burnt leaves and dirt." Many had worn-out boots, so they wrapped rags around their bloody feet to keep them from freezing.

Many Continental soldiers died from disease that winter. Others deserted the army. Those who stayed had such trust in General Washington that they were willing to put up with almost anything.

▲ Drums such as this were played to summon troops.

▼ A press to make musket balls

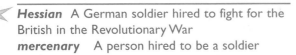

Hessian A German soldier hired to fight for the British in the Revolutionary War
mercenary A person hired to be a soldier

War in the West and South

While Washington was at Valley Forge, a young Virginian, George Rogers Clark, was preparing to attack British forts in the West. The British wanted to stir up the Indians against the Americans.

In the summer of 1778, Clark and his men took the British fort at Kaskaskia, in present-day Illinois. Later, Clark also took a fort at Vincennes

The first Purple Heart, a military decoration awarded to those wounded or killed in action, was designed by Washington and established in 1782. Today's Purple Heart is shown on the right.

(vihn SENZ) in what is now Indiana. Locate Kaskaskia and Vincennes on the map below. Clark's victories gave the United States control of much land between the Appalachian Mountains and the Mississippi River.

In 1778, fighting also shifted to the South. For the next two years, American forces suffered their worst defeats. The British captured Savannah, Georgia, and Charleston, South Carolina. They won control over a large part of the South.

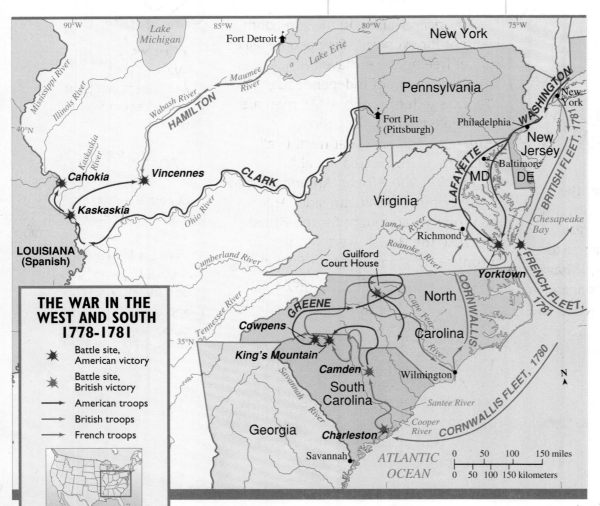

THE WAR IN THE WEST AND SOUTH 1778-1781

* Battle site, American victory
* Battle site, British victory
→ American troops
→ British troops
→ French troops

Victory at Sea

The Patriots had only a small navy. To help it, Congress allowed private owners of ships to arm their own vessels with cannons. These ships were called **privateers**. By the end of the war, American privateers had sunk or captured more than 600 British ships.

Although there were not many American warships, the privateers could put up a good fight against one British ship at a time.

One such battle came on September 23, 1779. The American warship *Bonhomme Richard* was fighting the British warship *Serapis* off the coast of

privateer A privately-owned armed ship having a government's permission to attack enemy ships

This painting shows the battle between *Bonhomme Richard* and HMS *Serapis*.

Britain. It seemed certain that the heavily armed *Serapis* would win. The British gave the *Bonhomme Richard's* captain, John Paul Jones, a chance to surrender. But Jones cried out, "I have not yet begun to fight!" After several more hours of bitter fighting, Jones and his men won.

Americans Win the War

Faced with such determination, the British finally gave up. They could hardly believe that the weak American army had beaten them. When General Cornwallis's troops surrendered to George Washington, the British band played "The World Turned Upside Down."

It did seem that everything had been scrambled. A scrawny string of colonies had taken on one of the world's great powers—and won! It was the first time in history that colonists had successfully broken away from their home country.

Freedom—But Not for All

Americans had won their freedom, but not for everyone. Few people talked about freeing the enslaved Africans. In the Declaration of Independence, Thomas Jefferson wrote, "All men are created equal. . . ." But most Americans thought that meant "all *white* men are created equal."

About 5,000 African Americans had fought on the American side. At least that many had fought for the British, because the British were the first to promise freedom in return for fighting. But no matter which side they chose, African Americans didn't have much hope for a better life.

Native Americans didn't have much to look forward to either. Many Native Americans stayed away from the fighting. Others, such as the Iroquois, fought for the British. They figured the British couldn't be any worse than the Americans who wanted to take over their land.

SHOW WHAT YOU KNOW!

REFOCUS
COMPREHENSION

1. What were some challenges that George Washington faced as head of the Continental army?

2. What was the significance of the victory at Saratoga?

THINK ABOUT IT
CRITICAL THINKING

What were some qualities that Americans had that helped them win the war?

WRITE ABOUT IT
ACTIVITY

Suppose you are a soldier spending the winter at Valley Forge. Write a letter home describing your living conditions. Reference and trade books may help give you more accurate detail.

WOMEN DURING THE REVOLUTION

FOCUS *During the time of the Revolutionary War, women were important participants in social, economic, political, and military activities.*

Women at Work

During the war, women took care of their families. Some also ran farms and businesses while their husbands were away at war. If her husband died on the battlefield, a woman would often carry on her husband's occupation.

Jane Burgess, a Maryland widow, advertised in a local paper in 1773 that she still carried on "the Blacksmith Business" of her husband. Women ran inns and were barbers and apothecaries (pharmacists) in the 1700s. In many cases women carried on trades their fathers or husbands had practiced. But women began to be recognized for their own accomplishments as well.

The Goddards were an interesting family of business women. Sarah Goddard of Providence lent her son William money to start the *Providence Gazette* in 1765, on the condition that she would be his partner. Several years later William and his sister Mary Katherine moved to Maryland and started a printing business as well as Baltimore's first newspaper. Because of Mary's skill, she was selected by the Congress to print the official copy of the Declaration of Independence.

▼ Making cannon balls

Volunteers and Activists

Women also played other important roles. Most women did not work outside the home and often spent time together spinning and sewing. Their hands were busy, but their minds were free to think about issues of the day. Since clothing for soldiers was needed, spinning became vital. Betsy Ross and others like her used their sewing skills to produce banners and flags.

The Daughters of Liberty, which you read about on page 164, organized **boycotts** of textiles and tea. In 1770 over 300 women in Boston vowed not to drink tea. They made and sold teas instead. Made from herbs or fruit leaves, these "liberty teas" were described as "bad-tasting." But people loved the idea of the boycotts, and the liberty teas were popular.

Poets and Playwrights

During this time period there were some well-known women writers. Phillis Wheatley, although enslaved, was treated well by her owners in Boston. She eventually became famous as America's first-known African American poet. In 1776 she wrote a poem praising George Washington and even met him when he camped nearby.

Mercy Otis Warren wrote popular political plays during the 1770s. Nasty

Phillis Wheatley was born in Africa around 1753. Captured by slave traders in 1761 and taken to Boston, she eventually became a celebrated poet.

characters in Warren's plays were Loyalists; nice ones were Patriots.

On the Battlefield

Some women became directly involved in the war. Women who were gunsmiths and blacksmiths helped make weapons. One group of women got hold of the statue of George III that had been pulled down by the Sons of Liberty. They melted it down to make bullets.

In 1777, Colonel Ludington, a local militia leader, heard that British troops were raiding a supply center in Danbury, Connecticut. Sybil Ludington, his 16-year-old daughter, volunteered to warn the militia. Despite the danger of being stopped by a British patrol, she rode many miles on horseback to spread the news.

Many women served as nurses and seamstresses. Others helped on the battlefield, carrying food and drink and comforting soldiers.

One woman, Mary "Molly" Hays, was at her husband's side during the battle at Monmouth. Because she brought pitchers of water to other Continental soldiers, she got the nickname Molly Pitcher. When Mary's husband was wounded during the fighting, she bravely took his place, firing the cannon.

boycott An organized campaign in which people refuse to have any dealings with a particular group or business

Hand in Hand: An American History Through Poetry

Collected by Lee Bennett Hopkins

During the Revolutionary War some women went to the front. One of them was Mary "Molly" Hays, known as Molly Pitcher, who was at her husband's side during the battle at Monmouth.

Molly Pitcher

All day the great guns barked and roared;

All day the big balls screeched and soared;

All day, 'mid the sweating gunners grim,

Who toiled in their smoke-shroud dense and dim,

Sweet Molly labored with courage high,

With steady hand and watchful eye,

Till the day was ours, and the sinking sun

Looked down on the field of Monmouth won,

And Molly standing beside her gun.

Now, Molly, rest your weary arm!

Safe, Molly, all is safe from harm.

Now, woman, bow your aching head,

And weep in sorrow o'er your dead!

Next day on that field so hardly won,

Stately and calm stands Washington,

And looks where our gallant Greene doth lead

A figure clad in motley weed—

A soldier's cap and a soldier's coat

Masking a woman's petticoat.

He greets our Molly in kindly wise;

He bids her raise her tearful eyes;

And now he hails her before them all

Comrade and soldier, whate'er befall,

"And since she has played a man's full part,

A man's reward for her loyal heart!

And Sergeant Molly Pitcher's name

Be writ henceforth on the shield of fame!"

Oh, Molly, with your eyes so blue!

Oh, Molly, Molly, here's to you!

Sweet honor's roll will aye be richer

To hold the name of Molly Pitcher.

Laura E. Richards

You can read other poems about the history of the United States by checking the book out of your school or public library.

SHOW WHAT YOU KNOW!

REFOCUS
COMPREHENSION

1. In what ways did women contribute to the war effort?

2. Who were the Daughters of Liberty and what did they do?

THINK ABOUT IT
CRITICAL THINKING

Why do you think so many women actively supported the revolution?

WRITE ABOUT IT
ACTIVITY

Read the poem "Molly Pitcher." Write a paragraph that summarizes the meaning of the poem.

SUMMING UP

1 DO YOU REMEMBER...
COMPREHENSION

1. Why did Great Britain raise taxes in 1763?

2. How did the first fighting of the revolution break out?

3. What did the Declaration of Independence formally announce?

4. What was the purpose of the Committees of Correspondence?

5. What did the Second Continental Congress accomplish?

6. What were some of George Washington's strengths as a leader?

7. What problems did Washington have as general of the American army?

8. Why was the American victory at Saratoga so important?

9. Why was the final outcome of the war surprising to so many people?

10. In what important ways did women help win the war?

2 SKILL POWER
UNDERSTANDING CAUSE AND EFFECT

List three examples of cause and effect in the events leading up to the start of the Revolutionary War. Then give three examples of cause and effect during the war itself.

3 WHAT DO YOU THINK?
CRITICAL THINKING

1. Could the differences between Great Britain and the colonies have been resolved without a war? Explain.

2. Why was the first shot fired at Lexington said to be "heard round the world"?

3. Washington had the ability to inspire his soldiers to do the impossible. What are some ways in which a leader inspires people?

4. What, do you think, was the greatest American advantage in the Revolutionary War? What was the greatest British advantage?

5. In what ways was being a soldier in the revolution different from being a soldier today?

4 SAY IT, WRITE IT, USE IT
VOCABULARY

Write newspaper headlines that might have appeared in a newspaper during revolutionary times. Use one or more of the vocabulary words in each headline, showing that you know the meanings of these words.

boycott	Minuteman
Declaration of Independence	Patriot
	privateer
Hessian	proclamation
Loyalist	revolution
mercenary	surveyor

5 GEOGRAPHY AND YOU
MAP STUDY

Look at the maps on pages 163 and 165 and below to answer the following questions.

1. List the 13 colonies.

2. Use the scale of miles and measure the distance from Boston to Concord.

3. Identify the battle sites of the war in Massachusetts.

4. What colonies did Cornwallis pass through as he went from Charleston to Yorktown?

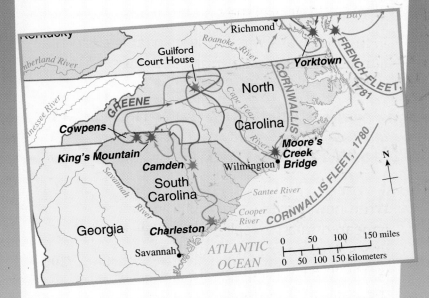

6 TAKE ACTION
CITIZENSHIP

Independence meant that the United States needed its own flag. With a group of classmates, draw pictures of some of our nation's early flags. Find out what the parts and colors of the flags stand for. Then make a list of rules that tell how we should honor and display our flag.

7 GET CREATIVE
LANGUAGE ARTS CONNECTION

The Declaration of Independence was written in beautiful handwriting on special parchment paper. Look at the text of the Declaration of Independence on pages 612–615. Find a passage from the declaration that means a lot to you. Use pen and ink to create a copy of the passage that you can post in your classroom.

LOOKING AHEAD

In the next chapter you will find out how the new nation set up a new government.

The New

Passing laws, raising taxes, making treaties—have you ever wanted to know how the government goes about accomplishing these things? Or have you ever wondered about the beginnings of our government? This chapter is about all that and more.

▲ How do the branches of our government balance each other? Find out on page 201.

CONTENTS

Nation

These books tell about some people, places, and events of interest during the time when the Constitution was written. Read one that interests you and fill out a book-review form.

READ AND RESEARCH

Shh! We're Writing the Constitution by Jean Fritz
(G. P. Putnam's Sons, 1987)
Did you know that Benjamin Franklin arrived at the Grand Convention for the Constitution in a sedan chair carried by four prisoners from a Philadelphia jail? Read all about the serious and ridiculous details involved in the making of the United States Constitution. *(nonfiction)*

Martha Washington by Joan Marsh (Franklin Watts, 1993)
Read about the life of Martha Washington from her childhood to her time as First Lady of the United States. *(biography)*

Benjamin Franklin, Scientist and Inventor by Eve B. Feldman (Franklin Watts, 1990)
Did you know that people once thought that lightning was caused by magic or heavenly powers? Find out about Benjamin Franklin's scientific experiments with electricity and his many practical inventions. *(biography)*

The Constitution by Marilyn Prolman (Childrens Press, 1995)
Journey back to 1787, when the 13 states were not in agreement about what the new government should be, and when a strong national government did not exist. Learn all about the making of the Constitution, a document that continues to guide our nation. *(nonfiction)*

Using a Flowchart

Knowing how to read a flowchart will help you understand the order of the steps in a process.

UNDERSTAND IT

People often use diagrams to explain how something works. One type of diagram, a flowchart, shows the steps involved in a process. Flowcharts are often used to explain how to do something or how a complicated system works.

If you have ever seen a chart of how to help a choking victim in a restaurant, you have seen a flowchart. You might also have seen flowcharts that show how newspapers can be recycled into paper that can be used again.

Flowcharts are also used to explain how different parts of our government work.

EXPLORE IT

The flowchart below shows how the President of the United States is elected. Study the flowchart for a minute. Are there some things that surprised you? Did you think, for example, that the citizens actually elect the President directly?

Look again at the chart. What problem might arise in this system? How do people know that an electoral college representative will vote for their candidate?

How the President Is Elected

In November, people vote for the candidate of their choice. Each candidate is represented by members of the electoral college.

⬇

In December the electoral college members vote for the President. In January the votes are counted.

↙ ↘

The candidate with the majority vote becomes President.

If there is no majority, the House of Representatives decides which candidate will be President.

With a group of your classmates, learn more about how your local government operates. Talk with parents and other adults in your community to find out as much as you can about one government task or operation. For example, you might look into how your community

- responds to a fire or medical emergency
- builds a new school or park
- recycles and/or disposes of trash
- puts in a new road
- hires a new school principal
- decides how much property tax to charge homeowners

Take notes on all the information you learn. Then make a flowchart to arrange the steps of the task or operation in order. Show what may or may not happen at each step. Include small drawings.

Collect all the flowcharts and fasten them together at the top. You can display your Flowchart Flip Book in your classroom.

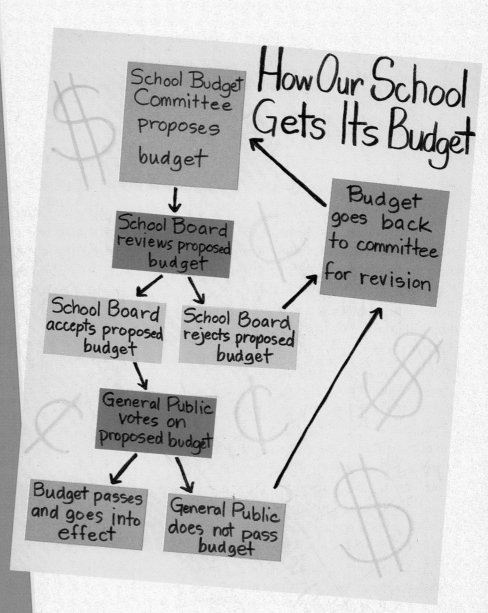

How Our School Gets Its Budget

School Budget Committee proposes budget

School Board reviews proposed budget

School Board accepts proposed budget

School Board rejects proposed budget

Budget goes back to committee for revision

General Public votes on proposed budget

Budget passes and goes into effect

General Public does not pass budget

SKILL POWER SEARCH *What other flowcharts can you find in this chapter? What processes do they show?*

Setting the Scene

KEY TERMS

republic
constitution
ratify
Bill of Rights
Cabinet
political party

A New Government

FOCUS *Americans designed a new kind of government. Through trial and error, hard work, and creative thinking, they wrote a constitution that still guides and protects us.*

Americans Create a Republic

Now that America was independent, what kind of government would it have? Americans didn't want a king and a parliament. They had seen those in action and didn't like what they saw. In fact, they didn't like any kind of government that was more powerful than the people it represented.

Americans chose a **republic** to protect their rights. Another name for a republic is a *representative democracy*. This type of government is based on the consent of the people. In other words, the American citizens would elect representatives to pass laws or govern their country.

The 13 former colonies were now states. Each state had its own **constitution**, or written set of laws. These constitutions told the exact powers of state governments. Most states also had bills of rights added to their constitutions so that Americans could have their freedoms written down.

A Weak Government

State constitutions seemed fine, but Americans also wanted a written constitution for the national government. In 1777, a Congressional committee created the Articles of Confederation. This document provided for the first

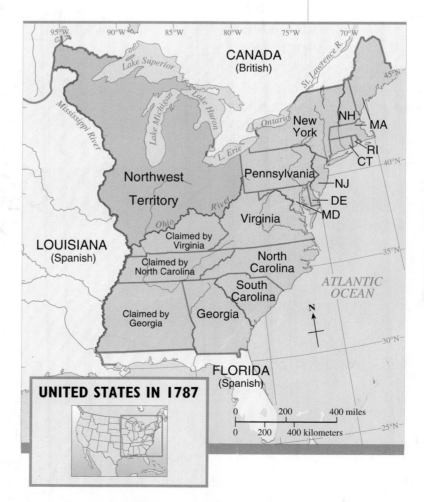

Each state printed its own money. But money from one state might not be accepted in another.

UNITED STATES IN 1787

★ **republic** A government in which the power to govern comes from the people, not a king
constitution A set of laws governing a state or nation

1777
Articles of Confederation
are created

1787
Constitutional Convention
meets in Philadelphia

1789
George Washington
is elected President

1791
Bill of Rights is added
to the Constitution

1775   1780   1785   1790   1795

government of the United States. There was to be no king and no parliament, and the national government was to be weaker than the state governments. Americans wanted state governments to have more power because they were considered closer to the people than the national government.

How weak was the first national government? It had no army, no court system, and no President. It did have a weak Congress that had to beg the states for money because it had no power to collect taxes. Usually the states refused, and Congress went further and further into debt. Congress couldn't even settle disputes between states. And if people wanted to make Congress stronger, *all* the states had to agree. One state could block the will of all the others.

Congress did have some accomplishments, one of which dealt with the Northwest Territory. Find this area on the map on page 188. Passed in 1787, the Northwest Ordinance divided the territory into "not less than three nor more than five states." (In fact, it became five states—Ohio, Indiana, Illinois, Michigan, and

Wisconsin.) The ordinance said that the new states would be equal to the original 13 states. And these new states would not have slavery.

Shays's Rebellion

Soon Congress's weaknesses outweighed its accomplishments. Massachusetts farmers had a hard year in 1786, and they couldn't pay their taxes. Judges ordered them to sell their land to get the tax money.

Shays's Rebellion ▶

189

A reenactment of the 1787 Constitutional Convention

You can read the United States Constitution on pages 616–635.

These delegates met throughout the summer. They argued back and forth. They fought bitterly with each other. In the end they wrote a new constitution, which made the national government more powerful. Now the government could raise an army and collect taxes. Still, the Constitution left the states with a great deal of power.

Constitutional Genius

This was the first time a nation had written its own constitution. No other nation had one. Even Great Britain didn't have a written constitution. Later our Constitution became a model for other nations to use. Today it remains the oldest constitution in use in the world.

The writers of the Constitution knew they weren't perfect. So they made it possible to *amend*, or change, the Constitution. This enabled future Americans to change part of the Constitution instead of getting rid of the whole thing.

Not everyone was pleased by the new Constitution. Some people didn't want power taken away from the states and given to the national government. This opposition didn't surprise the writers of the Constitution. They knew all along that it would be challenging to **ratify**, or pass, the new document.

The writers did two things to make ratification easier. First, only 9 states

This angered the farmers. One farmer, Daniel Shays, led an armed rebellion. Although it was crushed by the state militia, it scared many people. The national government, which had no army, just stood on the sidelines. It was so weak that it couldn't even deal with a small group of angry farmers.

The Constitutional Convention

People began to see a need to make the national government stronger. In May 1787 a group of delegates met in Philadelphia to strengthen the national government by fixing the Articles of Confederation. However, these men quickly saw that the Articles of Confederation couldn't do the job and a whole new government was needed.

 ratify To formally approve

had to ratify it, not all 13. Second, James Madison, Alexander Hamilton, and John Jay wrote a series of essays called *The Federalist* that tried to convince people to support the new Constitution.

The battle for ratification was fought from state to state. One problem was that the Constitution did not have a bill of rights. A bill of rights would clearly define people's rights. So the Constitution's supporters promised to add a bill of rights as soon as the Constitution was ratified.

This promise helped the process of ratification, but it still took a while. The map on this page shows what year each state approved the Constitution. It wasn't until June 21, 1788, that the ninth state, New Hampshire, voted yes. Virginia and New York soon followed. North Carolina held out until November 1789. Rhode Island didn't join the Union until May 1790. Finally, in 1791 the first ten amendments, known collectively as the **Bill of Rights**, were added to the Constitution.

You can read the Gallery of Presidents on pages 605–611.

Our First President

The Constitution provided for a President. But many Americans were concerned about the power of the President. Would the President really be a king with a different title? These fears were put to rest in 1789 when George Washington was unanimously elected President.

Washington was a great President. People watched his every move, knowing that he was setting the tone for future Presidents. Even the title Washington chose for himself, "Mr. President," is still used today. A Senate committee wanted to call him "His Highness, the President of the United States of America, and Protector of Liberties."

Washington chose a number of people to lead executive departments and advise him in important matters. He listened carefully to their advice. Today, certain advisors to the President are known as **Cabinet** members.

RATIFICATION OF THE CONSTITUTION

NH (1788)
New York (1788)
MA (1788)
RI (1790)
CT (1788)
Pennsylvania (1787)
NJ (1787)
DE (1787)
Virginia (1788)
MD (1788)
North Carolina (1789)
South Carolina (1788)
Georgia (1788)
ATLANTIC OCEAN

Bill of Rights The first ten amendments to the Constitution

Cabinet A group of advisors to the President

Political Parties

Two of his best-known Cabinet officers were Alexander Hamilton, his secretary of the treasury, and Thomas Jefferson, his secretary of state. The two men disagreed on almost everything.

Hamilton wanted to encourage manufacturing. He hoped the United States would soon have many large cities. In addition, he wanted a large and powerful national government.

Jefferson hoped for a nation with some factories. But he wanted the United States to remain a mostly rural nation of small farms. He also wanted a small national government.

The disputes between these leaders led to the birth of **political parties**. In the 1790s, people who favored many of Hamilton's ideas were called *Federalists*. Jefferson's supporters were called *Democratic-Republicans*.

The government that governs best governs least.
—**Thomas Jefferson**

 political party A group of people who hold certain beliefs about how the government should be run

Whiskey Rebellion

Meanwhile, farmers in western Pennsylvania were angered by a tax on whiskey. Many of these farmers made whiskey out of their corn because it was cheaper to ship whiskey than corn. And corn sometimes spoiled before it was sold. These farmers felt that the tax was unfair, because they were being taxed on the only practical product they could sell.

The protesting farmers resorted to violent attacks against the government officers who enforced the tax. Would this be just like Shays's Rebellion? No. When George Washington sent 13,000 troops, the farmers put down their guns and fled. President Washington showed the new national government's strength.

The Second President

Washington served two terms, or eight years, as President. He was so popular that he would have been elected again if he had run for reelection. But in 1797 he stepped down and returned to his home at Mount Vernon.

John Adams, a Federalist who had been Washington's Vice President, was elected the nation's second President. During Adams's presidency, the United States was almost dragged into a war between Great Britain and France.

Adams knew that going to war might make him popular, but he also knew that war was not good for the country. While President Adams avoided war, his decision was not looked upon favorably.

The new nation survived, despite the lack of popularity of its new President. The Constitution had provided well for change as needed, even in its provision for presidential elections every four years.

 The Whiskey Rebellion

SHOW WHAT YOU KNOW!

REFOCUS
COMPREHENSION

1. How was the government's response to Shays's Rebellion different from the response to the Whiskey Rebellion?

2. How did political parties begin in the United States?

THINK ABOUT IT
CRITICAL THINKING

Do you think the delegates should have written a new Constitution when they were only supposed to revise the Articles of Confederation? Give reasons for your answer.

WRITE ABOUT IT
ACTIVITY

Make a flowchart that shows the steps that led to the ratification of the Constitution.

Dealing With Other Nations

FOCUS *Once the United States became independent, it had to deal with other nations in a new way. Between 1784 and 1800 there were threats of war, but American leaders tried to avoid military conflicts.*

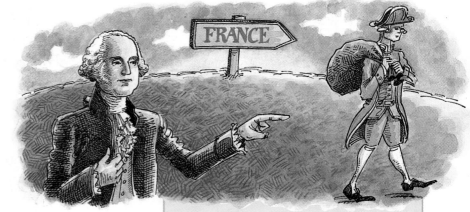

FIGHTING FOR THE LAND

America's independence didn't excite many Native Americans. They wanted to keep their land and protect their way of life. Americans moving west across the Appalachian Mountains wanted to push out the Native Americans. Between 1784 and 1786, Native Americans signed a series of treaties in which they gave up claims to some western lands.

Some Native Americans, however, wanted to fight for the land. As a result, several bloody battles were fought between Native Americans and white settlers throughout the late 1780s and early 1790s.

THE FRENCH REVOLUTION

It seemed as if the American ideals of freedom and equality had taken hold in France. In July 1789, the French people revolted against King Louis XVI. Later the French established a republic. Most Americans were overjoyed that the French, like themselves, had been successful in their revolution.

By 1793, however, the French Revolution had turned ugly. The king and queen were beheaded, and many others were killed in the "Reign of Terror."

This violence upset some Americans. Other Americans remembered how the French had helped America during its revolution and still supported the French in their revolution.

WAR AND GENÊT

In 1778 the United States had promised to help France in case of war. Then, in 1793, France went to war with Britain. Since the United States needed to continue trade with Britain, President Washington decided to remain *neutral*, or to stay out of the war completely.

Citizen Genêt (ZHUH ne), a Frenchman, came to America and pressured Americans into getting involved. Genêt tried to recruit Americans to fight the British.

Washington ordered Genêt to stop recruiting or be sent back to France. Genêt was afraid to return to Paris, because his political party had lost power. He obeyed Washington and stayed in the United States.

1784–1786	1789	1793	1793	1795
Treaties with	French Revolution	France and	British begin	Spain and U.S. sign treaty
Native Americans	begins	Britain at war	impressment of	regarding Mississippi River
			American sailors	

1784　1786　1788　1790　1792　1794　1796

TROUBLE WITH BRITAIN

The war between Great Britain and France affected the United States. According to the 1783 Treaty of Paris, British fur traders were to leave their forts in the Northwest Territory. Now, the British refused to leave. They did not recognize the right of a neutral United States to trade with France.

In 1793, British ships began stopping American ships at sea, forcing American sailors to serve in the British navy. Called *impressment*, this made some Americans angry enough to demand war. President Washington knew that America could not risk war so soon after its revolution. So the United States still remained neutral.

BETTER LUCK WITH SPAIN

Things went better with Spain than with France and Britain. Back in 1784, Spain had closed the port of New Orleans to American commerce. Later, in 1795, Spain feared Americans might attack Louisiana. So Spain signed a treaty allowing Americans to sail freely down the Mississippi River and to use the port of New Orleans. This treaty helped American farmers along the Mississippi River to ship their goods anywhere in the world.

REFOCUS
COMPREHENSION

1. How were Native Americans affected by America's independence?

2. How did the treaty between Spain and the United States benefit American farmers?

THINK ABOUT IT
CRITICAL THINKING

Do you think that the United States should have honored its promise to help France in case of war? Explain the reasons for your decision.

WRITE ABOUT IT
ACTIVITY

Suppose you are representing the United States in Great Britain. Write a speech that you would deliver to British leaders, protesting the impressment of American sailors.

The Constitutional Convention

FOCUS *Throughout the summer of 1787, delegates to the Constitutional Convention struggled to produce the Constitution of the United States.*

Philadelphia, 1787

You probably will arrive late. But so will almost everyone else. Except for James Madison and a few others, all the delegates to the 1787 Constitutional Convention in Philadelphia are late. Why? Well, eighteenth- century roads are awful. Buggies often get stuck in the muddy, rutted paths.

This is probably your first visit to Philadelphia. The city may seem noisy and dirty. Swarms of flies and other insects fill the air. Horses and wagons clog the streets. Smoke from wood-fired cooking stoves makes it hard to breathe.

You probably notice the heat the most. Philadelphia is having one of its hottest summers in 40 years. Everyone is sweating in the 90-degree heat.

Still, you feel a sense of excitement. There is so much to see and do. You can visit Peale's Museum. It's full of fossils, stuffed animal skins, and other "wonderful works of nature." You can

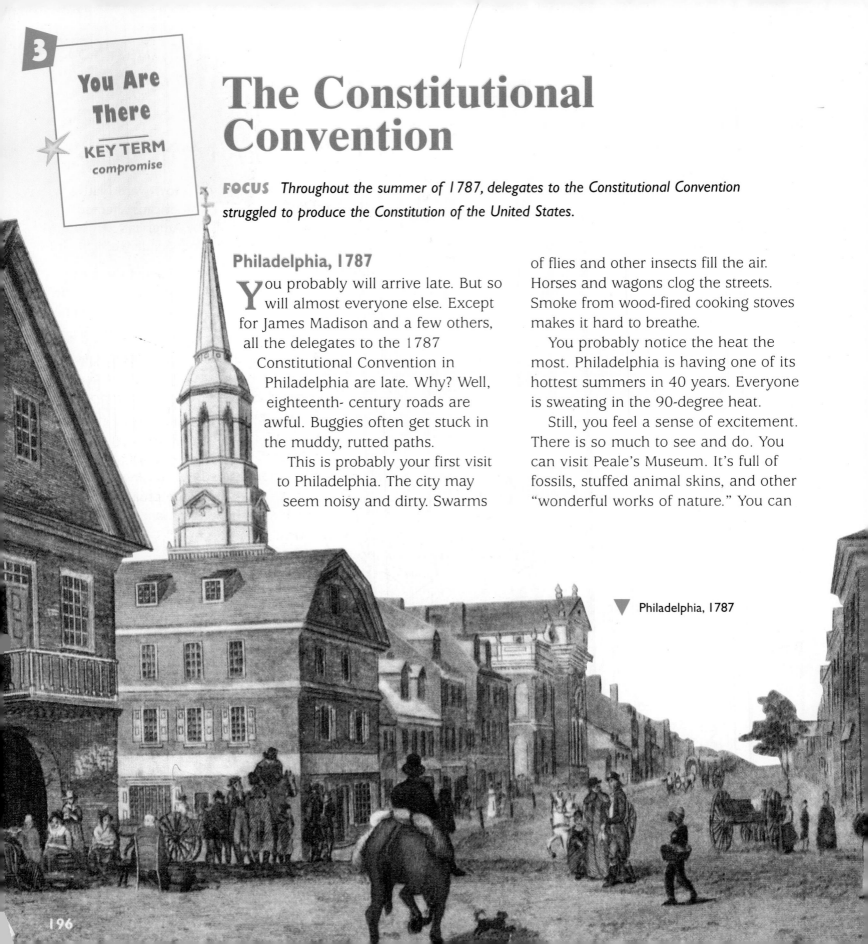

▼ Philadelphia, 1787

relax on the docks of the Delaware River and watch a demonstration of a new invention—the steam-powered boat. You might even visit a shop that's selling the latest fad from Europe—the toothbrush.

If you're hungry or thirsty, you can go to a tavern called the Indian Queen, where you'll see many other delegates. You all come here despite the huge open sewer being repaired across the street. And you never know which will be stronger—the smell of food cooking or the smell of the sewer. Despite the heat, you keep your windows closed at night to avoid the stinging flies while you sleep. You put up with these discomforts and remind yourself that you're here to do an important job.

Who's Here and Who's Not

The convention is scheduled to open on May 14, 1787, at the State House. It is May 25 before enough delegates reach the city to start the talks. Nineteen elected delegates never show up at all. Rhode Island doesn't want a strong national government, and doesn't send a delegate.

Looking at the other 54 delegates, you may notice that there are no

I was not absent a single day, nor more than a casual fraction of any hour in any day, so that I could not have lost a single speech, unless a very short one.
—James Madison

It was a "convention of the well-bred, the well-fed, the well-read, and the well-wed."
—James MacGregor Burns

▲ Benjamin Franklin

women, no Native Americans, and no African Americans. This meeting is for white men only—they are the only ones who can vote and hold office. Some well-known people are also missing. Patrick Henry, who had protested British taxes before the revolution, refuses to come, saying he "smelt a rat in Philadelphia." Others, such as Samuel Adams, are equally suspicious. Meanwhile, John Adams is in England and Thomas Jefferson is in France.

Still, many well-known people are here, including George Washington and the 81-year-old Benjamin Franklin. Franklin had spent a number of years in Europe, representing the interests of the colonies, and later, the new nation. And Alexander Hamilton has come to argue for the strongest possible national government.

Keeping a Secret

As the convention begins, you and the other delegates must decide if you should keep the windows open or closed in the sweltering heat. If you close the windows, you'll suffer even more from the heat, especially the New England delegates, in their heavy woolen suits and wigs. If you leave the windows open, you'll have to listen to the noise from the streets, your meetings won't be private, and more flies will get inside the building. Whatever you decide, it is important to keep the meetings secret. George Washington, as president of the convention, strictly bans the press and public from entering.

James Madison takes daily notes. Those notes will provide the greatest evidence of what goes on at these meetings in Philadelphia.

Each day, you see Benjamin Franklin being carried to the convention by prisoners from a local jail in a sedan chair with glass windows.

Not Everyone Agrees

Once the convention starts, you have hundreds of issues to consider. What powers will you give the President? Who will control commerce between the states? Should judges be elected or appointed? What, if anything, should be done about slavery? And so on. The big issue, however, is the new Congress—what will it look like?

Delegates from states with large populations prefer Madison's idea,

The Constitution allowed slavery. Yet, in 1787 in Philadelphia, Absalom Jones and Richard Allen began an abolition, or antislavery, society. The picture above is a logo for an early abolition society.

known as the Virginia Plan. Since this plan suggests that representation be based on population, it gives large states more power. And delegates from small states like William Paterson's idea, known as the New Jersey Plan. It calls for equal representation for all states.

You and other delegates argue about this for seven weeks. At last, people begin to consider Roger Sherman's compromise. Known as the Great Compromise, it calls for Congress to have two houses. In the Senate, or upper house, every state gets two senators. This protects small states. The House of Representatives, or lower house, favors large states. In this house, representation is based on a state's population. Not everyone likes this idea, but after all this time they realize it is a workable solution.

Making Another Compromise

The Great Compromise brings about a new problem. How do you count population? Southern states want to count enslaved people. This will give southern states more representatives. Northern states only want free people counted.

Again, you and the other delegates reach a compromise. The Three-fifths

---

★ *compromise* An agreement in which each side gives in a little

Compromise says that 5 enslaved people will be counted as the equivalent of 3 free people. So for this purpose, 100 enslaved people count as 60 free people.

On July 16, the Great Compromise, suggested by Sherman, and the Three-fifths Compromise are passed. The issue of slavery is largely ignored. Gouverneur Morris of New York and George Mason of Virginia speak against it. Few delegates listen, and nothing is done to change the system of slavery.

Agreement at Last

It's been a long and trying four months. But on September 17 you and your fellow delegates sign the new Constitution. Will it work? Benjamin Franklin thinks so. He has been studying a carving on the back of Washington's chair. It shows the sun on the horizon. Franklin wonders whether it is a rising or a setting sun. At the end of the convention he says, "I have the happiness to know that it is a rising and not a setting sun."

On July 26, 1788, people celebrated as the Constitution became the law of the land.

Alexander Hamilton ▶

HAMILTON. HAMILTON

REFOCUS
COMPREHENSION

1. List three issues that were discussed at the Constitutional Convention.

2. What groups were and were not represented at the convention?

THINK ABOUT IT
CRITICAL THINKING

Why is it sometimes necessary to make compromises in order to get things done?

WRITE ABOUT IT
ACTIVITY

It is September 1787. You and the other delegates have just signed the Constitution. Write a journal entry describing how you feel about what the convention has or has not accomplished.

4 **Citizenship**

KEY TERMS
executive branch
legislative branch
judicial branch
impeach
bill
federalism

How Our Government Works

FOCUS *Our government is limited because the people have freedoms that the government cannot take away and because no single person has all the political power.*

Basic Freedoms

In the Declaration of Independence, Thomas Jefferson wrote of "unalienable Rights." These are basic freedoms that Americans believe all people are born with. The Constitution's Bill of Rights is made up of ten amendments that provide many freedoms.

The five freedoms protected by the First Amendment are listed in the chart below. First is freedom of religion, which allows us to worship as we please. We can freely express our thoughts because we have freedom of speech. Freedom of the press enables us to freely express our ideas in writing. Freedom of assembly means that we can gather with other people to protest something. Last, we have freedom of petition, or the right to ask the government to change a law that we feel is wrong.

Freedoms Under the Constitution

Freedom of Religion	**Freedom of Speech**	**Freedom of the Press**	**Freedom of Assembly**	**Freedom of Petition**
The right to worship according to your own beliefs	The right to say what you believe	The right to publish newspapers, magazines, and books	The right to gather with other people and work for political action	The right to ask the government to right a wrong

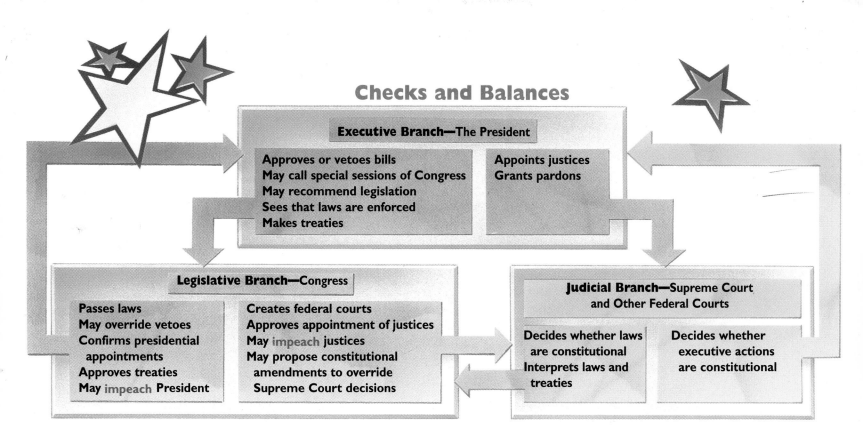

Checks and Balances

Executive Branch—The President

Approves or vetoes bills
May call special sessions of Congress
May recommend legislation
Sees that laws are enforced
Makes treaties

Appoints justices
Grants pardons

Legislative Branch—Congress

Passes laws
May override vetoes
Confirms presidential
  appointments
Approves treaties
May impeach President

Creates federal courts
Approves appointment of justices
May impeach justices
May propose constitutional
  amendments to override
  Supreme Court decisions

**Judicial Branch—Supreme Court
and Other Federal Courts**

Decides whether laws
are constitutional
Interprets laws and
treaties

Decides whether
executive actions
are constitutional

Separation of Powers

The federal government is separated into three branches. The **executive branch,** headed by the President, is responsible for carrying out laws. The President is helped by departments that have special jobs.

The **legislative branch,** or Congress, is made up of the Senate and the House of Representatives. Congress is responsible for making the laws.

The **judicial branch,** or the federal court system, is responsible for deciding the meaning of the laws. The highest court is the Supreme Court. Federal courts also handle cases involving federal laws, and they settle disputes between the states.

The Constitution also has a system of checks and balances that prevents any of the three branches of government from becoming too powerful. Each branch can "check" or limit the power of the other two.

The chart above shows how this works. For example, the President can veto, or refuse to sign, bills passed by Congress. On the other hand, Congress can override a President's veto.

What is a check that the Supreme Court has on Congress? What is a check that Congress has on the Supreme Court? Can you find a check that the President has on Congress? Can you find a check on the President from Congress?

executive branch The part of government that carries out laws
legislative branch The part of government that makes laws
judicial branch The part of government that decides the meaning of laws
impeach To charge a public official with having done something illegal while in office

How a Bill Becomes a Law

This flowchart shows how a **bill** becomes a law.

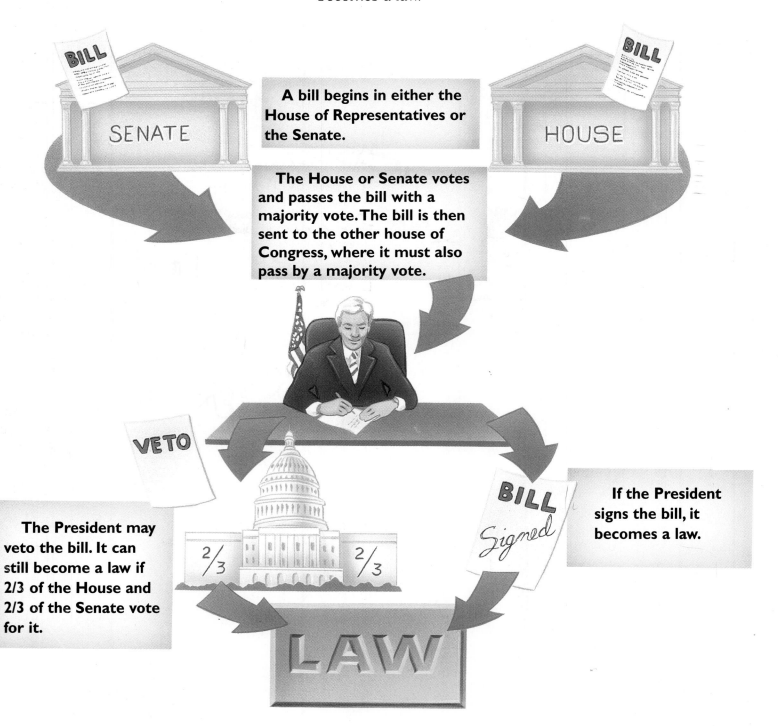

A bill begins in either the House of Representatives or the Senate.

The House or Senate votes and passes the bill with a majority vote. The bill is then sent to the other house of Congress, where it must also pass by a majority vote.

The President may veto the bill. It can still become a law if 2/3 of the House and 2/3 of the Senate vote for it.

If the President signs the bill, it becomes a law.

★ **bill**   An officially suggested law

The Federal System

Powers of the National Government

Make laws about immigration and citizenship
Control trade between states and with foreign countries
Set standard weights and measures
Make copyright and patent laws
Establish a postal system
Print and coin money
Make foreign policy
Create armed forces
Declare war

Concurrent Powers

Collect taxes and borrow money
Create laws to maintain health, safety, and welfare
Set up court systems
Set minimum wage
Charter banks

Powers of the State Governments

Control trade within the state
Control education
Create local governments
Set requirements for elected officials
Create laws regulating marriage and divorce
Set standards for professional licenses

Federalism

The writers of the Constitution had to decide how much power to give the states and the national government. They decided on a system of shared power called **federalism**. The chart above shows how it works.

Only state governments can run schools. Only the federal government can declare war or print money. Other powers, called *concurrent powers*, are shared. For example, both the federal government and the state government can collect taxes.

federalism A system of government that divides powers between the national and state governments

SHOW WHAT YOU KNOW!

REFOCUS
COMPREHENSION

1. What are five freedoms that are listed in the Bill of Rights?

2. What is the purpose of a system of checks and balances?

THINK ABOUT IT
CRITICAL THINKING

Which of the five freedoms listed on page 200 do you think is most important?

WRITE ABOUT IT
ACTIVITY

Discuss with a partner whether the national or the state government should be more powerful. Explain your conclusion in writing.

Two First Ladies

FOCUS *As the first two First Ladies, Martha Washington and Abigail Adams influenced the nation in different ways.*

Martha Washington

Martha Washington's public life began long before her husband, George, became President. During the Revolutionary War, while George was serving in the military, Martha managed their household at Mount Vernon in Virginia. Yet Martha Washington left Mount Vernon to be with General Washington during the winters, even during the harsh winter at Valley Forge.

Martha Washington sometimes helped the general by performing clerical duties. At that time there were no copy machines. People hand copied important documents. When the general was short of staff, Mrs. Washington sometimes hand copied his letters so that he would have a copy.

Martha Washington also became involved in the "Association," an organization that raised money for the Continental troops to thank them for fighting. The money was spent on the troops as General Washington saw fit. It was not to be spent on clothing, food, or other basic provisions.

After the war Martha and George entertained many guests at Mount Vernon. Martha enjoyed spending time with her grandchildren and being back home. But that didn't last long. In 1789, George was elected President. They had to move to New York City, the nation's temporary capital.

Since George Washington had already gone to New York, Mrs. Washington traveled there without him. Along the way, crowds honored her with parades, fireworks, and bands. Being **First Lady** was an honor, but it brought duties, such as hosting formal dinners. If people came to see Martha Washington and she was not at home, she made sure to see them within the next three days.

At last, in 1797, George gave his farewell speech as President. The Washingtons returned to Mount Vernon, and in 1799, George Washington died. Martha was devastated. Two years later her health

---

★ **First Lady** The President's wife

▲ Martha Washington and a quilt that she made

▲ Abigail Adams

States in France during the Revolutionary War, Abigail Adams managed the family farm in Massachusetts. She hired workers, collected rents, and did all that her husband normally did.

Abigail Adams wrote many letters about her ideas on public issues, even though she had never attended school. In letters to her husband, she argued for the rights of women. She wanted girls to be able to go to school. She wanted men to respect women and their work.

In one letter to her husband, Mrs. Adams argued for women's voting rights. She wrote, "Remember the Ladies . . . [We] will not hold ourselves bound by any laws in which we have no voice."

While First Lady, Mrs. Adams continued to write letters. Though most of her writings dealt with political issues of that time, she also wrote about life as First Lady.

Abigail and John Adams were the first family to live in the White House, even though it was not yet completed. There was no fence, no yard, no wood for the fireplace. The main staircase wasn't even built.

As First Ladies, Martha Washington and Abigail Adams had different personal interests. Even today, First Ladies have their own causes and particular interests.

failed. Wanting to protect her privacy, she burned all but two of the letters she and George had exchanged. In May 1802, Martha Washington died.

Abigail Adams

When John Adams became the second President, his wife, Abigail, became the second First Lady. Like Martha Washington's, Abigail Adams's story began long before she became First Lady. While John Adams was away serving in the Second Continental Congress or representing the United

SHOW WHAT YOU KNOW!

REFOCUS
COMPREHENSION

1. What are some jobs that Martha Washington did in her public life?

2. How do we know so much about Abigail Adams?

THINK ABOUT IT
CRITICAL THINKING

From reading about Martha Washington and Abigail Adams, what can you tell about what women could and could not do at this time?

WRITE ABOUT IT
ACTIVITY

Write a letter to the First Lady about an issue that is important to you.

SUMMING UP

1 DO YOU REMEMBER . . .
COMPREHENSION

1. Why did people want state governments to be stronger than the national government?

2. Why did Shays's Rebellion frighten people?

3. Why is the U.S. Constitution important?

4. What were the first two political parties?

5. How did Americans feel about the French Revolution?

6. What kept some leaders of the American Revolution from coming to the Constitutional Convention?

7. How did the New Jersey Plan and the Virginia Plan differ?

8. What was the Three-fifths Compromise?

9. What three branches of government did the Constitution create?

10. What were some goals Abigail Adams had for girls and women?

2 SKILL POWER
USING A FLOWCHART

In this chapter you learned how to use flowcharts. Using the flowchart on page 201, explain how the Constitution prevents any one branch of the government from becoming too powerful.

3 WHAT DO YOU THINK?
CRITICAL THINKING

1. Suppose the Constitution had never been written and the Articles of Confederation remained in effect. How might things be different today?

2. Support this statement with facts from this chapter: After the colonies became independent, the new nation had to learn to deal with other nations.

3. Why might some people have been disappointed by the results of the Constitutional Convention?

4. Why are the freedoms set forth in the Bill of Rights so important to Americans?

5. What do you think the American people expect of the First Lady?

4 SAY IT, WRITE IT, USE IT
VOCABULARY

Write a news story about the Constitutional Convention for a local newspaper. As you describe the delegates at work, use as many of the vocabulary words as possible.

bill	First Lady
Bill of Rights	impeach
Cabinet	judicial branch
compromise	legislative branch
constitution	political party
executive branch	ratify
federalism	republic

5 GEOGRAPHY AND YOU
MAP STUDY

Use the present-day map below and the maps on pages 188 and 191 to answer these questions.

1. What present-day states made up the land claimed by Georgia?

2. What river separated Spanish-held Louisiana and the United States?

3. What year did the first state ratify the Constitution? Name all the states that ratified the Constitution in that same year.

4. What bodies of water border on the Northwest Territory?

6 TAKE ACTION
CITIZENSHIP

The Constitution provides for the Senate and the House of Representatives. You have two senators and a representative in Washington, D.C. Do you know who they are? With a group of classmates, find out the names and addresses of your senators and representatives. Post this information on a classroom bulletin board. Then look for news articles that tell about their opinions and how they voted on issues. You may even wish to write to them explaining your ideas about an issue.

7 GET CREATIVE
ART CONNECTION

United States money honors many of the nation's founders and constitutional delegates. Design a new coin or bill that honors someone who you think has played an important part in the nation's heritage.

LOOKING AHEAD In the next unit explore what the new nation goes through as it expands and changes.

Expansion AND Conflict

How Do People Deal With Conflict?

This is a time of growth, change, and conflict. Examine the differences that led to conflict and eventually to a war that pitted American against American.

GROWTH AND

Between 1800 and 1830 the United States grew rapidly and in many ways. There were growing pains, however, as sectional differences arose and threatened the Union.

How did young workers use bobbins and spindles in the early 1800s? Find out on page 232.

CONTENTS

CONFLICT

These books tell about how the United States grew and changed in the early 1800s. Read one that interests you and fill out a book-review form.

READ AND RESEARCH

The Story of Sacajawea, Guide to Lewis and Clark
by Della Rowland (Dell Publishing, 1989)
When she was 16, Sacajawea met Lewis and Clark. She helped guide their team of explorers through the western United States. Explore the land with the group and find out how Sacajawea contributed to their expedition. *(biography)*
•*You can read a selection from this story on page 222.*

By the Dawn's Early Light: The Story of the Star-Spangled Banner **by Steven Kroll** (Scholastic, 1994)
Travel back to the War of 1812 and meet Francis Scott Key, a Washington lawyer. Follow him as he tries to rescue a friend from British troops and ends up inspired to write what became our national anthem. *(nonfiction)*

The Cherokees **by Elaine Landau** (Franklin Watts, 1992)
Follow the story of the Cherokees from long ago to today. Learn about their daily life, festivals, religion, and history. Find out why their removal to Oklahoma was known as the Trail of Tears. *(nonfiction)*

Samuel Slater's Mill and the Industrial Revolution
by Christopher Simonds (Silver Burdett Press, 1990)
In 1789, Samuel Slater came to the United States from Great Britain. Learn how he inspired a revolution that changed the United States. *(nonfiction)*

SKILL POWER

Preparing for an Oral Report

Knowing how to give an oral report lets you share important information with others.

UNDERSTAND IT

You're the explorer Meriwether Lewis in 1806. You've just returned from an incredible two-and-a-half-year journey across the continent. You've discovered rivers, mountain ranges, native peoples, and hundreds of animals and plants that you've never seen before. You're bursting with information to share with the President and Congress. A good way to do it, you decide, is to give an oral report.

When you give an oral report, you share what you've learned with others. It's different from a written report because you have to face your audience. An oral report can be about things you've seen personally or things you've researched in books.

Captain Lewis sent a live horned lizard to President Jefferson.

EXPLORE IT

Here's how Meriwether Lewis might have prepared his oral report. Use these steps to prepare your own report.

1. **Narrow the topic.** Lewis couldn't talk about all of his discoveries in one brief report. So he might narrow the topic to "Animals We Saw for the First Time."

2. **Gather information.** Examining his journals, Lewis found details about the animals he saw on the expedition. (To write about something you didn't see, you'd use textbooks, encyclopedias, and other sources.)

3. **Take notes and make an outline on cards.** Note cards are easy to hold and look at when speaking aloud. Lewis might make an outline showing the main ideas and details he will cover.

4. **Write an introduction and conclusion.** Beginning with a dramatic fact or quotation catches the audience's attention. Lewis might begin by describing the vast herds of buffaloes. The conclusion should quickly sum up the main points of the report.

INDEX CARDS

5. **Use visual aids.** Lewis could show his sketches and stuffed animals. Photos, maps, and charts will make your report more interesting, too.

6. **Practice.** Try out your oral report for a friend or in front of a mirror. Find ways to use your voice, face, and hands to help express your ideas.

Follow the steps in Explore It to prepare notes for your own oral report. You might want to report on something you have seen or done personally, such as visiting a museum or historical site. Or you can look through this chapter and choose and narrow a topic that interests you.

When you listen to your classmates' reports, be a good listener. Here's how.

● Look at the speaker and pay attention.

● Listen for the main points.

● Form questions in your mind to ask the speaker later.

SKILL POWER SEARCH What topics in this chapter would you like to know more about? Choose one for an oral report.

A CHANGING NATION

FOCUS *The United States grew in many ways in the early 1800s. Growth produced conflict and rising tensions with Great Britain as well as great expectations at home.*

Jefferson Arrives in Washington

On March 4, 1801, Thomas Jefferson walked slowly and confidently through the cheering crowded streets of Washington, D.C. He was on his way to be sworn in as the third President of the United States.

Jefferson wore a simple outfit—plain coat, plain pants. No powdered wig or fancy clothes for him. He wanted to show those who had voted for him that it was the ordinary American they had supported. The President, he felt, should get no special favors. But the crowds who lined his route knew exactly who he was—*their* President.

After taking the oath of office, Jefferson, a Democratic-Republican, spoke to the crowd. "Let us unite with one heart and one mind," he said.

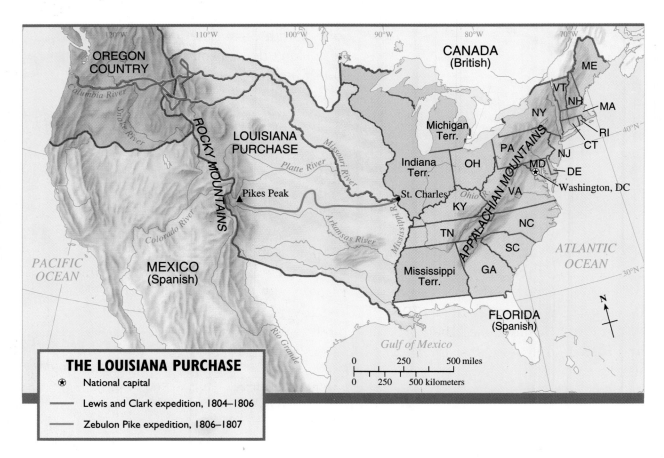

THE LOUISIANA PURCHASE

⊛ National capital

—— Lewis and Clark expedition, 1804–1806

—— Zebulon Pike expedition, 1806–1807

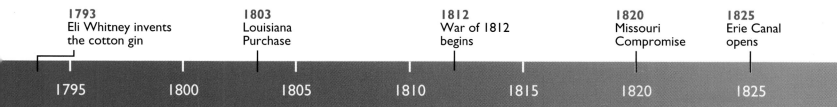

1793 Eli Whitney invents the cotton gin	1803 Louisiana Purchase	1812 War of 1812 begins	1820 Missouri Compromise	1825 Erie Canal opens

1795   1800   1805   1810   1815   1820   1825

"We are all Republicans—we are all Federalists." This meant that Jefferson wanted Americans to unite no matter which party they had voted for.

Thomas Jefferson and his fellow Democratic-Republicans undid many Federalist laws. They got rid of the hated whiskey tax. They cut government spending and reduced the size of the army and navy. But Jefferson's greatest accomplishment was to double the size of the country.

New Land Opportunities

By 1800, thousands of American hunters, trappers, and pioneers had crossed the Appalachian Mountains. The first settlers to cross the Appalachians were rewarded with fertile valleys and farmland. Word spread back east: The land west of the mountains was ripe for settlement. Native Americans, of course, had long been settled on the same land.

Spain had opened the port of New Orleans to American trade in 1795. But in 1802, Spain closed the port and then sold it to France. Americans wanted to gain control of New Orleans because it was the port through which all the goods from the Mississippi River valley were shipped.

The Louisiana Purchase

Jefferson wanted to purchase New Orleans from Napoleon, the French emperor. For years Napoleon had hoped to build an empire in America. But by 1800 he was preparing France for war with Great Britain. He knew he couldn't defend Louisiana against the British navy, and war was expensive. So he decided to sell it.

When the American representatives James Monroe and Robert Livingston offered $10 million for New Orleans, Napoleon's agents said no. But if the United States wanted to buy *all* of Louisiana, including New Orleans, for $15 million, a deal could be made.

Monroe and Livingston couldn't believe their ears. As you can see on the map on page 214, this area was huge. The Louisiana Purchase cost about three cents an acre. It was the greatest real estate bargain in history.

★ **Louisiana Purchase**   The purchase in 1803 of French lands in North America that doubled the size of the United States

215

Lewis and Clark drew pictures of animals they had never seen before. From top to bottom, they drew a white gull, a buzzard, and an American white-fronted goose.

The New Nation Expands

The Louisiana Purchase *doubled* the size of the United States. Americans had lots of questions about this new **territory**. Was it good for farming? How high were its mountains? In 1804, Jefferson sent Meriwether Lewis and William Clark off to find some answers. In May 1804, Lewis and Clark began to explore the Louisiana Territory by heading up the Missouri River by canoe. Some days they covered 15 miles. Other days they could travel only 3 or 4 miles. At last, in June 1805, they reached what is now Montana. Then they crossed the Rocky Mountains on horseback. From there they traveled down the Columbia River to the Pacific Ocean. On November 7, 1805, Clark wrote in his journal: "Ocean in view! O! the joy."

Soon after Lewis and Clark's successful expedition, the United States added parts of Florida to its territory. But Spain held on to the peninsula. Finally, in 1819 the United States bought the rest of Florida from Spain.

Britain—an Enemy Again

Meanwhile, the United States was once again having trouble with Great Britain. Even though Americans had won their revolution—or maybe *because* they had won their revolution—the British were provoking them. Britain still had claims to parts of North America. And the British encouraged Native Americans to fight Americans. The British also seized American ships and pressed American sailors into service, making them work on British ships.

President Jefferson persuaded Congress to pass an **embargo** against all foreign countries. This meant that the United States would no longer trade with any other nations. At the time, Britain was the main trading partner of the United States. Jefferson hoped the embargo would prove that the United States could survive without *any* European trade. But he was wrong. Americans needed to sell food, lumber, and other products to Europe. And they needed to purchase the finished goods that Europeans made from those raw materials.

The War of 1812

When the embargo failed and Great Britain resumed seizing America's ships, some Americans called for war. In June 1812 they got their way. President James Madison, who had been elected in 1808, asked Congress to declare war on Great Britain.

The War of 1812 started out on land but became known for its battles on water. It continued until January 1815. Commodore Oliver Perry's ships defeated a British force on Lake Erie and produced America's first victory in 1813. The British went on to capture

---

territory An area of land that has not yet become a state

embargo A government order that stops or slows trade with a particular nation

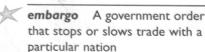

Washington, D.C., and to burn the White House. The map on the right shows several important battles. The battle of New Orleans was the largest. News traveled slowly in those days, so the battle was actually fought two weeks after both sides had signed a peace treaty.

The war itself didn't settle much. It wasn't a war over territories—no lands were won or lost. But Americans gained self-confidence. Twice now they had stood up to the mighty British Empire. Also, since Native Americans no longer had British support, it would now be easier for white settlers to move west.

During the war Francis Scott Key wrote a poem, "The Star-Spangled Banner." The words came to him as he watched Americans hold out against a British attack on Fort McHenry, in Maryland. Set to a familiar melody, his poem became so popular that it later became our national anthem.

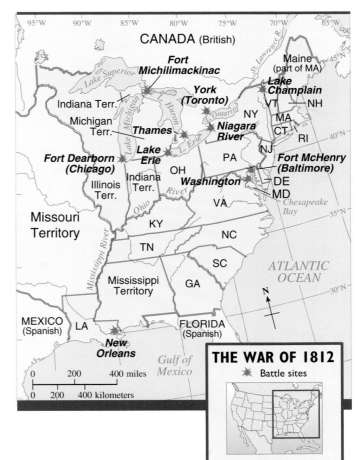

THE WAR OF 1812

★ Battle sites

The attack on Fort McHenry might have looked like this to Francis Scott Key.

Building a Nation

Since the United States was growing so much in the early 1800s, **internal improvements**, such as roads, canals, steamboats, and railroads, were built to link the new cities that sprang up. In 1807, Robert Fulton built the first successful steamboat, making it possible to sail *up* a river, against the current. The 363-mile-long Erie Canal opened in 1825. It linked the Great Lakes to New York City, so goods from Detroit and Buffalo could be carried by water instead of by more expensive overland routes. A great era of railroad building began during this time. Communications improved, too. In 1837, Samuel F. B. Morse demonstrated his telegraph, which carried messages quickly over long distances.

It wasn't just internal improvements that signaled a changing nation. Americans were used to weaving cloth by hand. But in Britain in the late 1700s, a new machine made it possible to spin cotton into thread. Another machine wove thread into cloth. These and other inventions were introduced to the United States and jump-started the **Industrial Revolution**. At first these machines ran on water power. Later they ran on steam.

---

internal improvement The building of transportation and communications systems to help a country's economy
Industrial Revolution The period of great change in how people lived and made products, brought about by power-driven machines

The Cotton Gin and the South

Southern planters had been growing cotton since the mid-1700s. But the kind of cotton that grew best in the South was filled with sticky seeds. It took a worker a whole day to clean one pound. That made cotton expensive to grow.

Eli Whitney's contribution to the Industrial Revolution changed that. In 1793 he invented the cotton gin. This little machine picked the seeds from cotton. It cleaned 50 pounds of cotton in one day. Thus, cotton became profitable to grow because it was easy to process.

Differences Arise

The United States was growing and changing. The North and the West

An early artist's image of enslaved people and masters working at a cotton gin

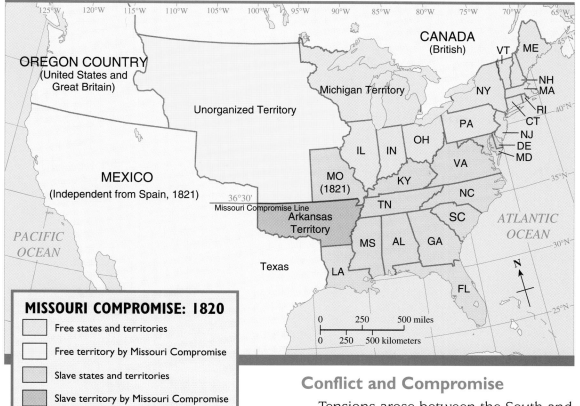

MISSOURI COMPROMISE: 1820

- Free states and territories
- Free territory by Missouri Compromise
- Slave states and territories
- Slave territory by Missouri Compromise

SHOW WHAT YOU KNOW!

REFOCUS
COMPREHENSION

1. Why was the Louisiana Purchase important to the growth and development of the United States?

2. How did the Industrial Revolution affect the North and the South?

THINK ABOUT IT
CRITICAL THINKING

How might history have been different had the cotton gin not been invented?

WRITE ABOUT IT
ACTIVITY

If you were a non-slaveholding farmer in Missouri in 1820, how would you react to the news of the Missouri Compromise?

were changing one way, the South another. In the North and the West, mills that turned cotton into fashions sprang up. Canals were dug, and railroads were constructed.

In the South, on the other hand, the cotton that fed the Industrial Revolution in the North was king. It quickly became the most important crop grown in the South. The South grew more cotton more cheaply than any other place on earth. By 1820 the South grew 100 times more cotton than in 1790. The booming cotton business led to a new dependence on slavery, which had almost died out in the 1790s, when tobacco had declined in importance. Now that cotton made money, it was profitable to keep enslaved people. They grew the cotton and worked the gins that cleaned it.

Conflict and Compromise

Tensions arose between the South and the North. One issue was tariffs, or extra charges added to the cost of imported goods. The North wanted high tariffs to protect its new industries. The South wanted low tariffs to keep imports— goods brought from other countries— less costly. Another issue was slavery. Most northerners weren't ready to fight slavery in the South. But they did want to keep it out of new territories, because they worried that white workers would not be able to compete with slave labor. In 1820 the **Missouri Compromise** stated that Missouri could enter the Union as a slave state in exchange for Maine's entrance as a free state. The compromise forbade slavery in the rest of the Louisiana Territory, north of 36°30' north latitude. Find this line on the map above. But the time would soon come when such compromises would become more difficult.

⭐ **Missouri Compromise** The 1820 ruling that admitted Missouri as a slave state

Map Adventure

★ KEY TERMS

corps
interpreter

LITERATURE

The Story of
Sacajawea

THE LEWIS AND CLARK EXPEDITION

FOCUS *The expedition led by Meriwether Lewis and William Clark traveled over 7,000 miles, giving America much information about lands west of the Mississippi.*

N
W *E*
S

Pacific Ocean

Fort Mandan

Lewis's Route

Clark's Route

Mandan village

Columbia River

Clearwater River

Yellowstone River

Missouri River

Mississippi River

8

5

7

6

4

3

2

1

THE LEWIS AND CLARK EXPEDITION

Louisiana Territory

Westward journey

Return journey

0   100   200   300 miles

0   100   200   300 miles

Adventure in the Louisiana Territory

The "Corps of Discovery" began its two-year-long journey to explore the Louisiana Territory in May 1804. Over 40 men handled the large keelboat and two flat-bottomed dugout canoes, called pirogues (pih ROHGZ). The cargo included compasses, tents, medical supplies, and 193 pounds of "portable soup," a kind of food. Their mission: Find an all-water route to the Pacific, meet and observe Native American groups, and map out the new territory.

Map Legend

1 **St. Louis** In 1804 this city was little more than a few scattered buildings. Later, as thousands of settlers from the East passed through, it was called the "Gateway to the West."

2 **Missouri River** The Corps struggled against the Missouri River's strong current. Called the "Big Muddy" because of the soil it carries from the mountains, the river hid many dangers, including fallen trees and rocks.

3 **Great Plains** Passing through these grassy plains, Lewis and Clark took notes on everything they saw. Many animals looked strange to them, including prairie dogs, which Lewis called "barking squirrels."

4 **Fort Mandan** The Corps built this fort as a winter camp, near a Mandan Indian village. When spring came, they set out again with a Shoshoni guide, Sacajawea; Charbonneau, her French trapper husband; and their newborn son.

5 **Great Falls** The Corps reached these mighty waterfalls on June 13. Forced to carry their boats and supplies around the falls, they suffered through a month of rattlesnakes, floods, and grizzlies.

6 **Three Forks** Sacajawea recognized this area as her home and served as an interpreter when the Corps met the Shoshonis. The Shoshonis sold horses to Lewis and Clark and showed them a mountain pass.

7 **Rocky Mountains** The towering height of the Rockies convinced the Corps that there was no all-water route to the Pacific. Horses carried the supplies across, while most of the men walked.

8 **Fort Clatsop** The Corps finally reached the Pacific Ocean in November 1805 and camped here for the winter. Come spring, they faced a long journey home.

corps A group of people who act together
interpreter A person who helps two people or groups understand the languages and customs of each other

MAP IT

1. You are a member of the Corps. As you follow the Missouri River, you wonder whether it will take you directly to the Pacific Ocean. What do you discover?
2. The Corps finally ends its long westward journey and sets up Fort Clatsop. What ocean can you see from Fort Clatsop?
3. In the spring the Corps begins the return journey. When Lewis and Clark split up, you go with Clark. In what direction does your group head first? Have you seen any of this area before?
4. What river do you follow before you rejoin Lewis's group?

EXPLORE IT

Write a letter to a relative in which you describe some of the highlights of the Lewis and Clark expedition.

The Story of Sacajawea, Guide to Lewis and Clark

by Della Rowland

Sacajawea was a young Shoshoni who had been captured and raised by the Minnetaree people. When Lewis and Clark met her, they knew they had found the person who could help them meet the people and explore the land of the western United States. Here we join Sacajawea and the exploration Corps as they are about to explore the land in which she grew up.

As they moved closer to the mountains, Captain Lewis worried that the river would become rocky. Sacajawea told him she knew this river and that it would not change or become dangerous. And she was right! Three days later, on July 28, 1805, they came safely to the Three Forks.

The Corps made camp right at the place where Sacajawea and her family had been camped when the Minnetarees captured her. With Charbonneau translating, she told the men how she and her people had been captured by the Minnetarees. She described to them how she had run for three miles up the widest of the three forks, hidden in the woods, and watched as many of her people were killed.

Sacajawea pointed out the spot where she had been grabbed up as she had tried to cross the river. That terrible moment had changed her whole life, but Sacajawea did not show her feelings about that fateful day. As a Shoshoni, she had been taught that it was weak and childish to act in an emotional way. . . .

The captains named the three forks of the rivers they had found the Jefferson, Madison, and Gallatin rivers, after three of the most important political leaders of the time. . . . Sacajawea had followed the Jefferson when she ran to escape the Minnetarees. Now the Corps followed it toward the mountains.

After they had traveled a few days along the river, Sacajawea looked up from her boat and pointed out a tall rock on a high plain. She said the Shoshoni called it Beaver's Head Rock because it looked like that familiar animal to them. To her, Beaver's Head Rock meant that they were near the pass where her people crossed the mountains each year in search of food. . . .

Sacajawea told the captains that to find her people, they should follow the Jefferson River until it divided. Then they should take the fork that went west. The Shoshoni would either be on the Jefferson River, or on the west fork. Then she showed them an Indian road beside the river. It was the road her people took back and forth from the mountains to the plains.

When Lewis heard this, he decided to cross the mountains immediately.

Find out more about how Sacajawea helped the expedition by checking the book out of your school or public library.

SHOW WHAT YOU KNOW!

REFOCUS
COMPREHENSION

1. What was the purpose of the Lewis and Clark expedition?

2. List some challenges and obstacles faced by the members of the expedition.

THINK ABOUT IT
CRITICAL THINKING

Describe how Sacajawea might have felt when the expedition reached the area where she had been captured.

WRITE ABOUT IT
ACTIVITY

Go to a local park or open space you've never been to before. Describe it as if you were Lewis or Clark, noting all that you see.

NATIVE AMERICANS RESPOND

FOCUS *Native Americans responded in different ways as westward expansion resulted in the loss of more and more of their land.*

To Blend In or Fight?

Was it possible to trade land for peace? Some Native Americans in the early 1800s hoped so. They thought that if they sold *some* land to the settlers streaming into their lands from the east, they could hold on to the rest. Then they could live in peace. So Native Americans sold vast sections of their lands. But they could never sell enough. As settlements grew, Native Americans were forced to choose between two other options: fight, or **assimilate** into white society.

Given these choices, most Native Americans preferred to fight. From the late 1780s through the early 1800s, they fought several bitter wars against United States Army troops. One great Native American leader was Tecumseh (tih KUM-suh), a Shawnee warrior from the area of the Ohio and Indiana territories. He wanted Native Americans to unite against the settlers. Some agreed with him, but others did not.

In 1811, General William Henry Harrison was governor of the Indiana Territory. (Later he became

assimilate To become absorbed into another culture

President of the United States.) He defeated a force of 1,000 Shawnees in a battle at Tippecanoe Creek in Indiana Territory. Tecumseh wasn't there. But he was killed two years later as he fought with the British against United States troops. Hopes for a united Indian resistance died with Tecumseh.

The Cherokee Story

Some Native Americans were willing to try to adapt to white culture. The

Unorganized Territory

Mississippi R.

IL   IN   OH

MO

VA

Indian Territory

Arkansas Territory

KY

TN

NC

MEXICO

SC

MS   AL

GA

NATIVE AMERICAN REMOVAL: 1830–1840

LA

Florida Territory

← Cherokees
← Chickasaws
← Choctaws
← Creeks
← Seminoles

0   100   200 miles

0   100   200 kilometers

Gulf of Mexico

Tecumseh

Cherokees, who lived in Georgia, Tennessee, and North Carolina, tried to combine white and Native American ways. They combined white laws with theirs. They gave up old ways of hunting and gardening and opened sawmills and blacksmith shops. Traditionally, the Cherokees shared property. Now they gave up shared property and moved to individual farms. Some stopped wearing buckskin shirts and dressed in cloth trousers. By adapting like this, they hoped they could keep their land.

But adaptation was *not* enough for many white Americans. They wanted Cherokee land. In 1828, Georgia's legislature declared Cherokee laws worthless. The Cherokees appealed to the Supreme Court. In 1832 the court ruled in their favor, saying that Georgia's laws did *not* apply to the Cherokee

nation. The court's ruling should have been final, but President Andrew Jackson refused to enforce it.

Trail of Tears

In 1835, President Jackson told the Cherokees it would be "impossible" for them to live on their land any longer. Like other Native Americans, as you can see on the map on page 224, they were to move west of the Mississippi River.

The Cherokees refused to leave their land. But the United States Army, in the winter of 1838, forced 15,000 of them to give up their homes. They began a long, painful journey west. Many suffered from disease, hunger, and bitter cold. Four thousand died. The Cherokees remember this journey as the **Trail of Tears**.

▼ The Trail of Tears—sad, long, and brutal

 Trail of Tears The removal of Cherokees from their homelands to what is now Oklahoma

SHOW WHAT YOU
KNOW!

REFOCUS
COMPREHENSION

1. What were three ways in which Native Americans responded to westward expansion?

2. How did the Cherokees adapt their ways of living to become assimilated?

THINK ABOUT IT
CRITICAL THINKING

Describe what you would feel if your community was forced to move across the country.

WRITE ABOUT IT
ACTIVITY

Write a letter to President Jackson urging him to rethink his decision to move the Cherokees.

FASTER AND BETTER

FOCUS *As Americans spread out across the continent, the nation became linked by better and better systems of transportation and communication.*

A RIVER HIGHWAY

In 1807, Robert Fulton chugged *up* the Hudson River in his new steamboat, the *Clermont*. Just 32 hours after leaving New York City, Fulton reached Albany, 150 miles away. Fulton turned the Hudson—and other rivers, as well—into a two-way highway. In 1820 about 60 steamboats operated on the Mississippi River. By 1860 there were more than 1,000.

Faster and more powerful boats were developed. Some were able to travel in very shallow water. This was essential along western rivers, which were full of sandbars and rocks. In 1841 the *Orphan Boy* set a steamboat record. It carried 40 tons of freight as well as passengers through water only two feet deep.

THE "BIG DITCH"

In 1817 the New York State legislature approved $7 million to build a canal to help connect the Great Lakes to the Atlantic Ocean. It would never happen, said many critics. Some people laughed. They made fun of Governor DeWitt Clinton, who came up with the idea. They called the canal "Clinton's big ditch." After all, no existing canal was more than 28 miles long, and Clinton wanted to build one 363 miles long, from Albany to Buffalo.

But in 1825 the Erie Canal opened and became a huge success. Because it was now easier to move goods from Great Lakes cities to New York City, the freight charge dropped from $100 a ton to $10 a ton.

MIGHTY TOM THUMB

Peter Cooper's *Tom Thumb* was the first American-built steam locomotive. Cooper hoped to convince railroad owners to use locomotives, instead of horses, to pull their trains. In 1830 he showed that *Tom Thumb* could travel at 18 miles an hour for 13 miles.

The railroad industry grew quickly. By 1840 there were as many miles of railroad track as there were of canals. In the 1850s, the number of miles of railroad track increased from 8,879 miles to 30,626 miles. People stopped talking about canals. Railroads were the future.

1807
The *Clermont* sails up the Hudson River

1825
Erie Canal opens

1830
Tom Thumb runs in Baltimore

1844
S.F.B. Morse sends message in Morse Code

1848
Cunard's steamships sail from New York to Europe in 10 to 14 days

1805 — 1820 — 1830 — 1840 — 1850 — 1860

SINGING WIRES

On May 24, 1844, Samuel F. B. Morse sent a simple message. It said, "What hath God wrought?" Morse sent these words from Washington, D.C., to Baltimore. But the amazing thing was that he sent them over a piece of wire! His message traveled in the form of Morse Code. This is a system in which each letter in the alphabet has its own pattern of dots and dashes.

Morse demonstrated his telegraph in 1837, but he didn't have the money to string telegraph wire. By 1844, Morse had proved that his invention really worked, and Congress had spent $30,000 to build a telegraph line.

TIME TRAVEL

The world was changing faster and faster by the 1840s. Older Americans could still remember when everything moved at a snail's pace. It once took 74 days to sail to Europe and back. In 1848, Samuel Cunard's steamships made the trip in just 20 to 28 days.

The Erie Canal turned a four-week trip from Detroit to New York into a two-week jaunt. By 1857, Detroit was just an overnight train ride from New York City. In 1800, thanks to better roads, a horse and rider could go from New York to Philadelphia in two days. By 1820, that time was cut to one day. When George Washington died in 1799, the people in Boston didn't find out for 11 days. With the telegraph the sad news would have reached Boston within seconds.

REFOCUS
COMPREHENSION

1. Why was the Erie Canal a success?

2. What were some ways in which transportation had improved by the 1850s?

THINK ABOUT IT
CRITICAL THINKING

The War of 1812 was over before the last battle was fought. What invention on this page could have brought the news of war's end sooner, and how?

WRITE ABOUT IT
ACTIVITY

Write about some forms of communication that are used today that were not available in the mid-1800s.

AMERICA ON THE MOVE

FOCUS *In the early 1800s, improvements in transportation and communication transformed the United States and changed the expectations of Americans.*

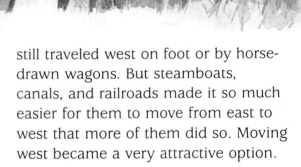

Getting Bigger—and Smaller

Between 1803 and 1853 what we know today as the continental United States was formed. The land area ruled by the United States had more than tripled. By 1853 the United States stretched from the potato fields of northern Maine to sunny California. It reached from the southern tip of Florida to beautiful Puget (PYOO jiht) Sound in what is now the state of Washington.

But at the same time, improvements in transportation and communication made the country *seem* smaller. Steamboats, canals, railroads, and the telegraph shrank distances. After all, for the traveler, the important measure of distance between point *A* and point *B* wasn't miles. It was time.

What did better transportation mean to the settlement of America's new territories? Well, many pioneers still traveled west on foot or by horse-drawn wagons. But steamboats, canals, and railroads made it so much easier for them to move from east to west that more of them did so. Moving west became a very attractive option.

Growing Markets

Equally important, steamboats, canals, and railroads opened up and linked new **markets**. Wheat and other grains that were grown in Ohio, Illinois, and Indiana were processed, and then shipped back to the East. From there they were shipped to markets around the world. New

---

⭐ **market** A place where a buyer meets a seller to purchase a product or service

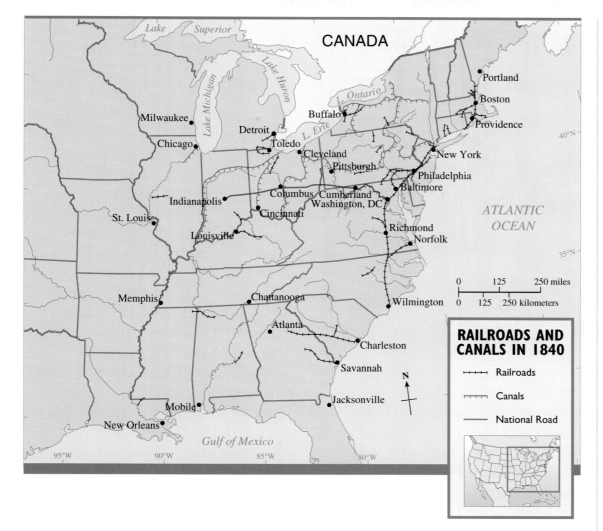

RAILROADS AND CANALS IN 1840

├┼┼┼┤ Railroads
├──┤ Canals
───── National Road

industries, such as flour processing, sprang up. And new industries meant more jobs for people.

More and More Cities

As industries grew, so did the number of cities. Some of the cities are shown on the map above. Cities no longer had to be on the ocean to export their goods. With steamboats, canals, and railroads, they could be on lakes or rivers, as long as they had workers and the products that people wanted.

Chicago developed on Lake Michigan as a grain center. Cincinnati seemed to spring up overnight on the Ohio River. St. Louis, on the

▼ The *DeWitt Clinton*, a very early locomotive, chugged 16 miles in New York State in 1831.

Occupations and opportunities for women began to increase by the early 1800s.

Mississippi, became a major trading center and the "Gateway to the West." These cities and many others helped to support the many smaller settlements in the West.

Industries Get a Boost

Americans in the early 1800s bubbled over with a "can-do" attitude. So much had been done since independence was won. The country had stood up to foreign powers, and the size of the country had doubled overnight in 1803. There seemed to be nothing Americans wouldn't tackle. They seemed to go out of their way to find a new problem. And, of course, every problem had a solution.

One great problem-solver was Eli Whitney. He developed the idea of **interchangeable parts**. This idea

called for a machine to make a part and then thousands of that part—all exactly alike.

Prior to 1800, for example, every gun was made by hand by a skilled worker called a gunsmith. But by 1800, Whitney showed that by mass producing each part, a gun could be assembled by anyone, even by an unskilled worker. Any barrel, any trigger, any firing pin for a particular kind of gun would fit. He built a gun factory in Connecticut to put his theory into practice.

The idea of interchangeable parts changed American industry drastically. It made **mass production** possible. Now factories could turn out vast quantities of identical goods.

Mass production was first used in gun factories. Later, it was used in making sewing machines and farm equipment. Even the machines that drove the factories were mass-produced, with interchangeable parts.

Women in the Workplace

New ways of doing things had a profound impact on women. Textile mills, for example, took some traditional work away from women. Clothes had been made at home by women who spun thread, wove cloth, and sewed shirts and dresses. By the early 1800s, fabrics of all sorts were being produced in mills.

---

interchangeable parts   Parts that can be used in place of each other

mass production   The ability to produce many goods of one kind quickly and efficiently

On the other hand, textile mills gave women work. When mill owners couldn't get male farmers to work in the mills, they turned to women. In the end, women still made the clothes. But they did it in a factory instead of by the fireplace at home. Women also slowly became accepted as shop owners and merchants. This is the period in American history when people first got used to the idea of women working outside their homes.

Demand for Education

The inventiveness that American industry became known for helped lead to a demand for more public education. It was thought that people who were better educated would be better workers. The Erie Canal, for example, needed some highly educated and skilled workers in its construction. In Massachusetts, Horace Mann fought for higher teacher pay, more interesting classes, and better teacher training.

Mill owners also began to support public education. They saw the need for literate workers. Such workers were more reliable and better able to handle complex machinery. Public schools, by now including both boys and girls, did well. Private female academies were established and flourished. By 1840, a large percentage of white Americans were able to read and write.

▼ The Erie Canal was a symbol of American inventiveness and expansion.

★ *literate*   Having the ability to read and write

SHOW WHAT YOU KNOW!

REFOCUS
COMPREHENSION

1. What factors helped the growth of cities in this period?

2. What effect did the growth of industry have on education in the United States?

THINK ABOUT IT
CRITICAL THINKING

Eli Whitney's theory of interchangeable parts changed the way that many people worked. How do you think a worker who was used to making a product by hand would feel about working in a factory?

WRITE ABOUT IT
ACTIVITY

Write a letter to your local paper asking for internal improvements that would make your neighborhood or community better.

THE "LOWELL GIRLS"

FOCUS *In the 1830s, owners of the Lowell mills hoped to create a new kind of working environment for young women.*

"With a Light Heart"

The factory bell is ringing. It's time to get up! You don't want to be late for your first day of work!

Getting ready for your new job in Lowell, Massachusetts, in 1831, you are so excited it's hard to believe you didn't awake at the crack of dawn. After all, the idea of working in a textile mill seems very glamorous. Perhaps you agree with Lucy Larcom, who wrote that she arrived for her first day of work "with a light heart."

There is good reason to have high hopes and few worries. The work isn't hard, even though the workdays are 12 hours long. As a new worker, your job is to change the bobbins on the spinning-frames every 45 minutes. That leaves time to laugh and tell stories with the friends you will make with other "Lowell girls." Most of the girls, like you, are in their teens or early twenties. You all enjoy being away from home, learning to be more independent and earning money.

You feel very lucky to be a Lowell girl in 1831. You can thank Francis Cabot Lowell for that. It was his idea to create a good working environment for young women. He had seen dirty mill cities in Great Britain, and he wanted to build something much better for American workers.

Lowell died in 1817, but his grand plan was carried out by others. In the 1820s they built six mills along the Merrimack River in Massachusetts, in a city they named after Lowell. They planted trees and shrubs and built boarding houses. Visitors compared the town to a college campus.

The Good Life

Most Lowell girls are like you, from a small New England farm. According to Mr. Lowell's plan, you will work in the mills, save some money, and then move on to get married and raise a family.

These few years, however, are well spent. You live in a clean room, under the watchful eye of an older woman who makes sure you don't get into any trouble. Your new friends tell you that she will probably get on your nerves with her watchfulness. The pay is good—$3 a week. That's more than you

> LOWELL OFFERING
> December, 1845.
>
> A REPOSITORY
> OF ORIGINAL ARTICLES, WRITTEN BY
> "FACTORY GIRLS."
>
> LOWELL: MISSES CURTIS & FARLEY.
> Boston: JORDAN & WILEY, 121
> Washington street.
> 1846.

▲ Lowell girls carried lunch in tin boxes like this. They read the *Lowell Offering* in their spare time.

▲ Lowell girls at work

SHOW WHAT YOU KNOW!

REFOCUS
COMPREHENSION

1. What was Francis Cabot Lowell's plan for his mills?

2. How did life change for the Lowell girls between the 1820s and 1840s?

THINK ABOUT IT
CRITICAL THINKING

About one in four Lowell workers were young men. Why, do you think, were there so few Lowell boys?

WRITE ABOUT IT
ACTIVITY

Write a story about a day in the life of a Lowell girl in the 1820s and 1830s.

might make teaching, cleaning house, or working on a farm. You also attend lectures, join a sewing circle, and go to church every Sunday. You even have time to read the magazine *Lowell Offering*, published for Lowell girls.

Time Brings Change

The Lowell plan works beautifully—for a few years. But the generous treatment of the Lowell girls comes with a price. The Lowell mills need to compete with other mills, so the owners have to cut costs. That means cutting wages. It also means getting more out of each worker. In the mid-1830s, you and other girls **strike** for better wages, but the strike is not very successful. By 1840 the mill owners

have turned up the speed of the machines. Workers like you have to change the bobbins more often and tend to more machines.

In a period of about 20 or 30 years, the Lowell mills go through a number of changes. The workday is harder and longer—for some, it is 14 hours. Lowell girls now have less free time for lectures and such. In time, many of them will quit. The mill owners will hire new workers to replace them. The replacements probably won't come from New England farms, as the early Lowell girls did. At about this time, many people were coming to America from Ireland. They had left their homeland because of a **famine**. Many of the jobs in the Lowell mills will be filled by young Irish workers.

---

 strike To refuse to work until certain demands, such as higher wages or better working conditions, are met

 famine A time when there is not enough food for everyone

233

SUMMING UP

1 DO YOU REMEMBER . . .
COMPREHENSION

1. Why did Thomas Jefferson say, "We are all Republicans—we are all Federalists"?

2. How did the United States acquire the Louisiana Territory and Florida?

3. Why didn't Jefferson's embargo work?

4. Why did the North and the South feel differently about tariffs in the early 1800s?

5. What was the purpose of the Lewis and Clark expedition?

6. What was the Trail of Tears?

7. How did the inventions of Robert Fulton and Peter Cooper improve transportation in the United States?

8. How did the idea of interchangeable parts change American industry?

9. How did the rise of factories affect education in the United States?

10. What kind of working environment did Francis Cabot Lowell want to create?

2 SKILL POWER
PREPARING FOR AN ORAL REPORT

In this chapter you learned how to give an oral report. Use what you learned to report on any topic in the chapter that interests you. Some possible topics are

Louisiana Purchase	Erie Canal
Trail of Tears	telegraph
Missouri Compromise	War of 1812

Use details in the chapter as well as in other sources to prepare your report.

3 WHAT DO YOU THINK?
CRITICAL THINKING

1. Why did the British provoke the United States into war in 1812?

2. Why was Sacajawea so important to Lewis and Clark's Corps of Discovery?

3. What do you see in the painting on page 225 that shows how the Cherokees adapted to living like white Americans? What do you think the painting cannot show about the Trail of Tears?

4. Which do you think had a greater impact on most Americans' everyday lives—faster transportation, with canals and railroads, or faster communication, with the telegraph?

5. What do you think were some negative effects that the rise of mass production had on workers' lives?

4 SAY IT, WRITE IT, USE IT
VOCABULARY

The title of this chapter is "Growth and Conflict." Choose six of the vocabulary words below and tell what they mean. Explain how these terms show America's emergence as a major nation.

assimilate	literate
corps	Louisiana Purchase
embargo	market
famine	mass production
Industrial Revolution	Missouri Compromise
interchangeable parts	strike
internal improvement	territory
interpreter	Trail of Tears

5 GEOGRAPHY AND YOU
MAP STUDY

Use the map on page 214 to answer these questions.

1. What mountain range is located in the Louisiana Purchase?

2. What river did Lewis and Clark mainly travel on before they reached the Rocky Mountains?

3. What two territories did Lewis and Clark explore?

4. Name another expedition that explored the Louisiana Territory.

6 TAKE ACTION
CITIZENSHIP

The rise of mass production and mills in the 1840s created a need for better-educated workers. Today's workers require even more specialized skills. What type of education will you need to become a productive citizen and worker?

With a group of classmates, list some typical occupations in your community. Talk with adults or do library research to find out about the skills and education needed for each career. Show what you find out on a chart called "Getting Ready for a Career."

7 GET CREATIVE
SCIENCE CONNECTION

Find out more about one of the inventions or developments that helped America grow—the steamboat, the telegraph, the cotton gin, the canal, the locomotive. What scientific and technical problems did the inventor or builder have to solve to make the invention work? Draw a diagram or sketch that shows the main parts of the invention and how it worked.

LOOKING AHEAD
In Chapter 11 learn about some of the differences between sections of the United States in the mid-1800s.

SURVEY

SECTIONALISM

With the acquisition of Mexican territory and the Oregon Country, the United States exhibited its "manifest destiny" by 1860. But the institution of slavery was raised as an issue every time the nation expanded.

CONTENTS

▼ What did settlers bring with them as they moved west? Find out on page 247.

AND EXPANSION

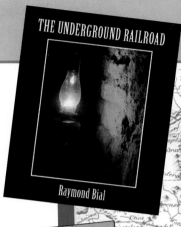

These books tell about people and places during the time that the United States expanded westward and had to address the issue of slavery. Read one that interests you and fill out a book-review form.

READ AND RESEARCH

The Underground Railroad by Raymond Bial
(Houghton Mifflin Co., 1995)
This book contains inspirational stories of men and women who risked their lives to help thousands of slaves find freedom. You will see photos of houses that were used to hide slaves on their dangerous journey. *(nonfiction)*

Dear Levi: Letters From the Overland Trail by Elvira Woodruff, illustrated by Beth Peck (Alfred A. Knopf, 1994)
Read the letters that 12-year-old Austin writes to his brother Levi as Austin travels west in his covered wagon to find his father's claim to gold in Oregon. *(historical fiction)*

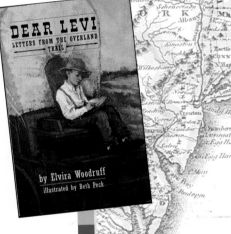

Remember the Ladies: The First Women's Rights Convention by Norma Johnston (Scholastic, 1995)
Just one hundred years ago, women were without any political power. They could not even vote. Read about several women who were determined to find ways to change the laws that restricted their rights. *(nonfiction)*

Sojourner Truth: Ain't I a Woman?
by Patricia and Fredrick McKissack (Scholastic, 1992)
Meet an amazing woman who was born into slavery but emerged as a strong and eloquent voice for the abolition movement and for women's rights. *(biography)*

SKILL POWER

Reading a Political Cartoon

Knowing how to interpret a political cartoon will help you understand different points of view on issues.

▲ A political cartoon of President Jackson

UNDERSTAND IT

Political cartoons have always been popular in the United States. In a clever, humorous way, a political cartoon presents one side, or point of view, of an issue.

For example, do you know that you have an Uncle Sam? Uncle Sam often shows up in political cartoons. He's a symbol of our country. If he is shown wearing worn-out clothes and with empty pockets, the person drawing the cartoon is probably saying our country has money problems. If Uncle Sam is polishing a gun, the cartoonist is showing readers that our country is preparing for war.

What is happening to Uncle Sam in this cartoon? ▶

EXPLORE IT

To appreciate a political cartoon, you need to know something about the issue or subject. Back in 1832, for example, Andrew Jackson was reelected President in spite of differences in how Americans viewed him and the presidency. Was Jackson really a "man of the people," or was he more like a king, forcing his own views on America?

This cartoon poked fun at President Jackson, who is pictured here as a king who holds no regard for the Constitution or the interests of Americans. Notice how each part of the cartoon stands for something. His clothes are typical of clothes worn by kings of the day. (Note the throne in the background.) In one hand, he holds a paper marked "veto," the strongest power a United States President has. One of the papers he is standing on is the United States Constitution. The other papers under his feet mention the U.S. banking system and improvements to roads and canals.

The caption of a political cartoon sums up a cartoonist's point of view in words. Write a caption that expresses this cartoonist's point of view.

TRY IT

In a newspaper or magazine, find a political cartoon about an issue that interests you. Discuss the cartoon with your parents, friends, or teacher to make sure you understand it. Then, in a paragraph, explain the issue and the cartoonist's point of view. Tape the cartoon and your explanation to chart paper. Draw arrows to the symbols in the cartoon and write what they stand for.

You may instead want to draw an original political cartoon. If so, pick a topic from current events, or choose a school situation or problem. Decide what symbols you will use to state your point of view. Remember: a good political cartoon makes its point without any extra explanation.

SKILL POWER SEARCH *Look for another political cartoon in this chapter. Can you determine the issue being illustrated and the cartoonist's point of view?*

KEY TERMS

Tejano
Manifest Destiny
annex
abolitionist
Fugitive Slave Law
Republican party

THE ROAD TO WAR

FOCUS *America's expansion westward during the early and mid-1800s provided new and exciting opportunities for millions of Americans. It also emphasized slavery as the issue that divided Americans, no matter where they settled.*

New Frontiers

In the first half of the 1800s, as you learned in the last chapter, Americans could not be stopped from moving to western parts of the continent. As a result, 15 new states joined the Union between 1803 and 1850. Vast new territories came under American rule.

By 1850 the nation stretched from the Atlantic to the Pacific. The map on this page shows this growth. The wide-open areas between the two oceans lured many people. Some saw this new frontier as a place to start new businesses or to own farms of their own. Others saw the frontier as a place to set up new plantations with their slaves.

The United States grew in other ways as well. A steady flow of immigrants, mostly German and Irish, arrived on the nation's Atlantic shores. Between 1790 and 1860, over 5 million people immigrated from Europe. At first they settled in the cities of the East. Then they joined other Americans in the move west.

Americans in Texas

In 1821, Mexico won its independence from Spain. Texas was a Mexican territory. Since very few people lived in Texas, the Mexicans invited Americans to settle there. Mexico sold huge tracts of land for almost nothing. In return, an American had to adopt the Roman Catholic

EXPANSION OF THE UNITED STATES
— Present-day boundaries

1836
The Battle of
the Alamo

1850
Compromise
of 1850

1852
*Uncle Tom's
Cabin* published

1854
Kansas-
Nebraska Act

1857
Dred
Scott decision

1835   1840   1845   1850   1855   1860

religion, learn Spanish, and become a Mexican citizen. In the early 1820s, Stephen F. Austin led 300 American families to eastern Texas.

By 1835, over 35,000 Americans were living in Texas. But they hung on to their old customs. Most did not learn Spanish, and they did not adopt the Catholic religion. Although they did become Mexican citizens, most resented Mexican customs and laws.

Many of the settlers were from the American South and were slaveholders. In 1829, Mexico outlawed slavery, increasing tension on both the American and Mexican sides. In 1835, fighting broke out.

"Remember the Alamo!"

The Mexican dictator General Antonio López de Santa Anna thought that Texas settlers should be proud Mexican citizens. So he tried to crush the American presence in Texas. At the Battle of the Alamo, he and more than 4,000 men attacked some 180 Texans and **Tejanos** (te HAH nohz). The Texans and Tejanos held on to their fort, the Alamo, for 13 days. But on March 6, 1836, the

Mexicans scaled the fort's walls and killed its defenders, including Davy Crockett and Jim Bowie.

The Mexicans had won the battle, but the Texans had gained momentum. Under the leadership of Sam Houston, and with the rallying cry "Remember the Alamo!" more Americans in Texas moved against Santa Anna. On April 21, 1836, Houston's men crushed the Mexican army at the battle of San Jacinto (juh SIHN toh). Santa Anna was captured. He was forced to grant what the Texas settlers had come to want: the independent Republic of Texas, the "Lone Star Republic."

The Alamo today looks much as it did before it was attacked in 1836.

★ **Tejano** A Texan of Mexican descent

State	Date
Vermont	1791
Kentucky	1792
Tennessee	1796
Ohio	1803
Louisiana	1812
Indiana	1816
Mississippi	1817
Illinois	1818
Alabama	1819
Maine	1820
Missouri	1821
Arkansas	1836
Michigan	1837
Florida	1845
Texas	1845
Iowa	1846
Wisconsin	1848
California	1850
Minnesota	1858
Oregon	1859

Oregon Country

During the early 1840s many Americans came down with a case of "Oregon fever." They had heard stories of the rich soil, the mild climate, and the natural beauty of what was known as Oregon Country. Oregon Country, as you can see on the map on this page, lay between the Rocky Mountains and the Pacific Ocean. Thousands wanted to load their wagons and follow the trail that missionaries and other early settlers had forged to Oregon.

There was one problem. Great Britain also had a claim to the Oregon Country. Americans wanted the entire area—from the northern California border to the southern tip of Alaska, at north latitude 54°40'. Some of them adopted the saying, "Fifty-four forty or fight." They felt that it was America's **Manifest Destiny** to expand as far as possible.

Clay and Polk

The issue of Oregon played a large role in the election of 1844. The Whig party nominated Henry Clay; the Democrats nominated James K. Polk.

Polk was not as well known to voters, but he was a man who knew

⭐ **Manifest Destiny** The belief that America should expand its territorial limits

just what he wanted. An avid expansionist, he wanted to **annex** the Lone Star Republic and take over the entire Oregon Country. Clay, on the other hand, opposed the annexation of Texas. He also feared war with Great Britain if the United States pushed its claims to Oregon too hard. Campaigning on the slogan "Fifty-four forty or fight," Polk won a close race.

President Polk got what he wanted. The United States annexed Texas in 1845. That led to a war with Mexico, which the United States won. In winning the war, the United States acquired a vast amount of land,

⭐ **annex** To add on or attach

THE OREGON COUNTRY

—— Present-day boundaries

ALASKA (Russia)

CANADA (Great Britain)

OREGON

Vancouver Island

Fort Victoria — Line of 1846 — Line of 1818

PACIFIC OCEAN

COUNTRY

Astoria
Portland — Columbia R. — Fort Walla Walla

UNITED STATES

Willamette R.

OREGON TRAIL

Fort Hall

MEXICO

including present-day California. Meanwhile, Polk avoided war with Great Britain. The two nations agreed to split the Oregon Country along the 49th parallel. Britain would control the area to the north; the United States would acquire the area to the south.

Expansion and Slavery

The issue of slavery had to be dealt with every time America moved to expand. As you have read, most Northerners opposed the spread of slavery into new territories. Southerners, on the other hand, supported the extension of slavery.

By the time Polk was elected, most Americans had an opinion about slavery. Americans took three basic positions on the issue. First, there were those, like John C. Calhoun of South Carolina, who strongly defended slavery. Second, there were those, like Daniel Webster of Massachusetts, who thought slavery was wrong but feared that any talk of abolishing it would divide the Union, another name for the United States. Webster didn't want to see slavery spread into new territories, though.

And third, there were **abolitionists**, who simply wanted to get rid of slavery, period. Two abolitionists were William Lloyd Garrison and Frederick Douglass. Many women were also outspoken supporters of abolition.

▲ A poster advertising a speech to be given by Frederick Douglass and a very early photograph of him

The Compromise of 1850

In 1849 there were 15 slave states and 15 free states in the Union, giving Southern and Northern states a balance of power in Congress. But that year, California asked to be admitted to the Union as a free state. This presented a problem, because the Missouri Compromise did not apply to California or other lands in the far western part of the country. The question that had to be answered was whether California was going to be allowed to enter the Union as a free state and upset the North-South balance of power.

Henry Clay, known as the Great Compromiser, suggested a plan to save the fragile balance. Eventually called the Compromise of 1850, his plan allowed California to be admitted as a free state. This pleased the North. The compromise also outlawed the slave trade (though not slavery itself) in Washington, D.C.

The South was pleased because the compromise called for a very tough **Fugitive Slave Law**. Now Northerners would *have to* return runaway slaves to their owners in the South. Also, the compromise created two new territories, called Utah and New Mexico. The Compromise of 1850 left

---

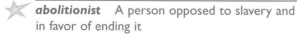

abolitionist   A person opposed to slavery and in favor of ending it

Fugitive Slave Law   A law that made it easier for slaveholders to get runaway slaves returned to them

An early copy of the book that brought attention to slavery

open the future of slavery in these territories, as you can see from the map on the left below.

Uncle Tom's Cabin and Slavery

The issue of slavery, however, didn't go away. The Fugitive Slave Law upset many Northerners. Many felt that it violated a "higher law" ensuring the freedom of all people.

In 1852, Harriet Beecher Stowe added fuel to the fire with her novel *Uncle Tom's Cabin*. It shocked Northern readers, and readers all around the world, by depicting the miserable lives of slaves. The impact of *Uncle Tom's Cabin* is hard to overstate. President Abraham Lincoln met Stowe during the war that would be fought between the North and the South in the 1860s. He supposedly greeted her by saying, "So you're the little woman who wrote the book that made this great war!"

A New Party Forms

Westward expansion also kept the issue of slavery alive. The Kansas-Nebraska Act of 1854 increased tensions. It repealed the Missouri Compromise by declaring that the citizens of the two new territories of Kansas and Nebraska could vote on whether to allow slavery or not. See the map on the right below. Under the Missouri Compromise there was to be *no* slavery in these territories. Now slavery in these lands was *possible*.

The Kansas-Nebraska Act set off firestorms of protest in the North. It led directly to the creation of the **Republican party**. The party's main goal was to fight the extension of slavery. One Republican was a lawyer

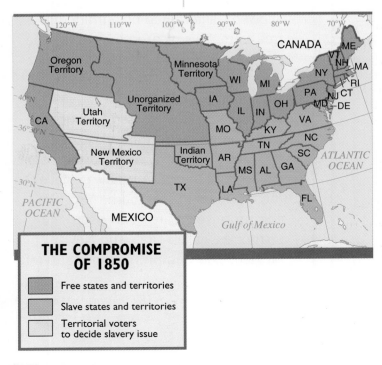

THE COMPROMISE OF 1850

Free states and territories

Slave states and territories

Territorial voters to decide slavery issue

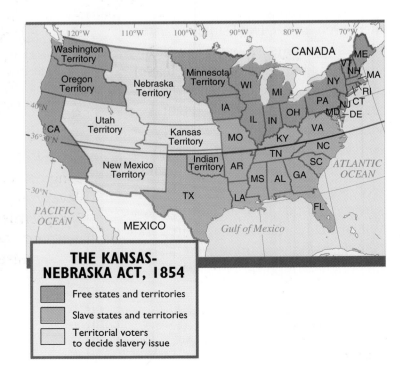

THE KANSAS-NEBRASKA ACT, 1854

Free states and territories

Slave states and territories

Territorial voters to decide slavery issue

These photographs of Douglas and Lincoln, attached by a ribbon, were given away to people who attended their debates in 1858.

from Illinois, Abraham Lincoln. In 1858 he ran for the United States Senate against Senator Stephen A. Douglas, the chief sponsor of the Kansas-Nebraska Act. In debates, Lincoln argued against the extension of slavery. Douglas felt that the issue should be decided by the people in the territories. Douglas won the election, but Lincoln—with his stance on slavery and his speaking skills—would be the Republican party presidential candidate in 1860.

Dred Scott

No More Compromises

Southerners and Northerners rushed to settle Kansas, bringing with them supporters and opponents of slavery. But guns, not ballots, ruled the day. In 1856 a proslavery mob burned the town of Lawrence. John Brown, an abolitionist, led a raid on a proslavery settlement, killing five men. In 1857 the Supreme Court made its Dred Scott decision. Scott, a slave, had moved with his master from Missouri, a slave state, to Illinois, a free state. They later moved back to Missouri. Scott sued for his freedom when his master died because Scott had lived as a free man in the North. The Supreme Court ruled that Dred Scott was still a slave, and that slaves were not citizens. So they had no rights under the law. The decision meant that Congress could not really outlaw slavery anywhere. The Missouri Compromise was therefore meaningless. Any hope for further compromise on the issue of slavery was dead.

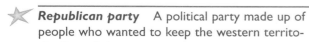

Republican party A political party made up of people who wanted to keep the western territories free of slavery

SHOW WHAT YOU KNOW!

REFOCUS
COMPREHENSION

1. Name two areas that became part of the United States as a result of the "Manifest Destiny" policy.

2. Explain how westward expansion and the slavery issue were connected.

THINK ABOUT IT
CRITICAL THINKING

Why do you think many people did not want to upset the balance of power between free states and slave states?

WRITE ABOUT IT
ACTIVITY

As a journalist for France, you have been asked to compare the three views on slavery common in America in the 1850s. Write a newspaper article comparing them.

2

LIFE ON THE OREGON TRAIL

FOCUS *Traveling the Oregon Trail was often hard and dangerous. But the hope for a better life at the end of the trail inspired people to face the challenge.*

Hopes and Fears

All kinds of thoughts are going through your mind as you get ready to leave all that you know behind. You and your family are headed for the green Willamette Valley in Oregon Country. To get there, you will be taking the **Oregon Trail**.

It is early spring. You and other families from your hometown have gathered at Independence, Missouri, and are meeting the many others who will start on the trail in about a month. You and your father have the chance to talk about your hopes and fears.

First of all, he tells you what to expect from the **terrain** of the trip. The first part, crossing the Great Plains, is relatively easy. You will be following the Platte River, and the land is fairly flat. But beyond the plains you must be ready to cross the Rocky Mountains at South Pass. On the other side of the mountains, the trail follows the Snake River and then the Columbia River, going through desert and scrub land before it takes you to your new home.

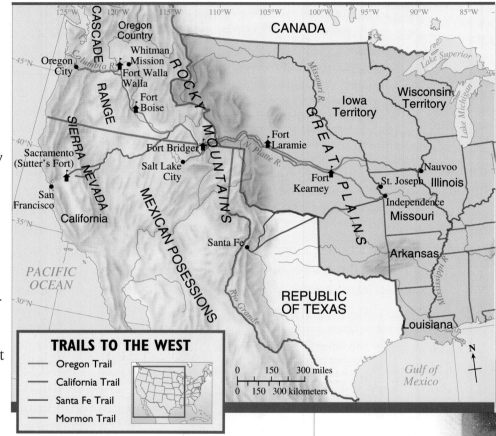

TRAILS TO THE WEST
— Oregon Trail
— California Trail
— Santa Fe Trail
— Mormon Trail

0   150   300 miles
0   150 300 kilometers

You feel sad about leaving your friends behind. On the other hand, you *are* pretty excited. You will see new parts of the country. And you will be going to a place where your family can make a better living. That is the reason your family is moving west.

Oregon Trail   The trail blazed by pioneers who moved from Missouri to Oregon Country
terrain   Land and landforms, including deserts, mountains, and valleys

Traveling the Trail

Packing for the trip hasn't been easy. You need to take almost everything you own. So into the covered wagon go the spinning wheel, the feather beds, and the iron stove. In goes your father's fiddle. You can't head west without cotton shirts, buckskin pants, sunbonnets, and boots. And of course you need guns, a kettle, and plenty of matches. Finally, you need hundreds of pounds of food. Most important are flour, salt, sugar, and bacon. By the time your wagon is fully loaded, it weighs 2,500 pounds!

Life on the trail is hard to get used to, especially in the beginning. Every day you must be up at sunrise. There is much to be done before the wagon train sets off. All day long, for the first month or so, you travel across endless prairie. The oxen move slowly under the heavy loads. On the best days you cover only 20 miles.

Sooner or later some travelers become sick. If your father and mother do, you will have to take over some of their duties. Your father cares for the animals, repairs the wagon, and hunts for food. Your mother cooks, washes, and takes care of the young children.

A New Home

The Rocky Mountain scenery is grand, but rainstorms make the ground soggy. Wagon wheels stick in the mud. Desperate to keep going, your parents drop the iron stove by the side of the trail to make the wagon lighter.

After the Rockies, just as your father said, comes the desert. The wagon train makes some of its slowest progress here. You are upset when you have to leave your bed by the side of the trail. It's hard, but you have to lighten your wagon even more. You begin to make out the green meadows of the Willamette Valley ahead. You're almost to your new home!

Pioneers tried to keep traditions, like eating on a tablecloth, alive on the trek west.

SHOW WHAT YOU KNOW!

REFOCUS
COMPREHENSION

1. What kinds of terrain did the Oregon Trail cover?

2. Why did pioneers need to pack so many items to travel west?

THINK ABOUT IT
CRITICAL THINKING

Why did people cross America on the Oregon Trail, in spite of all its hardships?

WRITE ABOUT IT
ACTIVITY

You are traveling on the Oregon Trail. Write a letter to a friend back home in which you describe life on the trail.

WESTWARD HO!

FOCUS *In the first half of the 1800s, the United States expanded its territory westward. This came largely at the expense of Mexico.*

AUSTIN BRINGS SETTLERS TO TEXAS

Thousands of Americans flocked to Texas beginning in 1821. Their leader, Stephen F. Austin, won a huge land grant from the Mexican government, allowing him to bring 300 American families to the Texas coast. Each family got an allotment of land and paid Austin just 12 1/2 cents per acre. That was quite a bargain, since land in the United States cost $1.25 an acre.

The fertile land of Texas allowed the settlers, mostly from the South, to plant cotton and other crops they already knew how to grow.

TEXAS INDEPENDENCE!

In 1836, Texas became an independent country. It called itself the Lone Star Republic. Texans wrote their own constitution, based on that of the United States. They elected Sam Houston their first president. They also made slavery legal to please settlers who had come from the southern United States.

WHAT ABOUT STATEHOOD?

Sam Houston wanted Texas to be one of the United States. He thought it was the only way to keep Texas protected from Mexico. Not everyone in Texas agreed with him. Some Texans wanted to keep their total independence.

One such person was Mirabeau Buonaparte Lamar (MIHR uh boh BOH-nuh pahrt luh MAHR), the second president of Texas. During his presidency Texans waged war on both Native Americans and Mexicans to expand Texas's influence. Houston, however, won back the presidency in 1841, and peace was restored. His likeness in the 1840s is captured in the painting below.

1821	1836	1841	1845
Stephen Austin settles Texas	Texas becomes an independent republic	Sam Houston wins back "Lone Star Republic" presidency	Texas joins the Union

1820   1822   1824   1836   1838   1840   1842   1844

"EXPANSION, EXPANSION, EXPANSION!"

James K. Polk's campaign message was simple: Expansion! Expansion! Expansion! He wanted to annex Texas. But that would cost him votes in the North. Maybe, he thought, he could get away with this position if he also favored the annexation of Oregon. That would win him support among northern voters.

Polk's plan worked. He won a narrow victory. But even before Polk took office, President John Tyler got Congress to pass a bill to annex Texas. On December 29, 1845, Texas joined the United States. And in 1846 the British backed down from their claim to the Oregon Country by signing the Oregon Treaty. In the treaty, Great Britain gave the United States all the territory west of the Rocky Mountains south of the 49th parallel. Cartoonists enjoyed portraying Britain as a looming bully and America as an underdog fighter.

WAR WITH MEXICO

The Mexicans claimed that the southern boundary of Texas was the Nueces (noo AY-says) River. The Americans said it was the Rio Grande, farther south. President Polk ordered troops to occupy the land between the two rivers. On April 26, 1846, angry Mexicans attacked the American troops and killed or wounded 16.

Congress declared war on Mexico. The Americans easily won the Mexican War (1846–1848). This was the first war in which some officers in the United States Army received medals, like the one on the left. In the Treaty of Guadalupe Hidalgo (GWAHD ul OOP hih-DAHL goh), the Mexicans gave up their claim to Texas. They also sold a vast area of land to the United States for just $15 million. Known as the Mexican Cession, it included California, Nevada, and Utah. It also included most of Arizona and parts of Wyoming, New Mexico, and Colorado.

1846	1846–1848	1847	1853
Oregon Treaty signed	Mexican War	Mormons settle Utah	Gadsden Purchase

| 1846 | 1848 | 1850 | 1852 | 1854 | 1856 |

MORMONS IN UTAH

The Mormons had tried for years to find a place where they could live in peace. Other Americans often found their beliefs strange. Mormons, for example, believed in holding all property in common. They also believed in the right of a husband to have more than one wife.

In July 1847, Brigham Young led the Mormons to the Great Salt Lake in present-day Utah. As Young looked at the dry and empty valley, he said, "This is the place." The hard-working Mormons moved in large groups to Utah and turned the former wasteland into a prosperous community.

GADSDEN PURCHASE

In 1853 another piece of land was added to the United States. This was done with the Gadsden Purchase, named for the minister to Mexico at the time. The United States bought this land from Mexico for $10 million. It was located south of the Gila River and makes up the southern parts of present-day Arizona and New Mexico. The Gadsden Purchase—so named because James Gadsden negotiated the purchase—gave the United States a fairly flat tract of land as a possible route for a transcontinental railroad.

SHOW WHAT YOU KNOW!

REFOCUS
COMPREHENSION

1. Why was Texas so attractive to Stephen Austin and his settlers?

2. Why did the Mormons have difficulty finding a place to settle in?

THINK ABOUT IT
CRITICAL THINKING

How might the United States have been different if the Gadsden Purchase had not been made?

WRITE ABOUT IT
ACTIVITY

Write a report about President James K. Polk. Discuss Polk's contributions to the expansion of the United States.

REFORM AND REFORMERS

Citizenship

★ **KEY TERMS**
common man
temperance

FOCUS *The spirit of reform spread across the nation, starting in the 1820s. This led to reform movements aimed at giving women more rights and ending the institution of slavery.*

The Rise of the Common Man

In the early days of the United States, only white men who owned property could vote. But in the early 1800s, attitudes changed. People wanted a democracy not just *for* the people but *by* the people. By the 1820s almost all adult white males had won the right to vote. These men wanted their voices to be heard on the issues of the day. Thus began "the rise of the **common man**."

Women, too, wanted to be involved in the issues of the day, even though they didn't have the right to vote. One of their targets was alcohol. Women believed men and teenagers drank too much. Those who opposed drinking felt that whiskey, rum, and hard cider made workers unreliable and kept people away from home and church. Women organized groups to promote **temperance**, or drinking less or not at all. These efforts paid off. By the mid-1830s more than a million men had signed pledges to cut down on drinking.

Women found that other issues could benefit from their involvement. In 1843, Dorothea Dix reported to the Massachusetts legislature on the condition of jails and poorhouses. Dix had found that mentally ill people were put "in cages, closets, cellars, stalls, pens!"

At first, people either didn't believe her or they didn't care enough. But Dix wouldn't quit. She got Massachusetts to build a larger state hospital. She spent the next 45 years working to get other states to build hospitals for the mentally ill.

Women's Rights

Women also fought for their own rights. In 1848, Lucretia Mott, Elizabeth Cady Stanton, and other women called for a meeting on women's rights. It was held in Seneca Falls, New York. Several hundred women attended. Stanton stirred the crowd when she read a declaration modeled on the Declaration of Independence. She announced, "We hold these truths to be self-evident: all men *and women* are created equal."

A pledge that would be signed by a man who promised to moderate his drinking

★ **common man** The "average" American citizen, whose concerns are represented in government
temperance Moderation in drinking alcohol or total abstinence from drinking alcohol

Elizabeth Cady Stanton addressing women at Seneca Falls ▶

For the rest of their lives, Stanton and Mott fought for women's rights. They were later joined by Susan B. Anthony, who fought to get women the right to vote. She and others saw some success in women's rights on the state level. But it would be a long time before women would win the rights they demanded.

The Abolitionists

Some Americans had always considered slavery wrong. As you have read, some settlers opposed it as far back as the 1600s. But for the most part, northerners hoped that slavery would just fade away—or they refused to think about it at all.

That started to change in the 1820s. Because of the cotton gin, it was clear that slavery wasn't going to just fade away. People who opposed slavery realized that they would have to speak out.

One leading abolitionist was William Lloyd Garrison. A deeply religious man, Garrison thought slavery was a sin in the eyes of God. Garrison started a newspaper called *The Liberator*. In article after article he pounded away at the cruelty of slavery.

Speaking Out Against Slavery

Garrison upset many people. They thought he was a troublemaker. But he was not a man to back down, even in the face of death threats. "I am in earnest," Garrison wrote. "I will not equivocate [compromise]—I will not excuse—I will not retreat a single inch—AND I WILL BE HEARD!" Garrison *was* heard. He caused many Americans to think for the first time about the true injustice of slavery.

Free African Americans had long spoken out against slavery. In 1827 the first black newspaper, *Freedom's Journal,*

◀ Susan B. Anthony

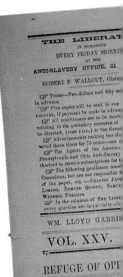

THE LIBERAT

IS PUBLISHED
EVERY FRIDAY MORNI
AT THE
ANTI-SLAVERY OFFICE, 21

ROBERT F. WALLCUT, GENE

WM. LLOYD GARRI

VOL. XXV.

REFUGE OF OPI

took up the fight. But it was Frederick Douglass who really moved people. A fugitive slave from Maryland who lived in Rochester, New York, Douglass spoke and wrote eloquently about the evils of slavery. His first-hand knowledge made him one of the most popular speakers in the country. Like Garrison, Douglass published an antislavery newspaper. It was called *The North Star*.

The Movement Grows

As time went by, more and more people joined the abolition movement. Women joined in large numbers. More than half the members of Garrison's American Anti-Slavery Society were women.

Among them were two sisters named Sarah and Angelina Grimké, who had grown up on a South Carolina plantation. They had lived with slavery, and they hated it. They felt so strongly about it that they left the South. In the 1830s they began to give talks against slavery in northern cities and towns. The sisters angered many men, who booed and hissed when the sisters spoke. The men were not so much bothered that the Grimkés were speaking out against slavery. It was considered improper for women to speak out in public.

The Grimké sisters, however, kept lecturing and writing. In 1837, Sarah Grimké wrote that "men and women were created equal" and that "whatever is right for man to do, is *right* for woman."

Abby Kelly felt the same way. She traveled the nation, speaking out against slavery while her husband stayed home and cared for their daughter. In trying to free the slaves, Kelly said, women found out how much work they had to do to free themselves.

SHOW WHAT YOU KNOW!

REFOCUS
COMPREHENSION

1. What were the major reform movements of this period?

2. List some reformers and the causes they supported.

THINK ABOUT IT
CRITICAL THINKING

What kind of risks did the abolitionists face?

WRITE ABOUT IT
ACTIVITY

Lay out your own anti-slavery newspaper. What features would it include? Who would be its guest columnists?

▼ An issue of *The Liberator*

ENSLAVED AND FREE

FOCUS *The story of slavery was a sad chapter in American history. Yet, despite the cruel nature of this institution, enslaved people maintained their dignity as well as their desire to be free.*

The Work of Slaves

While white people debated what to do about slavery, 4 million African Americans were enslaved. For them, slavery was not just an issue to be debated by white Americans and freed black people; it was their life.

Enslaved African Americans had to do anything and everything their masters told them to do. They were made to work as lumberjacks in the Carolina forests. They were sent into the gold, coal, and salt mines of Virginia and Kentucky. They could be found working as wagon drivers in Georgia and Louisiana. From time to time, slaves were also given jobs as skilled laborers. They were carpenters, blacksmiths, and silversmiths.

Most slaves, however, worked on farms and plantations. They often spent 14 hours a day—or more—working in the fields. But it wasn't just the number of hours that made field work so brutal. It was the nature of the work.

Slaves labored in sun that was

▼ Enslaved brothers, in a photo taken in the 1850s

sweltering, in heat that was unbearable. In cotton fields, slaves had to stoop over to pick balls of cotton. It was just as bad on sugar plantations. Slaves there had to dig drainage ditches across snake-filled land. The sugar cane was hard to cut and heavy to carry. In some ways, rice workers had the worst conditions of all. Since rice grows in water, slaves spent long hours standing in water up to their knees.

A Grim Life for Slaves

Slaves who worked as house servants also suffered their share of misery. While both men and women were field hands, most of the indoor workers were women. They didn't suffer in the sun. Nor did they have to spend all day bending and lifting. But they faced different problems. They could be commanded to work at any time, day or night. Because they came into such close contact with white people, they endured constant criticism. They were sometimes insulted—or even beaten—by their masters.

Without question, a slave's life was grim. Yet every slave was expected to turn a cheerful face to his or her master, who did not want angry or sullen slaves. Any sign of unhappiness was taken as a sign of independence. And that was not allowed. Masters punished any slave who showed dissatisfaction. Slaves learned to approach their masters in a humble way. They learned to appear happy, even when they were miserable.

Free African Americans

Many free black people lived in both the North and the South. Some had been freed when Northern states passed laws against slavery. Some had escaped from plantations and had made their way to free states. Others had been freed by their owners. Still others had managed to buy their freedom. They had a different kind of struggle to face, yet they also suffered many of the same hardships as enslaved African Americans.

They might have been free, but their lives weren't easy. Wherever they went, they faced **discrimination**, or unfair

treatment because of their skin color. All across the North, they ran into limits on their freedom. In most states they did not enjoy the same voting rights as white people. In several states they were not allowed to own land. And

◀ Slaves as well as free African Americans did backbreaking work under the hot sun.

AFRICAN AMERICANS IN THE SOUTH, 1820 AND 1860

	Enslaved African Americans		Free African Americans	
	1820	1860	1820	1860
Alabama	41,879	435,080	571	2,690
Arkansas	1,617	111,115	59	144
Delaware	4,509	1,798	12,958	19,829
Florida		61,745		932
Georgia	149,654	462,198	1,763	3,500
Kentucky	126,732	225,483	2,759	10,684
Louisiana	69,064	331,726	10,476	18,647
Maryland	107,397	87,189	39,730	83,942
Mississippi	32,814	436,631	458	773
Missouri	10,222	114,931	347	3,572
North Carolina	205,017	331,059	14,612	30,463
South Carolina	258,475	402,406	6,826	9,914
Tennessee	80,107	275,719	2,727	7,300
Texas		182,566		355
Virginia	425,153	490,865	36,889	58,042

★ **discrimination** Action or policies against a minority group

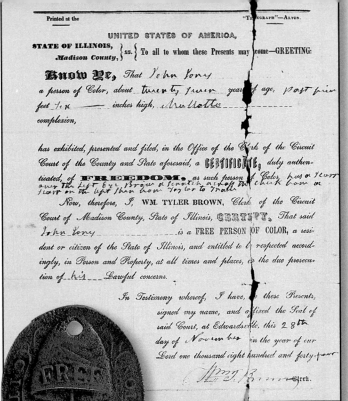

wherever they went, free African Americans were banned from white hotels, theaters, and churches.

Finding work was not easy. New England mills wanted nothing to do with free African Americans. Factories and stores wouldn't hire black males, except as janitors and handymen. African American women could work as servants and cooks. But these jobs paid very little.

Sojourner Truth was an outspoken freed slave who traveled to cities in the North, speaking out for the rights of African Americans. She was also a supporter of women's rights. Although she could neither read nor write, she gave speeches that spellbound every member of her audience.

It was much worse in the South. Here African Americans who had been freed or who had bought their freedom lived almost like slaves. They were living in a society that suspected any "free" black person to be a runaway, so their **certificates of freedom** were very important. Only a few jobs were open to them. Laws prevented them from being taught to read and write. Although many free black people lived in poverty, some became successful despite discrimination.

At the Mercy of the Owner

Slaves longed for freedom. They knew of and had heard stories of slaves who had escaped from their masters or bought their freedom. But for most slaves, freedom was a far-off dream.

Laws were designed to protect masters, not slaves. So owners were free to overwork their slaves. They could separate slave mothers and children by selling them to different plantations. They could feed slaves a diet lacking in meat, milk, and fresh vegetables. Finally, owners could punish their slaves almost any way they wanted to. Whippings, in front of family and friends,

This slave had to wear bells so that her master could track her movements.

▲ Two ways African Americans "proved" they were free: the certificate of freedom, and a badge, worn around the neck

---

certificate of freedom Paperwork that proved that a slave had been freed or had bought his or her freedom

Harriet Tubman

were a humiliating but common form of punishment. In a system that upheld the right of masters to treat their slaves inhumanely, it is surprising that slaves survived at all.

Slaves Revolt

Some slaves did more than survive. They fought back. In the early 1800s some planned revolts. The most famous was Nat Turner's Rebellion in 1831. Turner and fellow slaves in Virginia killed about 60 slaveholders before being captured and killed. After that, slaves were watched closely. Although it was hard for them to organize revolts, individual slaves fought for better treatment by destroying crops, breaking tools, and setting fires. Their actions showed that many would risk death rather than continue living in slavery.

Other slaves tried to escape to the North. If they made it, they could start new lives as free persons. But if they were caught and returned to their masters, they faced terrible punishments. They might have bones in their feet broken or be severely whipped. Despite the risks, slaves kept escaping. The **Underground Railroad** was organized to help them escape.

The Underground Railroad

The Underground Railroad was run by free black people and abolitionists. They created a series of "stations," or places where runaway slaves could hide on their way north. Called **conductors**, freed slaves led groups of runaways from one station to the next. It was risky. Yet they kept at it. One of the most remarkable Underground Railroad conductors was Harriet Tubman.

Tubman was born into slavery around 1820. In 1849 she escaped to freedom. In describing her decision, she later said, "There was one of two things I had a *right* to, liberty (freedom) or death; if I could not have one, I would have the other."

Tubman reached freedom by way of the Underground Railroad. After making it to safety, she became a conductor. Again and again, she risked her life, conducting at least 19 trips from the South. She helped more than 300 people escape from slavery. Not one of her "passengers" was ever caught.

 Underground Railroad A system set up by opponents of slavery to help slaves flee from the South to the North

conductor A person who helped runaway slaves to hide and escape

SHOW WHAT YOU KNOW!

REFOCUS
COMPREHENSION

1. Which freed slave spoke out in the North against slavery?

2. What was Nat Turner's Rebellion?

THINK ABOUT IT
CRITICAL THINKING

How was the Underground Railroad like a real railroad? What made it different?

WRITE ABOUT IT
ACTIVITY

If you were a conductor on the Underground Railroad, how would you lead slaves to freedom?

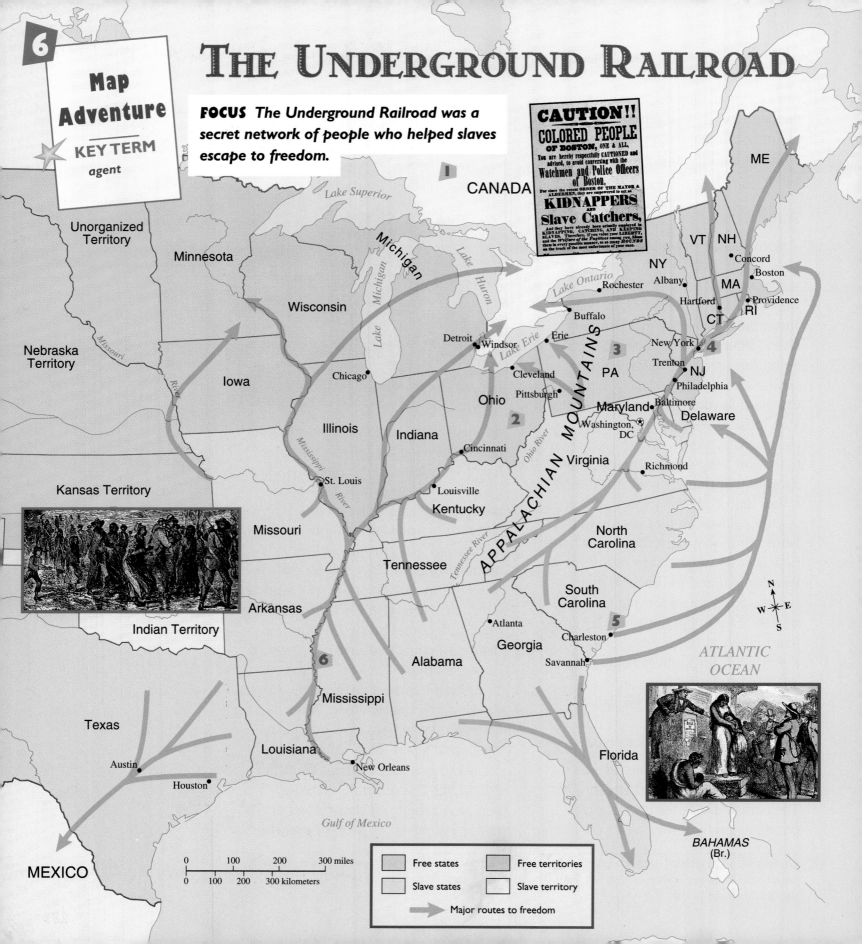

THE UNDERGROUND RAILROAD

6

Map Adventure

★ KEY TERM

agent

FOCUS The Underground Railroad was a secret network of people who helped slaves escape to freedom.

CAUTION!!
COLORED PEOPLE
OF BOSTON, ONE & ALL,
You are hereby respectfully CAUTIONED and advised, to avoid conversing with the
Watchmen and Police Officers of Boston,
For since the recent ORDER OF THE MAYOR & ALDERMEN, they are empowered to act as
KIDNAPPERS
AND
Slave Catchers,
And they have already been actually employed in KIDNAPPING, CATCHING, AND KEEPING SLAVES. Therefore, if you value your LIBERTY, and the Welfare of the Fugitives among you, Shun them in every possible manner, as so many HOUNDS on the track of the most unfortunate of your race.

CANADA

Unorganized Territory

Minnesota

Lake Superior

Michigan

Wisconsin

Lake Michigan

Lake Huron

1

ME

VT NH

NY

Concord
Boston

Albany

MA

Rochester

Lake Ontario

Hartford

Providence

CT   RI

Buffalo

Nebraska Territory

Iowa

Chicago

Detroit Windsor

Lake Erie

Erie

3

New York

4

Cleveland

PA

Trenton

NJ

Pittsburgh

Philadelphia

Ohio

Maryland

Baltimore

2

Delaware

Illinois

Indiana

Washington, DC

Kansas Territory

Cincinnati

Ohio River

Virginia

Richmond

Mississippi River

St. Louis

Louisville

Missouri

Kentucky

APPALACHIAN MOUNTAINS

North Carolina

Tennessee River

Tennessee

Arkansas

Atlanta

South Carolina

Indian Territory

Georgia

Charleston

5

6

Alabama

Savannah

ATLANTIC OCEAN

Texas

Mississippi

Louisiana

Austin

New Orleans

Houston

Florida

Gulf of Mexico

BAHAMAS (Br.)

MEXICO

| 0 | 100 | 200 | 300 miles |
| 0 | 100 | 200 | 300 kilometers |

N W E S

Free states
Free territories
Slave states
Slave territory
Major routes to freedom

Adventure on the Run!

After 1850, slaves who had run away from their masters were no longer free in the North. Only Canada, Mexico, and the Bahamas were truly safe for escaped slaves. Thousands of people secretly hid runaways in attics, under floors, in haystacks, and even in secret rooms while slave hunters and **agents** combed the docks, streets, and woods of the North. Conductors risked their lives to hide and guide slaves along the way.

Map Legend

1 Canada Slavery was illegal in Canada, and runaways were free once they crossed the border. Here, former slaves could vote and own property.

2 Ohio Most escaping slaves passed through Ohio because it was close to the slave states and to freedom in Canada. Slaves followed the North Star to cross the Ohio River and headed north for Lake Erie and Canada. Many brave people in Ohio gave the runaways shelter, food, and clothes.

3 Pennsylvania Bordering three slave states, Pennsylvania had many conductors in its Quaker community. Quakers did not believe in slavery and began helping runaway slaves soon after the United States won its independence.

4 New York City Slave hunters searched the streets of this city while runaways were sheltered by New York's large free African American community. From here, most runaways continued north, but some outsmarted the slave hunters and became conductors in the city.

5 Charleston Slave hunters patrolled Charleston's piers looking for runaways. But many ship captains hid the runaways and sailed to Philadelphia, New York, and Boston. In these cities, runaways could find food, shelter, and help in reaching Canada.

6 Mississippi River For slaves in the deep South, the Mississippi was a main route of escape. Hiding on steamboats or rowing upriver in canoes, runaways would not leave a trail as they floated toward Illinois, Indiana, and Ohio.

⭐ *agent* A person who acts for or represents another

MAP IT

You are a conductor on the Underground Railroad. You are planning routes to help slaves escape to freedom.
1. *If you were to lead escaping slaves from Georgia to Canada by way of Buffalo, New York, what slave states would you pass through?*
2. *If you were headed from Arkansas to Windsor, Canada, by way of Indiana and Ohio, what cities would you pass through?*
3. *What river would you follow to get from Louisiana to Minnesota?*
4. *You plan to go from Charleston, South Carolina to New England by water. What city in Massachusetts is your destination?*
5. *You want to help some slaves in Florida escape to freedom. You decide the trip to Canada would take too long. What is the closest place that you could lead slaves to freedom?*

EXPLORE IT

You have just escaped to freedom in Canada. Write a description of the route you took. Include some experiences you had on the Underground Railroad.

SUMMING UP

1 DO YOU REMEMBER . . .
COMPREHENSION

1. How was the issue of slavery related to the expansion of the United States?

2. Describe the three major positions on slavery taken by Americans in the 1800s.

3. What were some of the hardships faced by travelers along the Oregon Trail?

4. Why did the United States and Mexico go to war in the 1840s?

5. What land areas were added to the United States as a result of the Mexican Cession?

6. What were some of the issues that women reformers spoke out about?

7. Who was Frederick Douglass and why did so many people listen to him speak?

8. Describe some of the conditions that slaves on farms and plantations worked under.

9. What were some of the hardships faced by freed black Americans in the northern states?

10. Name three places outside the United States to which slaves escaped.

2 SKILL POWER
READING A POLITICAL CARTOON

In this chapter you saw that political cartoons can be used to express how people feel about issues. Look at political cartoons in your local paper or in a magazine. What do they tell you about the views of the cartoonist?

3 WHAT DO YOU THINK?
CRITICAL THINKING

1. How did the Dred Scott decision drive the nation further apart on the issue of slavery?

2. You and your family are moving to a part of the country you have never seen before. Write about how you feel.

3. Why did so many women become active abolitionists?

4. What effect do you think the abolitionists had on people's attitudes toward slavery?

5. How do you think slaveholders in America felt about Canada in the 1800s? Why?

CHAPTER 11

4 SAY IT, WRITE IT, USE IT
VOCABULARY

Suppose that you were with a group of fugitive slaves who risked their lives to reach freedom in the North. Write about your experience, describing the journey and the life you found in the North. Use as many vocabulary words as you can.

abolitionist
agent
annex
certificate of freedom
common man
conductor
discrimination
Fugitive Slave Law

Manifest Destiny
Oregon Trail
Republican party
Tejano
temperance
terrain
Underground Railroad

5 GEOGRAPHY AND YOU
MAP STUDY

Use the map on page 240 and the Atlas map on page 590 to answer these questions.

1. What present-day states made up the Mexican Cession?

2. What is the only territory shown on the map that does not touch a body of water?

3. What states besides Texas had land included in the Texas Annexation?

4. Which cessions or purchases touch the Pacific Ocean?

6 TAKE ACTION
CITIZENSHIP

Just like the reformers in the 1800s, there are people in your own community who think things should be changed. How do you think your community could be improved? Here are a few issues to think about: How well do different groups of people get along together? Are the parks and schools in good condition?

Is public transportation convenient and efficient? Choose an issue that you feel strongly about and talk to others about your ideas. By talking to people about community problems, you might figure out ways to do something about them.

7 GET CREATIVE
MATH CONNECTION

Portland, Oregon
500 miles

The journey along the Oregon Trail was long and hard. What would a trip from Missouri to the West Coast be like today? Using a road map, plan a car trip from Independence, Missouri, to Portland, Oregon. Choose the highways you would take. If you drove an average of 55 miles per hour, how many miles could you cover each day? How many days would the entire trip take?

LOOKING AHEAD

In the next chapter, you will find out how the United States went from a divided country to Civil War.

The War Between

The North took up arms to preserve the Union; the South, to preserve its way of life. The War Between the States, or Civil War, was long and bloody, and Reconstruction did little to bring the nation back together.

CONTENTS

▼ Who used the items this girl is holding? Turn to pages 274–275 to find out.

The States

These books tell about some people, places, and important events during the time of the Civil War. Read one that interests you and fill out a book-review form.

READ AND RESEARCH

Lincoln: A Photobiography by Russell Freedman
(Houghton Mifflin Co., 1987)
While reading the life of this great President, let the photographs help you picture the important events in our nation's history, especially the five years of the Civil War. *(biography)*
• *You can read a selection from this book on page 278.*

Clara Barton: Healing the Wounds
by Cathy East Dubowski (Silver Burdett Press, 1991)
Clara Barton, an army nurse during the Civil War, eased the suffering of many soldiers. Read about her courageous life both on and off the battlefield. *(biography)*

The Emancipation Proclamation: Why Lincoln Really Freed the Slaves by Robert Young (Silver Burdett Press, 1994)
Learn about the events leading up to Lincoln's famous Emancipation Proclamation. Then decide for yourself whether you think he issued the proclamation because of the evils of slavery or because he wanted the war to end and the Union to be preserved. *(nonfiction)*

Shades of Gray by Carolyn Reeder (Avon Books, 1991)
Will lost his entire family because of the Civil War. Now he must live with his Uncle Jed, a coward who refused to fight for the Confederacy. Can Will respect a man who would not defend his own Southern home? *(historical fiction)*

Skill Power

Analyzing a Document

Knowing how to analyze historical documents helps you understand the events of the past.

UNDERSTAND IT

The date is February 22, 1861. Newly-elected President Abraham Lincoln visits Independence Hall in Philadelphia. As he addresses the crowd, there is a question on everyone's mind. Will the nation soon be torn apart by a war?

Parts of Lincoln's speech are shown on this page. A speech is a kind of document. Documents take many forms. They can be speeches, letters, or even legal documents, like laws or treaties.

Documents provide firsthand accounts of events and show how people were thinking and feeling at a certain time.

EXPLORE IT

When you read the first part of a document, decide what the topic is. In this speech, for example, Lincoln stresses the importance of the Declaration of Independence.

As you continue to read, look for the main ideas of the document. In which part does Lincoln remind his listeners of the declaration's promise of equal freedom for all?

Each part of a document introduces new ideas. What idea does Lincoln express in part 3?

[1] . . . I have never had a feeling, politically, that did not spring from . . . the Declaration of Independence . . . I have often inquired of myself what great principle or idea it was that kept this Confederacy [the United States] so long together . . . .

[2] . . . the Declaration of Independence . . . gave promise that in due time the weights would be lifted from the shoulders of all men, and that all should have an equal chance . . . .

[3] . . . there is no need of bloodshed and war. There is no necessity for it. I am not in favor of such a course . . . .

THE GETTYSBURG ADDRESS

Four score and seven years ago our fathers brought forth, on this continent, a new nation, conceived in liberty, and dedicated to the proposition that "all men are created equal."

Now we are engaged in a great civil war, testing whether that nation, or any nation so conceived, and so dedicated, can long endure. We are met on a great battle field of that war. We have come to dedicate a portion of it, as a final resting place for those who died here that the nation might live. This we may in all propriety [proper behavior] do. But, in a larger sense, we can not dedicate— we can not consecrate—we can not hallow—this ground. The brave men, living and dead, who struggled here, have hallowed it far above our poor power to add or detract. The world will little note, nor long remember, what we say here, but it can never forget what they did here.

It is rather for us, the living, here to be dedicated to the great task remaining before us—that from these honored dead we take increased devotion to that cause for which they gave the last full measure of devotion—that we here highly resolve that these dead shall not have died in vain; that this nation, under God, shall have a new birth of freedom; and that government of the people, by the people, and for the people, shall not perish from the earth.

SKILL POWER SEARCH *Use what you know about analyzing documents to find out more about other historical events.*

The Nation Divides

1 Setting the Scene

KEY TERMS

secede
Confederacy
civil war
defensive war
blockade
Emancipation
Proclamation

FOCUS *All efforts at compromise between the North and the South ended in failure. The issue of slavery was finally settled on the battlefield in the bloodiest conflict in American history.*

Lincoln Is Elected

In November 1860, Abraham Lincoln was elected President. He had no plans to abolish slavery in the South. He had, however, promised that there would be "no slavery in the territories." This upset Southerners. They felt that, as Americans, they had as much right to the western territories as Northerners.

Southerners also believed that slavery in the territories was an issue for the

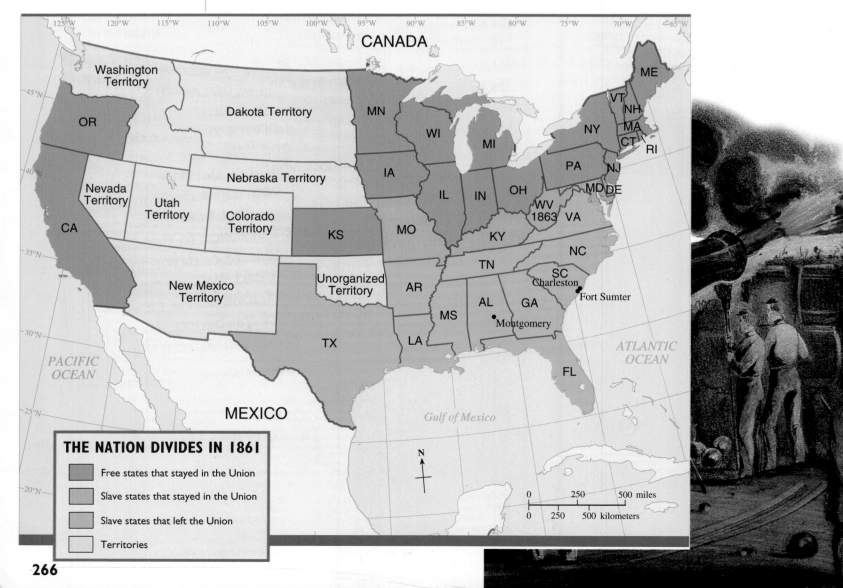

THE NATION DIVIDES IN 1861

- Free states that stayed in the Union
- Slave states that stayed in the Union
- Slave states that left the Union
- Territories

December 1860	February 1861	April 1861	January 1863	November 1863	April 1865
South Carolina secedes	Confederate States of America formed	Confederates fire on Fort Sumter	Emancipation Proclamation	Gettysburg Address	Lee surrenders

| 1860 | 1861 | 1862 | 1863 | 1864 | 1865 |

territories to decide, not the federal government. Lincoln argued that the federal government had the right to prohibit slavery in all the territories. Without new slave states, the Southerners would gradually lose their political power.

The Confederacy Is Born

To many Southerners, differences over slavery now seemed too great to resolve. In addition many Southerners believed in "states' rights." They thought that each state was independent and had the right to leave the Union if it wanted to. In December 1860, South Carolina **seceded** from the Union. Before Lincoln was inaugurated, six more states—Mississippi, Florida, Alabama,

▼ The Confederate battery at Fort Moultrie firing on Fort Sumter in Charleston Harbor

Georgia, Louisiana, and Texas—also voted to leave. You can find these states on the map on the facing page. Together they formed a new nation, the **Confederacy**, or the Confederate States of America, on February 4, 1861. The capital was established in Montgomery, Alabama. Jefferson Davis was chosen president.

Firing on Fort Sumter

When Lincoln became President in March 1861, many still hoped that war could be avoided. Four slave states still remained in the Union. And even within the Confederacy some people still supported the Union.

Abraham Lincoln wanted to avoid **civil war**. But as President, he had a duty to preserve the Union. He said no state could decide on its own to leave the Union. He also told the South that he would hold on to all property owned by the United States government.

Although Lincoln had decided to fight if necessary, he didn't want to fire the first shot. And as things turned out, he didn't. On the morning of April 12, 1861, Confederate soldiers opened fire on Fort Sumter in the harbor of Charleston, South Carolina.

 secede To withdraw from an organization or nation
Confederacy The nation formed by the states that seceded from the Union
civil war Armed fighting between groups within the same country

267

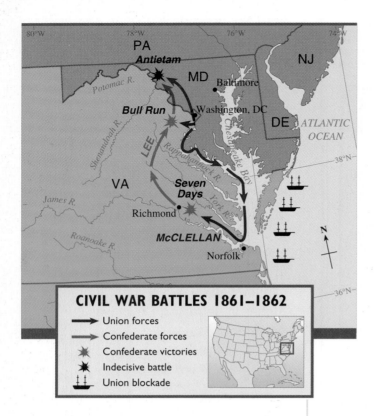

CIVIL WAR BATTLES 1861–1862

- → Union forces
- → Confederate forces
- ✹ Confederate victories
- ✸ Indecisive battle
- ⛵ Union blockade

Major Robert Anderson, the fort commander, had refused to hand the fort over to the Confederacy. Supplies at the fort were low, however, and Major Anderson told the President that he would have to give up the fort unless food arrived soon. Lincoln agreed to send supply ships to the fort. The President said the ships would not carry guns or troops, hoping that the Confederates would allow the ships to go through. But before the ships arrived, the Confederates demanded that Anderson surrender the fort. When he refused, Confederate cannons on shore opened fire. Major Anderson was forced to surrender.

Soon after, Lincoln called for Americans to join the army and help put down the rebellion. Even so, four more southern states—Virginia, North Carolina, Tennessee, and Arkansas— joined the Confederacy. The bloodiest war in America's history had begun.

Advantages and Disadvantages

Both the North and the South began the war in high spirits. The North had several advantages—a larger population, most of the industry, and many of the railroads. It also had more than 40 warships, while the South had none.

Even so, the South was hopeful. They had better-trained and more experienced generals, including Robert E. Lee. The South had another big advantage—fighting a **defensive war** on land they knew well. To win, the

▼ Union and Confederate soldiers at the battle of Bull Run

⭐ *defensive war* A war in which an army fights to defend its own territory

North would have to invade and conquer the South. Finally, the South didn't need long supply lines the way the North did. This gave the South the ability to move more quickly.

Battle of Bull Run

Only one soldier died at Fort Sumter. The real fighting started a few months later outside Manassas Junction, Virginia. Here 35,000 Union troops faced 25,000 Virginia soldiers. Many Union supporters traveled the 30 miles from Washington, D.C., to see this first battle of the war. They even brought picnic lunches.

The fighting began on July 21, 1861, near a small stream, Bull Run, shown on the map on page 268. The picnickers could hear the sound of cannon fire in the distance. "This should be quick," most of them thought. "We'll whip the Rebs [Rebels] here, and the war will be over."

At first the Union side was winning. Then fresh Confederate troops arrived, and the battle turned. The poorly trained Union soldiers began dropping their guns and retreating. Soon panicky picnickers and Union soldiers competed in dashing back to Washington. After the battle of Bull Run, both sides knew that the war would probably be long, bitter, and bloody.

War Strategies

The Union's plan for winning the war had several parts. First, Lincoln ordered a naval **blockade** of Southern ports so that the Confederacy could not get supplies from or sell its cotton to European countries. Second, the Union would try to invade the South and divide it into parts. And third, Union forces would attack Richmond, Virginia, the new capital of the Confederacy.

The Confederates had one basic plan—just hold on. Sooner or later the North would quit. Many thought that Northerners were too divided about the war to put up a good fight. Southerners also believed they were better fighters, boasting that one Rebel "could whip a half-dozen Yankees [Northerners] and not half try."

Fighting the War

In the early days of the war, the South looked strong. Under the leadership of General Robert E. Lee and General Thomas "Stonewall" Jackson, they beat the Union army again and again.

General George McClellan, leader of the Union troops, responded poorly. McClellan was a brilliant planner, but he hesitated to attack. Finally, Lincoln fired him. After trying several other generals, Lincoln found one that he felt could be

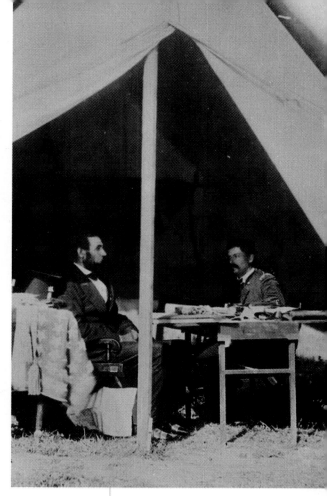

▲ President Abraham Lincoln with General George McClellan

blockade A blocking of a port or region to prevent entering or leaving

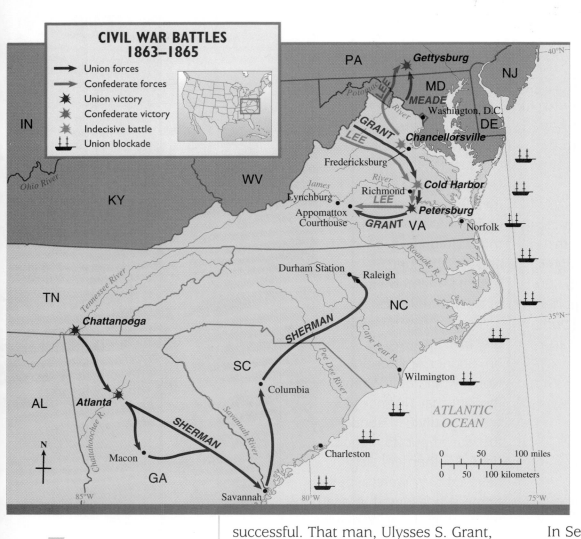

Union forces
Confederate forces
Union victory
Confederate victory
Indecisive battle
Union blockade

command of all Union armies.

Under Grant, the North continued trying to cut the South into thirds. General William Tecumseh Sherman led Union troops on a "march to the sea" through Georgia and then north through South Carolina. You can follow his route on the map at the left. Like Grant, Sherman believed in total war—destroying anything that might help the enemy. Crops, barns, bridges, and mills all became fair targets. Homes were ransacked and destroyed. Before General Sherman burned the city of Atlanta, he told the mayor, "War is cruelty."

Emancipation Proclamation

successful. That man, Ulysses S. Grant, had already won key victories. On March 9, 1864, Lincoln placed him in

In September 1862, President Lincoln announced that as of January 1, 1863, all slaves in the rebelling states

▼ Guard detail of the 107th United States Colored Infantry

This painting shows the surrender at Appomattox Court House, April 9, 1865.

SHOW WHAT YOU KNOW!

REFOCUS
COMPREHENSION

1. How did events at Fort Sumter lead to the firing of the first shot of the Civil War?

2. What was the purpose of the Union blockade?

THINK ABOUT IT
CRITICAL THINKING

How did the advantages of the North contribute to the Union's winning the war?

WRITE ABOUT IT
ACTIVITY

Make a chart with the headings *North* and *South*. List the advantages each side had in the Civil War.

would be "forever free." The **Emancipation Proclamation** changed the focus of the war. It was no longer just a battle to preserve the Union. It now became a war to free the slaves.

Some freed African Americans now joined the Union army. At first many served as cooks, drivers, and workers—not as soldiers or sailors. But later they joined in large numbers and served as soldiers. Before the war was over, more than 185,000 African Americans had fought in the army. Many died, and 21 received the Congressional Medal of Honor, our country's highest award.

War Ends and Lincoln Dies

By the spring of 1865, the South was badly weakened. Its armies were running out of men and supplies. On April 9, 1865, Lee surrendered to Grant in a private home in the village of Appomattox Court House, Virginia.

The Civil War was over. The Union was saved, and slavery was abolished. But the cost of the war was huge. Over 600,000 people died. More soldiers died in the Civil War than in any other American war. Over 250,000 others were crippled for life.

Five days after the war ended, while Lincoln attended a play at Ford's Theater in Washington, D.C., John Wilkes Booth slipped into the President's box. Booth, a Confederate radical, shot Lincoln in the back of the head. Lincoln died a few hours later.

A nation mourned and wondered what to do about the Confederate states. Lincoln had wanted to treat the South firmly but "with malice [bad feelings] toward none, with charity for all." What would happen now that Lincoln was gone?

⭐ **Emancipation Proclamation** An order that declared freedom for the slaves in all the states that had left the Union

North Versus South

FOCUS *Most battles of the Civil War were bloody affairs. Just when people thought the fighting couldn't get any worse, it did.*

MONITOR AND MERRIMACK

In March 1862 a Confederate vessel covered with iron plates sailed out of Norfolk, Virginia. Called the *Merrimack* (later renamed the *Virginia*), its mission was to break the Union blockade so that needed Confederate supplies from abroad could arrive.

Soon *Merrimack* guns blasted the Union's wooden ships. Union cannonballs just bounced off its sides. The next day the Union answered with its own ironclad ship, the *Monitor*. Neither ship could damage the other, and this historic battle ended in a draw. But it really was a Union victory because the blockade held. A few months later the Confederates sank the *Merrimack* to keep it from falling into enemy hands when Union forces captured Norfolk.

BATTLE OF SHILOH

On April 6, 1862, the South attacked Grant's army at Shiloh, Tennessee. Grant rallied his men and drove the Confederates back the next day. Although the battle had no clear winner, it showed just how bloody the war would be. At Bull Run, casualties were light, but Shiloh was a slaughter. Over 13,000 Union soldiers were killed, wounded, or captured. The South had almost 11,000 killed, wounded, or captured. More men died in this one battle than in America's three previous wars.

BATTLE OF ANTIETAM

In September 1862, General Robert E. Lee decided to invade the North. He hoped to win a quick victory and force the North to quit. On September 17 he came up against General George McClellan at Antietam Creek, near Sharpsburg, Maryland. McClellan almost surrounded Lee but moved too slowly. Fresh Confederate troops arrived in time to save Lee and his army. Antietam was not really the victory Lincoln was looking for, but Lee's advance into the North was stopped.

There were even more casualties at Antietam than at Shiloh. In just one awful day, the two armies had almost 23,000 killed, wounded, or captured. September 17, 1862, was the bloodiest day of the war.

March 1862	April 1862	September 1862		July 1863	July 1863
Monitor and *Merrimack*	Battle of Shiloh	Battle of Antietam		Battle of Gettysburg	Battle of Vicksburg

JANUARY 1862   JULY   JANUARY 1863   JULY   JANUARY 1864

BATTLE OF GETTYSBURG

On July 1, 1863, General Lee invaded the North for the last time. At Gettysburg, Pennsylvania, he clashed with a Union army led by General George Meade. The battle lasted three days and became the best-known battle of the war. Wave after wave of Southern soldiers attacked Union positions. On July 3, Lee ordered General George Pickett to make one final charge. The Union army drove the Confederates back. This battle was often looked on as the turning point in the war. After this, Lee ordered his army to retreat into Virginia.

Four months later President Lincoln dedicated a cemetery in Gettysburg in honor of the soldiers who had died there. His Gettysburg Address, which took less than five minutes to deliver, expressed the meaning of the horrible conflict for the whole world. He promised "that these dead shall not have died in vain; that this nation, under God, shall have a new birth of freedom; and that government of the people, by the people, and for the people, shall not perish from the earth."

BATTLE OF VICKSBURG

A day after the victory at Gettysburg, President Lincoln received more good news from the West. Union armies, led by General Grant, had captured the Confederate stronghold of Vicksburg, Mississippi. This was a critical victory for the Union. The North at last controlled the entire Mississippi River. Arkansas, Texas, and most of Louisiana were now cut off from the rest of the Confederacy. These states could no longer send troops and supplies across the Mississippi River to the main Confederate armies.

The victory also made General Grant a Northern war hero. Unlike some other Union generals, Grant showed a grim determination to do what had to be done. Lincoln now chose him to destroy Lee's army.

Ulysses S. Grant

REFOCUS
COMPREHENSION

1. Why can it be said that the battle of Antietam was not a victory for either side?

2. Why was it important for the Union to capture Vicksburg?

THINK ABOUT IT
CRITICAL THINKING

Why is a civil war especially tragic?

WRITE ABOUT IT
ACTIVITY

Read and analyze the quote from the Gettysburg Address. Then write in your journal, explaining the meaning of the words.

Life as a Soldier

FOCUS *Young soldiers on both sides in the Civil War believed in their cause, fought bravely, and suffered mightily.*

Hoping to Be a Hero

To young men looking for adventure, war sounds thrilling. How excited you must be if you are a 17- or 18-year-old farm boy in 1861. Until now your time has been spent plowing fields and milking cows. You might have dreamed of doing something heroic, but there aren't many chances to be a hero on the family farm.

Now, war is breaking out. If you join the army, you have a chance to put on a uniform, march into battle, and fight for a glorious cause. In the case of a New England farm boy, that means saving the Union. For a Southern farm boy, it is defending states' rights.

The Reality of Army Camps

If you are one of the tens of thousands of young boys and men who join the Confederate or Union army, you soon learn that war is not what you expected. Life in an army camp is hard. You become dirtier with each passing day; there is little time to wash clothes or

take a bath. Soon your body is covered with lice.

As time passes, if you are lucky enough to have a uniform, it becomes ragged. Your boots wear out, but new ones are often impossible to get. You might find yourself marching through miles of sharp, tangled bushes in bare feet. The lack of tents means that you have to sleep on the ground, without regard to the weather. You and your fellow soldiers huddle under thin blankets—some so poorly made that they fall apart in the rain.

Food is another problem. It is usually scarce; even when you have some, it is often spoiled. A meal might consist of moldy bread and rotten meat. If there is no time to cook bacon, you have to eat it raw or go hungry.

▼ A Union cavalry trooper

Long, Lonely Days

As the weeks pass, your dreams of glory begin to slip away. Most of the time you aren't standing proudly on the battlefield but are marching through the rain or waiting around a campsite. You write long letters to your family back home, telling them of your loneliness. You try to keep up your spirits as this war drags on and on.

The Horrors of Battle

When fighting occurs, misery turns to horror. Most battles are chaotic. Smoke from guns and cannons fills the air. You hear the agonizing screams of wounded men. You might see friends shot or taken prisoner. As one Confederate soldier writes, "It is a sad sight to see the dead and if possible more sad to see the wounded—shot in every possible way you can imagine."

You yourself might end up among the dead or wounded. If you are wounded, you have to hope the injury isn't serious. Medical knowledge is very limited. Nurses can bandage wounds, and doctors can amputate shattered arms or legs. But beyond that, there isn't much anyone can do. Many soldiers die from infections and loss of blood. Also, there is the threat of dying from deadly **epidemic** diseases that are in the filthy, crowded army camps. In fact, for every Civil War soldier killed in battle, two die from disease.

⭐ **epidemic** The spread of disease to a large number of people in a short period of time

▼ A Confederate private

SHOW WHAT YOU KNOW!

REFOCUS
COMPREHENSION

1. Why did many young men volunteer for the army?

2. What were some of the problems that soldiers faced daily?

THINK ABOUT IT
CRITICAL THINKING

If you had lived during the time of the Civil War, would you have wanted to serve in the military? Give your reasons.

WRITE ABOUT IT
ACTIVITY

Suppose you are a Union or Confederate soldier. Write a letter home telling of life in your army camp.

Abraham Lincoln

FOCUS *Born in a log cabin, Abraham Lincoln rose to become President of the United States. His bold and courageous leadership helped the Union win the Civil War.*

Lincoln, "The Rail Splitter" ▶

Humble Beginnings

When Abraham Lincoln was born in 1809, his future didn't look particularly bright. After all, his parents were poor farmers who had very little education. They lived in a log cabin in the woods of Kentucky.

As a child Lincoln spent much of his time helping his father scratch a living out of their small plot of land. When Lincoln was seven, the family moved to Indiana. Here he helped to farm and build a log cabin for the family. With all the chores to be done, little time was left for "book learning." In fact, in his entire childhood, Lincoln only spent about a year in school.

Yet he loved books. He read whenever and wherever he got the chance. He would walk miles to borrow a book. Often he tucked one into his pocket before heading out to split wood or plow a field.

Lawyer and Family Man

When Lincoln was a young adult, he moved to Illinois. After studying law books on his own and earning a license to practice, he became a successful lawyer. At the age of 25, he was elected to the Illinois state legislature and became a leader of the Republican party.

In 1842, Lincoln married Mary Todd of Lexington, Kentucky. The two were almost opposite in background. Mary was from a well-known, well-to-do family. By the time Lincoln ran for President, the couple had had four sons. Abraham Lincoln and Mary Todd were devoted to their family. They shared the tragedy of the deaths from disease of two of their four children.

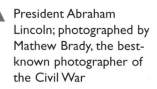

Abraham Lincoln was often seen wearing his top hat.

President Lincoln

When the Civil War broke out, no one knew what kind of President Lincoln would be. He had been in office a little more than a month when the fighting started. At times over the next four years, many people had their doubts about President Lincoln. In the end, however, he proved to be a brilliant politician and an inspiring leader.

Lincoln possessed several great qualities. He was intelligent, shrewd, and courageous. His goal was to preserve the Union, and he was ready to do whatever it took to accomplish this goal. Again and again he angered Congress by acting without their consent. He used his power as President to do what he believed was necessary. Sometimes this meant spending more money than Congress had planned. Sometimes it meant throwing troublemakers in jail. In 1863 he announced that slaves in the rebelling states would be freed. Each of these actions met with criticism. But once Lincoln settled on a course of

President Abraham Lincoln; photographed by Mathew Brady, the best-known photographer of the Civil War

Mary Todd Lincoln in formal dress; photographed by Brady in 1864

action, he rarely backed down.

One of Lincoln's talents was his ability to express himself. Speaking out in his high-pitched voice, he could state his ideas in ways that kept people spellbound. Two of the greatest speeches in American history were written by this self-taught man from the frontier—the Gettysburg Address and Lincoln's second **inaugural address**

inaugural address The speech made at the start of a term of office

Lincoln: A Photobiography

by Russell Freedman

Abraham Lincoln rose from humble beginnings to greatness. Through photographs and text, you will come to know the real Mr. Lincoln.

Abraham Lincoln wasn't the sort of man who could lose himself in a crowd. After all, he stood six feet four inches tall, and to top it off, he wore a high silk hat.

His height was mostly in his long bony legs. When he sat in a chair, he seemed no taller than anyone else. It was only when he stood up that he towered above other men.

At first glance, most people thought he was homely. Lincoln thought so too, referring once to his "poor, lean, lank face." As a young man he was sensitive about his gawky looks, but in time, he learned to laugh at himself. When a rival called him "two-faced" during a political debate, Lincoln replied: "I leave it to my audience. If I had another face, do you think I'd wear this one?"

According to those who knew him, Lincoln was a man of many faces. In repose, he often seemed sad and gloomy. But when he began to speak, his expression changed. "The dull, listless features dropped like a mask," said a Chicago newspaperman. "The eyes began to sparkle, the mouth to smile, the whole countenance was wreathed in animation, so that a stranger would have said, 'Why, this man, so angular and solemn a moment ago, is really handsome!'"

Lincoln may have seemed like a common man, but he wasn't. His friends agreed that he was one of the most ambitious people they had ever known. Lincoln struggled hard to rise above his log-cabin origins, and he was proud of his achievements. By the time he ran for president he was a wealthy man, earning a large income from his law practice and his many investments. As for the nickname Abe, he hated it. No one who knew him well ever called him Abe to his face. They addressed him as Lincoln or Mr. Lincoln.

It's true that Lincoln had little formal "eddication," as he would have pronounced it. Almost everything he "larned" he taught himself. All his life he said "thar" for *there,* "git" for *get,* "kin" for *can.* Even so, he became an eloquent public speaker who could hold a vast audience spellbound, and a great writer whose finest phrases still ring in our ears. He was known to sit up late into the night, discussing Shakespeare's plays with White House visitors.

Lincoln is best known as the Great Emancipator, the man who freed the slaves. Yet he did not enter the war with that idea in mind. "My paramount object in this struggle *is* to save the Union," he said in 1862, "and is *not* either to save or destroy slavery." As the war continued, Lincoln's attitude changed. Eventually he came to regard the conflict as a moral crusade to wipe out the sin of slavery.

Want to read more? You can by checking the book out of your school or public library.

SHOW WHAT YOU KNOW!

REFOCUS
COMPREHENSION

1. Describe Lincoln's early life.

2. What were some of Lincoln's accomplishments as a young man?

THINK ABOUT IT
CRITICAL THINKING

Why is Lincoln considered to have been a great President?

WRITE ABOUT IT
ACTIVITY

Based on your reading of the literature selection, write a description of Abraham Lincoln.

Women and the War Effort

FOCUS *Although few actually fought, women in the North and the South aided the Civil War effort in many important ways.*

▼ Civil War nurses

Raising Money and Running Farms

While men faced each other on the battlefield, women had struggles of their own. Most women did not take up arms, but they found other ways to serve.

In both the North and the South, women raised money to aid injured troops. Over 10,000 soldiers' aid societies were organized. Women rolled bandages, made tents, and sewed clothing to send to the troops. In addition, they took on much of the work that men ordinarily did, such as plowing fields, planting crops, and gathering harvests.

Helping the Wounded and Aiding the Fighting

Some women traveled to the battlefields to help the sick and wounded. In 1861, Dorothea Dix became the superintendent of nurses for the Union army. Under her direction, thousands of Northern women waded through blood and dirt to nurse soldiers in pain. One, Clara Barton, many years later used the skills she gained during the war to found the American branch of the **Red Cross**. Southern women also became nurses, cleaning wounds and comforting dying men. Sally Tompkins ran a private hospital in Richmond, Virginia, where she cared for both Confederate and Union soldiers.

Other women, eager to help the war cause, became spies. One of the North's spies was Harriet Tubman, the famed "conductor" on the Underground Railroad. Still others carried mail for the armies. Some women even went so far as to disguise themselves as men so that they could reach the battlefield.

Coping in the South

As the war dragged on, Southern women faced additional burdens. Many lost food supplies when the

⭐ **Red Cross** An international society for the relief of suffering in times of war or disaster

Clara Barton, Civil War nurse and founder of the American Red Cross

War and Death

In addition to all else, both Northern and Southern women lived every day with the knowledge that war meant death. They knew that the men who marched off to battle might never return. To keep track of Union soldiers, Northerners started the United States Sanitary Commission. Many women worked for this organization. But news traveled slowly, and sometimes messages didn't get through at all.

One Southern woman wrote in her journal: "I have no heart to keep this journal or tell of the dreadful, fatal battles in Virginia. My heart is too heavy. I am entirely miserable. Many whom I know are killed and wounded."

Union army marched through. The army simply confiscated, or took, their crops. Some saw their farms burned and their fields destroyed.

Even women who lived far from the battle sites faced huge problems. They had to manage slaves who were becoming more and more restless. They also had to cope with the breakdown of wagons and plows. Since no one could get spare parts from the North, many farm implements just lay rusting in the fields.

Pauline Cushman (left) was a Union spy. Rose O'Neal Greenhow and her daughter (right) were spies for the Confederate cause.

Spotlight

⭐ **KEY TERMS**

Reconstruction
Radical Republican
black codes
carpetbagger
sharecropper
Jim Crow laws

Reconstruction

FOCUS *President Andrew Johnson and Congress often clashed over how the defeated South should be treated. Meanwhile, newly freed slaves faced many challenges and difficulties.*

▼ The ruins of Richmond after the Civil War

READMISSION OF STATES TO THE UNION

Mar. 30, 1870 Date of readmission

VA *Jan. 26, 1870*
TN *July 24, 1866*
NC *June 25, 1868*
AR *June 22, 1868*
SC *June 25, 1868*
MS *Feb. 23, 1870*
TX *Mar. 30, 1870*
AL *June 25, 1868*
GA *July 15, 1870*
LA *June 25, 1868*
FL *June 25, 1868*

0   150   300 miles
0   150   300 kilometers

The South in Ruins

By the end of the Civil War, the South was a wasteland. Cities such as Richmond and Atlanta lay in ruins. Railroad tracks were ripped up. Blackened chimneys were all that remained of burned factories. Fields, once filled with crops, had been reclaimed by weeds. Clearly, the people of the South—black and white— needed help. The plan to rebuild the South became known as **Reconstruction**.

Presidential Plan

With Lincoln's death, Vice President Andrew Johnson became President. Johnson presented a plan, known as the presidential plan, for bringing the South back into the Union. First, 10 percent of voters in each state had to take an oath of loyalty to the Union. Second, each state had to form a new government, with a new constitution. Third, the states had to ratify, or formally approve, the Thirteenth Amendment to the Constitution, which outlawed slavery.

When Johnson became President, he began pardoning many of the Confederate leaders. Some of these leaders were even elected to Congress. This upset many members of Congress, especially a group known as **Radical**

▲ Andrew Johnson

Republicans. This group was also angered to hear that the new Southern governments were passing **black codes**—laws that limited the rights of black citizens. The codes declared, for example, that African Americans couldn't travel without passes, couldn't change jobs, and couldn't vote.

Congressional Plan

Radical Republicans and Johnson fought bitterly over Reconstruction. Under Republican leadership, Congress passed a plan for reconstruction. This plan called for the Union army to occupy the South. It got rid of the all-white state governments that were being formed in the South. New state constitutions were to be written by conventions made up of black Americans as well as white Americans. Also, former Confederate leaders could not vote or hold office.

Congress's plan also required all Southern states to ratify the Fourteenth Amendment to the Constitution. This amendment made African Americans citizens and promised them "equal protection of the laws." When a state did these things, it could rejoin the Union. Only then would the United States army leave that state.

Later, in 1870, Congress passed the Fifteenth Amendment. This said

---

⭐ **Reconstruction** The name given to the plan to rebuild the South following the Civil War, 1865–1877

⭐ **Radical Republican** A member of the Republican party who wanted to punish the South and give land to black citizens
black codes Southern laws passed after the Civil War, aimed at limiting the rights and opportunities of African Americans

283

that no state could keep a person from voting because of his race or color. However, at this time neither black nor white women were allowed to vote.

Reconstruction Brings Change

By 1870 all states in the South had rejoined the Union. African Americans held public office for the first time, although most officeholders were still white. Some African Americans served in state governments and in the United States Congress. Three were elected lieutenant governors. About half had been free blacks before the war, but the other half had been slaves just a few years earlier.

To help needy black citizens and white citizens in the South, Congress created the Freedmen's Bureau. Freedmen were former slaves. The bureau provided food, medical care, and legal advice. It set up schools and hospitals. Many Northern women who were once abolitionists went south to teach in bureau schools. They taught thousands of African Americans,

young and old, to read and write.

Unlike the teachers who came to the South to help, others came hoping to make money from the South's misery. Most Southerners didn't like these people and called them **carpetbaggers**. A carpetbag is a cheap suitcase made out of pieces of carpet. Southerners said these people hoped to fill their carpetbags with riches.

Anger in the South

Many Southerners disliked Reconstruction. They were opposed to having their former slaves take part in government, to giving equal rights to African Americans, and to sending black children to school. Some white Southerners formed secret societies, such as the Ku Klux Klan. These groups tried to frighten freed African Americans and their white supporters. Wearing white sheets, the Klan usually struck at night. They beat or killed people and burned down homes as well as black schools and churches.

▲ "The Carpet Bagger": song sheet music cover of 1869

★ **carpetbagger** The name given to a Northern white person who moved to the South after the Civil War

◀ The first African American senators and representatives in the 41st and 42nd Congresses of the United States

The Newly Freed

Southern agriculture was in shambles after the war. Some freed black citizens left the plantations to find work elsewhere. Some went searching for relatives separated during the days of slavery. Many stayed on the plantations to work the fields.

Their former owners, however, couldn't pay them wages. The newly freed citizens had no money to pay rent, so each agreed to share at harvest time. The **sharecropper** would get some of the crop, and the landowner would get the rest.

This sounded fair, but it wasn't. African Americans had to go into debt to buy seeds and other materials. Their half of the crop was just enough to pay off this debt and provide food for their families. Without money the only way they could survive was to stay in their current arrangement. To them, sharecropping seemed like slavery, only with a different name.

The End of Reconstruction

Newly freed African Americans worked hard to improve their lives. Family and church were the foundations of community life. Churches provided help to the poor and others in need and also helped people learn to

 Primary school for Freedmen

read. Black churches did even more teaching than the Freedmen's schools. Much of the money used for education came from within the African American community itself.

In 1877 the last United States troops left the South. White citizens who wanted to return to the old ways now controlled the Southern states. Reconstruction was over. So, too, was the progress black citizens had made. Over the next 20 years, African Americans lost nearly every right they had won during Reconstruction. **Jim Crow laws** segregated, or separated, black citizens and white citizens in restaurants and other public places. New laws made it nearly impossible for black citizens to vote or hold office. It would be many years before African Americans would regain the rights they had lost.

★ **sharecropper** A person who farms land owned by another and gives part of the crop in return for seeds, tools, and other supplies

★ **Jim Crow laws** Laws that segregated and discriminated against African Americans

SHOW WHAT YOU KNOW!

REFOCUS
COMPREHENSION

1. What did the congressional plan require for a Confederate state to reenter the Union?

2. What were some ways in which Jim Crow laws took away rights gained by African Americans?

THINK ABOUT IT
CRITICAL THINKING

What might have happened had the United States troops not left the South?

WRITE ABOUT IT
ACTIVITY

Describe how you think a Southern child might have felt about learning to read and write for the first time at a Freedmen's Bureau school.

SUMMING UP

1 DO YOU REMEMBER . . .
COMPREHENSION

1. How did the battle of Bull Run change the North's attitude toward the war?

2. How did the Emancipation Proclamation change the focus of the war?

3. What similar attitude toward war did General Grant and General Sherman share?

4. Why was the draw between the *Monitor* and the *Merrimack* really a victory for the Union?

5. What causes were most Union and Confederate soldiers fighting for?

6. What was the cause of death for most Civil War soldiers?

7. Give examples of how Lincoln used his powers as President to do what he thought was right despite Congress's objections.

8. How did the Civil War place greater burdens on the South than on the North?

9. What were the purposes of the Thirteenth and Fourteenth Amendments?

10. Why did many white Southerners dislike Reconstruction?

2 SKILL POWER
ANALYZING A DOCUMENT

Analyzing the Gettysburg Address helped you understand how President Lincoln felt about the war and the United States. Find other documents, such as speeches, letters, or even legal documents. Analyze each document by asking what is the topic and what are the main ideas. Share your findings.

3 WHAT DO YOU THINK?
CRITICAL THINKING

1. Which of the North's three strategies for winning the war was most important? Explain.

2. Why was the battle of Gettysburg seen as the turning point in the Civil War?

3. Suppose you were a typical Civil War soldier. Tell how your attitudes toward the war probably changed over time.

4. Would you agree that the Emancipation Proclamation was only a start in the direction of freeing slaves? Explain.

5. Do you think Reconstruction would have been a success if the presidential plan had been followed?

4 SAY IT, WRITE IT, USE IT
VOCABULARY

Write five questions that you might have asked President Lincoln about the Civil War. Write the answers that Lincoln might have given. Use one or more of the vocabulary words in each question and answer.

black codes
blockade
carpetbagger
civil war
Confederacy
defensive war
Emancipation Proclamation
epidemic
inaugural address
Jim Crow laws
Radical Republican
Reconstruction
Red Cross
secede
sharecropper

5 GEOGRAPHY AND YOU
MAP STUDY

Use the maps in this chapter to answer the following questions.

1. What slave states remained in the Union in 1861?

2. List the free states that stayed in the Union and the slave states that left the Union.

3. Make a list of the sites where battles were fought between the Union and Confederate forces.

4. In what states were the battles of Antietam and Gettysburg fought?

6 TAKE ACTION
CITIZENSHIP

During the Civil War, Northerners and Southerners alike raised money to aid injured troops. Today, citizens also raise money for worthwhile causes. Find out about an organization in your community that raises money to achieve its goals. Talk to a member of the group to find out more about this work. Then share what you learn with the class.

7 GET CREATIVE
MUSIC CONNECTION

"Battle Cry of Freedom" was written during the Civil War. It was a popular rallying song of the North. Soldiers sang it in battle, in camps, and on long marches. The Confederates also liked this spirited tune and had a version of their own. With a group of classmates, find the words, music, and a recording of this song as well as other songs that came out of the Civil War. After reading about and listening to the songs, choose a few and share them with your class.

LOOKING AHEAD In the next chapter discover how people traveled westward and found new frontiers.

REFERENCE

CONTENTS

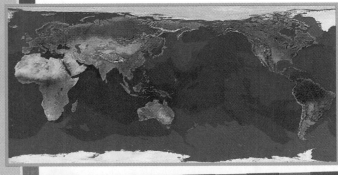

SECTION

RESEARCH AND REFERENCE

While studying the history of our United States, you can use these books to locate where an event took place, to learn more about the people and places involved, and to discover the role that each of our Presidents played in the growth of our country.

The Kingfisher Young People's Encyclopedia of the United States **edited by William E. Shapiro**
(Kingfisher, 1994)
Colorful illustrations and photographs will help you get to know the people, places, and events that contribute to the uniqueness of the United States.

Encyclopedia of the Presidents and Their Times **by David Rubel** (Scholastic, 1994)
Fun-filled facts and illustrations will introduce you to America's 42 Presidents of the past and present. Find out where they were born, their nicknames, and what they have done to help our country.

The Reader's Digest Children's World Atlas **edited by Nicola Barber and Nicholas Harris**
(The Reader's Digest Association, 1995)
Maps, photographs, and illustrations will enrich your study of our country's history. You will realize how important the United States is to the rest of the world.

ARCTIC OCEAN

Greenland
(Den.)

Arctic Circle

Alaska (U.S.)

60°N

80°N   160°W   140°W   120°W   100°W   80°W   60°W   40

ALEUTIAN IS. (U.S.)

CANADA

NORTH

AMERICA

UNITED STATES

40°N

See inset below

AZORES
(Port.)

Midway I. (U.S.)

Bermuda (U.K.)

ATLANTIC OCEAN

Tropic of Cancer

MEXICO

20°N

HAWAII (U.S.)

Caribbean Sea

CAPE VERDE

VENEZUELA   GUYANA
SURINAME
French Guiana
(Fr.)

COLOMBIA

SOUTH

GALÁPAGOS IS.
(Ecuador)

0°   Equator

ECUADOR

AMERICA   BRAZIL

WESTERN
SAMOA

PACIFIC OCEAN

PERU

AMERICAN
SAMOA (U.S.)

FRENCH POLYNESIA
(Fr.)

BOLIVIA

TONGA

20°S

Pitcairn I. (U.K.)   PARAGUAY

COOK IS. (N.Z.)   Tropic of Capricorn

Easter I.
(Chile)

CHILE

URUGUAY

N

ARGENTINA

W   E

S

40°S

International Date Line

FALKLAND IS.
(U.K.)

60°S

Antarctic Circle

80°S

WEST INDIES AND CENTRAL AMERICA

0   150   300 miles

0   150   300 kilometers

UNITED STATES

30°N

N

W   E

S

Gulf of Mexico

ATLANTIC OCEAN

25°N

B
A
H
A
M
A
S

Tropic of Cancer

CUBA

TURKS AND
CAICOS IS. (U.K.)

20°N

Hispaniola   *BR. VIRGIN IS.*
(U.K.)

MEXICO

CAYMAN
ISLANDS
(U.K.)

HAITI

DOMINICAN
REPUBLIC

Puerto Rico
(U.S.)

ANTIGUA
AND BARBUDA

BELIZE

GREATER ANTILLES

JAMAICA

VIRGIN ISLANDS (U.S.)

Guadeloupe (Fr.)

GUATEMALA

ST. KITTS AND NEVIS

DOMINICA

Martinique (Fr.)

15°N

HONDURAS

Caribbean Sea

ST. LUCIA

EL SALVADOR

NICARAGUA

NETH. ANTILLES (Neth.)

ARUBA

ST. VINCENT AND
THE GRENADINES

BARBADOS

GRENADA

LESSER ANTILLES

COSTA
RICA

10°N

PANAMA

COLOMBIA

VENEZUELA

TRINIDAD
AND
TOBAGO

90°W   85°W   80°W   75°W   70°W   65°W   60°W

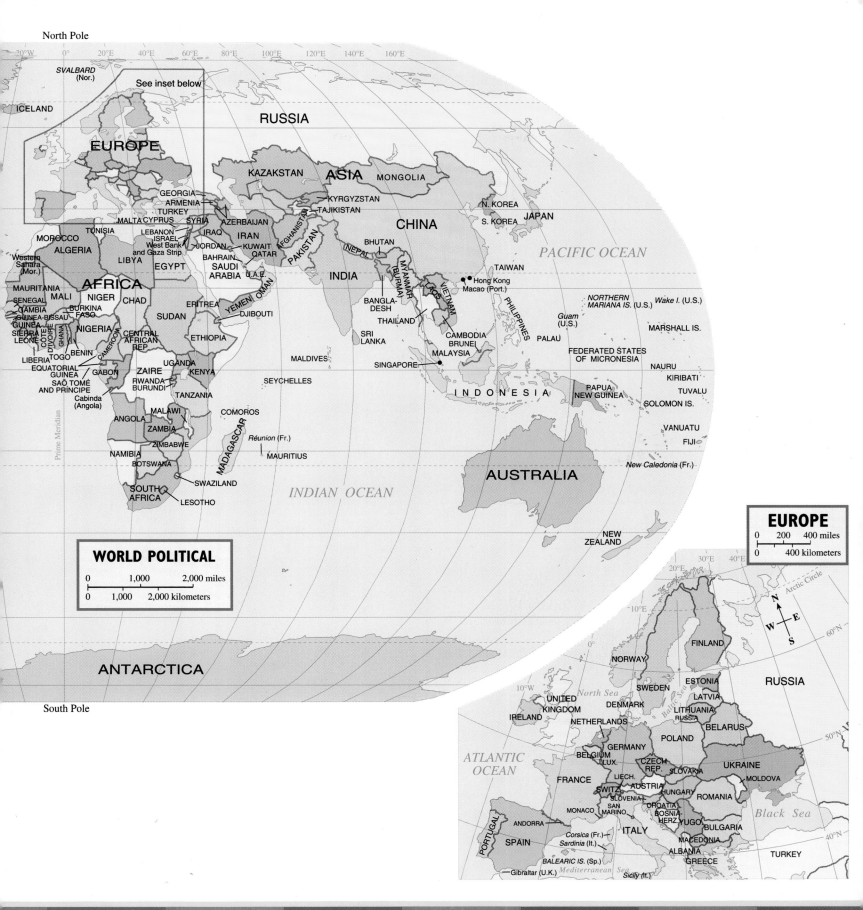

North Pole

20°W 0° 20°E 40°E 60°E 80°E 100°E 120°E 140°E 160°E

SVALBARD
(Nor.)

See inset below

ICELAND

RUSSIA

EUROPE

KAZAKSTAN ASIA MONGOLIA

GEORGIA
ARMENIA
TURKEY
MALTA CYPRUS SYRIA
LEBANON
ISRAEL
West Bank
and Gaza Strip
MOROCCO
TUNISIA
ALGERIA
Western
Sahara
(Mor.)
LIBYA
EGYPT

AZERBAIJAN
IRAQ
IRAN
JORDAN
KUWAIT
BAHRAIN
QATAR
SAUDI
ARABIA
U.A.E.
AFGHANISTAN
PAKISTAN
KYRGYZSTAN
TAJIKISTAN

CHINA

N. KOREA JAPAN
S. KOREA

PACIFIC OCEAN

AFRICA

MAURITANIA
SENEGAL MALI NIGER CHAD
GAMBIA
GUINEA-BISSAU BURKINA
GUINEA FASO
SIERRA GHANA
LEONE
COTE
DIVOIRE
LIBERIA TOGO BENIN
EQUATORIAL CAMEROON
GUINEA GABON
SAO TOME ZAIRE
AND PRINCIPE
Cabinda
(Angola)

NIGERIA

CENTRAL
AFRICAN
REP.

SUDAN

ERITREA
DJIBOUTI
YEMEN OMAN

ETHIOPIA

UGANDA
RWANDA KENYA
BURUNDI

BHUTAN

NEPAL

INDIA

MYANMAR
(BURMA)

BANGLA-
DESH

THAILAND

SRI
LANKA

MALDIVES

LAOS
VIETNAM

CAMBODIA
BRUNEI
MALAYSIA

SINGAPORE

TAIWAN

Hong Kong
Macao (Port.)

PHILIPPINES

PALAU

NORTHERN
MARIANA IS. (U.S.)

Guam
(U.S.)

Wake I. (U.S.)

MARSHALL IS.

FEDERATED STATES
OF MICRONESIA

NAURU

KIRIBATI

TUVALU

TANZANIA

SEYCHELLES

INDONESIA

PAPUA
NEW GUINEA

SOLOMON IS.

ANGOLA

MALAWI

ZAMBIA

ZIMBABWE

COMOROS

MADAGASCAR

Réunion (Fr.)

MAURITIUS

VANUATU

FIJI

NAMIBIA

BOTSWANA

SOUTH
AFRICA

SWAZILAND

LESOTHO

INDIAN OCEAN

AUSTRALIA

New Caledonia (Fr.)

Prime Meridian

WORLD POLITICAL

0 1,000 2,000 miles

0 1,000 2,000 kilometers

NEW
ZEALAND

ANTARCTICA

South Pole

EUROPE

0 200 400 miles

0 400 kilometers

20°E 30°E 40°E

Arctic Circle

10°W 10°E 60°N

NORWAY FINLAND

North Sea SWEDEN ESTONIA RUSSIA

UNITED DENMARK LATVIA
KINGDOM Baltic Sea
IRELAND LITHUANIA
NETHERLANDS RUSSIA BELARUS

50°N

ATLANTIC
OCEAN

GERMANY
BELGIUM
LUX.

POLAND

CZECH
REP. SLOVAKIA

UKRAINE

FRANCE

LIECH.

SWITZ. AUSTRIA HUNGARY
SLOVENIA
SAN CROATIA
MARINO BOSNIA-
HERZ. YUGO.
ITALY

MOLDOVA

ROMANIA

BLACK SEA

MONACO

PORTUGAL

ANDORRA

SPAIN

Corsica (Fr.)
Sardinia (It.)

BALEARIC IS. (Sp.)

Gibraltar (U.K.)

BULGARIA

MACEDONIA
ALBANIA GREECE

TURKEY

40°N

Sicily (It.) Mediterranean Sea

Black Sea

160°W   140°W   120°W   100°W   80°W   60°W   40°W   20°W

80°N

ARCTIC OCEAN
Beaufort Sea

Greenland

Iceland

Arctic Circle

▲ Mt. McKinley

60°N

Yukon

Bering Sea

Gulf of Alaska

Hudson Bay

Baffin Bay

NORTH AMERICA

Great Lakes

Newfoundland

ALEUTIAN ISLANDS

ROCKY MOUNTAINS

GREAT PLAINS

Missouri R.

St. Lawrence R.

Ohio R.

APPALACHIAN MTS.

BRITISH ISLES

PYRENEES

40°N

Mt. Whitney ▲

Colorado R.

Rio Grande

Bermuda

Azores

Strait of Gibraltar

Madeira Is.

ATLAS MTS.

Canary Is.

Gulf of Mexico

BAHAMAS

ATLANTIC OCEAN

Tropic of Cancer

20°N

HAWAIIAN ISLANDS

YUCATÁN PEN.

Cuba

Hispaniola

WEST INDIES

SAHEL

Caribbean Sea

CENTRAL AMERICA

Cape Verde Is.

Equator

0°

GALÁPAGOS ISLANDS

LLANOS

Orinoco R.

GUIANA HIGHLANDS

Amazon R.

AMAZON BASIN

PACIFIC OCEAN

SOUTH AMERICA

ATLANTIC OCEAN

20°S

POLYNESIA

ANDES MOUNTAINS

BRAZILIAN HIGHLANDS

Tropic of Capricorn

ATACAMA DESERT

Paraná R.

International Date Line

WORLD PHYSICAL

Land Elevation

Feet		Meters
Over 9,841		Over 3,001
6,581–9,840		2,001–3,000
3,281–6,580		1,001–2,000
661–3,280		201–1,000
0–660		0–200
Below sea level		Below sea level

☐ Ice-covered land

▲ Mountain peak

0   500   1,000   1,500   2,000 miles

0   1,000   2,000 kilometers

Mt. Aconcagua ▲

PAMPAS

Río de la Plata

N
W   E
S

40°S

PATAGONIA

Strait of Magellan

FALKLAND ISLANDS (U.K.) (MALVINA IS.)

Cape Horn

Drake Passage

60°S

Antarctic Circle

80°S

20°E 40°E 60°E 80°E 100°E 120°E 140°E 160°E

SVALBARD

Barents Sea

ARCTIC OCEAN

Novaya Zemlya

Baltic Sea

North Sea

EUROPE

CARPATHIANS

URAL MTS.

Ob R.

Volga R.

Ural R.

Yenisey R.

SIBERIA

Lena R.

Irtysh R.

▲ ALPS

Mt. Blanc

BALKAN PEN.

Black Sea

CAUCASUS MTS.

Mt. Ararat ▲

Caspian Sea

Aral Sea

ALTAI MTS.

ASIA

GOBI

L. Baikal

Amur R.

Sea of Okhotsk

KAMCHATKA PENINSULA

Sakhalin

Hokkaido

Mediterranean Sea

Mt. Damavand ▲

Indus R.

THAR DESERT

Ganges R.

TIBETAN PLATEAU

▲ Mt. Everest

Huang He

Chang Jiang (Yangzi) R.

Honshu

Sea of Japan

Shikoku

Kyushu

SAHARA

Nile R.

Red Sea

ARABIAN PENINSULA

NUBIAN DESERT

Persian Gulf

DECCAN PLATEAU

East China Sea

Taiwan

Hainan

South China Sea

PHILIPPINE ISLANDS

MICRONESIA

SUDAN

Niger R.

AFRICA

Arabian Sea

Bay of Bengal

Sri Lanka

MALAY PEN.

PACIFIC OCEAN

GREAT RIFT VALLEY

(Congo) R.

L. Victoria

▲ Mt. Kenya

▲ Mt. Kilimanjaro

Sumatra

Borneo

INDONESIA

Celebes

New Guinea

ZAIRE BASIN

SEYCHELLES

INDIAN OCEAN

Java

Timor

MELANESIA

Zambezi R.

Madagascar

GREAT SANDY DESERT

KALAHARI DESERT

AUSTRALIA

NULLARBOR PLAIN

Darling R.

North Island

Orange R.

Cape of Good Hope

Tasmania

South Island

NEW ZEALAND

ANTARCTICA

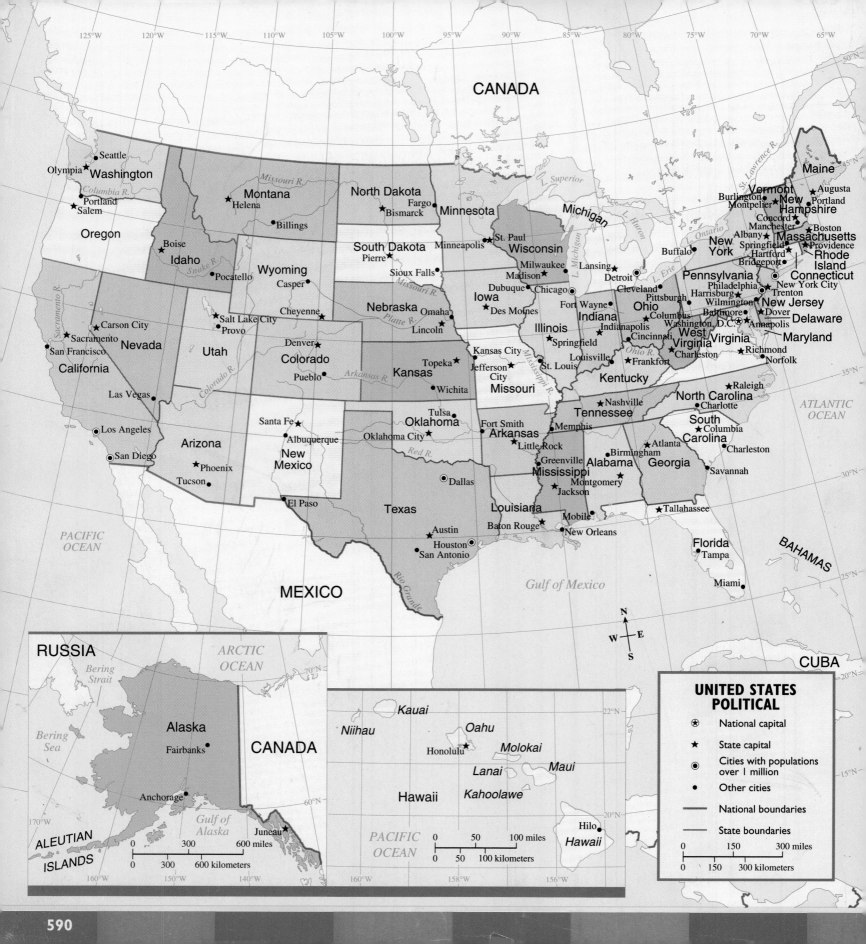

UNITED STATES POLITICAL

- ⊛ National capital
- ★ State capital
- ⊙ Cities with populations over 1 million
- • Other cities
- ⎯⎯ National boundaries
- ⎯⎯ State boundaries

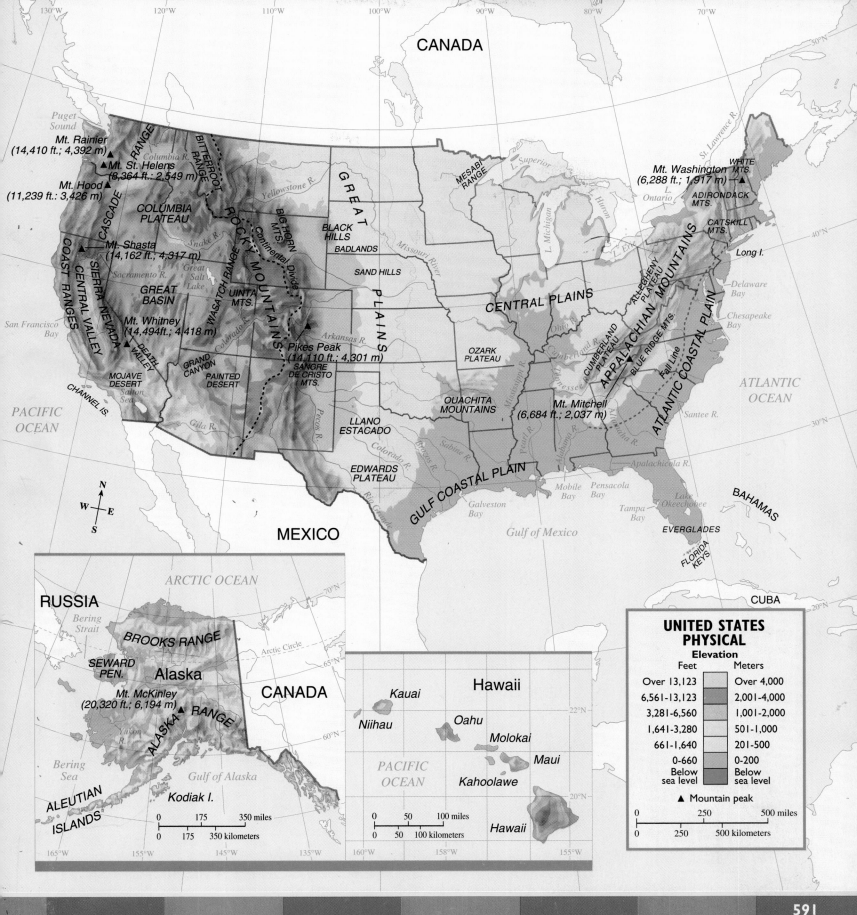

CANADA

Puget Sound

Mt. Rainier
(14,410 ft.; 4,392 m) ▲

▲ Mt. St. Helens
(8,364 ft.; 2,549 m)

Mt. Hood ▲
(11,239 ft.; 3,426 m)

CASCADE RANGE

BITTERROOT RANGE

Columbia R.

Yellowstone R.

COLUMBIA
PLATEAU

ROCKY MOUNTAINS

BIG HORN MTS.

Continental Divide

GREAT

BLACK
HILLS

BADLANDS

MESABI RANGE

L. Superior

L. Huron

L. Michigan

WHITE MTS.

Mt. Washington
(6,288 ft.; 1,917 m) — ▲

ADIRONDACK
MTS.

CATSKILL
MTS.

Mt. Shasta ▲
(14,162 ft.; 4,317 m)

Snake R.

Sacramento R.

Great Salt Lake

WASATCH RANGE

UINTA
MTS.

SAND HILLS

Missouri River

P

L

Long I.

L. Ontario

L. Erie

SIERRA NEVADA

COAST RANGES

CENTRAL VALLEY

GREAT
BASIN

A

I

N

CENTRAL PLAINS

ALLEGHENY PLATEAU

Delaware
Bay

San Francisco
Bay

Mt. Whitney
(14,494 ft.; 4,418 m) ▲

DEATH VALLEY

Colorado R.

Pikes Peak
(14,110 ft.; 4,301 m)

Arkansas R.

S

OZARK
PLATEAU

Ohio R.

CUMBERLAND PLATEAU

APPALACHIAN MOUNTAINS

BLUE RIDGE MTS.

Fall Line

Chesapeake
Bay

PACIFIC
OCEAN

CHANNEL IS.

MOJAVE
DESERT

Salton
Sea

GRAND
CANYON

PAINTED
DESERT

SANGRE
DE CRISTO
MTS.

Gila R.

Pecos R.

LLANO
ESTACADO

OUACHITA
MOUNTAINS

Mississippi R.

Tennessee R.

Cumberland R.

Mt. Mitchell
(6,684 ft.; 2,037 m)

Altamaha R.

ATLANTIC COASTAL PLAIN

Santee R.

ATLANTIC
OCEAN

N

W   E

S

MEXICO

EDWARDS
PLATEAU

Colorado R.

Rio Grande

GULF COASTAL PLAIN

Sabine R.

Brazos R.

Pearl R.

Alabama R.

Mobile
Bay

Pensacola
Bay

Apalachicola R.

Galveston
Bay

Tampa
Bay

EVERGLADES

BAHAMAS

Gulf of Mexico

FLORIDA
KEYS

ARCTIC OCEAN

RUSSIA

Bering
Strait

BROOKS RANGE

SEWARD
PEN.

Alaska

CANADA

Arctic Circle

70°N

65°N

CUBA

Bering
Sea

Mt. McKinley
(20,320 ft.; 6,194 m) ▲

ALASKA RANGE

Yukon R.

Gulf of Alaska

60°N

ALEUTIAN
ISLANDS

Kodiak I.

0   175   350 miles

0   175   350 kilometers

165°W   155°W   145°W   135°W

Hawaii

Kauai

Niihau

Oahu

Molokai

Maui

Kahoolawe

22°N

PACIFIC
OCEAN

0   50   100 miles

0   50   100 kilometers

160°W   158°W   155°W

Hawaii

20°N

UNITED STATES PHYSICAL

Elevation

Feet	Meters
Over 13,123	Over 4,000
6,561–13,123	2,001–4,000
3,281–6,560	1,001–2,000
1,641–3,280	501–1,000
661–1,640	201–500
0–660	0–200
Below sea level	Below sea level

▲ Mountain peak

0   250   500 miles

0   250   500 kilometers

ASIA

EUROPE

Bering Sea

Bering Strait

Barrow

ARCTIC OCEAN

Alaska (U.S.)

Arctic Circle

Yukon R.

Anchorage

Beaufort Sea

Mackenzie R.

Baffin Bay

Qaanaaq

Greenland (Kalaalit Nunaat) (Den.)

Gulf of Alaska

Whitehorse

Great Bear Lake

Nuuk

Juneau

Yellowknife

Great Slave Lake

Iqaluit

Labrador Sea

CANADA

Churchill

Hudson Bay

Goose Bay

PACIFIC OCEAN

Edmonton

Victoria *Vancouver* *Calgary*

Seattle

Saskatoon

Lake Winnipeg

Sept-Îles

Gander *St. John's*

Portland *Spokane*

Columbia R.

Regina

ST. PIERRE-MIQUELON (Fr.)

Missouri R.

Winnipeg

Great Lakes

Quebec

San Francisco

Great Salt Lake

Salt Lake City

Minneapolis ★*St. Paul*

Montreal ★ *Ottawa*

St. John

Halifax

Denver

Omaha

Milwaukee

Toronto

Detroit *Buffalo*

Boston

Los Angeles *San Diego*

Colorado R.

Chicago

Cleveland *Pittsburgh*

New York

UNITED STATES

Kansas City

Arkansas R.

St. Louis *Cincinnati*

Philadelphia

★*Washington, D.C.*

Phoenix

Ohio R.

Norfolk

El Paso

Dallas

Memphis

Mississippi R.

ATLANTIC OCEAN

Tropic of Cancer

Rio Grande

San Antonio

Houston *New Orleans*

Atlanta

Bermuda (U.K.)

Monterrey

MEXICO

Gulf of Mexico

Miami

BAHAMAS

NORTH AMERICA POLITICAL

⊛ National capitals

⊙ Cities with populations over 1 million

• Major cities

— National boundaries

— State boundaries

0   300   600 miles

0   300   600 kilometers

Guadalajara

Mexico City

Orizaba

Clipperton Island (Fr.)

Nassau

Havana

CUBA

Santiago

CAYMAN ISLANDS (U.K.)

DOMINICAN REPUBLIC

VIRGIN IS. (U.S.-U.K.)

Puerto Rico (U.S.)

ANTIGUA AND BARBUDA

HAITI

Port-au-Prince

★*Santo Domingo*

ST. KITTS AND NEVIS

Guadeloupe (Fr.)

JAMAICA

Kingston

DOMINICA

Martinique (Fr.)

Belmopan

BELIZE

Caribbean Sea

ST. LUCIA

BARBADOS

GUATEMALA

HONDURAS

NETH. ANTILLES (Neth.)

ST. VINCENT AND THE GRENADINES

Guatemala ★

San Salvador ★

Tegucigalpa ★

ARUBA

GRENADA

Panama Canal

EL SALVADOR

NICARAGUA

TRINIDAD AND TOBAGO

Managua ★

San José ★

PANAMA

COSTA RICA

★ *Panama*

SOUTH AMERICA

N W E S

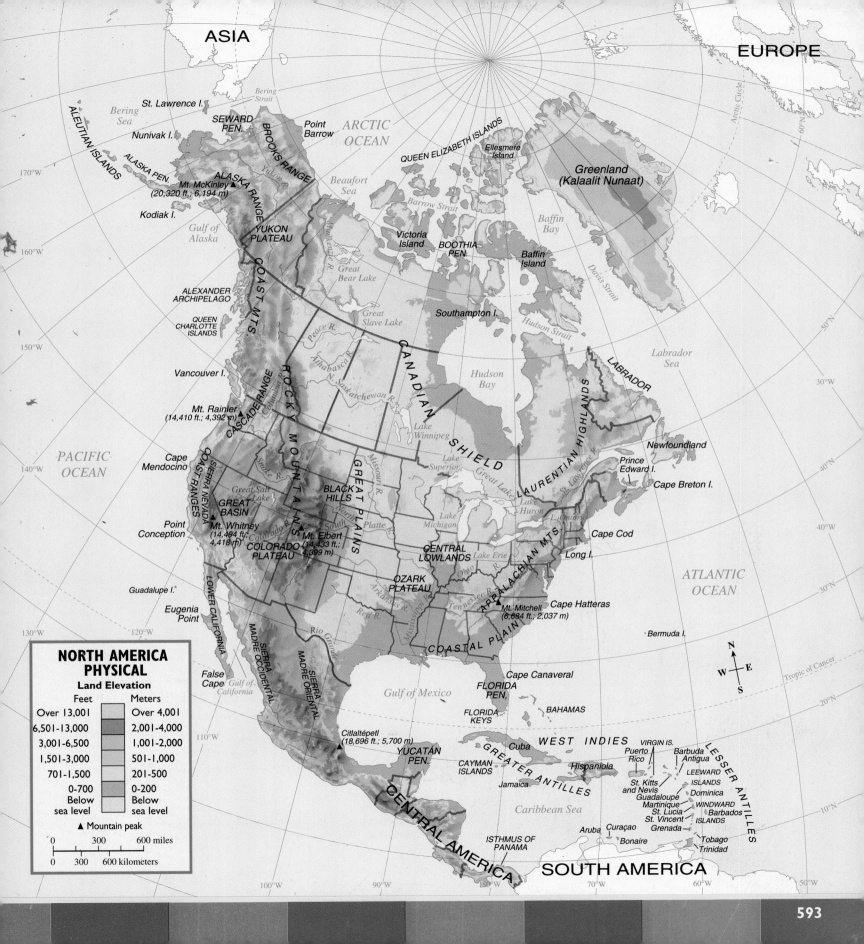

ASIA

EUROPE

ALEUTIAN ISLANDS

Bering Sea

St. Lawrence I.

Bering Strait

ARCTIC OCEAN

Nunivak I.

SEWARD PEN.

Point Barrow

QUEEN ELIZABETH ISLANDS

Ellesmere Island

Arctic Circle

ALASKA PEN.

BROOKS RANGE

Beaufort Sea

Greenland (Kalaalit Nunaat)

Mt. McKinley ▲ (20,320 ft.; 6,194 m)

ALASKA RANGE

Yukon R.

Kodiak I.

Gulf of Alaska

YUKON PLATEAU

Mackenzie R.

Great Bear Lake

Victoria Island

BOOTHIA PEN.

Barrow Strait

Baffin Island

Baffin Bay

Davis Strait

ALEXANDER ARCHIPELAGO

COAST MTS.

Great Slave Lake

Southampton I.

Hudson Strait

Labrador Sea

QUEEN CHARLOTTE ISLANDS

Peace R.

CANADIAN SHIELD

Hudson Bay

LABRADOR

Vancouver I.

Athabasca R.

N. Saskatchewan R.

LAURENTIAN HIGHLANDS

Newfoundland

ROCKY MOUNTAINS

CASCADE RANGE

Columbia R.

Lake Winnipeg

Prince Edward I.

Mt. Rainier (14,410 ft.; 4,392 m)

COAST RANGES

Snake R.

Missouri R.

Lake Superior

St. Lawrence R.

Cape Breton I.

Cape Mendocino

SIERRA NEVADA

Great Salt Lake

GREAT PLAINS

BLACK HILLS

Great Lakes

LAURENTIAN MTS.

PACIFIC OCEAN

GREAT BASIN

N. Platte R.

S. Platte R.

Lake Michigan

Lake Huron

Cape Cod

Point Conception

Mt. Whitney (14,494 ft.; 4,418 m)

COLORADO PLATEAU

Mt. Elbert (14,433 ft.; 4,399 m)

CENTRAL LOWLANDS

Lake Erie

L. Ontario

Long I.

ATLANTIC OCEAN

Guadalupe I.

OZARK PLATEAU

Ohio R.

APPALACHIAN MTS.

Eugenia Point

LOWER CALIFORNIA

Arkansas R.

Tennessee R.

Mt. Mitchell (6,684 ft.; 2,037 m)

Cape Hatteras

Red R.

Mississippi R.

Bermuda I.

SIERRA MADRE OCCIDENTAL

Rio Grande

SIERRA MADRE ORIENTAL

COASTAL PLAIN

False Cape

Gulf of California

Cape Canaveral

FLORIDA PEN.

Citlaltépetl (18,696 ft.; 5,700 m)

Gulf of Mexico

FLORIDA KEYS

BAHAMAS

YUCATÁN PEN.

CAYMAN ISLANDS

Cuba

WEST INDIES

VIRGIN IS.

Puerto Rico

Barbuda Antigua

GREATER ANTILLES

Hispaniola

LEEWARD ISLANDS

LESSER ANTILLES

Jamaica

St. Kitts and Nevis

Guadaloupe

Dominica

Martinique

WINDWARD

Caribbean Sea

St. Lucia

St. Vincent

Barbados

ISLANDS

CENTRAL AMERICA

Grenada

Aruba

Curaçao

Bonaire

Tobago

Trinidad

ISTHMUS OF PANAMA

SOUTH AMERICA

Tropic of Cancer

N
W   E
S

NORTH AMERICA PHYSICAL

Land Elevation

Feet	Meters
Over 13,001	Over 4,001
6,501–13,000	2,001–4,000
3,001–6,500	1,001–2,000
1,501–3,000	501–1,000
701–1,500	201–500
0–700	0–200
Below sea level	Below sea level

▲ Mountain peak

0   300   600 miles

0   300   600 kilometers

Caribbean Sea

Barranquilla
Cartagena
Maracaibo
Valencia
Caracas
Cúcuta
Barquisimeto
San
Cristóbal
VENEZUELA
GUYANA
SURINAME
Bucaramanga
Georgetown
French Guiana
(Fr.)
Medellín
Bogotá
Paramaribo
Cayenne
Cali
Orinoco R.
COLOMBIA

ATLANTIC OCEAN

Mapelo I.
(Colombia)

Quito
ECUADOR
Equator
Belém
GALÁPAGOS IS.
(Ecuador)
Manaus
Amazon R.
São Luís
Guayaquil
Fortaleza
Iquitos
Madeira R.
Xingu R.
Tocantins R.
Recife
Trujillo
PERU
B R A Z I L
Maceió
Lima
Cuzco
Araguaia R.
São Francisco R.
Salvador
Callao
Brasília
Arequipa
L. Titicaca
La Paz
BOLIVIA
Paraguay R.
Sucre
Belo
Horizonte
Chuquicamata
PARAGUAY
Paraná R.
Rio de Janeiro
Tropic of Capricorn
São Paulo
Niterói
Antofagasta
Tucumán
Asunción
Santos
San Felix I.
(Chile)
San Ambrosio I.
(Chile)
Curitiba
Uruguay R.
Pôrto Alegre
CHILE
Córdoba
Santa Fe
Juan Fernández Is.
(Chile)
Rosario
Paraná
URUGUAY
Valparaíso
Buenos Aires
Santiago
La Plata
Montevideo
Concepción
ARGENTINA
Mar del Plata
Bahía Blanca

PACIFIC OCEAN

ATLANTIC OCEAN

Strait of
Magellan
FALKLAND IS. (U.K.)
(MALVINAS IS.)
Punta Arenas

N
W E
S

SOUTH AMERICA POLITICAL

⊛ National capitals
◉ Cities with populations over one million
• Other cities
— International boundaries

0   400   800 miles
0   400   800 kilometers

10°N

0°

10°S

20°S

30°S

40°S

50°S

100°W   90°W   80°W   70°W   60°W   50°W   40°W   30°W   20°W   10°W

Caribbean Sea

GUAJIRA PEN.

Margarita I.

ORINOCO RIVER
DELTA

Lake
Maracaibo

Orinoco R.

C. Orange

Gulf of
Panama

LLANOS

Mt. Tolima
(17,105 ft.; 5,215 m) ▲

GUIANA HIGHLANDS

Mapelo I.

Magdalena R.

AMAZON
RIVER DELTA

Equator   0°

GALÁPAGOS IS.

Mt. Chimborazo
(20,561 ft.; 6,267 m) ▲

Rio Negro

AMAZON

Amazon R.

Marajó
Island

C. São Roque

Gulf of
Guayaquil

Marañón R.

BASIN

Xingu R.

Negra Pt.

Ucayali R.

SOUTH

10°S

▲ Mt. Huascarán
(22,205 ft.; 6,763 m)

AMERICA

MATO
GROSSO
PLATEAU

PACIFIC
OCEAN

ANDES

MOUNTAINS

L. Titicaca

Mt. Ancohuma
(20,958 ft.; 6,388 m) ▲

Araguaia R.

Tocantins R.

São Francisco R.

▲ Mt. Bandeira
(9,479 ft.; 2,890 m)

L. Poopó

20°S

GRAN CHACO

BRAZILIAN

C. Frio

Tropic of Capricorn

San Felix I.

San Ambrosio I.

ATACAMA DESERT

Paraguay R.

Paraná R.

HIGHLANDS

ATLANTIC
OCEAN

30°S

Mt. Aconcagua
(22,831 ft.; 6,959 m)

Paraná R.

Uruguay R.

Juan Fernández Is.

PAMPAS

Río de
la Plata

Blanca Bay

SOUTH AMERICA PHYSICAL

San Matías Gulf

Chiloé I.

VALDÉS PEN.

Land Elevation

CHONOS
ARCHIPELAGO

TAITAO PEN.

Feet	Meters
Over 13,121	Over 4,001
6,561-13,120	2,001-4,000
3,281-6,560	1,001-2,000
661-3,280	201-1,000
0-660	0-200

40°S

N
W   E
S

PATAGONIA

Gulf of
San Jorge

C. Tres Puntas

▲ Mountain peak

0   400   800 miles

0   400   800 kilometers

FALKLAND IS. (U.K.)
(MALVINAS IS.)

Grande Bay

50°S

Strait of
Magellan

Tierra Del Fuego

Cape Horn

South Georgia

90°W   80°W   70°W   60°W   50°W   40°W   30°W   20°W   10°W

EUROPE

ASIA

Mediterranean Sea

Tangier
Algiers
Tunis

Rabat
Oran

Casablanca

MADEIRA IS. (Port.)

Marrakech

MOROCCO

Tripoli

Benghazi

Alexandria
Cairo

EGYPT

Suez Canal

CANARY IS. (Sp.)

El Aaiún

Western Sahara (Morocco)

ALGERIA

LIBYA

Tropic of Cancer

L. Nasser

Red Sea

Nile R.

MAURITANIA

Nouakchott

MALI

Timbuktu

Niger R.

NIGER

CHAD

SUDAN

Khartoum

Port Sudan

ERITREA

Asmara

Dakar

SENEGAL

Banjul

GAMBIA

Bissau

GUINEA-BISSAU

Bamako

BURKINA FASO

Ouagadougou

Niamey

N'Djamena

L. Chad

White Nile R.

Blue Nile R.

DJIBOUTI

Djibouti

Gulf of Aden

Conakry

GUINEA

Freetown

SIERRA LEONE

Monrovia

LIBERIA

CÔTE D'IVOIRE

Yamoussoukro

Accra

GHANA

TOGO

BENIN

Lomé

Porto-Novo

NIGERIA

Abuja

Lagos

CAMEROON

Malabo

EQUATORIAL GUINEA

Yaoundé

CENTRAL AFRICAN REPUBLIC

Bangui

ETHIOPIA

Addis Ababa

SOMALIA

Mogadishu

SÃO TOMÉ AND PRÍNCIPE

São Tomé

Libreville

GABON

CONGO

Brazzaville

Kinshasa

Cabinda (Angola)

ZAIRE

Zaire (Congo) River

UGANDA

Kampala

RWANDA

Kigali

Bujumbura

BURUNDI

L. Turkana

KENYA

Nairobi

Mombasa

L. Victoria

0° Equator

Ascension (Br.)

Luanda

ATLANTIC OCEAN

ANGOLA

L. Tanganyika

TANZANIA

Dar es Salaam

SEYCHELLES

Victoria

INDIAN OCEAN

St. Helena (Br.)

L. Nyasa

ZAMBIA

Lusaka

L. Kariba

MALAWI

Lilongwe

COMOROS

Moroni

Harare

ZIMBABWE

Zambezi River

MOZAMBIQUE

Antananarivo

MADAGASCAR

MAURITIUS

Réunion (Fr.)

Port-Louis

NAMIBIA

Windhoek

Tropic of Capricorn

BOTSWANA

Gaborone

Pretoria

Johannesburg

Maputo

Mbabane

SWAZILAND

Maseru

LESOTHO

Durban

SOUTH AFRICA

Umtata

Cape Town

Port Elizabeth

AFRICA POLITICAL

⊛ National capitals

⊙ Cities with populations over one million

• Other cities

— International boundaries

···· Disputed boundaries

0   500   1,000 miles

0   500   1,000 kilometers

596

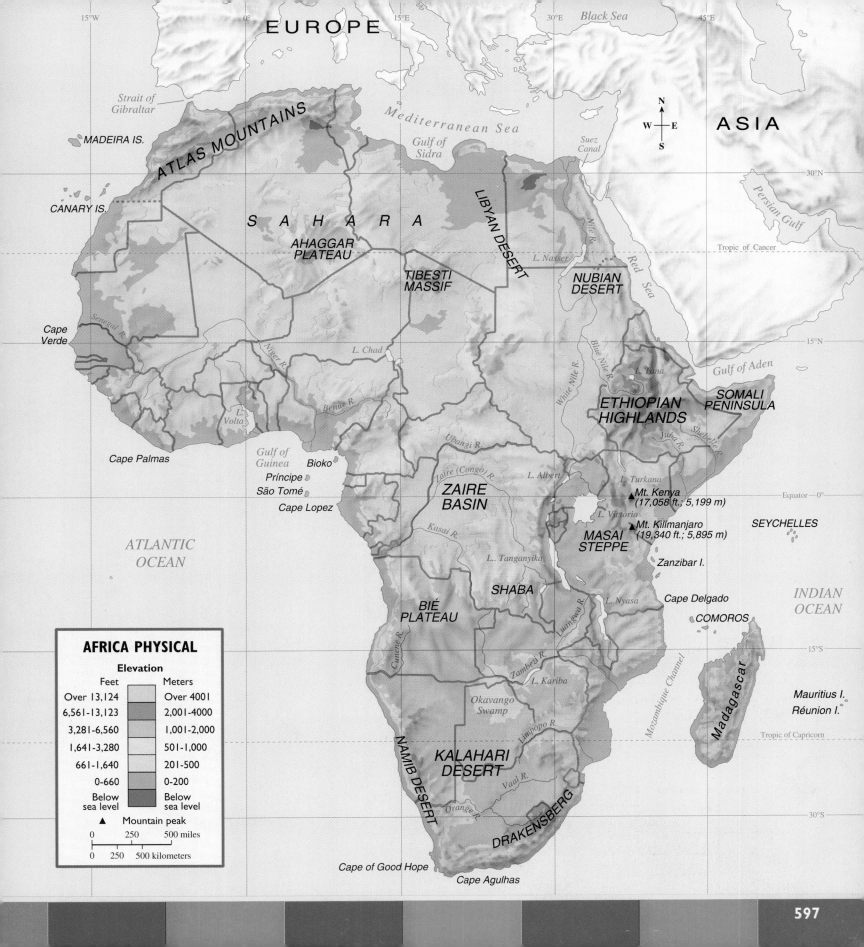

EUROPE

ASIA

Black Sea

Mediterranean Sea

Strait of Gibraltar

Gulf of Sidra

Suez Canal

Persian Gulf

15°W

0°

15°E

30°E

45°E

N
W   E
S

MADEIRA IS.

ATLAS MOUNTAINS

CANARY IS.

S A H A R A

AHAGGAR PLATEAU

TIBESTI MASSIF

LIBYAN DESERT

L. Nasser

Nile R.

NUBIAN DESERT

30°N

Tropic of Cancer

Cape Verde

Senegal R.

Niger R.

L. Chad

15°N

Red Sea

Gulf of Aden

White Nile R.

Blue Nile R.

L. Tana

ETHIOPIAN HIGHLANDS

SOMALI PENINSULA

Cape Palmas

Benue R.

L. Volta

Gulf of Guinea

Bioko

Príncipe

São Tomé

Cape Lopez

Ubangi R.

Zaire (Congo) R.

ZAIRE BASIN

Kasai R.

L. Albert

L. Turkana

Juba R.

Shebelle R.

▲ Mt. Kenya
(17,058 ft.; 5,199 m)

L. Victoria

▲ Mt. Kilimanjaro
(19,340 ft.; 5,895 m)

MASAI STEPPE

SEYCHELLES

Zanzibar I.

Equator — 0°

ATLANTIC OCEAN

L. Tanganyika

SHABA

BIÉ PLATEAU

Cunene R.

Luangwa R.

L. Nyasa

Cape Delgado

COMOROS

INDIAN OCEAN

15°S

AFRICA PHYSICAL

Elevation

Feet		Meters
Over 13,124		Over 4001
6,561–13,123		2,001–4000
3,281–6,560		1,001–2,000
1,641–3,280		501–1,000
661–1,640		201–500
0–660		0–200
Below sea level		Below sea level

▲ Mountain peak

0   250   500 miles

0   250   500 kilometers

Zambezi R.

L. Kariba

Okavango Swamp

Mozambique Channel

Madagascar

Mauritius I.

Réunion I.

Tropic of Capricorn

NAMIB DESERT

KALAHARI DESERT

Limpopo R.

Vaal R.

Orange R.

DRAKENSBERG

30°S

Cape of Good Hope

Cape Agulhas

597

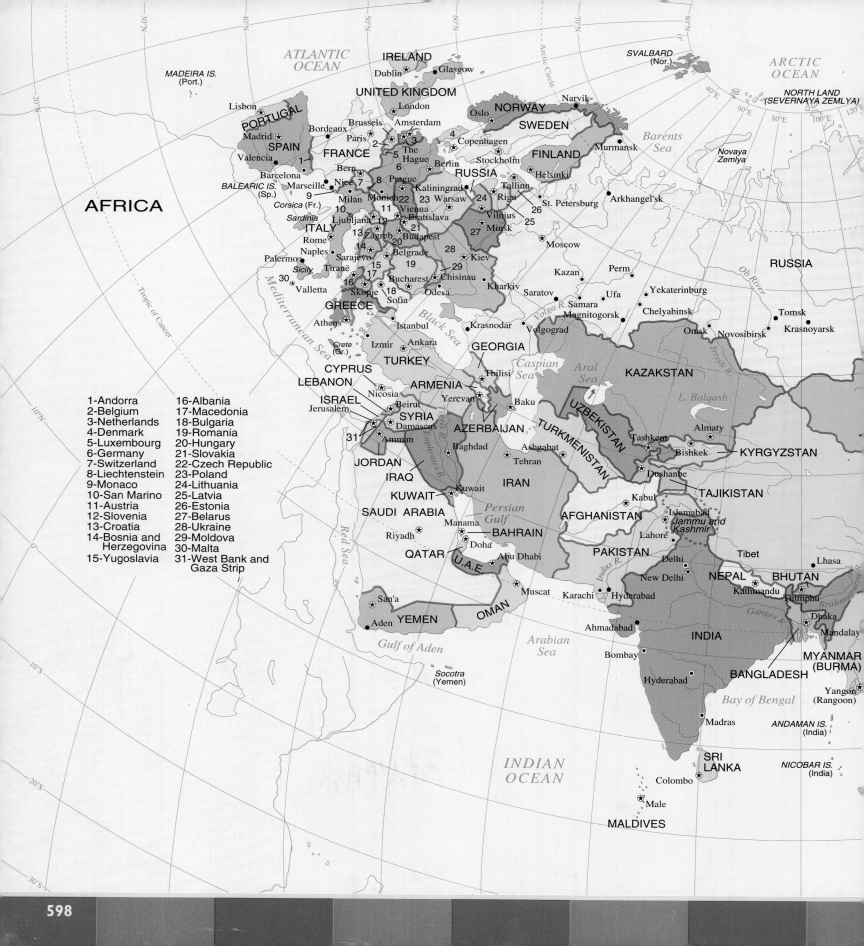

ATLANTIC
OCEAN

IRELAND

Dublin ⭐ ⭐ Glasgow

SVALBARD
(Nor.)

ARCTIC
OCEAN

MADEIRA IS.
(Port.)

UNITED KINGDOM

London ⭐

NORTH LAND
(SEVERNAYA ZEMLYA)

Lisbon ⭐

Narvik ⭐

NORWAY

PORTUGAL

Brussels

Amsterdam

Oslo ⭐

SWEDEN

Bordeaux ⭐

Paris ⭐

2

3

4

Copenhagen ⭐

Barents
Sea

Novaya
Zemlya

Madrid ⭐

SPAIN

FRANCE

5

The
Hague

Berlin ⭐

Stockholm ⭐

FINLAND

Murmansk ⭐

Valencia ⭐

1

Bern ⭐

6

Prague ⭐

RUSSIA

Helsinki ⭐

AFRICA

Barcelona ⭐

Nice ⭐

7

8

Munich ⭐

Kaliningrad ⭐

Tallinn ⭐

St. Petersburg ⭐

Arkhangel'sk ⭐

BALEARIC IS.
(Sp.)

Marseille ⭐

9

22

23

Warsaw ⭐

24

Riga ⭐

Corsica (Fr.)

Milan ⭐

Vienna ⭐

26

Sardinia

10

11

Bratislava ⭐

Vilnius ⭐

Moscow ⭐

RUSSIA

Ljubljana ⭐

12

21

25

Minsk ⭐

ITALY

Rome ⭐

13

Zagreb ⭐

20

Budapest ⭐

27

Kazan ⭐

Perm ⭐

14

Belgrade ⭐

28

Kiev ⭐

Naples ⭐

Sarajevo ⭐

15

19

Yekaterinburg ⭐

Palermo ⭐

Sicily

Tiranë ⭐

17

29

Chisinau ⭐

Saratov ⭐

Samara ⭐

Ufa ⭐

Omsk ⭐

Chelyabinsk ⭐

Novosibirsk ⭐

Tomsk ⭐

30

16

Valletta ⭐

Skopje ⭐

18

Bucharest ⭐

Odesa ⭐

Kharkiv ⭐

Krasnodar ⭐

Volgograd ⭐

Magnitogorsk ⭐

Krasnoyarsk ⭐

GREECE

Sofia ⭐

Black Sea

Athens ⭐

Istanbul ⭐

GEORGIA

Caspian
Sea

Aral
Sea

L. Balqash

KAZAKSTAN

Izmir ⭐

Ankara ⭐

Tbilisi ⭐

CYPRUS

TURKEY

LEBANON

ARMENIA

Nicosia ⭐

Beirut ⭐

Yerevan ⭐

Baku ⭐

UZBEKISTAN

Almaty ⭐

ISRAEL

Jerusalem ⭐

SYRIA

Damascus ⭐

AZERBAIJAN

TURKMENISTAN

Tashkent ⭐

Bishkek ⭐

KYRGYZSTAN

31

Amman ⭐

Baghdad ⭐

Ashgabat ⭐

Dushanbe ⭐

JORDAN

IRAQ

Tehran ⭐

IRAN

Kabul ⭐

TAJIKISTAN

KUWAIT

Kuwait ⭐

Islamabad ⭐

Jammu and
Kashmir

SAUDI ARABIA

Persian
Gulf

AFGHANISTAN

Lahore ⭐

PAKISTAN

Manama ⭐

BAHRAIN

Delhi ⭐

Tibet

Lhasa ⭐

Riyadh ⭐

Doha ⭐

New Delhi ⭐

NEPAL

BHUTAN

QATAR

Abu Dhabi ⭐

U.A.E.

Kathmandu ⭐

Thimphu ⭐

Red Sea

Muscat ⭐

Karachi ⭐

Hyderabad ⭐

Dhaka ⭐

San'a ⭐

OMAN

Ahmadabad ⭐

INDIA

Mandalay ⭐

YEMEN

Aden ⭐

Bombay ⭐

MYANMAR
(BURMA)

Gulf of Aden

Arabian
Sea

Hyderabad ⭐

BANGLADESH

Yangon ⭐
(Rangoon)

Socotra
(Yemen)

Madras ⭐

ANDAMAN IS.
(India)

INDIAN
OCEAN

SRI
LANKA

NICOBAR IS.
(India)

Colombo ⭐

Male ⭐

MALDIVES

1-Andorra
2-Belgium
3-Netherlands
4-Denmark
5-Luxembourg
6-Germany
7-Switzerland
8-Liechtenstein
9-Monaco
10-San Marino
11-Austria
12-Slovenia
13-Croatia
14-Bosnia and
   Herzegovina
15-Yugoslavia

16-Albania
17-Macedonia
18-Bulgaria
19-Romania
20-Hungary
21-Slovakia
22-Czech Republic
23-Poland
24-Lithuania
25-Latvia
26-Estonia
27-Belarus
28-Ukraine
29-Moldova
30-Malta
31-West Bank and
   Gaza Strip

ATLANTIC
OCEAN

ARCTIC
OCEAN

Ireland
BRITISH ISLES

SVALBARD

NORTH
LAND

MADEIRA IS.

Great Britain

SCANDINAVIAN
PENINSULA

LAPLAND

*Novaya
Zemlya*

TAYMYR
PEN.

*North
Sea*

KOLA
PEN.

*Barents
Sea*

YAMAL
PEN.

*Kara
Sea*

*Strait of
Gibraltar*

IBERIAN
PENINSULA

PYRENEES

Baltic Sea

CENTRAL
SIBERIAN
PLATEAU

BALEARIC IS.

ALPS

NORTH EUROPEAN PLAIN

URAL MOUNTAINS

WEST
SIBERIAN
PLAIN

SIBERIA

Corsica

CARPATHIAN MTS.

Sardinia

*Tyrrhenian
Sea*

ADRIATIC MTS.

Volga R.

Sicily

BALKAN
PENINSULA

Malta

*Ionian
Sea*

Aegean Sea

Black Sea

ALTAI MTS

Crete

ANATOLIAN
PLATEAU

CAUCASUS
MOUNTAINS

KIRGIZ
STEPPE

KAZAK
UPLANDS

L. Balqash

Cyprus

Caspian Sea

*Aral
Sea*

TURAN LOWLAND

Mediterranean Sea

*Suez
Canal*

SINAI
PENINSULA

SYRIAN
DESERT

ELBURZ MTS.

TIAN SHAN

TARIM
BASIN

AFRICA

Tigris R.

ZAGROS MTS.

PLATEAU
OF
IRAN

PAMIRS

HINDU KUSH

KUNLUN SHAN

Euphrates R.

ARABIAN
PENINSULA

Persian Gulf

Red Sea

Indus R. (Sutlej R.)

TIBETAN PLATEAU

Salween R.

Gulf of Oman

GREAT
INDIAN
DESERT

HIMALAYAS

Mt. Everest
(29,028 ft.
8,848 m)

RUB AL' KHALI
DESERT

GANGES PLAIN

Brahmaputra R.

Ganges R.

Gulf of Aden

*Arabian
Sea*

DECCAN

Godavari R.

*Bay of
Bengal*

Equator

WESTERN GHATS

PLATEAU

EASTERN GHATS

LAKSHADWEEP

ANDAMAN
IS.

*Sri
Lanka*

NICOBAR
IS.

MALDIVE IS.

N
W E
S

INDIAN
OCEAN

EAST
SIBERIAN
SEA

NEW
SIBERIAN
ISLANDS

*Laptev
Sea*

*Bering
Sea*

CHERSKI RANGE

KOLYMA RANGE

VERKHOYANSK RANGE

CENTRAL RANGE

KAMCHATKA
PENINSULA

SIBERIA

*Sea of
Okhotsk*

L. Baikal

Aldan R.

Lena R.

Amur R.

Sakhalin

KURIL ISLANDS

GREATER KHINGAN RANGE

MANCHURIAN
PLAIN

Hokkaido

Honshu

*Sea of
Japan*

MONGOLIAN
PLATEAU

GOBI

Great Wall

KOREAN
PEN.

Korea Strait

Mt. Fuji
(12,389 ft.; 3,776 m)

Shikoku

Kyushu

JAPANESE
ARCHIPELAGO

NAN SHAN

*Huang He
(Yellow R.)*

*Yellow
Sea*

NORTH
CHINA
PLAIN

*Changjiang
(Yangzi R.)*

RYUKYU IS.

*East
China
Sea*

Okinawa

BOHEA HILLS

Xijiang (West R.)

Taiwan

*Luzon
Strait*

*Philippine
Sea*

MARSHALL
IS.

*PACIFIC
OCEAN*

GILBERT IS.

MARIANA
IS.

Guam

CAROLINE IS.

Luzon

Hainan

*South
China
Sea*

Mindoro

Samar

Panay

PHILIPPINE
ISLANDS

PALAU IS.

Palawan

Negros

Mindanao

INDOCHINA
PENINSULA

Mekong R.

ADMIRALTY
IS.

New
Ireland

SOLOMON IS.

New Britain

VANUATU
(NEW HEBRIDES)

*Gulf of
Thailand*

*Celebes
Sea*

Halmahera

MOLUCCAS

New Guinea

MAOKE
MTS.

MALAY
PENINSULA

Ceram

ARU
IS.

*Coral
Sea*

New Caledonia

*Strait of
Malacca*

Celebes

Buru

Sumatra

Borneo

*Java
Sea*

*Arafura
Sea*

Bangka

E A S T   I N D I E S

MENTAWAI
IS.

GREATER SUNDA ISLANDS

Sumbawa

Flores

Timor

Lombok

Sumba

AUSTRALIA

Java

Bali

LESSER SUNDA ISLANDS

<table>
<tr><td colspan="3" align="center">**EURASIA PHYSICAL**</td></tr>
<tr><td colspan="3" align="center">Elevation</td></tr>
<tr><td>Feet</td><td></td><td>Meters</td></tr>
<tr><td>Over 13,120</td><td></td><td>Over 4,000</td></tr>
<tr><td>6,561–13,120</td><td></td><td>2,001–4,000</td></tr>
<tr><td>3,281–6,560</td><td></td><td>1,001–2,000</td></tr>
<tr><td>1,641–3,280</td><td></td><td>501–1,000</td></tr>
<tr><td>661–1,640</td><td></td><td>201–500</td></tr>
<tr><td>0–660</td><td></td><td>0–200</td></tr>
<tr><td>Below
sea level</td><td></td><td>Below
sea level</td></tr>
</table>

0   500   1,000 miles

0   500   1,000 kilometers

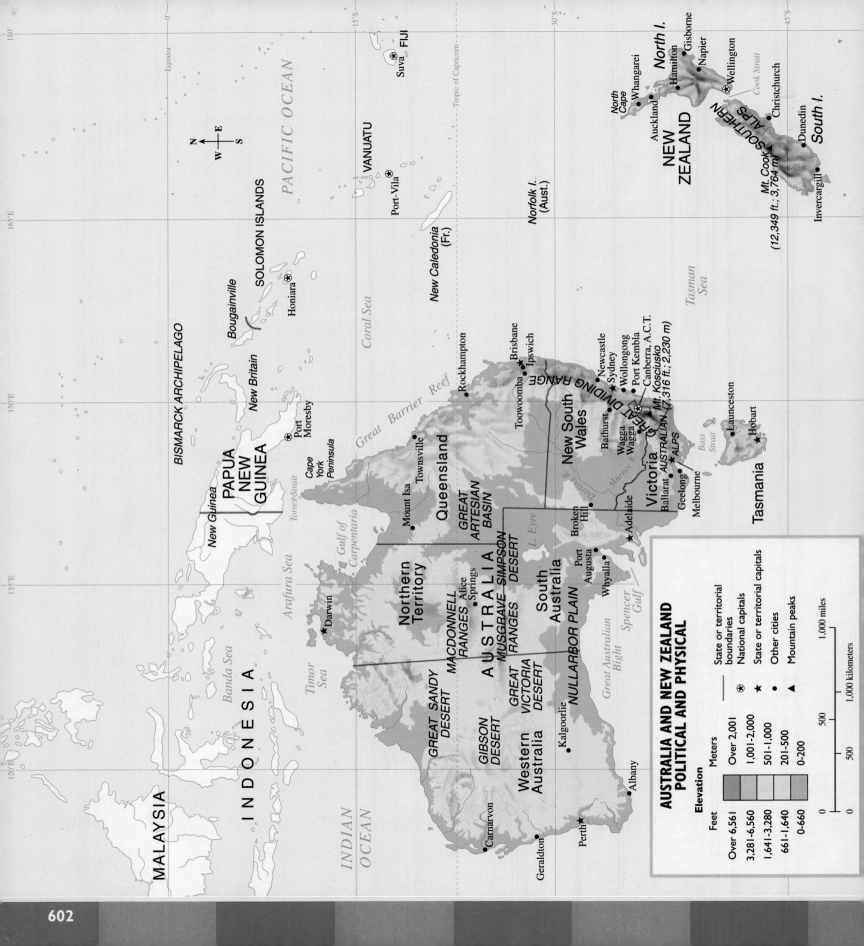

MALAYSIA

INDONESIA

PACIFIC OCEAN

Banda Sea

Timor Sea

Arafura Sea

BISMARCK ARCHIPELAGO

Bougainville

New Britain

SOLOMON ISLANDS

Honiara ⊛

New Guinea

PAPUA NEW GUINEA

Port Moresby ⊛

Torres Strait

Gulf of Carpentaria

Cape York Peninsula

Great Barrier Reef

Coral Sea

VANUATU

Port-Vila ⊛

New Caledonia (Fr.)

Norfolk I. (Aust.)

FIJI

Suva ⊛

Tasman Sea

North Cape

Whangarei
Auckland ● Hamilton
Napier
NEW ZEALAND
Wellington ⊛

North I.
Gisborne

Cook Strait
Christchurch ●

SOUTHERN ALPS

Mt. Cook ▲
(12,349 ft.; 3,764 m)

South I.
Dunedin ●

Invercargill ●

Darwin ★

Northern Territory

Alice Springs ●

MACDONNELL RANGES

MUSGRAVE RANGES

AUSTRALIA

GREAT SANDY DESERT

GIBSON DESERT

GREAT VICTORIA DESERT

Western Australia

Kalgoorlie ●

Carnarvon ●

Geraldton ●

Perth ★

Albany ●

Great Australian Bight

NULLARBOR PLAIN

South Australia

SIMPSON DESERT

L. Eyre

Port Augusta ●
Whyalla ●

Spencer Gulf

Adelaide ★

Broken Hill ●

Mount Isa ●

Queensland

GREAT ARTESIAN BASIN

Townsville ●

Rockhampton ●

Brisbane ★
Ipswich ●

Toowoomba ●

New South Wales

Darling R.

Murray R.

Newcastle ●
Sydney ★
Wollongong ●
Port Kembla ●
Canberra, A.C.T. ⊛

GREAT DIVIDING RANGE

Bathurst ●
Wagga Wagga ●

GREAT AUSTRALIAN ALPS
Mt. Kosciusko ▲
(7,316 ft.; 2,230 m)

Victoria

Ballarat ●
Geelong ●
Melbourne ★

Bass Strait

Launceston ●

Tasmania

Hobart ★

INDIAN OCEAN

AUSTRALIA AND NEW ZEALAND POLITICAL AND PHYSICAL

⎯	State or territorial boundaries
⊛	National capitals
★	State or territorial capitals
●	Other cities
▲	Mountain peaks

Elevation

Feet	Meters	
Over 6,561	Over 2,001	
3,281–6,560	1,001–2,000	
1,641–3,280	501–1,000	
661–1,640	201–500	
0–660	0–200	

0   500   1,000 miles

0   500   1,000 kilometers

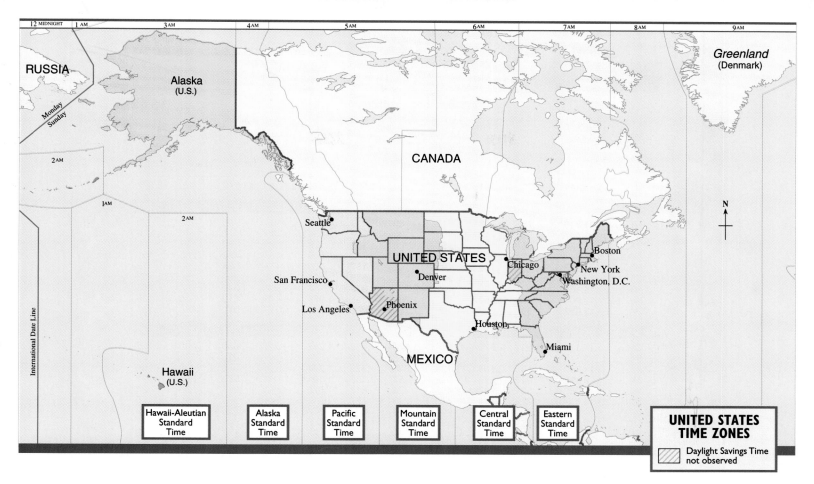

UNITED STATES TIME ZONES

12 MIDNIGHT | 1 AM | 3 AM | 4 AM | 5 AM | 6 AM | 7 AM | 8 AM | 9 AM

RUSSIA

Alaska (U.S.)

Monday / Sunday

International Date Line

CANADA

Greenland (Denmark)

N

Seattle

UNITED STATES

San Francisco

Denver

Los Angeles

Phoenix

Chicago

Boston

New York

Washington, D.C.

Houston

Miami

MEXICO

Hawaii (U.S.)

Hawaii-Aleutian Standard Time

Alaska Standard Time

Pacific Standard Time

Mountain Standard Time

Central Standard Time

Eastern Standard Time

Daylight Savings Time not observed

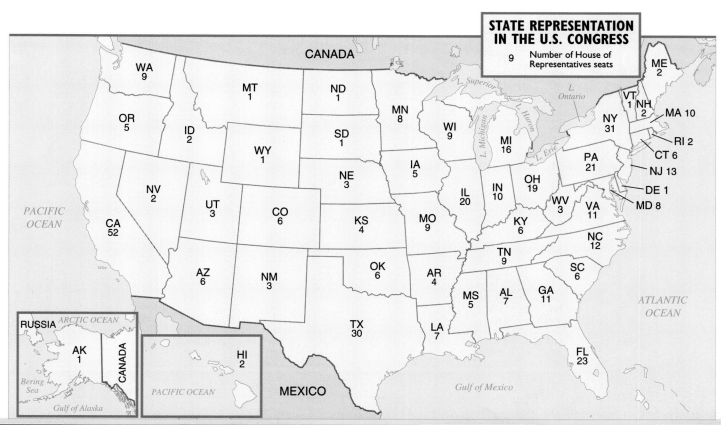

STATE REPRESENTATION IN THE U.S. CONGRESS

9   Number of House of Representatives seats

CANADA

WA 9
MT 1
ND 1
MN 8
ME 2
L. Superior
L. Ontario
VT 1
NH 2
MA 10
NY 31
RI 2
CT 6
NJ 13
DE 1
MD 8
OR 5
ID 2
WY 1
SD 1
WI 9
L. Michigan
L. Huron
MI 16
L. Erie
PA 21
NV 2
UT 3
CO 6
NE 3
IA 5
IL 20
IN 10
OH 19
WV 3
VA 11
CA 52
KS 4
MO 9
KY 6
NC 12
AZ 6
NM 3
OK 6
AR 4
TN 9
SC 6
PACIFIC OCEAN
MS 5
AL 7
GA 11
ATLANTIC OCEAN
TX 30
LA 7
FL 23

RUSSIA
ARCTIC OCEAN
AK 1
CANADA
Bering Sea
Gulf of Alaska

HI 2
PACIFIC OCEAN

MEXICO
Gulf of Mexico

STATE POPULATION BY AGE

(In thousands; as of July 1, 1994)

REGION AND STATE	Total	Under 5 years	5 to 17 years	18 to 24 years	25 to 34 years	35 to 44 years	45 to 54 years	55 to 64 years	65 to 74 years	75 to 84 years	85 years and over
U.S.	260,341	19,727	48,291	25,263	41,354	41,659	29,871	21,018	18,712	10,925	3,522
Northeast	51,396	3,681	8,853	4,711	8,224	8,265	6,077	4,347	4,037	2,411	790
ME	1,240	78	228	115	183	210	150	104	95	57	20
NH	1,137	80	212	100	190	203	134	83	76	44	16
VT	580	38	108	57	88	102	72	45	39	23	8
MA	6,041	423	1,001	566	1,058	972	699	473	460	288	101
RI	997	71	169	97	161	157	109	77	84	53	18
CT	3,275	231	557	281	531	538	401	271	253	159	53
NY	18,169	1,382	3,129	1,702	2,987	2,875	2,147	1,552	1,341	784	268
NJ	7,904	579	1,352	688	1,264	1,301	966	676	612	356	109
PA	12,052	799	2,099	1,105	1,760	1,906	1,399	1,066	1,077	644	197
Midwest	61,394	4,444	11,699	5,940	9,370	9,796	6,992	5,046	4,456	2,716	935
OH	11,102	784	2,070	1,079	1,673	1,773	1,287	945	850	486	155
IN	5,752	407	1,066	591	878	919	674	483	413	241	80
IL	11,752	915	2,168	1,128	1,886	1,878	1,341	955	818	499	164
MI	9,496	701	1,824	932	1,457	1,539	1,101	762	673	385	121
WI	5,082	350	997	483	771	817	570	412	364	236	84
MN	4,567	327	914	416	723	757	511	348	300	198	75
IA	2,829	188	541	274	393	434	316	246	226	152	59
MO	5,278	376	1,003	498	792	816	600	448	405	249	91
ND	638	43	129	66	90	99	66	52	47	34	13
SD	721	54	154	70	97	108	73	58	55	36	14
NE	1,623	116	326	158	232	253	176	133	119	79	32
KS	2,554	184	506	247	378	403	278	203	187	120	47
South	90,692	6,786	16,824	9,076	14,283	14,285	10,440	7,468	6,614	3,749	1,167
DE	706	51	124	68	120	114	81	58	54	27	8
MD	5,006	379	884	441	876	861	616	391	330	175	55
DC	570	43	76	58	114	91	65	46	43	25	9
VA	6,552	469	1,134	670	1,135	1,098	804	517	426	229	70
WV	1,822	108	321	190	235	286	225	176	160	92	28
NC	7,070	510	1,246	733	1,143	1,119	834	599	521	280	83
SC	3,664	274	678	394	576	576	430	301	262	135	38
GA	7,055	549	1,344	729	1,207	1,161	830	527	413	228	69
FL	13,953	962	2,300	1,174	2,069	2,077	1,543	1,256	1,441	873	257
KY	3,827	261	709	400	577	604	455	333	278	159	52
TN	5,175	366	931	518	799	822	630	452	375	215	69
AL	4,219	302	778	446	631	648	491	371	317	179	56
MS	2,669	207	549	304	382	390	287	219	187	109	36
AR	2,453	172	468	247	343	357	284	219	199	124	40
LA	4,315	337	898	458	642	663	476	347	287	157	50
OK	3,258	237	643	328	459	489	374	285	244	147	52
TX	18,378	1,559	3,742	1,919	2,975	2,929	2,014	1,371	1,078	594	196
West	56,859	4,816	10,915	5,536	9,478	9,313	6,362	4,157	3,604	2,049	629
MT	856	59	179	80	106	141	104	74	62	40	12
ID	1,133	87	252	120	149	177	127	89	72	46	14
WY	476	33	104	49	60	82	57	39	30	17	5
CO	3,656	270	700	344	575	660	453	286	212	117	39
NM	1,654	140	358	162	238	261	183	131	106	58	17
AZ	4,075	344	795	392	633	612	436	317	317	180	49
UT	1,908	181	491	232	283	261	173	118	96	56	17
NV	1,457	115	261	124	250	238	179	126	106	48	10
WA	5,343	394	1,014	492	845	929	649	402	345	208	65
OR	3,086	209	574	278	440	528	386	249	232	145	45
CA	31,431	2,833	5,844	3,085	5,615	5,109	3,403	2,195	1,921	1,084	342
AK	606	56	136	61	98	118	73	37	19	7	2
HI	1,179	95	209	116	186	199	138	94	86	43	12

Source: Statistical Abstracts of the United States, 1995

PRESIDENTS

George Washington (1789–1797)

BORN Feb. 22, 1732 **DIED** Dec. 14, 1799
EARLY CAREER Surveyor; head of Virginia militia; plantation owner
MARRIED Martha Dandridge Custis; one stepdaughter, one stepson
POLITICAL PARTY Federalist
VICE PRESIDENT John Adams
HOBBIES Fox hunting; raising mules; daily walks
ADMINISTRATION Departments of Foreign Affairs, Treasury, and War created; Attorney General established; Post Office continued
ANECDOTES Disapproved of swearing; commander in chief of Continental Army; lived at No. 1 Cherry Street, New York City, the first presidential mansion

John Adams (1797–1801)

BORN Oct. 30, 1735 **DIED** July 4, 1826
EARLY CAREER Schoolteacher; lawyer
MARRIED Abigail Smith; three sons, two daughters
POLITICAL PARTY Federalist
VICE PRESIDENT Thomas Jefferson
HOBBIES Reading; keeping diaries; walking five miles a day; fishing; playing whist
ADMINISTRATION Library of Congress, Marine Corps, Navy, and Public Health Services established
ANECDOTES Read seven languages; was married more than 54 years, longer than any other President; lived more than 90 years, longer than any other President; died on fiftieth anniversary of the signing of the Declaration of Independence

Thomas Jefferson (1801–1809)

BORN April 13, 1743 **DIED** July 4, 1826
EARLY CAREER Lawyer; plantation owner; writer
MARRIED Martha Wayles Skelton; one son, five daughters
POLITICAL PARTY Democratic-Republican
VICE PRESIDENT Aaron Burr; George Clinton
HOBBIES Playing the violin; cooking (introduced ice cream, waffles, and macaroni to the U.S.); inventing; designing Monticello, his home; scientist; book collecting
ADMINISTRATION Made the Louisiana Purchase; authorized Lewis and Clark Expedition; African slave import ended
ANECDOTES Ranked writing the Declaration of Independence as his finest achievement; died on the same day as John Adams; his personal library became part of the Library of Congress

James Madison (1809–1817)

BORN March 16, 1751 **DIED** June 28, 1836
EARLY CAREER Farmer; lawyer
MARRIED Dolley Payne Todd; one stepson
POLITICAL PARTY Democratic-Republican
VICE PRESIDENT George Clinton, Elbridge Gerry
HOBBIES Horseback riding; playing chess; reading Latin and Greek texts
ADMINISTRATION First war bonds issued; U.S. defeated England in the War of 1812
ANECDOTES The shortest President, 5' 4"; wrote nine of the ten amendments that are the Bill of Rights; Dolley, his wife, packed a valuable portrait of George Washington before the British burned the White House; his portrait is on the $5,000 bill

James Monroe (1817–1825)

BORN April 28, 1758 **DIED** July 4, 1831
EARLY CAREER Lawyer; farmer; writer; soldier
MARRIED Elizabeth Kortright; two daughters, one son
POLITICAL PARTY Democratic-Republican
VICE PRESIDENT Daniel D. Tompkins
HOBBIES Horseback riding; hunting
ADMINISTRATION Purchased Florida; issued Monroe Doctrine; Missouri Compromise; Era of Good Feeling
ANECDOTES Wounded as a soldier in Continental Army by a bullet that remained in his shoulder; the only President to have a foreign capital city named after him: Monrovia, in Liberia

John Quincy Adams (1825–1829)

BORN July 11, 1767 **DIED** February 23, 1848
EARLY CAREER Lawyer; private secretary
MARRIED Louise Catherine Johnson; three sons, one daughter
POLITICAL PARTY Democratic-Republican
VICE PRESIDENT John C. Calhoun
HOBBIES Swimming daily in Potomac River; playing billiards; growing mulberry trees; raising silkworms
ADMINISTRATION Smithsonian Institution established
ANECDOTES Read Shakespeare at age 10; attended schools in France and Holland; at 14, served as private secretary to first U.S. diplomat in Russia; only son of a President to become President; received fewer electoral and popular votes than his opponent

Andrew Jackson (1829–1837)

BORN March 15, 1767 **DIED** June 8, 1845
EARLY CAREER Lawyer; soldier; landowner; saddler
MARRIED Rachel Donelson Robards; one stepson
POLITICAL PARTY Democratic
VICE PRESIDENTS John C. Calhoun; Martin Van Buren
HOBBIES Owning racehorses; playing practical jokes; collecting pipes from all over the world; reading newspapers
ADMINISTRATION Introduced spoils system so that friends could get government jobs
ANECDOTES A poor orphan, at 13 he joined Continental Army; was quick tempered; dressed fashionably in Washington; 20,000 supporters jammed his inaugural reception at the White House

Martin Van Buren (1837–1841)

BORN Dec. 5, 1782 **DIED** July 24, 1862
EARLY CAREER Lawyer
MARRIED Hannah Hoes; four sons
POLITICAL PARTY Democratic
VICE PRESIDENT Richard M. Johnson
HOBBIES Attending theater and opera; fishing
ADMINISTRATION Created independent treasury system to deal with economic panic of 1837
ANECDOTES Grew up speaking Dutch; first President born a U.S. citizen, not a British subject; not popular because he wore expensive clothes and rode in a luxury coach when many citizens had lost their jobs; created the Blue Room in the White House

William Henry Harrison (1841)

BORN Feb. 9, 1773 **DIED** April 4, 1841
EARLY CAREER Army officer
MARRIED Anna Symmes; six sons, four daughters
POLITICAL PARTY Whig
VICE PRESIDENT John Tyler
HOBBIES Brisk walks; horseback riding; reading the Bible
ADMINISTRATION Did not make one major decision during his 35 days in office; hoped to end the spoils system
ANECDOTES Quit premedical studies and became a soldier when his father died; during a storm, while making longest inaugural speech (1 hour 45 minutes), he caught a cold and died one month later

John Tyler (1841–1845)

BORN March 29, 1790 **DIED** Jan. 18, 1862
EARLY CAREER Lawyer; militia captain
MARRIED Letitia Christian; three sons, five daughters. Julia Gardiner; five sons, two daughters
POLITICAL PARTY Whig
VICE PRESIDENT None
HOBBIES Playing the violin; fox hunting; caring for pets
ADMINISTRATION Annexation of Texas; signed trade treaty with China
ANECDOTES First Vice President to become President through death of a President; enjoyed giving parties for his 15 children; youngest child was born when Tyler was 70 years old

James K. Polk (1845–1849)

BORN Nov. 2, 1795 **DIED** June 15, 1849
EARLY CAREER Store clerk; lawyer
MARRIED Sarah Childress; no children
POLITICAL PARTY Democratic
VICE PRESIDENT George M. Dallas
HOBBIES None, he worked 14 hours a day
ADMINISTRATION Manifest Destiny; Mexican-American War of 1846; Department of Interior established; laid cornerstone of Washington Monument
ANECDOTES At 10, moved 500 miles from North Carolina to Tennessee in a covered wagon; first President whose inaugural address was reported by telegraph, as Samuel F. B. Morse sent the speech by wire to Baltimore, MD

Zachary Taylor (1849–1850)

BORN Nov. 24, 1784 **DIED** July 9, 1850
EARLY CAREER Farmer; army officer
MARRIED Margaret Sackall Smith; five daughters, one son
POLITICAL PARTY Whig
VICE PRESIDENT Millard Fillmore
HOBBIES Riding; being with friends
ADMINISTRATION Compromise of 1850; signed treaty with Hawaiian Islands
ANECDOTES The only President who never voted in an election, he first voted when he was 62 years old; allowed his favorite war horse, Whitey, to graze on the White House lawn; was second cousin of James Madison

Millard Fillmore (1850–1853)

BORN Jan. 7, 1800 **DIED** March 8, 1874
EARLY CAREER Apprenticed to clothmaker; teacher; lawyer
MARRIED Abigail Powers; one son, one daughter. Caroline Carmichael McIntosh; no children
POLITICAL PARTY Whig
VICE PRESIDENT None
HOBBIES Collecting books; civic volunteer
ADMINISTRATION Sent Commodore Perry to Japan to open up trade; Fugitive Slave Act became law; California admitted to Union
ANECDOTES His first wife had been his teacher; did not attend college; created first permanent library in the White House; the last Whig President; installed first bathtub in the White House

Franklin Pierce (1853–1857)

BORN Nov. 23, 1804 **DIED** Oct. 8, 1869
EARLY CAREER Lawyer
MARRIED Jane Means Appleton; three sons
POLITICAL PARTY Democratic
VICE PRESIDENT William R. King
HOBBIES Fishing
ADMINISTRATION Signed trade treaty with Japan; Gadsden Purchase of Mexican borderland; Kansas-Nebraska Act
ANECDOTES Nicknamed Handsome Frank; made no speeches during campaign; the only President elected to office who was not renominated by his political party for a second term; kept same Cabinet for four years

James Buchanan (1857–1861)

BORN April 23, 1791 **DIED** June 1, 1868
EARLY CAREER Lawyer
MARRIED The only bachelor President
POLITICAL PARTY Democratic
VICE PRESIDENT John Breckinridge
HOBBIES Reading; entertaining friends; playing cards
ADMINISTRATION Dred Scott decision enacted; Pony Express begun
ANECDOTES Tilted his head when he spoke because one eye was nearsighted and the other eye was farsighted; gave all presidential gifts to the Patent Office; raised his orphaned niece, Harriet Lane, who later served as White House hostess

Abraham Lincoln (1861–1865)

BORN Feb. 12, 1809 **DIED** April 15, 1865
EARLY CAREER Rail-splitter; ferryboat captain; store clerk; postmaster; lawyer
MARRIED Mary Todd; four sons
POLITICAL PARTY Republican
VICE PRESIDENTS Hannibal Hamlin; Andrew Johnson
HOBBIES Reading; memorizing poetry; swapping jokes; attending theater; wrestling; walking
ADMINISTRATION Civil War fought; Emancipation Proclamation; Department of Agriculture established; signed Homestead Act
ANECDOTES The tallest President, 6' 4"; did not attend college; first President assassinated

Andrew Johnson (1865–1869)

BORN Dec. 29, 1808 **DIED** July 31, 1875
EARLY CAREER Tailor
MARRIED Eliza McCardle; three sons, two daughters
POLITICAL PARTY Union
VICE PRESIDENT None
HOBBIES Playing checkers; tending own vegetable garden; attending circus and minstrel shows
ADMINISTRATION 13th Amendment abolished slavery; 14th Amendment passed; purchased Alaska
ANECDOTES Never attended school and was illiterate at 17 when he opened a tailor shop; married at 18, his wife taught him to read, write, and figure math; the only President who was impeached

Ulysses Simpson Grant (1869–1877)

BORN April 27, 1822 **DIED** July 23, 1885
EARLY CAREER Farmer; store clerk; commanding general of the Union army at the end of the Civil War
MARRIED Julia Dent; three sons, one daughter
POLITICAL PARTY Republican
VICE PRESIDENTS Schuyler Colfax; Henry Wilson
HOBBIES Drawing; painting; riding horses
ADMINISTRATION Department of Justice created; first national park, Yellowstone, established
ANECDOTES Changed his name from Hiram, because his initials, HUG, bothered him; died penniless, four days after completing his autobiography, which earned his family nearly half a million dollars

Rutherford B. Hayes (1877–1881)

BORN Oct. 4, 1822 **DIED** Jan. 17, 1893
EARLY CAREER Lawyer; major general
MARRIED Lucy Ware Webb; seven sons, one
  daughter
POLITICAL PARTY Republican
VICE PRESIDENT William A. Wheeler
HOBBIES Morning exercise; hunting; fishing;
  shooting; playing chess and croquet; landscaping; reading
ADMINISTRATION Women permitted to practice law before U.S.
  Supreme Court; last federal troops removed from South
ANECDOTES Distinguished himself in the Civil War (wounded four
  times); his wife was the first First Lady to graduate from college;
  first President to install a telephone in the White House; first
  President to visit the West Coast (in 1880)

James A. Garfield (1881)

BORN Nov. 19, 1831 **DIED** Sept. 19, 1881
EARLY CAREER Farmer; carpenter; college professor
  and president; lawyer; Civil War general
MARRIED Lucretia Rudolph; five sons, two
  daughters
POLITICAL PARTY Republican
VICE PRESIDENT Chester A. Arthur
HOBBIES Reading, especially to Molly, his daughter; hunting; fishing;
  playing chess and billiards
ADMINISTRATION American Red Cross established
ANECDOTES One of youngest Civil War generals; could write Greek
  with one hand and Latin with the other at the same time; died 80
  days after he was shot, the second of four Presidents assassinated

Chester A. Arthur (1881–1885)

BORN Oct. 5, 1829 **DIED** Nov. 18, 1886
EARLY CAREER Teacher; lawyer
MARRIED Ellen Lewis Herndon; two sons, one
  daughter
POLITICAL PARTY Republican
VICE PRESIDENT none
HOBBIES Fishing, once catching an 80-pound
  bass
ADMINISTRATION Civil Service Commission organized; Washington
  Monument dedicated; standard time adopted
ANECDOTES Enjoyed fine clothes and fashionable surroundings;
  moved into the White House only after the old furniture was
  removed and the rooms were redecorated

Grover Cleveland (1885–1889 and 1893–1897)

BORN March 18, 1837 **DIED** June 24, 1908
EARLY CAREER Store clerk; teacher at school
  for the blind; book editor; lawyer; sheriff
MARRIED Frances Folsom; three daughters,
  two sons
POLITICAL PARTY Democratic
VICE PRESIDENT Thomas A. Hendricks
HOBBIES Fishing; morning walks; playing poker
ADMINISTRATION Interstate Commerce Commission established;
  gold standard maintained; homesteaders settled the West
ANECDOTES Did not attend college; the only President married in the
  White House; the only President to serve two nonconsecutive
  terms; the candy bar Baby Ruth was named after his daughter

Benjamin Harrison (1889–1893)

BORN Aug. 20, 1833 **DIED** March 13, 1901
EARLY CAREER Lawyer
MARRIED Caroline Lavinia Scott; one son, one
  daughter. Mary Lord Dimmick; one daughter
POLITICAL PARTY Republican
VICE PRESIDENT Levi P. Morton
HOBBIES Daily walks; duck hunting; playing billiards
ADMINISTRATION Pan-American Conference held; Sherman Antitrust
  Act passed; six states entered the Union
ANECDOTES The only grandson of a President to become a
  President; had the first billion dollar national budget; loved pets
  and kept a goat named Old Whiskers for his grandchildren

William McKinley (1897–1901)

BORN Jan. 29, 1843 **DIED** Sept. 14, 1901
EARLY CAREER Teacher; post office clerk;
  Civil War captain; lawyer
MARRIED Ida Saxton; two daughters
POLITICAL PARTY Republican
VICE PRESIDENTS Garret A. Hobart; Theodore
  Roosevelt
HOBBIES Attending opera and theater;
  playing cribbage
ADMINISTRATION Spanish-American War won, U.S. acquired the
  Philippines, Puerto Rico, Guam, Samoa; Hawaii became U.S. territory
ANECDOTES Always wore a red carnation in his lapel for good luck;
  was devoted to his invalid wife; campaigned from his front porch
  in Canton, Ohio, where 750,000 people came to hear him; at an
  exposition in Buffalo, NY, he was shot; died 8 days later, the third
  of four Presidents assassinated

Theodore Roosevelt (1901–1909)

BORN Oct. 27, 1858 **DIED** Jan. 6, 1919
EARLY CAREER Cowboy; deputy sheriff; Rough Riders colonel
MARRIED Alice Hathaway Lee; one daughter. Edith Kermit Carow; four sons, one daughter
POLITICAL PARTY Republican
VICE PRESIDENT Charles W. Fairbanks
HOBBIES Horseback riding; hiking; swimming; hunting; boxing; reading
ADMINISTRATION Departments of Commerce and Labor created; Panama Canal Zone leased
ANECDOTES The youngest President; first American to win Nobel Peace Prize; was shot, but finished delivering speech before going to hospital to remove bullet; the original teddy bear was named after him because he refused to shoot a bear cub while hunting

William H. Taft (1909–1913)

BORN Sept. 15, 1859 **DIED** March 8, 1930
EARLY CAREER Reporter; lawyer; judge; professor and dean of law school
MARRIED Helen Herron; two sons, one daughter
POLITICAL PARTY Republican
VICE PRESIDENT James S. Sherman
HOBBIES Attending theater, playing golf
ADMINISTRATION Established parcel post; income tax established
ANECDOTES The heaviest President, weighing more than 330 pounds; once became stuck in bathtub; first President to throw out ball on opening day of baseball season; kept a cow named Pauline Wayne on the White House grounds; first President to become Chief Justice of U.S. Supreme Court, a job he enjoyed more than being President

Woodrow Wilson (1913–1921)

BORN Dec. 28, 1856 **DIED** Feb. 3, 1924
EARLY CAREER Lawyer; professor; president of Princeton University
MARRIED Ellen L. Axson; three daughters. Edith Bolling Galt; no children
POLITICAL PARTY Democratic
VICE PRESIDENT Thomas R. Marshall
HOBBIES Playing golf (painted golf balls black to see them in snow); horseback riding; attending musical comedies
ADMINISTRATION Purchased Virgin Islands; Federal Reserve Act passed; 19th Amendment guaranteed women's right to vote
ANECDOTES First President to earn a doctoral (PhD) degree and to hold a news conference; kept sheep to trim the White House lawn; because of a stroke, his wife Edith helped him complete his second term

Warren G. Harding (1921–1923)

BORN Nov. 2, 1865 **DIED** Aug. 2, 1923
EARLY CAREER Teacher; newspaper editor and publisher
MARRIED Florence Kling DeWolfe; one stepson
VICE PRESIDENT Calvin Coolidge
POLITICAL PARTY Republican
HOBBIES Playing golf; attending baseball games; boxing
ADMINISTRATION Teapot Dome scandal
ANECDOTES First President to give a speech over radio; first President to visit Alaska and Canada; interrupted a game of golf to sign peace treaty ending World War I and then resumed playing; loved his dog, Laddie Boy, an Airedale; complained his "friends. . . [are] the ones that keep me walking the floors nights"

Calvin Coolidge (1923–1929)

BORN July 4, 1872 **DIED** Jan. 5, 1933
EARLY CAREER Lawyer
MARRIED Grace Anna Goodhue; two sons
POLITICAL PARTY Republican
VICE PRESIDENT Charles G. Dawes
HOBBIES Playing the harmonica; fishing; playing golf; exercising with Indian clubs and mechanical horse
ADMINISTRATION U.S. Foreign Service created; U.S. citizenship granted to Native Americans
ANECDOTES Coolidge was sworn in by his father, a notary, by the light of a kerosene lamp, at 2:45 A.M., at his Vermont farm; first President born of Indian ancestry; walked his pet raccoon on a leash; had reputation for never wasting a penny or a word

Herbert C. Hoover (1929–1933)

BORN Aug. 10, 1874 **DIED** Oct. 20, 1964
EARLY CAREER Newsboy; mining engineer; supervisor of refugee relief in Europe during World War I
MARRIED Lou Henry; two sons
POLITICAL PARTY Republican
VICE PRESIDENT Charles Curtis
HOBBIES Fly-fishing; tossing medicine ball with Cabinet members
ADMINISTRATION Veterans Administration created; Great Depression occurred; "Star-Spangled Banner" adopted as national anthem
ANECDOTES Born poor, he was an orphan at nine; became a successful engineer and was worth $4 million by the age of 40; China's chief mining engineer; spoke Chinese with his wife in the White House for privacy; son had two alligators that sometimes wandered loose around the White House

Franklin D. Roosevelt (1933–1945)

BORN Jan. 30, 1882 **DIED** April 12, 1945

EARLY CAREER Lawyer

MARRIED Anna Eleanor Roosevelt, a distant cousin; five sons, one daughter

POLITICAL PARTY Democratic

VICE PRESIDENTS John N. Garner; Henry A. Wallace; Harry S Truman

HOBBIES Collecting stamps; sailing; swimming; playing poker

ADMINISTRATION New Deal of government relief and work programs; World War II

ANECDOTES Elected to four terms, more than any other President; appointed first woman Cabinet officer, Frances Perkins, Secretary of Labor; paralyzed from the waist down by polio; spoke to the people by radio in "fireside chats"

Harry S Truman (1945–1953)

BORN May 8, 1884 **DIED** Dec. 26, 1972

EARLY CAREER Railroad timekeeper; farmer; haberdasher; judge

MARRIED Bess Wallace; one daughter

POLITICAL PARTY Democratic

VICE PRESIDENT Alben W. Barkley

HOBBIES Playing the piano; early morning walks; architecture; playing poker; swimming

ADMINISTRATION Atomic bomb dropped, ending World War II; Truman Doctrine; NATO organized; ratified 22nd Amendment

ANECDOTES The only President of the 20th century who did not attend college; his middle initial, S, did not stand for anything; sign on his desk read "The Buck Stops Here," meaning he took responsibility for decisions

Dwight D. Eisenhower (1953–1961)

BORN Oct. 14, 1890 **DIED** March 28, 1969

EARLY CAREER West Point cadet; supreme Allied commander in Europe during World War II; President, Columbia University; organized NATO

MARRIED Marie "Mamie" G. Doud; two sons

POLITICAL PARTY Republican

VICE PRESIDENT Richard M. Nixon

HOBBIES Playing golf, cooking, landscape painting; reading westerns

ADMINISTRATION NASA established; Alaska and Hawaii became states; 1st U.S. satellite launched

ANECDOTES The third of six sons, all nicknamed "Ike"; superstitious, he carried three lucky coins: a silver dollar, five-guinea gold piece, and a French franc; lived in 28 different homes before his retirement; first President to be a licensed airplane pilot

John F. Kennedy (1961–1963)

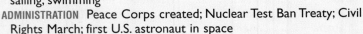

BORN May 29, 1917 **DIED** Nov. 22, 1963

EARLY CAREER Navy lieutenant; journalist

MARRIED Jacqueline Lee Bouvier; one daughter, two sons

POLITICAL PARTY Democratic

VICE PRESIDENT Lyndon B. Johnson

HOBBIES Playing touch football and golf; sailing; swimming

ADMINISTRATION Peace Corps created; Nuclear Test Ban Treaty; Civil Rights March; first U.S. astronaut in space

ANECDOTES First President born in 20th century; was a Boy Scout as a youth; could read 2,000 words per minute and understand most of it; only President to win a Pulitzer Prize, for *Profiles in Courage,* a biography; fourth of four Presidents assassinated

Lyndon B. Johnson (1963–1969)

BORN Aug. 27, 1908 **DIED** Jan. 22, 1973

EARLY CAREER Teacher; rancher

MARRIED Claudia "Lady Bird" Taylor; two daughters

POLITICAL PARTY Democratic

VICE PRESIDENT Hubert H. Humphrey

HOBBIES Enjoying life on his ranch; horseback riding; fishing; hunting

ADMINISTRATION Signed Civil Rights Act; proposed Great Society; Department of Housing and Urban Development created; increased number of troops sent to Vietnam; appointed first African American justice of the U.S. Supreme Court, Thurgood Marshall

ANECDOTES Took oath of office on jet airplane after the assassination of President Kennedy; first President sworn in by a woman

Richard M. Nixon (1969–1974)

BORN Jan 9, 1913 **DIED** April 22, 1994

EARLY CAREER Naval officer; lawyer; owned frozen-orange-juice company

MARRIED Thelma Catherine "Pat" Ryan; two daughters

POLITICAL PARTY Republican

VICE PRESIDENT Spiro T. Agnew; Gerald R. Ford

HOBBIES Playing the piano; bowling; playing golf; swimming; reading history

ADMINISTRATION Established relations with China; withdrew troops from Vietnam; first U.S. astronauts walk on moon; voting age lowered from 21 to 18

ANECDOTES First President to visit Communist China; only President to resign from office, which he did on Aug. 9, 1974, to avoid impeachment for his part in Watergate scandal

Gerald R. Ford (1974–1977)

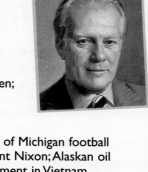

BORN July 14, 1913
EARLY CAREER National Park ranger; college football coach; naval officer; lawyer
MARRIED Elizabeth (Betty) Bloomer Warren; three sons, one daughter
POLITICAL PARTY Republican
VICE PRESIDENT Nelson A. Rockefeller
HOBBIES Skiing; swimming; playing golf; fan of Michigan football
ADMINISTRATION Pardoned former President Nixon; Alaskan oil pipeline constructed; ended U.S. involvement in Vietnam
ANECDOTES Became Vice President when Spiro Agnew resigned and became President when President Nixon resigned; first Eagle Scout to become President; voted Most Valuable Player in college football in 1934

James Earl "Jimmy" Carter (1977–1981)

BORN Oct. 1, 1924
EARLY CAREER Naval officer; owned peanut farm
MARRIED Rosalynn Smith; one daughter, three sons
POLITICAL PARTY Democratic
VICE PRESIDENT Walter F. Mondale
HOBBIES Jogging; fishing; playing tennis; reading
ADMINISTRATION Human rights in foreign policy; Camp David accords; recognized China; Department of Energy created
ANECDOTES First President born in a hospital; graduated with honors from U.S. Naval Academy; helped develop first nuclear-powered submarine; at first presidential phone-in, more than 9 million people tried to speak to Carter, and 42 actually got through

Ronald Reagan (1981–1989)

BORN Feb. 6, 1911
EARLY CAREER Radio announcer; actor; union president; corporate spokesman
MARRIED Jane Wyman; one son, one daughter. Anne "Nancy" Davis; one son, one daughter
POLITICAL PARTY Republican
VICE PRESIDENT George H.W. Bush
HOBBIES Horseback riding; ranching; exercising
ADMINISTRATION Reaganomics; appointed first woman justice of U.S. Supreme Court; Iran-Contra scandal; invasion of Grenada; Strategic Defense Initiative (Star Wars)
ANECDOTES Oldest man elected President; as a lifeguard in Illinois (1927–1932), he saved 77 people from drowning, and the town put up a plaque in his honor; kept jar of jelly beans for Cabinet meetings; after assassination attempt and before doctors removed a bullet from his lung, he said, "Please assure me you are all Republicans."

George H.W. Bush (1989–1993)

BORN June 12, 1924
EARLY CAREER Navy pilot; founded oil companies
MARRIED Barbara Pierce; four sons, two daughters
POLITICAL PARTY Republican
VICE PRESIDENT J. Danforth Quayle
HOBBIES Boating; fishing; hunting; playing horseshoes and tennis
ADMINISTRATION Concluded North American Free Trade Agreement; Persian Gulf War; first U.S.-Russia summit; savings and loan crisis; Americans With Disabilities Act
ANECDOTES Awarded the Distinguished Flying Cross for heroism in World War II; was ambassador to the United Nations and CIA director; headed U.S. Liaison Office in Beijing, China

William J. "Bill" Clinton (1993–

BORN August 19, 1946
EARLY CAREER Law professor
MARRIED Hillary Rodham; one daughter
POLITICAL PARTY Democratic
VICE PRESIDENT Albert Gore, Jr.
HOBBIES Jogging; playing golf; reading; playing tenor saxophone
ADMINISTRATION Anticrime law passed; joint space effort with Russia; appointed first female U.S. Attorney General, Janet Reno; troops sent to Haiti and Bosnia
ANECDOTES First President born after World War II; named after his father, he was adopted by his stepfather; at 17, as delegate to American Legion Boys Nation, he went to White House and shook hands with President Kennedy; first President who had been a Rhodes scholar

The Declaration of Independence

In Congress, July 4, 1776

When, in the course of human events, it becomes necessary for one people to dissolve the political bands which have connected them with another, and to assume, among the powers of the earth, the separate and equal station to which the laws of nature and nature's God entitle them, a decent respect to the opinions of mankind requires that they should declare the causes which impel them to the separation.

We hold these truths to be self-evident; that all men are created equal, that they are endowed by their Creator with certain unalienable rights, that among these are life, liberty, and the pursuit of happiness. That to secure these rights, governments are instituted among men, deriving their just powers from the consent of the governed; that whenever any form of government becomes destructive of these ends, it is the right of the people to alter or to abolish it, and to institute new government, laying its foundation on such principles, and organizing its powers in such form, as to them shall seem most likely to effect their safety and happiness. Prudence, indeed, will dictate that governments long established should not be changed for light and transient causes; and accordingly all experience hath shown that mankind are more disposed to suffer, while evils are sufferable, than to right themselves by abolishing the forms to which they are accustomed. But when a long train of abuses and usurpations, pursuing invariably the same object, evinces a design to reduce them under absolute despotism, it is their right, it is their duty, to throw off such government, and to provide new guards for their future security.

Such has been the patient sufferance of these colonies; and such is now the necessity which constrains them to alter their former systems of government. The history of the present king of Great Britain is a history of repeated injuries and usurpations, all having in direct object the establishment of an absolute tyranny over these states. To prove this, let facts be submitted to a candid world.

He has refused his assent to laws the most wholesome and necessary for the public good.

Why the Declaration of Independence Was Issued
This paragraph states that it has become necessary for the American colonists to break their political ties with Great Britain, and that it is only proper to explain why they are taking this step. (One reason was that the colonists hoped to get help from other nations.)

The Purposes of Government
This paragraph is the very heart of the Declaration of Independence. It states that all men are born with equal claims to "life, liberty, and the pursuit of happiness." These rights, given by the Creator, are "unalienable," that is, they cannot be given away, nor can a government take them away.

The paragraph goes on to state that governments were created to protect these human rights. Whenever a government interferes with them, its citizens have the right as well as the duty to change or do away with the government. A government must be based on the consent of the governed. Changing or doing away with a government will be carried out, however, only after events have proved that the government has abused its powers.

The Charges Against the British King
Here the Declaration of Independence reviews the years between 1763 and 1776, stating that the colonists believed the king's government had many times denied their basic human rights. King George III and his government are charged with committing a long list of misdeeds. Because of these acts, the declaration states that the king is no longer entitled to rule the American colonies. He no longer has the consent of the governed.

He has forbidden his governors to pass laws of immediate and pressing importance, unless suspended in their operation till his assent should be obtained; and when so suspended, he has utterly neglected to attend to them.

He has refused to pass other laws for the accommodation of large districts of people, unless those people would relinquish the right of representation in the legislature, a right inestimable to them, and formidable to tyrants only.

He has called together legislative bodies at places unusual, uncomfortable, and distant from the depository of their public records, for the sole purpose of fatiguing them into compliance with his measures.

He has dissolved representative houses repeatedly, for opposing, with manly firmness, his invasions on the rights of the people.

He has refused, for a long time after such dissolutions, to cause others to be elected; whereby the legislative powers, incapable of annihilation, have returned to the people at large for their exercise; the state remaining, in the meantime, exposed to all the dangers of invasion from without and convulsions within.

He has endeavored to prevent the population of these states; for that purpose obstructing the laws for the naturalization of foreigners, refusing to pass others to encourage their migrations hither, and raising the conditions of new appropriations of lands.

He has obstructed the administration of justice, by refusing his assent to laws for establishing judiciary powers.

He has made judges dependent on his will alone for the tenure of their offices, and the amount and payment of their salaries.

He has erected a multitude of new offices, and sent hither swarms of officers to harass our people and eat out their substance.

He has kept among us, in times of peace, standing armies, without the consent of our legislatures.

He has affected to render the military independent of, and superior to, the civil power.

He has combined with others to subject us to a jurisdiction foreign to our constitution and unacknowledged by our laws, giving his assent to their acts of pretended legislation:

For quartering large bodies of armed troops among us;

For protecting them, by a mock trial, from punishment for any murders which they should commit on the inhabitants of these states;

For cutting off our trade with all parts of the world;

For imposing taxes on us without our consent;

For depriving us, in many cases, of the benefits of trial by jury;

For transporting us beyond seas, to be tried for pretended offenses;

For abolishing the free system of English laws in a neighboring province, establishing therein an arbitrary government, and enlarging its boundaries, so as to render it at once an example and fit instrument for introducing the same absolute rule into these colonies;

For taking away our charters, abolishing our most valuable laws, and altering fundamentally the forms of our governments;

For suspending our own legislatures, and declaring themselves invested with power to legislate for us in all cases whatsoever.

He has abdicated government here, by declaring us out of his protection and waging war against us.

He has plundered our seas, ravaged our coasts, burned our towns, and destroyed the lives of our people.

He is at this time transporting large armies of foreign mercenaries to complete the works of death, desolation, and tyranny already begun with circumstances of cruelty and perfidy scarcely paralleled in the most barbarous ages, and totally unworthy the head of a civilized nation.

He has constrained our fellow-citizens, taken captive on the high seas, to bear arms against their country, to become the executioners of their friends and brethren, or to fall themselves by their hands.

He has excited domestic insurrection among us, and has endeavored to bring on the inhabitants of our frontiers, the merciless Indian savages, whose known rule of warfare is an undistinguished destruction of all ages, sexes, and conditions.

In every stage of these oppressions we have petitioned for redress in the most humble terms; our repeated petitions have been answered only by repeated injury. A prince whose character is thus marked by every act which may define a tyrant is unfit to be the ruler of a free people.

Nor have we been wanting in attentions to our British brethren. We have warned them, from time to time, of attempts by their legislature to extend an unwarrantable jurisdiction over us. We have reminded them of the circumstances of our emigration and settlement here. We have appealed to their native justice and magnanimity; and we have conjured them, by the ties of our common kindred, to disavow these usurpations, which would inevitably interrupt our connections and correspondence. They, too, have been deaf to the voice of justice and consanguinity. We must, therefore, acquiesce in the necessity which denounces our separation, and hold them, as we hold the rest of mankind, enemies in war; in peace, friends.

We, therefore, the representatives of the United States of America, in General Congress assembled, appealing to the Supreme Judge of the world for the rectitude of our intentions, do, in the name and by the authority of the good people of these colonies, solemnly publish and declare that these United Colonies are, and of right ought to be, free and independent states; that they are absolved from all allegiance to the British crown, and that all political connection between them and the state of Great Britain is, and ought to be, totally dissolved; and that, as free and independent states, they have full power to levy war, conclude peace, contract alliances, establish commerce, and do all other acts and things which independent states may of right do. And, for the support of this declaration, with a firm reliance on the protection of Divine Providence, we mutually pledge to each other our lives, our fortunes, and our sacred honor.

The Attempts to Obtain Justice
These two paragraphs state that the American colonists have asked the British king for justice. They have also appealed to the British people. Yet neither the king nor the British people have responded to the colonists' pleas.

The Colonies Declare Their Independence
This final paragraph actually proclaims independence. It also lists those things that the new United States of America may do as an independent country.

In the last sentence the signers pledge their lives and all they own to support the cause of independence. This was a serious matter, for as Benjamin Franklin said, "Now we must all hang together, or we will all hang separately." Still, they took the risk and signed the document that proclaimed to the world the independence of the United States of America.

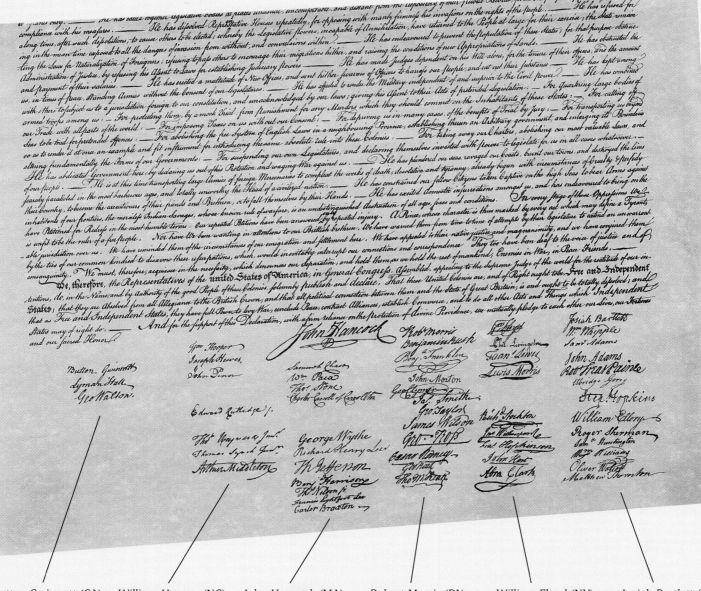

Button Gwinnett (GA)
Lymann Hall (GA)
George Walton (GA)

William Hooper (NC)
Joseph Hewes (NC)
John Penn (NC)

Edward Rutledge (SC)

Thomas Heyward, Jr.
(SC)
Thomas Lynch, Jr. (SC)
Arthur Middleton (SC)

John Hancock (MA)

Samuel Chase (MD)
William Paca (MD)
Thomas Stone (MD)
Charles Carroll
of Carrollton (MD)

George Wythe (VA)
Richard Henry Lee (VA)
Thomas Jefferson (VA)
Benjamin Harrison (VA)
Thomas Nelson, Jr. (VA)
Francis Lightfoot Lee
(VA)
Carter Braxton (VA)

Robert Morris (PA)
Benjamin Rush (PA)
Benjamin Franklin (PA)
John Morton (PA)
George Clymer (PA)
James Smith (PA)
George Taylor (PA)
James Wilson (PA)
George Ross (PA)
Caesar Rodney (DE)
George Read (DE)
Thomas McKean (DE)

William Floyd (NY)
Philip Livingston (NY)
Francis Lewis (NY)
Lewis Morris (NY)

Richard Stockton (NJ)
John Witherspoon (NJ)
Francis Hopkinson (NJ)
John Hart (NJ)
Abraham Clark (NJ)

Josiah Bartlett (NH)
William Whipple (NH)
Samuel Adams (MA)

John Adams (MA)
Robert Treat Paine (MA)
Elbridge Gerry (MA)
Stephen Hopkins (RI)
William Ellery (RI)
Roger Sherman (CT)
Samuel Huntington
(CT)
William Williams (CT)
Oliver Wolcott (CT)
Matthew Thornton (NH)

The Constitution of the United States of America

We the people of the United States, in order to form a more perfect union, establish justice, insure domestic tranquility, provide for the common defense, promote the general welfare, and secure the blessings of liberty to ourselves and our posterity, do ordain and establish this Constitution for the United States of America.

ARTICLE I

SECTION 1.

All legislative powers herein granted shall be vested in a Congress of the United States, which shall consist of a Senate and House of Representatives.

SECTION 2.

The House of Representatives shall be composed of members chosen every second year by the people of the several States, and the electors in each State shall have the qualifications requisite for electors of the most numerous branch of the State legislature.

No person shall be a representative who shall not have attained to the age of twenty-five years, and been seven years a citizen of the United States, and who shall not, when elected, be an inhabitant of that State in which he shall be chosen.

Representatives and direct taxes shall be apportioned among the several States which may be included within this Union, according to their respective numbers, which shall be determined by adding to the whole numbers of free persons, including those bound to service for a term of years, and excluding Indians not taxed, three fifths of all other persons.* The actual enumeration shall be made within three years after the first meeting of the Congress of the United States, and within every subsequent term of ten years, in such manner as they shall by law direct. The number of representatives shall not exceed one for every thirty thousand, but each State shall have at least one representative; and until such enumeration shall be made, the State of New Hampshire shall be entitled to choose three, Massachusetts eight, Rhode Island and Providence Plantations one, Connecticut five, New York six, New Jersey four, Pennsylvania eight, Delaware one, Maryland six, Virginia ten, North Carolina five, South Carolina five, and Georgia

---

The Preamble
This Constitution has been written and put into practice for the following reasons:
- To have a better government than that under the Articles of Confederation
- To see that everyone is treated fairly
- To keep peace within the country
- To defend the country from enemies
- To see that people live comfortably and well
- To keep people free both now and in the future.

Article I
The Legislative Branch
Section 1
All legislative, or law making, powers are given to the Congress. It has two parts, or houses: the Senate and the House of Representatives.

Section 2
Members of the House of Representatives serve a 2-year term. A term is a length of time. A representative must have been a citizen of the United States for at least 7 years, must be at least 25 years old, and must live in the state he or she will represent when elected.

The number of representatives from each state depends on that state's population. Each state has at least one representative. The total membership of the House of Representatives is limited to 435 voting members.

To decide the number of representatives from each state, the national government must count the number of people every 10 years. This count of population is called a census.

three. (*Changed by the Fourteenth Amendment*)

When vacancies happen in the representation from any State, the executive authority thereof shall issue writs of election to fill such vacancies.

The House of Representatives shall choose their speaker and other officers, and shall have the sole power of impeachment.

SECTION 3.

The Senate of the United States shall be composed of two senators from each State, chosen by the legislature thereof,* for six years; and each senator shall have one vote. (*Changed by the Seventeenth Amendment*)

Immediately after they shall be assembled in consequence of the first election, they shall be divided as equally as may be into three classes. The seats of the senators of the first class shall be vacated at the expiration of the second year, of the second class at the expiration of the fourth year, and of the third class at the expiration of the sixth year, so that one third may be chosen every second year; and if vacancies happen by resignation, or otherwise, during the recess of the legislature of any State, the executive thereof may make temporary appointments until the next meeting of the legislature, which shall then fill such vacancies.* (*Changed by the Seventeenth Amendment*)

No person shall be a senator who shall not have attained to the age of thirty years, and been nine years a citizen of the United States, and who shall not, when elected, be an inhabitant of that State for which he shall be chosen.

The Vice President of the United States shall be president of the Senate, but shall have no vote, unless they be equally divided.

The Senate shall choose their other officers, and also a president pro tempore, in the absence of the Vice President, or when he shall exercise the office of President of the United States.

The Senate shall have the sole power to try all impeachments. When sitting for that purpose, they shall be an oath or affirmation. When the President of the United States is tried, the Chief Justice shall preside: and no person shall be convicted without the concurrence of two thirds of the members present.

Judgment in cases of impeachment shall not extend further than to removal from office, and disqualification to hold any office of honor, trust or profit under the United States: but the party convicted shall nevertheless be liable and subject to indictment, trial, judgment and punishment, according to law.

SECTION 4.

The times, places, and manner of holding elections for senators and representatives shall be prescribed in each State by the legislature thereof; but the Congress may at any time by law make or alter such regulations, except as to the places of choosing senators.

The Congress shall assemble at least once in every year, and such

Section 3
The Senate is made up of two senators from each state. A senator serves a 6-year term. One third of the total membership of the Senate is elected every 2 years.

A senator must have been a citizen of the United States for at least 9 years, must be at least 30 years old, and must live in the state he or she will represent.

The Vice President of the United States is in charge of the Senate but may vote only to break a tie vote.

Both the House and the Senate have roles in the process known as impeachment. It is the House of Representatives that charges a government official with misconduct. The Senate then acts as a court to decide if the official is guilty. If two thirds of the senators agree that the official is guilty, he or she is removed from office. If the official is the President, then the Chief Justice of the United States acts as the judge.

Sections 4–7
Rules for running the House and the Senate are described here. Each house must keep a daily record of its actions. This is published so that people can find out how their representatives voted on bills. Members of Congress are paid by the government.

meeting shall be on the first Monday in December,* unless they shall by law appoint a different day. (*Changed by the Twentieth Amendment*)

SECTION 5.

Each house shall be the judge of the elections, returns and qualifications of its own members, and a majority of each shall constitute a quorum to do business; but a smaller number may adjourn from day to day, and may be authorized to compel the attendance of absent members, in such manner, and under such penalties as each house may provide.

Each house may determine the rules of its proceedings, punish its members for disorderly behavior, and, with the concurrence of two thirds, expel a member.

Each house shall keep a journal of its proceedings, and from time to time publish the same, excepting such parts as may in their judgment require secrecy; and the yeas and nays of the members of either house on any question shall, at the desire of one fifth of those present, be entered on the journal.

Neither house, during the session of Congress, shall, without the consent of the other, adjourn for more than three days, nor to any other place than that in which the two houses shall be sitting.

SECTION 6.

The senators and representatives shall receive a compensation for their services, to be ascertained by law, and paid out of the Treasury of the United States. They shall in all cases, except treason, felony and breach of the peace, be privileged from arrest during their attendance at the session of their respective houses, and in going to and returning from the same; and for any speech or debate in either house, they shall not be questioned in any other place.

No senator or representative shall, during the time for which he was elected, be appointed to any civil office under the authority of the United States, which shall have been created, or the emoluments thereof shall have been increased during such time; and no person holding any office under the United States shall be a member of either house during his continuance in office.

SECTION 7.

All bills for raising revenue shall originate in the House of Representatives; but the Senate may propose or concur with amendments as on other bills.

Every bill which shall have passed the House of Representatives and the Senate, shall, before it become a law, be presented to the President of the United States; if he approve he shall sign it, but if not he shall return it, with his objections to that house in which it shall have originated, who shall enter the objections at large on their journal, and proceed to reconsider it. If after such reconsideration two thirds of that house shall agree to pass the bill, it shall be sent, together with the objections, to the other house, by which it shall likewise be reconsidered, and if approved by two thirds of that house, it shall become a law. But in all such cases the votes of both houses shall be determined by yeas and nays, and the names of the persons voting for and against the bill shall be entered on the journal of each house respectively. If any bill shall not be returned by the President within ten days (Sundays excepted) after it shall have been presented to him, the same shall be a law, in like manner as if he had signed it, unless the Congress by their adjournment prevent its return, in which case it shall not be a law.

Every order, resolution, or vote to which the concurrence of the Senate and House of Representatives may be necessary (except on a question of adjournment) shall be presented to the President of the United States; and before the same shall take effect, shall be approved by him, or being disapproved by him, shall be repassed by two thirds of the Senate and House of Representatives, according to the rules and limitations prescribed in the case of a bill.

SECTION 8.

The Congress shall have power to lay and collect taxes, duties, imposts and excises, to pay the debts and provide for the common defense and general welfare of the United States; but all duties, imposts and excises shall be uniform throughout the United States;

To borrow money on the credit of the United States;

To regulate commerce with foreign nations, and among the several States, and with the Indian tribes;

To establish a uniform rule of naturalization, and uniform laws on the subject of bankruptcies through the United States;

To coin money, regulate the value thereof, and of foreign coin, and fix the standard of weights and measures;

To provide for the punishment of counterfeiting the securities and current coin of the United States;

To establish post offices and post roads;

To promote the progress of science and useful arts by securing for limited times to authors and inventors the exclusive right to their respective writings and discoveries;

To constitute tribunals inferior to the Supreme Court;

To define and punish piracies and felonies committed on the high seas, and offenses against the law of nations;

To declare war, grant letters of marque and reprisal, and make rules concerning captures on land and water;

To raise and support armies, but no appropriation of money to that use shall be for a longer term than two years;

To provide and maintain a navy;

To make rules for the government and regulations of the land and naval forces;

To provide for calling forth the militia to execute the laws of the Union, suppress insurrections and repel invasions;

Section 8
The powers and duties of Congress are listed here. Congress makes all laws concerning money and trade. Congress decides how people become citizens of the United States. It has the power to declare war.

The last paragraph of Section 8 is the "elastic clause." It gives Congress the power to make whatever laws it thinks necessary to carry out the powers listed in Section 8.

To provide for organizing, arming, and disciplining the militia, and for governing such part of them as may be employed in the service of the United States, reserving to the States respectively the appointment of the officers, and the authority of training the militia according to the discipline prescribed by Congress;

To exercise exclusive legislation in all cases whatsoever, over such district (not exceeding ten miles square) as may, by cession of particular States and the acceptance of Congress, become the seat of the government of the United States, and to exercise like authority over all places purchased by the consent of the legislature of the State in which the same shall be, for the erection of forts, magazines, arsenals, dockyards, and other needful buildings; and

To make all laws which shall be necessary and proper for carrying into execution the foregoing powers, and all other powers vested by this Constitution in the government of the United States, or in any department or officer thereof.

SECTION 9.

The migration or importation of such persons as any of the States now existing shall think proper to admit, shall not be prohibited by the Congress prior to the year one thousand eight hundred and eight, but a tax or duty may be imposed on such importation, not exceeding ten dollars for each person.

The privilege of the writ of habeas corpus shall not be suspended, unless when in cases of rebellion or invasion the public safety may require it.

No bill of attainder or ex post facto law shall be passed.

No capitation, or other direct,* tax shall be laid, unless in proportion to the census or enumeration herein before directed to be taken. (*Changed by the Sixteenth Amendment)

No tax or duty shall be laid on articles exported from any State.

No preference shall be given by any regulation of commerce or revenue to the ports of one State over those of another; nor shall vessels bound to, or from, one State be obliged to enter, clear, or pay duties in another.

No money shall be drawn from the Treasury, but in consequence of appropriations made by law; and a regular statement and account of the receipts and expenditures of all public money shall be published from time to time.

No title of nobility shall be granted by the United States: and no person holding any office of profit or trust under them, shall, without the consent of the Congress, accept of any present, emolument, office, or title of any kind whatever, from any king, prince, or foreign State.

SECTION 10.

No State shall enter into any treaty, alliance, or confederation; grant letters of marque and reprisal; coin money; emit bills of credit; make anything but gold and silver coin a tender in payment of debts;

Section 9
There are actions that Congress may not take. This section protects the people of the United States against injustice.

Section 10
The states may not assume any of the powers that are specifically given to Congress. The states also may not do certain things that the national government cannot do.

pass any bill of attainder, ex post facto law, or law impairing the obligation of contracts, or grant any title of nobility.

No State shall, without the consent of the Congress, lay any imposts or duties on imports or exports, except what may be absolutely necessary for executing its inspection laws: and the net produce of all duties and imposts laid by any State on imports or exports, shall be for the use of the Treasury of the United States; and all such laws shall be subject to the revision and control of the Congress.

No State shall, without the consent of Congress, lay any duty of tonnage, keep troops, or ships of war in time of peace, enter into any agreement or compact with another State, or with a foreign power, or engage in war, unless actually invaded, or in such imminent danger as will not admit of delay.

ARTICLE II

SECTION 1.

The executive power shall be vested in a President of the United States of America. He shall hold his office during the term of four years, and, together with the Vice President chosen for the same term, be elected as follows:

Each State shall appoint, in such manner as the legislature thereof may direct, a number of electors, equal to the whole number of senators and representatives to which the State may be entitled in the Congress: but no senator or representative, or person holding an office of trust or profit under the United States, shall be appointed an elector.

The electors shall meet in their respective States, and vote by ballot for two persons, of whom one at least shall not be an inhabitant of the same State with themselves. And they shall make a list of all the persons voted for, and of the number of votes for each; which they shall sign and certify, and transmit sealed to the seat of the government of the United States, directed to the president of the Senate. The president of the Senate shall, in the presence of the Senate and House of Representatives, open all the certificates, and the votes shall then be counted. The person having the greatest number of votes shall be the President, if such number be a majority of the whole number of electors appointed; and if there be more than one who have such majority, and have an equal number of votes, then the House of Representatives shall immediately choose by ballot one of them for President; and if no person have a majority, then from the five highest on the list the said house shall in like manner choose the President. But in choosing the President, the votes shall be taken by States, the representation from each State having one vote; a quorum for this purpose shall consist of a member or members from two thirds of the States, and a majority of all the States shall be necessary to a choice.

Article II
The Executive Branch
Section 1
The executive branch is the President, Vice President, and those who help carry out the laws passed by Congress. The President manages the government. The President and Vice President are elected to a 4-year term. The Vice President takes office if the President dies or resigns.
A President must have been born in the United States, must be at least 35 years old, and must have lived in the United States for at least 14 years.

In every case, after the choice of the President, the person having the greatest number of votes of the electors shall be the Vice President. But if there should remain two or more who have equal votes, the Senate shall choose from them by ballot the Vice President.*

(*Changed by the Twelfth Amendment)

The Congress may determine the time of choosing the electors, and the day on which they shall give their votes; which day shall be the same throughout the United States.

No person except a natural-born citizen, or a citizen of the United States, at the time of the adoption of this Constitution, shall be eligible to the office of President; neither shall any person be eligible to that office who shall not have attained to the age of thirty-five years, and been fourteen years a resident within the United States.

In case of the removal of the President from office, or of his death, resignation, or inability to discharge the powers and duties of the said office, the same shall devolve on the Vice President, and the Congress may by law provide for the case of removal, death, resignation, or inability, both of the President and Vice President, declaring what officer shall then act as President, and such officer shall act accordingly, until the disability be removed, or a President shall be elected.

The President shall, at stated times, receive for his services a compensation, which shall neither be increased nor diminished during the period for which he shall have been elected, and he shall not receive within that period any other emolument from the United States, or any of them.

Before he enter on the execution of his office, he shall take the following oath or affirmation:—"I do solemnly swear (or affirm) that I will faithfully execute the office of President of the United States, and will to the best of my ability, preserve, protect and defend the Constitution of the United States."

SECTION 2.

The President shall be commander in chief of the army and navy of the United States, and of the militia of the several States, when called into the actual service of the United States; he may require the opinion, in writing, of the principal officer in each of the executive departments, upon any subject relating to the duties of their respective offices, and he shall have power to grant reprieves and pardons for offenses against the United States, except in cases of impeachment.

He shall have power, by and with the advice and consent of the Senate, to make treaties, provided two thirds of the senators present concur; and he shall nominate, and by and with the advice and consent of the Senate, shall appoint ambassadors, other public ministers and consuls, judges of the Supreme Court, and all other officers of the United States, whose appointments are not herein otherwise provided for, and which shall be established by law: but the Congress may by law vest the appointment of such inferior officers, as they think proper, in the President alone, in the courts of law, or in the heads of

Sections 2–4
Some of the President's duties include carrying out the laws made by Congress, commanding all the armed forces, pardoning crimes, and reporting to Congress at least once a year on the overall condition of the nation. The President makes treaties and appoints government leaders with the approval of the Senate.

departments.

The President shall have power to fill up all vacancies that may happen during the recess of the Senate, by granting commissions which shall expire at the end of their next session.

SECTION 3.

He shall from time to time give to the Congress information of the state of the Union, and recommend to their consideration such measures as he shall judge necessary and expedient; he may, on extraordinary occasions, convene both houses, or either of them, and in case of disagreement between them with respect to the time of adjournment, he may adjourn them to such time as he shall think proper; he shall receive ambassadors and other public ministers; he shall take care that the laws be faithfully executed, and shall commission all the officers of the United States.

SECTION 4.

The President, Vice President, and all civil officers of the United States, shall be removed from office on impeachment for, and conviction of, treason, bribery, or other high crimes and misdemeanors.

ARTICLE III

SECTION 1.

The judicial power of the United States shall be vested in one Supreme Court, and in such inferior courts as the Congress may from time to time ordain and establish. The judges, both of the Supreme and inferior courts, shall hold their offices during good behavior, and shall, at stated times, receive for their services, a compensation which shall not be diminished during their continuance in office.

SECTION 2.

The judicial power shall extend to all cases, in law and equity, arising under this Constitution, the laws of the United States, and treaties made, or which shall be made, under their authority;—to all cases affecting ambassadors, other public ministers and consuls;—to all cases of admiralty and maritime jurisdiction;—to controversies to which the United States shall be a party;—to controversies between two or more States;—between a State and citizens of another State;—between citizens of different States;—between citizens of the same State claiming lands under grants of different States, and between a State, or the citizens thereof, and foreign States, citizens or subjects.

In all cases affecting ambassadors, other public ministers and consuls, and those in which a State shall be party, the Supreme Court shall have original jurisdiction. In all the other cases before mentioned, the Supreme Court shall have appellate jurisdiction, both as to law and

Article III
The Judicial Branch
Section 1
The federal court system is the judicial branch of government. The Supreme Court is the nation's highest court. It makes the final decisions in all matters of law. Federal judges are not elected. They are the only officials of the national government who may hold office for life.

Section 2
Federal courts handle certain kinds of cases. Only a few are handled directly by the Supreme Court. The judgment of the Supreme Court is final.

One of the great powers of our federal courts is their right to declare an act of Congress or a state legislature unconstitutional. This right is not mentioned specifically in any part of the Constitution.

fact, with such exceptions, and under such regulations as the Congress shall make.

The trial of all crimes, except in cases of impeachment, shall be by jury; and such trial shall be held in the State where the said crimes shall have been committed; but when not committed within any State, the trial shall be at such place or places as the Congress may by law have directed.

SECTION 3.

Treason against the United States shall consist only in levying war against them, or in adhering to their enemies, giving them aid and comfort. No person shall be convicted of treason unless on the testimony of two witnesses to the same overt act, or on confession in open court.

The Congress shall have power to declare the punishment of treason, but no attainder of treason shall work corruption of blood, or forfeiture except during the life of the person attained.

ARTICLE IV

SECTION 1.

Full faith and credit shall be given in each State to the public acts, records, and judicial proceedings of every other State. And the Congress may by general laws prescribe the manner in which such acts, records, and proceedings shall be proved, and the effect thereof.

SECTION 2.

The citizens of each State shall be entitled to all privileges and immunities of citizens in the several States.

A person charged in any State with treason, felony, or other crime, who shall flee from justice, and be found in another State, shall on demand of the executive authority of the State from which he fled, be delivered up to be removed to the State having jurisdiction of the crime.

No person held to service or labor in the State, under the laws thereof, escaping into another, shall, in consequence of any law or regulation therein, be discharged from such service or labor, but shall be delivered up on claim of the party to whom such service or labor may be due.* (*Changed by the Thirteenth Amendment)

SECTION 3.

New States may be admitted by the Congress into this Union; but no new State shall be formed or erected within the jurisdiction of any other State; nor any State be formed by the junction of two or more States, or parts of States, without the consent of the legislatures of the

---

Section 3
The crime of treason—that is, of trying to overthrow the government—is explained.

Article IV
The States
Sections 1–2
All states must accept acts, records, and laws of other states. A citizen of one state must be given the same rights as a citizen of another state when visiting that other state. The governor of one state has the power to send someone accused of a crime in another state back to that state for trial.

Sections 3–4
New states may be added to the United States. The United States government will protect all states from enemies.

States concerned as well as of the Congress.

The Congress shall have power to dispose of and make all needful rules and regulations respecting the territory or other property belonging to the United States; and nothing in this Constitution shall be so construed as to prejudice any claims of the United States, or of any particular State.

SECTION 4.

The United States shall guarantee to every State in this Union a republican form of government, and shall protect each of them against invasion; and on application of the legislature, or of the executive (when the legislature cannot be convened) against domestic violence.

ARTICLE V

The Congress, whenever two thirds of both houses shall deem it necessary, shall propose amendments to this Constitution, or, on the application of the legislatures of two thirds of the several States, shall call a convention for proposing amendments, which, in either case, shall be valid to all intents and purposes, as part of this Constitution, when ratified by the legislatures of three fourths of the several States, or by conventions in three fourths thereof, as the one or the other mode of ratification may be proposed by the Congress; provided [that no amendment which may be made prior to the year one thousand eight hundred and eight shall in any manner affect the first and fourth clauses in the ninth section of the first article, and] that no State, without its consent, shall be deprived of its equal suffrage in the Senate.

ARTICLE VI

All debts contracted and engagements entered into, before the adoption of this Constitution, shall be as valid against the United States under this Constitution, as under the Confederation.

This Constitution, and the laws of the United States which shall be made in pursuance thereof; and all treaties made, or which shall be made, under the authority of the United States, shall be the supreme law of the land; and the judges in every State shall be bound thereby, anything in the Constitution or laws of any State to the contrary notwithstanding.

The senators and representatives before mentioned, and the members of the several State legislatures, and all executive and judicial officers, both of the United States, and of the several States, shall be bound by oath or affirmation to support this Constitution; but no religious test shall ever be required as a qualification to any office or public trust under the United States.

Article V
Making Changes
The Constitution may be amended, or changed. The ways of amending the Constitution are explained. Only 26 amendments have been made since the Constitution was adopted.

Article VI
The Highest Law
The Constitution of the United States is the highest law of the land. State laws must be in agreement with the laws of the Constitution. All national and state lawmakers must support the Constitution.

ARTICLE VII

The ratification of the conventions of nine States shall be sufficient for the establishment of this Constitution between the States so ratifying the same.

Done in Convention by the unanimous consent of the States present the seventeenth day of September in the year of our Lord one thousand seven hundred and eighty-seven, and of the independence of the United States of America the twelfth. In witness whereof we have hereunto subscribed our names.

GEORGE WASHINGTON, PRESIDENT (VIRGINIA)

Massachusetts
Nathaniel Gorham
Rufus King

New York
Alexander Hamilton

Georgia
William Few
Abraham Baldwin

Delaware
George Read
Gunning Bedford
John Dickinson
Richard Bassett
Jacob Broom

Virginia
John Blair
James Madison

Pennsylvania
Benjamin Franklin
Thomas Mifflin
Robert Morris
George Clymer
Thomas FitzSimons
Jared Ingersoll
James Wilson
Gouvernor Morris

New Hampshire
John Langdon
Nicholas Gilman

New Jersey
William Livingston
David Brearley
William Paterson
Jonathan Dayton

Connecticut
William Samuel
Johnson
Roger Sherman

North Carolina
William Blount
Richard Dobbs
Spaight
Hugh Williamson

South Carolina
John Rutledge
Charles Cotesworth
Pinckney
Charles Pinckney
Pierce Butler

Maryland
James McHenry
Daniel of St. Thomas
Jenifer
Daniel Carroll

FIRST AMENDMENT — 1791

Congress shall make no law respecting an establishment of religion, or prohibiting the free exercise thereof; or abridging the freedom of speech, or of the press; or the right of the people peaceably to assemble, and to petition the government for a redress of grievances.

SECOND AMENDMENT — 1791

A well-regulated militia, being necessary to the security of a free State, the right of the people to keep and bear arms, shall not be infringed.

THIRD AMENDMENT — 1791

No soldier shall, in time of peace, be quartered in any house, without the consent of the owner, nor in time of war, but in a manner to be prescribed by law.

FOURTH AMENDMENT — 1791

The right of the people to be secure in their persons, houses, papers, and effects, against unreasonable searches and seizures, shall not be violated, and no warrants shall issue, but upon probable cause, supported by oath or affirmation, and particularly describing the place to be searched, and the persons or things to be seized.

FIFTH AMENDMENT — 1791

No person shall be held to answer for a capital or otherwise infamous crime, unless on a presentment or indictment of a grand jury, except in cases arising in the land or naval forces, or in the militia, when in actual service in time of war or public danger; nor shall any person be subject for the same offense to be twice put in jeopardy of life or limb; nor shall be compelled in any criminal case to be a witness against himself, nor be deprived of life, liberty, or property, without due process of law; nor shall private property be taken for public use without just compensation.

SIXTH AMENDMENT — 1791

In all criminal prosecutions, the accused shall enjoy the right to a speedy and public trial, by an impartial jury of the State and district wherein the crime shall have been committed, which district shall have been previously ascertained by law, and to be informed of the nature and cause of the accusation; to be confronted with the witnesses against him; to have compulsory process for obtaining witnesses in his favor, and to have the assistance of counsel for his defense.

The Bill of Rights
The first ten amendments are known as the Bill of Rights. They protect the basic freedoms of the American people.

First Amendment (1791)
Congress may not make rules to take away freedom of religion, freedom of speech, freedom of the press, or the right of people to come together in a peaceful way or to send petitions to their government.

Second Amendment (1791)
In order to have a prepared military, the people have the right to keep and bear arms.

Third Amendment (1791)
During peacetime the government cannot make citizens feed and house soldiers in their homes.

Fourth Amendment (1791)
People or their homes may not be searched without a good reason.

Fifth Amendment (1791)
Only a grand jury can accuse people of serious crimes. People cannot be forced to give evidence against themselves. If one is found not guilty of a crime, he or she cannot be tried again for the same crime. People's lives, freedom, and property may not be taken from them unfairly. The government must pay the owner for any property taken for public use.

Sixth Amendment (1791)
Persons accused of serious crimes have the right to a speedy and public trial. They must be told what they are accused of. They have the right to have a lawyer and to see and question those who accuse them.

Seventh Amendment (1791)
In most cases, people have the right to a jury trial.

Eighth Amendment (1791)
Punishment may not be cruel or unusual.

Ninth Amendment (1791)
The people may have rights that have not been listed in the Constitution.

Tenth Amendment (1791)
If the Constitution does not give a certain right to the United States government and also does not forbid a state government to have that right, then the states and the people have that right.

Eleventh Amendment (1795)
The power of the judicial branch is limited to certain kinds of cases.

Twelfth Amendment (1804)
Electors vote for President and Vice President separately. An elector is a person chosen by the state legislature to elect the President.

SEVENTH AMENDMENT — 1791

In suits at common law, where the value in controversy shall exceed twenty dollars, the right of trial by jury shall be preserved, and no fact tried by a jury shall be otherwise reexamined in any court of the United States, than according to the rules of the common law.

EIGHTH AMENDMENT — 1791

Excessive bail shall not be required, nor excessive fines imposed, nor cruel and unusual punishments inflicted.

NINTH AMENDMENT — 1791

The enumeration in the Constitution of certain rights shall not be construed to deny or disparage others retained by the people.

TENTH AMENDMENT — 1791

The powers not delegated to the United States by the Constitution, nor prohibited by it to the States are reserved to the States respectively, or to the people.

ELEVENTH AMENDMENT — 1795

The judicial power of the United States shall not be construed to extend to any suit in law or equity, commenced or prosecuted against one of the United States, by citizens of another State, or by citizens or subjects of any foreign State.

TWELFTH AMENDMENT — 1804

The electors shall meet in their respective States, and vote by ballot for President and Vice President, one of whom, at least, shall not be an inhabitant of the same State with themselves; they shall name in their ballots the person voted for as Vice President, and they shall make distinct lists of all persons voted for as President and of all persons voted for as Vice President, and of the number of votes for each, which lists they shall sign and certify, and transmit sealed to the seat of government of the United States, directed to the president of the Senate;—The president of the Senate shall, in the presence of the Senate and House of Representatives, open all the certificates and the votes shall then be counted;—The person having the greatest number of votes for President shall be the President, if such number be a majority of the whole number of electors appointed; and if no person have such majority, then from the persons having the highest numbers not exceeding three on the list of those voted for as President, the House of Representatives shall choose immediately, by ballot, the

President. But in choosing the President, the votes shall be taken by States, the representation from each State having one vote; a quorum for this purpose shall consist of a member or members from two thirds of the States, and a majority of all the States shall be necessary to a choice. And if the House of Representatives shall not choose a President whenever the right of choice shall devolve upon them, before the fourth day of March next following,* then the Vice President shall act as President, as in the case of the death or other constitutional disability of the President. The person having the greatest number of votes as Vice President shall be the Vice President, if such number be a majority of the whole number of electors appointed, and if no person have a majority, then from the two highest numbers on the list, the Senate shall choose the Vice President; a quorum for the purpose shall consist of two thirds of the whole number of senators and a majority of the whole number shall be necessary to a choice. But no person constitutionally ineligible to the office of President shall be eligible to that of Vice President of the United States. (*Changed by the Twentieth Amendment)

THIRTEENTH AMENDMENT — 1865

SECTION 1.

Neither slavery nor involuntary servitude, except as a punishment for crime whereof the party shall have been duly convicted, shall exist within the United States, or any place subject to their jurisdiction.

SECTION 2.

Congress shall have power to enforce this article by appropriate legislation.

FOURTEENTH AMENDMENT — 1868

SECTION 1.

All persons born or naturalized in the United States, and subject to the jurisdiction thereof, are citizens of the United States and of the State wherein they reside. No State shall make or enforce any law which shall abridge the privileges or immunities of citizens of the United States; nor shall any State deprive any person of life, liberty, or property, without due process of law; nor deny to any person within its jurisdiction the equal protection of the laws.

SECTION 2.

Representatives shall be apportioned among the several States according to their respective numbers, counting the whole number of persons in each State, excluding Indians not taxed. But when the right to vote at any election for the choice of electors for President and Vice

Thirteenth Amendment (1865)
Slavery is forbidden in the United States. Congress has the power to make laws to do away with slavery.

Fourteenth Amendment (1868)
People who are born in the United States or who are granted citizenship are United States citizens. They are also citizens of the states they live in.
States may not make laws that limit the rights of citizens of the United States. They may not take away a person's life, freedom, or property unfairly. They must treat all people equally under the law.

President of the United States, representatives in Congress, the executive and judicial officers of a State, or the members of the legislature thereof, is denied to any of the male inhabitants of such State, being twenty-one years of age, and citizens of the United States, or in any way abridged, except for participation in rebellion, or other crime, the basis of representation therein shall be reduced in the proportion which the number of such male citizens shall bear to the whole number of male citizens twenty-one years of age in such State.

SECTION 3.

No person shall be a senator or representative in Congress, or elector of President and Vice President, or hold any office, civil or military, under the United States, or under any State, who, having previously taken an oath, as a member of Congress, or as an officer of the United States, or as a member of any State legislature, or as an executive or judicial officer of any State, to support the Constitution of the United States, shall have engaged in insurrection or rebellion against the same, or given aid or comfort to the enemies thereof. But Congress may by a vote of two thirds of each house, remove such disability.

SECTION 4.

The validity of the public debt of the United States, authorized by law, including debts incurred for payment of pensions and bounties for services in suppressing insurrection or rebellion, shall not be questioned. But neither the United States nor any State shall assume or pay any debt or obligation incurred in aid of insurrection or rebellion against the United States, or any claim for the loss or emancipation of any slave; but all such debts, obligations and claims shall be held illegal and void.

SECTION 5.

The Congress shall have power to enforce, by appropriate legislation, the provisions of this article.

FIFTEENTH AMENDMENT — 1870

Fifteenth Amendment (1870)
No citizen may be denied the right to vote because of race or color.

SECTION 1.

The right of citizens of the United States to vote shall not be denied or abridged by the United States or by any State on account of race, color, or previous condition of servitude.

SECTION 2.

The Congress shall have power to enforce this article by appropriate legislation.

SIXTEENTH AMENDMENT — 1913

The Congress shall have power to lay and collect taxes on incomes, from whatever source derived, without apportionment among the several States, and without regard to any census or enumeration.

Sixteenth Amendment (1913)
Congress is allowed to pass a tax on income.

SEVENTEENTH AMENDMENT — 1913

The Senate of the United States shall be composed of two senators from each State, elected by the people thereof, for six years; and each senator shall have one vote. The electors in each State shall have the qualifications requisite for electors of the most numerous branch of the State legislatures.

When vacancies happen in the representation of any State in the Senate, the executive authority of such State shall issue writs of election to fill such vacancies: Provided, that the legislature of any State may empower the executive thereof to make temporary appointments until the people fill the vacancies by election as the legislature may direct.

Seventeenth Amendment (1913)
United States senators are to be elected directly by the people.

EIGHTEENTH AMENDMENT* — 1919 (*REPEALED BY THE TWENTY-FIRST AMENDMENT)

SECTION 1.

After one year from the ratification of this article the manufacture, sale, or transportation of intoxicating liquors within, the importation thereof into, or the exportation thereof from the United States and all territory subject to the jurisdiction thereof for beverage purposes is hereby prohibited.

SECTION 2.

The Congress and the several States shall have concurrent power to enforce this article by appropriate legislation.

SECTION 3.

This article shall be inoperative unless it shall have been ratified as an amendment to the Constitution by the legislatures of the several States, as provided in the Constitution, within seven years from the date of the submission hereof to the States by the Congress.

Eighteenth Amendment (1919)
Liquor cannot be manufactured or sold in the United States.

NINETEENTH AMENDMENT — 1920

SECTION 1.

The right of citizens of the United States to vote shall not be denied or abridged by the United States or by any State on account of sex.

Nineteenth Amendment (1920)
No citizen may be denied the right to vote because of sex.

SECTION 2.

Congress shall have power, by appropriate legislation, to enforce the provisions of this article.

SECTION 1.

The terms of the President and Vice President shall end at noon on the 20th day of January, and the terms of senators and representatives at noon on the 3d day of January, of the years in which such terms would have ended if this article had not been ratified; and the terms of their successors shall then begin.

SECTION 2.

The Congress shall assemble at least once in every year, and such meeting shall begin at noon on the 3d day in January, unless they shall by law appoint a different day.

SECTION 3.

If, at the time fixed for the beginning of the term of the President, the President-elect shall have died, the Vice President-elect shall become President. If a President shall not have been chosen before the time fixed for the beginning of his term, or if the President-elect shall have failed to qualify, then the Vice President-elect shall act as President until a President shall have qualified; and the Congress may by law provide for the case wherein neither a President-elect nor a Vice President-elect shall have qualified, declaring who shall then act as President, or the manner in which one who is to act shall be selected, and such persons shall act accordingly until a President or Vice President shall have qualified.

SECTION 4.

The Congress may by law provide for the case of the death of any of the persons from whom the House of Representatives may choose a President whenever the right of choice shall have devolved upon them, and for the case of the death of any of the persons from whom the Senate may choose a Vice President whenever the right of choice shall have devolved upon them.

SECTION 5.

Sections 1 and 2 shall take effect on the 15th day of October following the ratification of this article.

SECTION 6.

This article shall be inoperative unless it shall have been ratified as an amendment to the Constitution by the legislatures of three fourths of the several States within seven years from the date of its submission.

TWENTY-FIRST AMENDMENT — 1933

SECTION 1.

The eighteenth article of amendment to the Constitution of the United States is hereby repealed.

SECTION 2.

The transportation or importation into any State, territory, or possession of the United States for delivery or use therein of intoxicating liquors, in violation of the laws thereof, is hereby prohibited.

SECTION 3.

This article shall be inoperative unless it shall have been ratified as an amendment to the Constitution by conventions in the several States, as provided in the Constitution, within seven years from the date of submission hereof to the States by the Congress.

TWENTY-SECOND AMENDMENT — 1951

No person shall be elected to the office of the President more than twice, and no person who has held the office of President, or acted as President, for more than two years of a term to which some other person was elected President shall be elected to the office of the President more than once.

But this Article shall not apply to any person holding the office of President when this Article was proposed by the Congress, and shall not prevent any person who may be holding the office of President, or acting as President, during the term within which this Article becomes operative from holding the office of President or acting as President during the remainder of such term.

TWENTY-THIRD AMENDMENT — 1961

SECTION 1.

The District constituting the seat of government of the United States shall appoint in such manner as the Congress may direct:

A number of electors of President and Vice President equal to the whole number of senators and representatives in Congress to which the District would be entitled if it were a State, but in no event more than the least populous state; they shall be in addition to those appointed by the States, but they shall be considered, for the purposes of the election of President and Vice President, to be electors appointed by a State; and they shall meet in the District and perform such duties as provided by the twelfth article of amendment.

Twenty-first Amendment (1933)
This repeals, or cancels, the Eighteenth Amendment to the Constitution.

Twenty-second Amendment (1951)
A President is limited to two terms in office.

Twenty-third Amendment (1961)
Residents of Washington, D.C., have the right to vote for President.

SECTION 2.

The Congress shall have power to enforce this article by appropriate legislation.

TWENTY-FOURTH AMENDMENT — 1964

Twenty-fourth Amendment (1964)
Citizens cannot be asked to pay a tax in order to vote in national elections.

SECTION 1.

The right of citizens of the United States to vote in any primary or other election for President or Vice President, for electors for President or Vice President, or for senator or representative in Congress, shall not be denied or abridged by the United States or any State by reason of failure to pay any poll tax or other tax.

SECTION 2.

The Congress shall have power to enforce this article by appropriate legislation.

TWENTY-FIFTH AMENDMENT — 1967

Twenty-fifth Amendment (1967)
If the President becomes too ill to carry on the job, the Vice-President will take over as Acting President until the President is better.

SECTION 1.

In case of the removal of the President from office or his death or resignation, the Vice President shall become President.

SECTION 2.

Whenever there is a vacancy in the office of the Vice President, the President shall nominate a Vice President who shall take the office upon confirmation by a majority vote of both houses of Congress.

SECTION 3.

Whenever the President transmits to the president pro tempore of the Senate and the speaker of the House of Representatives his written declaration that he is unable to discharge the powers and duties of his office, and until he transmits to them a written declaration to the contrary, such powers and duties shall be discharged by the Vice President as Acting President.

SECTION 4.

Whenever the Vice President and a majority of either the principal officers of the executive departments or of such other body as Congress may by law provide, transmit to the president pro tempore of the Senate and the speaker of the House of Representatives their written declaration that the President is unable to discharge the powers and duties of his office, the Vice President shall immediately assume the powers and duties of the office as Acting President.

Thereafter, when the President transmits to the president pro tempore of the Senate and the speaker of the House of Representatives his